Praise for *Reagan's Secret War*

"Persuasive evidence of Ronald Reagan's decisive role in ending the Cold War. Important research impressively assembled." —*Kirkus Reviews*

"Say goodbye to the caricature of Reagan as a clueless but unaccountably lucky cowboy . . . the Andersons reveal a determined and shrewd statesman who propelled America to triumph in the Cold War while also negotiating huge cuts in the world's nuclear arsenals." —*Booklist*

"Ronald Reagan's steadfast commitment to abolish all nuclear weapons is brought to life in Martin and Annelise Anderson's captivating narrative. . . . If the world makes it to the nuclear-free mountaintop, we will have President Reagan to thank for inspiring our climb."
—**Sam Nunn, former senator and cochairman, Nuclear Threat Initiative**

"Artfully and accurately explains how, when, and where . . . All who are interested in the elimination of nuclear weapons should read *Reagan's Secret War*." —**James A. Baker III, 61st U.S. secretary of state**

"A significant read not only for presidential historians but anyone who cares about how we got where we are now, free of the Cold War."
—**Dan K. Thomasson,** Scripps Howard News Service

"Superb . . . the authors' unique access to previously classified materials and to the president's personal documents enabled them to write the most complete and accurate account of this historic effort."
—**Ed Meese, former U.S. attorney general**

"Our new president dreams of abolishing nuclear weapons. [This] book reveals classified secrets on how Ronald Reagan outwitted the Russians—it could give Obama a game plan." —**David A. Patten,** Newsmax.com

"A meticulous compilation of the president's methodical pursuit of a victorious but unrancorous end to the Cold War and a steady reduction and even removal of the threat of nuclear weapons . . . a very powerful argument for why Reagan was one of America's great presidents."

—**Conrad Black**, *American Spectator*

"How Reagan's rhetoric and his policies defeated the Soviets . . . The Andersons' discovery of secret Cabinet notes and minutes show a president in complete command."   —**Rowan Scarborough**, *Human Events*

"Martin and Annelise Anderson shed new light on the Reagan–John Paul II relationship by using previously classified U.S. government files."

—**George Weigel**, *The Observer*

"Takes the reader from the first meeting of the National Security Council all the way to Reagan's farewell address, and it's an enjoyable ride."

—**Sterling C. Beard**, *Dartmouth Review*

"As he ponders his response to unfolding events in Iran, President Obama would do well to consult *Reagan's Secret War.*"

—**Joseph Shattan**, *American Thinker*

REAGAN'S SECRET WAR

THE UNTOLD STORY OF HIS FIGHT
TO SAVE THE WORLD
FROM NUCLEAR DISASTER

Martin Anderson and Annelise Anderson

THREE RIVERS PRESS
NEW YORK

Published in the United States by Three Rivers Press, an imprint of the
Crown Publishing Group, a division of Random House, Inc., New York.
www.crownpublishing.com

Three Rivers Press and the Tugboat design are
registered trademarks of Random House, Inc.

Originally published in hardcover in the United States by Crown Publishers,
an imprint of the Crown Publishing Group, a division of Random House, Inc., in 2009.

Grateful acknowledgment is made to the Ronald Reagan Presidential Foundation for
permission to reprint handwritten excerpts from Ronald Reagan's diary.

All photographs in this book are courtesy of the Ronald Reagan Presidential Library.

Library of Congress Cataloging-in-Publication Data

Anderson, Martin, 1936–
Reagan's secret war / Martin Anderson and Annelise Anderson.
p. cm.
1. United States—Foreign relations—Soviet Union.   2. Soviet Union—Foreign
relations—United States.   3. United States—Foreign relations—1981–1989.
4. Reagan, Ronald.   5. Cold War.   6. Nuclear arms control.
I. Anderson, Annelise Graebner.   II. Title.
E876.A556 2008
327.73047—dc22   2008050918

ISBN 978-0-307-23863-4

Printed in the United States of America

Design by Leonard Henderson

10 9 8 7 6 5 4 3 2 1

First Paperback Edition

For Nancy Reagan and George Shultz

Nancy, who was at Ronald Reagan's side
for more than fifty years,
helping him as he shaped
our country—and then the world

And George, who as secretary of state
was with Reagan at every step he took
on the path to defeat the Soviet Union

CONTENTS

FOREWORD

~

By George P. Shultz

How do you judge a presidency and a president?

Accomplishments are one yardstick. In the case of Ronald Reagan, you can point to ample successes, both during his presidency and throughout his life. He was successful as a negotiator when he was head of the Screen Actors Guild. He was successful as an actor, mastering the art of inhabiting a character or role. As a two-term governor of California, he left the state in much better shape than he found it and was even more popular when he left office than when he entered.

During the Reagan presidency, I had the privilege of close association with Ronald Reagan as he changed our country for the better. Rather than looking for political glory, he always seemed motivated by his view of what was best for America. His was a nonpartisan way of thinking.

I saw Reagan inherit an economy in shambles with inflation in the teens and the prime rate at 20 percent. I watched as he worked closely with Paul Volcker, chairman of the Federal Reserve Board, to fight inflation and put us back on the right track. (Reagan was fond of telling what were, in some respects, old chestnuts. I remember him saying, when people warned that a serious effort to get rid of inflation might well lead to a recession, "If not us, who? If not now, when?")

In the areas of national security and foreign policy, there was a dramatic change for the better between the beginning and end of Reagan's presidency. When Reagan entered office, the Cold War was as cold as it could get, and when he left, it was all over but the shouting. Sometimes you hear doubters argue that whatever happens just happens—that Reagan's policies of strength, realism, and diplomacy (let alone his skill in negotiations) had nothing to do with it. But looking at his long list of accomplishments, most people feel that he must have had something special to offer.

A president's real legacy is ultimately about *more* than accomplishments, though—no matter how impressive they may be. Most actions of consequence are, in the end, based on ideas. If the ideas are good, they have staying power.

Ronald Reagan was very much a man of ideas, and one of his key convictions was that nuclear weapons are so destructive they should not be in the hands of mankind. He recognized the arguments for deterrence through mutual assured destruction. But he thought this strategy was immoral. I heard him ask on many occasions, "What's so good about a peace kept by the threat of destroying each other?"

Close as I was to Reagan, I learned a lot about the depth and long history of his thinking on the nuclear threat from reading Martin and Annelise Anderson's thorough and illuminating analysis of the record—much of it hidden until now in secret files. Thanks to the Andersons' truly vast accumulation of essays, stories, and letters in the president's own handwriting, we learn that Reagan committed his thoughts to paper almost continuously. This is significant because the act of writing is fundamentally an act of thinking. Reagan was a thinker as well as a doer.

Reagan made no secret of his view that we should abolish nuclear weapons. But most people did not take this idea seriously—until Reykjavik. I had the privilege of sitting beside Ronald Reagan in that tiny room in Hofdi House as we talked for two days with

Mikhail Gorbachev and Eduard Shevardnadze. There it emerged that the leaders of the two countries that jointly controlled more than 90 percent of the world's nuclear weapons were calling for the abolition of those weapons.

I remember vividly the reaction when we returned to Washington. Almost immediately, Margaret Thatcher summoned me to the British ambassador's residence. There I learned the meaning of a British verb that derives from Thatcher's characteristically carrying a stiff handbag, for I was "handbagged."

"How could you let the president agree to abolish nuclear weapons?" she accused.

"But Margaret, he's the *president*."

"Yes, but you're supposed to be the one who has his feet on the ground."

"Margaret, I agreed with him."

I emerged from the ambassador's residence bloodied. And over the next few days, as I heard similar reactions from others, I came to realize that this idea of abolishing all nuclear weapons was one whose time had not yet come. But I still believed in the concept, and more important, so did Ronald Reagan.

Today, Reykjavik can be seen as a watershed meeting. Maybe it was the beginning of the end of the Cold War. Clearly, the number of nuclear weapons in the hands of the United States and Russia has been sharply reduced since that time (although huge numbers still remain and the possibility of proliferation is all too apparent).

The contrast between the resistance to nuclear abolition among the political intelligentsia during Reagan's presidency and the current growing acceptance that this might just be possible was brought home to me in 2006, when my colleague Sid Drell, a physicist, and I decided to hold a conference marking the twentieth anniversary of the Reykjavik meeting with the objective of exploring its implications. Many outstanding individuals joined us and another of our colleagues, Bill Perry, at this conference, and in other ways we included our friends Henry Kissinger and Sam Nunn in the effort. Among the results was an essay in the *Wall Street Journal* published on January 4, 2007, calling for a world free of nuclear weapons.

Of course, the essay caused some to speak out in opposition, but the overwhelming response globally was positive. In the United States, some two-thirds of the former secretaries of state and defense, as well as national security advisers, have publicly expressed support for this effort.

Many people have commented on how refreshing it is to have something advanced on a bipartisan basis. Those leading the initiative all reply that this effort isn't bipartisan; it's *non*partisan. That was always the spirit of Ronald Reagan, who asked himself what was good for the country and, in the case of nuclear weapons, what was good for mankind.

Ultimately, the true test of a man and his presidency is whether his ideas have staying power. And as Martin and Annelise Anderson incisively argue in these pages, Reagan's idea of abolishing nuclear weapons once and for all was of immense importance. The public was hesitant to embrace it. Advisers Reagan trusted and who were experts in this arena didn't support it. But none of that diminished Reagan's conviction, and now we see that his idea lives on and is attracting support in the United States and around the world.

This book will make an immense contribution to the thinking on this subject because the authors have defied assumptions about what Reagan thought and said and conducted painstaking research to get at the truth of what he *really* planned and executed. All of us who are gripped by the transcendent importance of the nuclear threat will learn, and be inspired by, this account.

REAGAN'S SECRET WAR

INTRODUCTION

~

One eyewitness
is worth more than ten who
tell you what they have heard.
—PLAUTUS, ROMAN PLAYWRIGHT, C. 190 B.C.

Ronald Reagan accomplished so much with such apparent ease that the casual observer often assumes he had nothing to do with it, nothing to do with the resurgence of the economy or the reduction in nuclear arsenals or the end of the Cold War.

Perhaps he had advisers whose lines he read with such skill. Perhaps it was Gorbachev or Thatcher or the Pope. Or maybe it was just plain luck.

We think not.

The evidence for this conclusion comes primarily from Reagan himself—what he wrote and what he said, his own words, written in his own hand or spoken extemporaneously. This evidence shows that throughout his presidency, Reagan carried out goals he had long held, carefully plotted the strategy that brought about the ends he achieved, and made all the major decisions of his administration. He did not always reveal to friends, family, the press, or his closest advisers how he intended to accomplish his objectives or the purpose of his actions. Yet with the benefit of hindsight, we see intent, planning, and timing. And as we look back we begin to understand the origins of the ambitious goals he brought to his presidency.

Especially important to this understanding is a new block of evidence declassified for use in this book: the minutes of the National Security Council (NSC), documents previously classified as Top Secret or Secret, unavailable to researchers or the public until now. The NSC is the group that advises the president on the most difficult decisions he must make—those about national security. In the Reagan White House, the meetings of the NSC were not tape-recorded, but a scribe usually took careful notes on what each of the participants said, including the president. In quoting Reagan, these minutes reveal his decisions and directions to his staff on national defense, arms control negotiations, and U.S. strategy with respect to the Soviet Union, the Middle East, and Latin America.

Reagan chaired 355 meetings of the NSC or its smaller and more secretive component, the National Security Planning Group (NSPG). Minutes were found for 192 of them, and of these more than 80 have been declassified for use in this book—those most revealing of Reagan's thinking and decision making on national defense, arms control, and dealing with the Soviets.

Martin Anderson was given access to these minutes (and to other classified documents) in a rare confluence of events: he had the necessary clearances, and both the office of President Reagan (where Nancy Reagan was making the final decisions) and the current president had to agree. So did the Central Intelligence Agency, the National Security Council, the National Security Agency, and the departments of State and Defense. Each wrote a letter granting access and giving conditions.

To access the documents, Martin went into the vault at the Reagan Library through four locked and secured steel doors and was given a small desk in the archivists' workroom at which he could take notes—notes that were immediately classified and could not be taken out of the library. He had to leave his cell phone behind, and was always accompanied by one of the few archivists at the Reagan Library authorized to handle classified documents, an additional burden on these hardworking people. Security became even touchier a short time after Martin began his work, when President Clinton's former national security adviser, Samuel "Sandy" Berger, was caught extracting documents from the Clinton Presidential Library by concealing them in his clothing, even hiding them in his socks. Henceforth Martin's library visits involved pulling up his pant legs to demonstrate that there were no precious papers concealed in his socks.

The NSC minutes are critical to knowing who Reagan was and how he accomplished his goals, and they are the final block of evidence necessary to understanding Ronald Wilson Reagan. Only in these records do we find out what Reagan decided, how he handled controversy among advisers, and what instructions he gave on negotiating with the most formidable foe of the United States during the Cold War, the Soviet Union. They are the ultimate evidence of Reagan's own role in dealing with the threat of nuclear catastrophe and ultimately ending the Cold War.

They will not come as a surprise to his closest staff and advisers, who, after all, were there and have always said that he made all the decisions, but they will astonish many others, even those who already admire Reagan as a communicator, a politician, and a man with firm convictions.

Martin Anderson had access to other classified documents in the Reagan Library, including memorandums of conversations, known as "memcons" for short, prepared as a record when the president met foreign leaders or talked to them on the phone. One of the documents declassified for this book is a memcon of Reagan's December 15, 1981, meeting with the representative of Pope John Paul II, Vatican Secretary of State Agostino Cardinal Casaroli.

Of special interest are the transcripts of the four historic U.S.-Soviet summit meetings where Reagan and Mikhail Gorbachev debated and negotiated. The transcripts record not only the plenary sessions, attended by staff and advisers, but also the private sessions between the two men, where only translators and note takers were present. Many Soviets and Americans worked on the negotiations, but the man-to-man negotiations between the two leaders were of key importance. We have excerpted many of these transcripts to give the reader a feel for what happened at these summits and why.

Also of great interest and importance are the dozens of letters that went back and forth between Reagan and the four men who led the Soviet Union while he was president—Leonid Brezhnev, Yuri Andropov, Konstantin Chernenko, and finally Mikhail Gorbachev. Reagan took up his own pen to write some of these letters. Now declassified, they give us a strong understanding of Reagan's approach to the Soviets and how much was accomplished before Gorbachev ever took office.

Other evidence abounds, but much of it did not begin to become available until long after Reagan had left the presidency. As this information became available, even Reagan's own staff was surprised at the extent to which he had been developing his own policy views and crafting his own speeches over the years. They did not know that Reagan was, in truth, a writer. Whatever else he was doing—as student, sportscaster, Hollywood actor, representative for General Electric, governor, private citizen, president—Ronald Reagan wrote. He wrote short stories, articles, radio commentaries, speeches, letters, two autobiographies, and, during his years in the White House, a personal diary.

Even we, the co-authors of this book, did not know how much Reagan had written over the years until we began researching him. And we were intimately acquainted with Reagan's political life. We had worked in Reagan's presidential campaigns of 1976 and 1980, the 1980 transition to the new administration, and the Reagan White House. Martin Anderson joined Reagan's 1976 campaign in October 1975, taking a leave of absence from Columbia's Graduate School of Business. Martin was in charge of policy development and traveled with Reagan, travels that ended at the 1976 convention when Reagan lost his challenge to sitting president

Gerald R. Ford for the Republican nomination. Annelise Anderson joined the Reagan campaign in the summer of 1976 when her teaching responsibilities at California State University, Hayward, were over for the school year, and staffed a policy research center at the 1976 convention.

In 1979 Martin, again on leave, was back on the campaign trail, often traveling with Reagan. Both of us were heavily involved with the Republican Party platform at the convention. During the fall 1980 campaign, Martin traveled with Reagan, and Annelise was selected to travel with vice presidential candidate George H. W. Bush as his policy adviser and a link to the Reagan campaign. In the transition following Reagan's November 4, 1980, victory, Annelise was the lead person in developing recommendations for presidential appointments in the departments of Treasury, Commerce, and Transportation. When the administration took office, Martin became assistant to the president for policy development, and Annelise became an associate director of the Office of Management and Budget with responsibility for overseeing the budgets of five cabinet departments and forty agencies with $80 billion in discretionary spending.

Despite our years working with Reagan, neither of us knew that he had written—in his own hand, usually on yellow tablets—685 essays on domestic and foreign policy for his five-days-a-week radio commentary program, which was on the air every weekday from 1975 through 1979 except when he was a declared candidate for the presidency. The handwritten commentaries were discovered in Reagan's personal pre-presidential papers in the Reagan Presidential Library. Some were in dated folders, but more than sixty had been unceremoniously dumped in one cardboard box, and the task was to figure out which handwritten drafts went with which typed broadcasts—found in the Ronald Reagan Subject Collection in the Hoover Institution Archives—so that we knew what Reagan had himself written. At the same time we were finding handwritten drafts of speeches on foreign policy, national defense, agriculture, and much more. Suddenly it was obvious that Reagan himself had written most of the lines he was delivering. (Many of the commentaries and some handwritten speeches were published in the book *Reagan, In His Own Hand.*)

But we found much more than radio commentaries. Another treasure trove was Reagan's correspondence—handwritten letters or drafts of letters on yellow pads to be typed up for signature, and sometimes letters dictated on tape. Our search went far beyond the Reagan Library, and we collected copies of handwritten letters from other archives and from people who had collections of letters because they had corresponded with Reagan frequently. Reagan wrote hundreds of letters a year while governor of California (1967–75) and hundreds a year while president. (We selected more than a thousand of these letters for publication in *Reagan: A Life in Letters,* but this amounts to only about 10 percent of his total handwritten or dictated correspondence.) In many of these letters, Reagan wrote about policy and politics, often with ideas and viewpoints that had not yet made their way into public speeches.

The final treasure trove of Reagan's own words is the personal diary he kept as president. He used—from the very beginning— blank books: leather-bound volumes with $8\frac{1}{2}$-by-11-inch pages. He could not add or replace a page. By the end of his presidency there were five volumes, all filled with his own script. He was concise and to the point, and he wrote about everything—events, policy decisions, working with the Congress, impressions of foreign leaders, personality conflicts in his administration, family, friends, horseback riding, the weather, and social engagements. For years no one—except Nancy—knew he was keeping a diary. The diary is invaluable as a contemporaneous account and as a record of the consistency of his policies and the persistence of his efforts to make those policies reality on issues such as taxes, the budget, and national defense. Many of the diary entries become clear only in the context of events.

Another major resource mined by the authors are the transcripts of Reagan's frequent meetings with members of the press. Reagan gave a number of formal news conferences during his presidency, five or six a year, but he also met with various members of the press or particular groups—foreign correspondents, radio correspondents, regional groups, editorial boards of newspapers—on many occasions. He also did question-and-answer sessions with students and other citizen groups where the press was present. Including his formal news conferences, he met more than eighty times a year with one or more members of the press—a total of 678 meetings during the eight years. The transcripts of these interactions alone are massive, over three thousand pages. All are included in the official public papers of Ronald Reagan, but they are difficult to search either in printed form or online. Yet they are important, as Reagan often revealed his positions on issues and objectives in these less formal meetings before he made official statements. We have made a special collection of these transcripts and created our own index.

Reagan's speeches and Saturday radio addresses are also important, not only because they embody his skills in communicating with the public but also because he wrote so many of them himself, even though he had superb speechwriters. Reagan had always drafted many of his own speeches, and he continued to write a considerable number of them when he was president. In addition, he held meetings with his speechwriters to give them direction. Several specific instructions survive in his own hand, as well as his own editing on speeches drafted by others. The Presidential Handwriting File of Speeches at the Reagan Presidential Library includes 2,639 speeches—almost one a day for the 2,922 days of his presidency—that his hand touched in one way or another. Of these, sixty-four have significant sections (sometimes the entire speech) drafted in his own hand, and almost half include his own edits and rewriting.

A final resource for us has been the White House Daily Diary, not to be confused with Reagan's personal diary. The daily diary is actually a by-the-minute log of the president's comings and goings, his phone contacts, and his meetings, listing all participants—including those attending meetings of the NSC and the NSPG. The log is maintained by representatives of the National Archives stationed in the White House. The entire log is some eighteen thousand pages. A classified electronic copy is maintained by the Ronald Reagan Library. The declassified log, which excludes some family matters and private information such as Social Security numbers of White House guests, was copied, and Lawrence Livermore National Laboratory agreed to use its best scanning technology to create a searchable electronic copy, so we could check the times and attendance of meetings, phone conversations, travel, and so forth. It has proved invaluable for us in such tasks as determining how often he met with given members of Congress, where he was when he recorded his weekly radio broadcasts, and with whom he met in the press.

Chapter 1

~

REAGAN THE MAN

Ronnie became a loner. . . .
He doesn't let anybody get too close.
There's a wall around him.
—NANCY REAGAN, 1989

The best clue to understanding Ronald Reagan is Nancy Reagan. She is a graduate of Smith College in Massachusetts, a highly intelligent woman, an actress who met Ronald Reagan in Hollywood and married him in 1952. They were happily in love for more than fifty years. Nancy was also his closest friend, perhaps his only real friend, and she knew far more about him than anyone else in the world.

In 1989, just after they had left office, Nancy wrote a book about her life in which she told us more about Ronald Reagan than anyone. She knew the key to his self-assurance—he was a loner. Here is how she explained Reagan in her book:

It's hard to make close friends or to put down roots when you're always moving, and I think this—plus the fact that everybody knew his father was an alcoholic—explained why Ronnie became a loner. Although he loves people, he often seems remote, and he doesn't let anybody get too close.

There's a wall around him. He lets me come closer than anyone else, but there are times when even I feel that barrier.

Ronnie's closest friends and advisers have often been disappointed that he keeps this distance. . . .

Ronnie is an affable and gregarious man who enjoys other people, but unlike most of us, he doesn't need them for companion-
ship or approval.

As he himself has told me, he seems to need only one other
person—me.[1]

Despite all appearances, then, Reagan was a very private man.
His pollster, Richard Wirthlin, met with him one day in March
1983, to give him the latest results. It was good news; the national
polls were showing that Reagan's policies were widely supported.
While he was reporting the polls, Reagan interrupted in midsen-
tence and said:

> You know what I really want to be remembered for?
> I want to be remembered as the President of the United
> States who brought a sense and reality of peace and security. I
> want to eliminate that awful fear that each of us feels some-
> times when we get up in the morning knowing that the world
> could be destroyed through a nuclear holocaust.[2]

As far as we know he only said that once, in private. His usual
answer about his legacy was a response about restoring the American economy.

Another foundation for Reagan's actions, perhaps, was his
high intelligence—and his ability to hide it. He was an extraordi-
narily bright pupil who even taught himself how to read a newspaper when he was five years old.[3] But as time went on, he seemed to
quickly learn something that most highly intelligent people learn
as they grow older: a child who seems to know all the answers soon

has few friends. So he spent more time playing ball and being a regular student.

Unlike many intelligent people, Reagan's self-confidence was also great enough that he never felt he had to demonstrate his knowledge or his quickness. Indeed, on the front of his desk in the White House was a small sign that carried the words "There's no limit to what a man can do or where he can go if he doesn't mind who gets the credit."

One of Reagan's key tactics while deep in long and arduous negotiations was to accept what his opponent had offered. He never crowed over what he was given; he just said thanks. As he explained it one day in *Fortune* magazine:

> I've never understood people who want me to hang in there for a hundred percent or nothing. Why not take seventy percent or eighty percent, and then come back another day for the other twenty or thirty percent.[4]

One of the few people who seemed to understand how Reagan managed the White House was *Washington Post* editor Meg Greenfield. In 1984 she wrote an essay for *Newsweek* titled "How Does Reagan Decide?" As a liberal Democrat, she observed something that even many of Reagan's closest conservative supporters failed to understand—that he made decisions like a labor negotiator for a workers' union. She summed up part of his decision-making style like this:

> The long waiting out of the adversary, the immobility meanwhile, the refusal to give anything until the last moment, the willing-ness—nonetheless—finally to yield to superior pressure or force or particular circumstance on almost everything, but only with something to show in return, and only if the final deal can be in-terpreted as furthering the original Reagan objective.[5]

Reagan was also an unusual boss. Those who worked for him liked him. They did not necessarily agree with all of his policies, but they still found him pleasant and friendly. He didn't criticize his advisers in front of others. He didn't chew people out. He didn't reprimand them, he didn't complain to them face-to-face—and he never yelled at them. Sometimes he might look a little disappointed when things went wrong, but you rarely felt a sense of failure or humiliation.

When people first met Reagan, they often thought he was too easygoing and friendly to be tough. The impression was like a soft down pillow. What people failed to see was the two-inch-thick rod of steel right down the inside of the pillow.

Perhaps the most important key to Reagan's success was the quality of his advisers and staff. Individually the men and women in his staff were very different, and they all had skills that matched the jobs they held. But the one thing they all shared was that they were all smart and sensible. Some presidents have felt uncomfortable with brilliant men and women; Reagan thrived on them.

Even his political opponents noted that the group of advisers and staff was unusual. Robert Strauss, perhaps the most savvy Democrat around when Reagan was elected, called Reagan's staff "simply spectacular. It's the best White House staff I've ever seen."[6]

President Reagan's management philosophy was best summed up when a reporter asked: "Your friend Roger Smith, chairman of General Motors, says that you've done a great job of focusing on the big picture without getting bogged down in detail. How do you decide which problems to address personally, and which to leave to subordinates?" Reagan replied:

You surround yourself with the best people you can find, delegate authority, and don't interfere as long as the overall policy that you've decided upon is being carried out.

In the Cabinet meetings—and some members of the Cabinet who have been members of other Cabinets told me there have never been such meetings—I use a system in which I want to hear what everybody wants to say honestly. I want the decisions made on what is right or wrong, what is good or bad for the people of this country. I encourage all the input I can get. . . .

And when I've heard all that I need to make a decision, I don't take a vote.

I make the decision.

Then I expect every one of them, whether their views have carried the day or not, to go forward together in carrying out the policy.[7]

All this does not mean that Reagan was some kind of superhuman who could not be riled or upset. In fact, one of the most unappreciated facets of Reagan's character was his temper; it flared rarely, but was memorable when it did. If Reagan was crossed—crossed badly—he exploded into what could be called a black Irish rage. His face darkened, his jaw muscles clenched and bulged, and his lips got thin and tight. In public he might show sporadic flashes of displeasure, but never real anger. It wasn't that he did not get angry, but rather that he usually covered it up.

During his presidential campaign, on one of those rare occasions of real fury—a well-justified one, we might add—we watched him lean back a bit, reach up and grab the right side of his eyeglasses, rip the glasses off, and fling them across the room into the wall closest to him. After he smashed his glasses into the wall, he calmed down quickly and carried on. No one who was there can remember what happened to the eyeglasses. That kind of outburst didn't happen often—but it did happen.

Once during the campaign in 1976 Reagan was holding an impromptu press conference outside a building with a narrow alley. Some of the reporters were asking questions that had an insulting tone. After Reagan finished answering the last question, he turned and headed through the alley into the building, with the Secret

Service clearing the way. When he was about halfway down the alley, one of the reporters, a particularly provocative one, yelled: "What's the matter? Are you afraid to answer the question?"

Reagan stopped, his face turning red. Abruptly he turned and headed back out through the alley. His eyes were blazing, focused on the heckler waiting outside. As he moved through the alley, one of the advisers was standing in the way. Reagan, with one swift thrust of his arm, shoved him aside, slamming him against the wall. Outside he angrily answered the reporter's question, then turned back and went into the building. (The fellow he "moved" was fine.)

Another rare example of what could make Reagan upset was a rewritten draft of one of his speeches. One day, Peter Hannaford, one of his oldest and most valued speechwriters, handed him a new redraft of a major speech for him to read on the plane. Reagan smiled, slipped on his reading glasses, and started to read. After two or three pages, his eyebrows narrowed and his jaw tightened. Then, after reading the next page, he lifted it, raised it high in the air, and slammed it down hard onto the small pile he had just read. He continued to read, slamming each succeeding page down harder and harder. It was clear he didn't like the redraft of the speech.[8]

After Reagan had been in office for nearly six months, very few people understood his foreign policy. It especially bothered some of the reporters writing about him. They feared that he was on a course that could be dangerous, even leading the United States to a nuclear war. It was true that Reagan had never spelled out a detailed picture of what he wished to do in foreign policy, but it did not seem to bother him. A letter he dictated to a friend, John O. Koehler, on July 9, 1981, explains his reluctance to do so—and serves as a perfect example of his quietly self-confident approach:

> I know I'm being criticized for not having made a great speech outlining what would be the Reagan foreign policy. I have a foreign policy; I'm working on it.

I just don't happen to think that it's wise to always stand up and put in quotation marks in front of the world what your foreign policy is. I'm a believer in quiet diplomacy and so far we've had several quite triumphant experiences by using that method.

The problem is, you can't talk about it afterward or then you can't do it again.[9]

Chapter 2

~

THE AWESOME POWER
OF A PRESIDENT

A man's wisdom is most conspicuous
when he is able to distinguish
among dangers and
make choice of the least.
—MACHIAVELLI, *THE PRINCE,* 1513

The first thing Ronald Reagan received after taking the oath of office as president of the United States was the "football." The first part of the football was a small, plastic-coated card he could hold in his hand, a card that he would have with him for as long as he was the president.

The card contained awesome power. It held the Top Secret codes that could activate a black leather satchel—the other half of the football. That fairly large briefcase could order the Pentagon to launch the nuclear missiles poised and aimed at U.S. enemies. The only person who could authorize a nuclear strike, the only man with the codes, was the president.

In 1981 the United States had an estimated stockpile of 23,464 nuclear warheads. The Soviet Union stockpile was considerably larger, with 32,049 warheads. However, when you considered the most threatening nuclear warheads, those deliverable on intercontinental ballistic missiles (ICBMs), the Soviets had 5,977, and the United States had only 38 percent that number, 2,251. On the other hand, the United States had 5,090 warheads on sea-launched ballistic missiles (SLBMs), while the Soviets had only 1,956. The number of strategic warheads on U.S. bombers was more than ten times those on Soviet bombers—6,244 to 596.[1]

Even a small number of the warheads on either side, properly aimed, was many times over what was necessary to destroy civilization. In the event of a first strike by either superpower, the other could be expected to strike back. It was power that weighed heavily on both.

Here is how Reagan described it:

> As president, I carried no wallet, no money, no driver's license, no keys in my pocket—only secret codes that were capable of bringing about the annihilation of much of the world as we knew it.
>
> On inauguration day, after being briefed a few days earlier on what I was to do if ever it became necessary to unleash American nuclear weapons, I'd taken over the greatest responsibility of my life—of any human being's life.

This was his first understanding of the massive power that flows to every one of our presidents. For some of them there is no stark danger to cope with, no reason in the world why they would ever order nuclear missiles toward other countries, ripping apart millions of people far, far away. But Reagan and others faced a real and present danger—and every president who held that tiny card with the Top Secret numbers probably shivered a bit as he took possession.

> The plastic-coated card, which I carried in a small pocket in my coat, listed the codes I would issue to the Pentagon

confirming that it was actually the president of the United States who was ordering the unleashing of our nuclear weapons.

The decision to launch the weapons was mine alone to make.

We had many contingency plans for responding to a nuclear attack. But everything would happen so fast that I wondered how much planning or reason could be applied in such a crisis. The Russians sometimes kept submarines off our East Coast with nuclear missiles that could turn the White House into a pile of radioactive rubble within six or eight minutes.

Six minutes to decide how to respond to a blip on a radar scope and decide whether to unleash Armageddon!

How could anyone apply reason at a time like that?

There were some people in the Pentagon who thought in terms of fighting and *winning* a nuclear war. To me it was simple common sense: A nuclear war couldn't be won by either side. It must never be fought. But how do we go about trying to prevent it and pulling back from this hair-trigger existence?[2]

Besides the football, Reagan, like every U.S. president, was given another tremendous power. Every president can, if he wishes, take charge of deciding each and every policy. Every man and woman who works for him must carry out those decisions, no matter his or her own opinion.

Reagan made it clear how he would use that power the first time he chaired the National Security Council (NSC) meeting. The message he drove home during that first meeting was clear and simple:

I will make the decisions.

That first meeting took place on February 6, 1981, in the Cabinet Room. Reagan gave that order to a small group of key advisers. His words—and the words of everyone else in the room—were secret. Yet those five words would shape the foreign policy of the United States for the next eight years.[3]

That day Reagan also told his advisers:

> The NSC should meet frequently and help to formulate our policies. I urge cooperation at all levels. No one should stand on ceremony. During the campaign, I pledged to implement a new foreign policy and restore the margin of safety. I look to this group to help me. The Intelligence Community has a vital role. I intend to restore the vigor and effectiveness of our intelligence services.
>
> I will use the National Security Council structure to obtain your guidance, but I will make the decisions.
>
> Once made, I expect the Departments to implement them. Sub-cabinet appointments will play a vital role in effective implementation. The NSC is not just another cabinet agency. Although the decisions will be mine, you are the obvious source for good ideas.
>
> I want good advice.[4]

Few in the room seemed to take Reagan seriously that first day. They all were aware of the dangers they faced, the complexities and difficulties that lay ahead, but for some in that room it was probably a bit difficult to think of Reagan as a strong personality, a leader who would decree what was to be done and when. He was seventy years old that very day. He had a reputation for being easygoing and friendly, a man who many believed relied on his advisers.

But they would soon become aware that Reagan was dead serious. He was confident in his own judgments, he knew where he wanted to go, and he was keenly aware of the immense power he held in his hands as president.

How Reagan, as a president of the United States, would wield the awesome power he held would determine the country's fate.

As Ronald Reagan took the reins of the United States govern-

NATIONAL SECURITY COUNCIL MEETING

February 6, 1981

~~SECRET/SENSITIVE~~

Time and Place:	1:30 p.m. - 2:40 p.m., The Cabinet Room
Subject:	Caribbean Basin; Poland (S)

Participants

The President
The Vice President

State:
Secretary Alexander A. Haig, Jr.

Defense:
Caspar T. Weinberger

Treasury:
Secretary Donald T. Regan

Justice:
Attorney General William French Smith

DCI:
Mr. William J. Casey

JSC:
General David Jones

White House:
Mr. Edwin Meese, III, Counsellor to the President
Mr. James A. Baker, III, Chief of Staff to the President
Mr. Richard Allen, Assistant to the President for National
  Security Affairs
Adm. James Nance, Deputy Assistant to the President for
  National Security Affairs

Vice President's Office:
Adm. Daniel J. Murphy, Chief of Staff

National Security Council:
Janet Colson
Timothy E. Deal
Charles Tyson

~~SECRET/SENSITIVE~~
Review on February 6, 1987

MINUTES

The President: Interagency groups are reviewing the items on today's
agenda. Their work is not complete, but they will have issues for
decision shortly. The NSC should meet frequently and help to formulate
our policies. I urge cooperation at all levels. No one should stand on
ceremony. During the campaign, I pledged to implement a new foreign
policy and restore the margin of safety. I look to this group to help
me. The Intelligence Community has a vital role. I intend to restore
the vigor and effectiveness of our intelligence services. (C)

I will use the NSC structure to obtain your guidance, but I will make
the decisions. Once made, I expect the Departments to implement them.
Subcabinet appointments will play an vital role in effective implementation
The NSC is not just another cabinet agency. Although the decisions will
be mine, you are the obvious source for good ideas. I want good advice.
The NSC staff functions as an integral part of the White House, and Dick
Allen places a premium on good management. (C)

President Reagan opens the first NSC meeting.

ment in 1981, he was confronted with a number of dangers and difficulties. The greatest danger came from abroad. Totalitarian countries seemed to be becoming more powerful. Communist dictatorships, especially the Soviet Union, that had killed and enslaved millions were growing stronger and more threatening. The Communist ideal was on the march, as country after country fell to its wiles. Most ominous was the growing nuclear missile arsenal of the main U.S. enemy, the Soviet Union. As the Communist tide swelled, the threat of an all-out nuclear war between the superpowers—the Soviet Union and the United States—was real.

Many Americans, in particular Reagan, feared such a war could lead to Armageddon, a devastating conflict that would destroy civilization as we know it, sending the few who survived back into a stone age. In his autobiography, he wrote:

> During the Spring of 1981, the arms race was moving ahead at a pell-mell pace based on the MAD [mutually assured destruction] policy. Investing a far larger portion of their national wealth on arms than we were, the Soviets were piling new weapon upon new weapon. . . .
>
> There didn't seem any end to it, no way out of it.
>
> There had to be some way to remove this threat of annihilation and give to the world a greater chance of survival . . . [A]s I went back and forth from these thoughts . . . I reflected that in the past, man had been able to devise a defense against every other weapon thrown against him.
>
> I wondered if it might be possible to develop a defense against missiles other than the fatalistic acceptance of annihilation that was implicit under the MAD policy.
>
> We couldn't continue this nervous standoff forever, I thought; we couldn't lower our guard, but we had to begin the process of peace. . . . I spent a lot of time wondering what I could do to get the process started.[5]

The expectations for Reagan's presidency were low. For the past twenty years the task of being president had crushed some of our most able men. John Kennedy was assassinated before he could finish his first term. Lyndon Johnson was driven from the White House by the debacle of the Vietnam War. Richard Nixon was forced to resign by the bungling of the Watergate scandal. President Ford, who succeeded to the post after being appointed vice president, was defeated after serving two years. And President Carter just couldn't seem to cope with the awesome complexities of the Oval Office and was voted out of office after one term. Our political system is not used to rapid turnovers, and the turmoil of those administrations in such a short time was telling.

The chilling conclusion of many of our most learned men and women was that the office of the presidency had become unmanageable. President Eisenhower (1953–61) had been the last president to complete two full terms in office. The power of the president to work his will, to change policy, and to guide and lead the nation was thought to have been weakened irreparably as the 1980 election loomed.

The American political system, once marveled at throughout the world, had become shaky. It had been hammered in the years leading to the 1980s. The Vietnam War had left a painful stain on the reputation of our policy makers and our military. More than 47,000 young men and women had been killed in action and more than 153,000 wounded; many of these had been conscripted and forced to serve.

There was talk about the malaise that had infected the country. People began to openly ask whether or not the government was manageable, whether a president, in our current system, could govern. A few even looked longingly at the powers held by dictators in countries such as China or the Soviet Union, and many more questioned whether an open society with free markets and democratic elections could compete effectively with countries that controlled their economies from the center and repressed dissent. The idea that the Communist world and the free world were converging was in the air.

For Reagan, the expectations were even lower than for the others who were vying for the presidency. Remember, Reagan was a former movie actor with little apparent expertise in national security issues, someone whom people liked as a nice man, but not tough enough to step into the president's shoes. On the other hand, he had been a successful governor of California for eight years, and he could give a speech with mesmerizing force.

Still, as it was put by Richard Nathan, a highly respected political analyst at Princeton University: "Most close observers of the Washington scene and system saw Reagan as a media success who would be overwhelmed by the immense substantive and managerial demands of the presidency."[6] Reagan's official welcome to Washington, D.C., was cool and a bit contemptuous. While he was still in the ten-week transition, Thomas "Tip" O'Neill, the Democratic Speaker of the House of Representatives, issued a stinging warning:

> The governor of a state plays in the minor leagues. When you're president, you're in the big leagues. Things may not move as fast as you want them to.

It was not an unreasonable viewpoint.

One of the most serious issues Reagan faced when he took office was the decline in U.S. armed forces. The strain of the Vietnam War and the failure to fully support the needs of the military had led to a sharp decline in both strength and morale.

But before he could even think about the strength of the military and how he should deal with the increasing possibility of a war fought with nuclear-tipped missiles, Reagan had to solve one even more basic problem—the U.S. economy. As he took the oath of office in January 1981 it was clear that the economy was in deep trouble. The Dow Jones stock average hovered around 800. Taxes were high and rising, and price controls on gasoline and oil forced millions of drivers to wait in line for hours. Bringing the economy back to life, creating powerful growth and new and better jobs, was the necessary key to continued prosperity and peace.

Aside from national security and the economy, there were two other major challenges. The first was political. Reagan, as a Republican, would inherit a House of Representatives controlled by Democrats. The powers of the House were substantial, and Reagan would be unable to govern at will. He would have to cajole and convince his political enemies.

The second problem was Reagan himself. While a majority of the voters liked him, many feared and distrusted him. Many saw him as a reckless cowboy, an old actor, a fellow who, while pleasant and nice, was not too bright and relied on staff to tell him what to do. Some politicians held him in contempt. As noted, Tip O'Neill scoffed at his ability to play in the "big leagues," while Clark Clifford, secretary of defense for President Carter, dismissed Reagan as an "amiable dunce."[7]

When Ronald Reagan took the oath in 1981 he knew the United States needed change, and in political terms Reagan was a radical. As a former Democrat who had switched parties, he did not fit neatly into the usual Republican or Democrat molds. What eventually became Reaganism was a brew of policy—one that won the agreement of the voters who twice made him governor of California and twice president of the United States.

And Reagan surprised and baffled all the experts, friend and foe alike. Within a year Tip O'Neill's contempt would turn to relatively silent awe, and there would be no more talk about the "big leagues."

Chapter 3

~

JUGGLING PRIORITIES: 1981

The only sure way to avoid war is to surrender without fighting. . . .
The other way is based on the belief
that in an all-out race our system is stronger,
and eventually the enemy gives up the race as a hopeless cause.
Then a noble nation believing in peace
extends the hand of friendship
and says there is room in the world for both of us.
—SPEECH BY RONALD REAGAN, 1963

Reagan's top priority on taking office was defending the United States and avoiding nuclear war, but the most *urgent* matter was restoring economic prosperity in the United States. A strong economy was crucial not only for domestic policy but also for foreign policy. He made this clear in a March 17, 1980, campaign speech:

> We cannot meet our world responsibilities without a strong economic policy which is effective at home and in the world marketplace. . . . We must put our economic house in order so that we can once again show the world by example that ours is the best system for all who want security and freedom.[1]

On June 18, 1980, he had told editors and reporters of the *Washington Post* that a rapid U.S. arms buildup would be good for the United States because it would force the Soviets, with an already heavy burden of defense, to the arms-control bargaining table.[2] But in order to sustain such a buildup, Reagan would first have to put the U.S. economy back on a strong, robust footing.

THE ECONOMY

As Reagan took office, both inflation and unemployment were high. Unemployment was at 7.4 percent. The consumer price index had increased 13.3 percent in 1979 and 12.4 percent in 1980—two consecutive years of double-digit inflation. Interest rates were also high; the mortgage rate on new homes was over 13 percent and banks were charging their best business customers 20.5 percent for short-term loans. Price controls and allocations had left people waiting in lines at gas pumps, and the country continued to be subject to the whims of Middle East oil policy. As had happened with the stagflation in Britain in the 1970s, the trade-off between higher inflation and lower unemployment seemed not to be working.

Reagan's proposals for economic recovery were well established and had been presented in detail in a major campaign speech on September 9, 1980, in Chicago.[3] The four essential parts of the economic program, which would become known among the staff as the "four pillars," were straightforward: reducing tax rates for individuals and business, controlling federal spending, reducing and making more reasonable federal regulations, and reducing inflation and ultimately interest rates by controlling the money supply and balancing the budget. It was important, too, to stick with it. The outgoing president, Jimmy Carter, had had five economic programs in his single term.

Reagan's January 20, 1981, inaugural address focused on his two main goals, national security and economic growth.

We suffer from the longest and one of the worst sustained inflations in our national history. . . . In this present crisis, government is not the solution to our problem; government is the problem. . . .

It is time to reawaken this industrial giant, to get government back within its means, and to lighten our punitive tax burden. . . . And as we renew ourselves here in our own land, we will be seen as having greater strength throughout the world. We will again be the exemplar of freedom and a beacon of hope for those who do not now have freedom.[4]

As he began to conclude the speech, he laid out his most important priority, the one that would increasingly dominate his administration in the years ahead:

As for the enemies of freedom, those who are potential adversaries, they will be reminded that peace is the highest aspiration of the American people. We will negotiate for it, sacrifice for it; we will not surrender for it—now or ever. . . . We will maintain sufficient strength to prevail if need be, knowing that if we do we have the best chance of never having to use that strength.[5]

Once in office, Reagan wasted no time in beginning work on his economic and fiscal policies. In his first ten days in office, he established a presidential task force on regulatory relief, eliminated by executive order the price and allocation controls on crude oil and refined petroleum products that had existed in one form or another since 1973, terminated the remnants of the wage and price regulatory program, and froze pending regulations of the federal government for sixty days.[6] He went to the Department of the Treasury for his first of many meetings with Paul Volcker, then chairman of the Federal Reserve Board of Governors, to encourage and support a monetary policy that would control inflation.

He took a few symbolic actions to control federal expenditures, freezing the hiring of civilian federal employees and limiting federal travel. But the real work of controlling expenditures and reducing taxes would require sending legislation and a revised budget to Congress.

Reagan had come into Washington as an outsider, but once in town he reached out to the Congress and worked closely with them. He had a very good reason for this. Reagan knew what he wanted to do, but he would have to get the agreement of the Congress before any of his ideas would become reality.

When Reagan won the presidency by a large margin in November 1980, he swept in a surprising number of Republican senators, wresting power from the Democrats, who'd previously held the majority. The new Senate had fifty-three Republicans, forty-six Democrats, and one independent. While the Democrats lost the Senate, they held on to the House of Representatives. That meant they had control over all the money the government spent. In the first two years of Reagan's term the Democrats held 56 percent of the House of Representatives, and Reagan was fully aware of the fact that he would need to convince some of the Democrats to vote with him on key issues if he was to succeed. By the end of March Reagan had met more than fifty times with members of Congress and made a flurry of phone calls.

Congressional passage of revisions to the entire budget and the tax legislation was not likely to be easy; Democrats typically wanted less defense spending, more domestic spending, and higher taxes, but some southern Democrats favored Reagan's plans, and if Reagan had strong public support, Congress was more likely to bend to his will. Reagan's first speech to the nation as president, delivered February 5, 1981, from the Oval Office, was on the economy.[7] He was unhappy enough with the draft from his speechwriters that he got his secretary to clear his schedule for a few hours so he could work on it himself. Reagan specifically disavowed the trade-off between higher inflation and higher unemployment that had been a staple of economic policy for decades:

> In the past we've tried to fight inflation one year and then, with unemployment increased, turn the next year to fighting unemployment with more deficit spending as a pump primer. So, again, up goes inflation. It hasn't worked. We don't have to choose between inflation and unemployment—they go hand in hand. It's time to try something different, and that's what we're going to do.[8]

A few days later, on February 10, 1981, Reagan held the organizing meeting of the President's Economic Policy Advisory Board (PEPAB). George Shultz chaired the group, and the members were no less distinguished: Arthur Burns, Milton Friedman, and Alan Greenspan, among others. They would meet five more times in 1981, providing encouragement for resisting political pressure to reverse course on the economic program—especially the tax cuts.

Reagan was pleased with the work of his "inside" economic team—Donald T. Regan was secretary of the treasury; David Stockman was the director of the Office of Management and Budget; Murray Weidenbaum chaired the Council of Economic Advisers; and Martin Anderson was assistant to the president for policy development.

Reagan addressed, for the first time, a joint session of Congress on February 18, 1981, and like his first address to the nation from the Oval Office, the subject was the economy. Reagan had spent the weekend before the speech at Camp David, but it was not a weekend of rest and relaxation. It was the third speech in a few weeks he wrote himself. He wrote in his diary on February 15, 1981:

> I was at Camp David but I was indoors all day writing my speech for Wed. nite in Cong. . . . Finished speech by bedtime.[9]

The speech argued for Reagan's economic program, but Reagan wanted more than tax cuts and spending reductions: he wanted more money for national defense. Economists were still forecasting good economic growth, so it was possible, with spending control, to cut taxes and increase defense expenditures:

> This plan is aimed at reducing the growth in government spending and taxing, reforming and eliminating regulations which are unnecessary and unproductive or counterproductive, and encouraging a consistent monetary policy aimed at maintaining the value of the currency. . . .
>
> Our proposal is for a 10-percent across-the-board cut every year for 3 years in the tax rates for all individual income taxpayers, making a total cut in the tax-cut rates of 30 percent . . . it's actually only a reduction in the tax increase already built into the system.
>
> I'm sure there's one department you've been waiting for me to mention, the Department of Defense. . . . I believe that my duty as President requires that I recommend increases in defense spending over the coming years.[10]

On the same day a 280-page document summarizing the economic program was sent to the Congress, and the word from Reagan's pollster, Richard Wirthlin, was good. On March 2 Reagan noted:

> 95 percent support our budget cuts. Almost as many the tax cuts.[11]

More specific budget revisions were sent on March 10, which included a 1981 budget supplemental for national defense and additional funds for 1982.[12] Although Reagan's September 1980 speech had called for 5 percent real growth in defense spending, when it came time to send Congress revised budget requests for

1982, Secretary of Defense Caspar "Cap" Weinberger asked for larger increases, and he and David Stockman agreed on 7 percent. Each year, of course, the numbers would be revised to reflect budget pressures, inflation, and program needs. Congress did not give the president everything he asked for, but especially in the first few years, it gave him most of it. He asked for almost $7 billion in additional funds for 1981 (primarily for military pay and readiness) and $26 billion for 1982.

THE MILITARY BUILDUP

Reagan did not yet have all the precise details of his military buildup worked out when he sent the request to Congress for additional funds, but he knew they were needed, for three reasons. U.S. military strength had declined; Soviet military strength, both conventional and nuclear, had increased, and the Soviets were active throughout the world; and Reagan wanted to negotiate from a position of strength.

In a three-hour speech to the Twenty-sixth Congress of the Soviet Communist Party on February 24, 1981, in the Kremlin, Leonid Brezhnev proposed meeting with Reagan.[13] Walter Cronkite of CBS News asked Reagan about it on March 3, 1981. Reagan responded with words that foretold the strategy he would follow with the Soviets.

Cronkite asked, "What conditions do you have to be satisfied before you would agree to a summit meeting with Brezhnev?"

Reagan replied:

> I have said that I will sit and negotiate with them for a reduction in strategic nuclear weapons to lower the threshold of danger that exists in the world today. . . . I think one of them [conditions] would be some evidence on the part of the Soviet Union that they are willing to discuss that.

Cronkite then asked, "They're anxious to get arms control discussions going. . . . They're fearful you're not going to want to negotiate until such time as you get your defense program and your economic program through Congress and feel that you're negotiating from strength."

Reagan told him:

> I do believe this: that it is rather foolish to have unilaterally disarmed, you might say, as we did by letting our defensive, our margin of safety deteriorate, and then you sit with the fellow who's got all the arms. What do you have to negotiate with? You're asking him to come down to where you are, or you build up to where he is, but you don't have anything to trade. So, maybe realistic negotiations could take place. When? We can say, "Well, all right, this thing we're building—we'll stop if you'll stop doing whatever it is you're really doing."[14]

Between February 6, 1981, and March 26, 1981, Reagan chaired ten meetings of the National Security Council or the smaller National Security Planning Group; the latter group advised the president on, among other things, covert actions. Reagan was finding out from the inside the extent to which the Soviets were on the move around the world and the capabilities of the United States for dealing with them. Central America, the Caribbean, Poland, Cuba, Libya, the Middle East, Pakistan, South Africa—all came up in those early days. These meetings belie the idea that Reagan paid little attention to foreign affairs.

The February 6, 1981, meeting of the NSC took up the Caribbean basin and Central America, where the Soviet client state of Cuba was heavily involved. The Soviet Union was methodically trying to subvert the nations of Central America, the nations that lay just below the belly of the United States. If some of these nations became platforms for Soviet weapons, perhaps even nuclear missiles aimed at the United States, they could prove to be much more dangerous than the Soviet missiles President Kennedy had forced out of Cuba. A growing pack of Soviet client nations, armed to the teeth, was a potential threat that Reagan could not allow. Meanwhile, Cuba was shipping arms through Nicaragua to guerrillas trying to overthrow the military government in El Salvador.

William Casey, CIA director, pointed out that "there have been 100 planeloads of arms from Cuba over the past 90 days. The Nicaraguans can't be ignorant of that." General David Jones, the chairman of the Joint Chiefs, added: "In 1970, we had 500 advisers in Latin America. That number has now fallen to 65. The Soviets have more military advisers in Peru than we have in all of Latin America."[15]

Reagan expressed his views:

My own feeling—and one about which I have talked at length—is that we are way behind, perhaps decades, in establishing good relations with the two Americas. We must change the attitude of our diplomatic corps so that we don't bring down governments in the name of human rights. None of them is as guilty of human rights violations as are Cuba and the Soviet Union.

We don't throw out our friends just because they can't pass the "saliva test" on human rights. I want to see that stopped. We need people who recognize that philosophy. In Angola, for example, Savimbi holds a large chunk of Angolan territory. With some aid, he could reverse the situation. We should also reestablish relations with countries like Chile who have made substantial progress—and stop worrying about Allende's fate. . . . El Salvador is a good starting point. A victory there could set an example.[16]

We can't afford a defeat. El Salvador is the place for a victory. . . . For too many years, we have been telling adversaries what we can't do. It's time we make them start wondering what we will do.[17]

The concerns were very much the same in the February 11 meeting of the National Security Council. There were added worries, expressed by Al Haig, secretary of state, that "if the Soviets move into Poland, we must get them somewhere else first—and that means Cuba."[18] As the roles of Cuba and the Soviet Union were discussed, President Reagan asked one question three different times:

What can we do specifically about Cuba? . . . What specific pressures can be placed on Cuba—the source of the problem? . . . What kind of military action specifically?[19]

President Reagan never got a concrete answer. Since the Bay of Pigs fiasco under President Kennedy, nothing effective had been done about Cuba. And apparently no one had figured out a better solution. Over time, Reagan worked assiduously against the source of funds to Cuba (the Soviets) and the nations Cuba was giving arms to.

Reagan also made it crystal clear that he would never accept a Soviet-inspired takeover of Latin America. Toward the end of the meeting he said:

If the Junta falls in El Salvador, it will be seen as an American defeat. We will go with the first plan, but we must not let Central America become another Cuba on the mainland.

It cannot happen.[20]

The issues taken up on the March 19 National Security Council meeting involved another part of the world, the Mideast. A hangover from the agreement engineered by President Carter between Egypt and Israel called for Israel to withdraw from the Sinai Peninsula. Israeli foreign minister Shamir wanted a totally U.S. peacekeeping force, but Reagan was clearly skeptical.[21]

Pakistan was another issue on which Reagan pushed back at his advisers. Pakistan was considered by the United States to be a vital strategic friend, but its economy was in bad shape, it was pressing to develop a nuclear bomb, and it desperately needed money. Reagan's advisers suggested $2 billion in aid. After strenuous debate led by the director of OMB, David Stockman, President Reagan noted that:

> My silence on this matter is not from lack of interest but rather because I am afflicted with two allergies: the allergy of wanting to control government spending and the allergy of wanting to increase our national security posture. . . . Let's see what can be done from the current budget.[22]

Later Reagan jokingly asked:

> [Is] there some real estate the federal government owns that could be sold? I wonder how much we could get if we sold Rhode Island?[23]

He was sharply aware of the extent to which the reputation and capabilities of the United States had eroded in the 1970s. The Soviets had invaded Afghanistan in late 1979. The Soviets were also active directly or through Cuban proxies in Angola, Ethiopia, and Nicaragua. The Iranians had held fifty-two hostages in the U.S. embassy in Tehran from November 4, 1979, until the day Reagan was inaugurated; one rescue attempt had failed.

At the same time, the Soviet Union was targeting SS-20 missiles on Europe, and the United States had agreed with NATO in 1979 that if the Soviets persisted in their deployment, they would counter the Soviet buildup with the introduction of their own intermediate-range missiles in Europe.

Meanwhile the defense budget declined in the late 1970s to less than 5 percent of GNP, the lowest it had been since the war-production factories were shut down and the troops sent home after World War II. The Carter administration canceled production of Minuteman missiles and the B-1 bomber, the upgrade to the aging B-52s. It delayed cruise missiles, the MX multiple-warhead missile, Trident submarines, and the Trident II missile. Shipbuilding was cut back and the armed forces were underpaid.

By 1979 the Congress, with the Democrats in the majority in both houses, grew alarmed about the weakening U.S. national defense and appropriated more funds than President Carter had initially requested; they also provided funding for a new bomber.[24] But Reagan's March 1981 request upped the national defense budget by another 7 percent a year.

The United States had been cutting its military expenditures, but the Soviet Union was not. Experts estimated that their annual defense spending had exceeded that of the United States since the early 1970s. In comparison to NATO, as of 1980 the Warsaw Pact nations—the Soviet Union and its Eastern European satellites—had 2.7 times as many tanks, 20 percent more armored personnel carriers, and over twice as much artillery.[25]

On the nuclear front, the imbalance was no better: at the time of the Cuban missile crisis in 1963, the Soviets had had 4,238 nuclear weapons, compared to the U.S. total of 29,459. The U.S. arsenal had peaked at 32,040 warheads in 1966, but the Soviets had continued to build, and especially to construct missiles with multiple warheads; by 1972, the Soviets had just over half as many nuclear weapons as the United States. Now, in 1981, Reagan found a U.S. nuclear stockpile of 23,464 warheads—its lowest point in twenty years—while the Soviets' stockpile held 32,049 warheads and continued to grow.[26]

Against this growing arsenal, Reagan would reverse the Carter decisions to cancel and postpone weapons systems. Reagan's diary entries provide insight into the decisions he was making on the national defense program. One of the issues was whether to build one hundred B-1 bombers or wait for the development of the more advanced Stealth (ATB—advanced technology bomber) plane. For example, on June 30, 1981, he noted in his diary:

> This afternoon met with Cap. W. [Caspar Weinberger] on the B-1. He leans toward going for the "Stealth" which would leave a several year gap with only the aging B-52's. I tend to favor filling the gap with B-1's while we develop the "Stealth."[27]

How to base the MX missile so that it would not be vulnerable to Soviet missiles was also an issue. Following a National Security Planning Group meeting on August 3, 1981, he wrote in his diary:

> An N.S.C. meeting concerned mainly with the defense plans. Our task force has reported to Cap that we need a worldwide communications system for reaching our Subs, missile sites & Air Forces. They recommend going ahead with 100 B-1's while we develop the ATB plane. Go for the new D5 missile for our Tridents & go for the MX without the race track but put some in Silos and in airplanes.[28]

PEACE WITHOUT SURRENDER

Everything Reagan was doing in these early days of his presidency—from economic policy to his defense spending—can be traced back to his fundamental belief about how to achieve peace.

His conviction was that peace could be achieved in only two

ways: by strength great enough to prevent aggression by enemies or by surrender. The "peace through strength" slogan of his 1980 campaign was borne out of a long-standing conviction. As early as March 1964, he said:

> The thing that our well-meaning liberal friends refuse to recognize is that their whole reasonable "let's talk this over" solution to the threat of the bomb is appeasement, and appeasement does not give you a choice between peace and war. It gives you only a choice between flight or surrender. I commend to you the words of Winston Churchill who said to his own people when they were faced with a fiery trial, "If you will not fight for the right when you can without bloodshed; if you will not fight when your victory will be sure and not too costly, you may come to the moment when you will have to fight with all the odds against you and only a precarious chance of survival." There may be a worst case. You may have [to] fight when there is no chance of victory because it is better to perish than to live as slaves.[29]

And in 1975, just a few months after concluding his second term as governor of California, he asked rhetorically in a radio commentary:

> How much is it worth to not have World War III?

His answer was that:

> Enough evidence of weakness or lack of will power could tempt the Soviets as it once tempted Hitler and the rulers of Japan. . . . Power is not only sufficient military strength but a sound economy, a reliable energy supply, and credibility—the belief by any potential enemy that you will not choose surrender as the way to maintain peace.[30]

Peace

How much is it worth to not have W W III

Of course the over taxed citizenry in Europe & America want govt. spending reduced. But if we are told the truth, namely that enough evidence of weakness or lack of will power on our front could tempt the Soviet U. as it once did Hitler & the mil. rulers of Japan to believe our decision would be in favor of an ounce of prevention.

Power is not only sufficient mil. strength but it is also a sound economy, a reliable energy supply and credibility — the belief by any potential enemy that you will not choose surrender as the way to maintain peace.

Selections from Reagan's 1975 radio commentary on peace.

Reagan was even more explicit in his 1980 campaign:

I've called for whatever it takes to be so strong that no other nation will dare violate the peace . . . world peace must be our number one priority. . . . But it must not be peace at any price; it must not be a peace of humiliation and gradual surrender. . . . It is important, also that the Soviets know we are going about the business of building up our defense capability pending an agreement by both sides to limit various kinds of weapons.

Reagan did not think the Soviets wanted war. They wanted, he thought, victory without war. In the same speech he said:

The Soviets want peace and victory. . . . They seek a superiority in nuclear strength that, in the event of a confrontation, would leave us with a choice of surrender or die . . . but if we have the will and the determination to build a deterrent capability we can have real peace because we will never be faced with such an ultimatum. Indeed, the men in the Kremlin could in the face of such determination decide that true arms limitation makes sense.[31]

Reagan kept a file of 4-by-6-inch cards in his desk on which he had copied quotations he liked to use, and it included one from Dwight D. Eisenhower that summed up Reagan's own defense philosophy: "The vital element in keeping the peace is our mil. establishment. Our arms must be mighty, ready for instant action, so that no potential aggressor may be tempted to risk its own destruction."[32]

In 1963 Reagan had written a prophetic summary of his views about the U.S. economic and political system and the Soviet challenge:

The only sure way to avoid war is to surrender without fighting. . . . The other way is based on the belief that in an all out race our system is stronger, and eventually the enemy gives up the race as a hopeless cause. Then a noble nation believing in peace extends the hand of friendship and says there is room in the world for both of us.[33]

Chapter 4

~

NEAR DEATH FROM
AN ASSASSIN

I'm a little wounded
but I am not slain;
I will lay me down
for to bleed awhile,
Then I'll rise and
fight with you again.
—RONALD REAGAN'S FAVORITE POEM,
SIR ANDREW BARTON, 1466–1511

For Reagan, March 1981 began with a threatening letter from the Soviet Union and ended with an assassin's bullet lodged in his chest, next to his heart.

On March 6, national security went to the top of Reagan's agenda when he received a nine-page letter from Leonid Brezhnev, the general secretary of the Soviet Union. The brief honeymoon was over; now Reagan's work became serious. The letter was direct, almost insulting, with Brezhnev beginning by saying to Reagan:

I suppose you are aware that the Congress of our Party, which re-
cently took place in Moscow, devoted paramount attention to analysis

and evaluation of the international situation. . . . and to ensure for present and future generations the most basic right of each person—the right to life.

Then, with no hint of irony, Brezhnev added this:

The Soviet Union has not sought, and does not seek superiority. But neither will we permit such superiority to be established over us. Such attempts, as well as attempts to talk to us from a position of strength, are absolutely futile . . . to attempt to win in the arms race, to count on victory in an atomic war—would be dangerous madness.

Brezhnev continued by warning the United States not to get involved in Afghanistan, demanding that the United States limit the deployment of new submarines and that it agree to:

. . . a moratorium now of the deployment in Europe of new medium-range nuclear missile facilities . . . and cease all preparations for deployment . . . of the American Pershing II missiles and ground-based strategic cruise missiles.

Brezhnev then warned against "the vital necessity of averting a nuclear catastrophe," asserted the need for "improving the international atmosphere and preventing war," and closed with a touch of contempt when he told Reagan that "We expect, Mr. President, that you will regard our proposals with appropriate attention."[1]

Between the lines, it was a threatening, bullying letter designed to intimidate a new U.S. president, a man the Soviets knew had little experience dealing with hostile foreigners.

Initially, Reagan turned the letter over to his national security advisers—primarily Al Haig, the secretary of state, a man who had long experience dealing with the Soviets. Haig was not surprised at the tone and substance of Brezhnev's letter, and he set to work answering it in the same tough style.

The Brezhnev letter—what it said and how it was to be answered—surpassed in importance all the other national security issues facing Reagan. Yes, the U.S. economy was crucial; yes, there were dozens of issues that required his urgent attention. But it was the Soviet Union that had thousands of nuclear missiles targeted on the United States, able to wipe most of the country from the face of the earth.

Nineteen days later a suggested State Department reply from Haig was sent to the White House. Reagan's national security advisers were appalled at the draft. Even Richard Pipes, Reagan's hard-line adviser from Harvard, thought it was "fundamentally negative and in places undiplomatic in language" and "would be perceived by Moscow as deliberately insulting." Pipes suggested it be "rethought and rewritten."[2]

Richard Allen, the national security adviser, agreed with Pipes and others who had read the Haig draft. Reagan signed a decision memorandum returning the letter to the State Department for redrafting, but the next draft was still objectionable. Allen thought it was a terrible letter. He brought it to the attention of James Baker, the chief of staff, and Edwin Meese, the counselor to the president, on Monday morning, March 30.[3] The stage was set for a nasty staff fight between Allen, who said he had "no interest in locking horns with State over this issue," and Haig.

But that squabble never happened. Far more momentous events intervened.

At 2:25 p.m. on March 30, Reagan was gunned down by an assassin in a Washington, D.C., street, just after speaking to an AFL-CIO luncheon at the Washington Hotel. The bullet ripped into his chest, missing his heart by a fraction of an inch.

The White House security chief, Jerry Parr, immediately slammed Reagan into the backseat of his limousine and sped to George Washington University Hospital. Parr may have saved Reagan's life, for after they pulled up in front of the hospital, Reagan attempted to walk in but collapsed. Blood was filling Reagan's lungs as he stumbled through the front door of the hospital, close to death.

The spray of bullets from the assassin cut down three other men. His gun, a Rohm RG-14 .22 caliber revolver, spoke for only a few seconds, but the damage was massive. James Brady, the White House press secretary, took a bullet in his skull and was brain-damaged the rest of his life. One Secret Service agent, Timothy McCarthy, and a District of Columbia policeman, Thomas Delanty, took bullet wounds but recovered.

When word of the assassination attempt reached the White House, some of his advisers walked to the Situation Room, sat at the small table, and waited to hear whether Reagan was dead or alive. Thoughts raced through everyone's head. If Reagan died, the group's many plans and dreams would die with him. Who had shot him? Could it be a KGB assassin? Cap Weinberger had already increased the United States' military readiness. Were we going to war with the Soviet Union? Slowly the room filled up with about twenty men.

It turned into a very long day. As everyone in the Situation Room waited—and prayed—the last sixty-nine days flickered by. So much had been started, so much had been done; what would happen now?

The doctors in the hospital began operating at 3:30 p.m. It was a difficult operation. As one of the doctors later told a close aide, "It took me forty minutes to get through that chest. I have never in my life seen a chest like that on a man his age."[4] Almost two hours later the operation was over.

Reagan remained in the hospital for eleven days. He was a model patient. Despite grievous injury, he'd even joked with the doctors as he was wheeled into the operating room, saying:

I hope you all are Republicans.

While the operation to remove the bullet was successful, a serious infection settled in a few days later. The infection raged for almost a week and came close to killing him a second time. But Reagan had a determined will to live, and a surprisingly strong body for a seventy-year-old man.

When Reagan walked out of the hospital, waving, on April 11, 1981, people all over the world sighed and relaxed.

Reagan's recovery from the assassination attempt soon gave him an aura that, for a while, turned into political awe. An outpouring of affection and warmth from the American people swept over him like a warm, soft blanket. The people of the United States, and many around the world, had fallen in love with him. For a while, he could do no wrong. Even as the love waned and he made mistakes, he became known as the "Teflon president," the man to whom bad things simply did not stick.

After Reagan had left the hospital and returned to the White House, he sat down with his personal diary and wrote about what he had been through.

Getting shot hurts. Still my fear was growing because no matter how hard I tried to breathe it seemed I was getting less & less air. I focused on that tiled ceiling and prayed.

But I realized I couldn't ask for Gods help while at the same time I felt hatred for the mixed up young man who had shot me. Isn't that the meaning of the lost sheep? We are all Gods children & therefore equally beloved by him. I began to pray for his soul and that he would find his way back to the fold.

I opened my eyes once to find Nancy there.

I pray I'll never face a day when she isn't there. Of all the ways God has blessed me giving her to me is the greatest and beyond anything I can ever hope to deserve.[5]

getting shot hurts. Still my fever was growing because no matter how hard I tried to breathe it seemed I was getting less & less air. I focused on that tiled ceiling and prayed. But I realized I couldn't ask for Gods help while at the same time I felt hatred for the mixed up young man who had shot me. Isn't that the meaning of the lost sheep? We are all Gods children & therefore equally beloved by him. I began to pray for his soul and that he would find his way back to the fold.

I opened my eyes once to find Nancy there. I pray I'll never face a day when she isn't there. Of all the ways God has blessed me giving her to me is the greatest and beyond anything I can ever hope to deserve.

• • • •

Whatever happens now I owe my life to God and will try to serve him in every way I can.

Reagan's personal diary on the shooting.

He finished his diary entry that Saturday night with a few prophetic words that would have a deep, abiding effect on the rest of his presidency. Everything he had dreamed about and fought for as he ran for the office of president of the United States had been suddenly solidified. Now he knew not only what he wanted to do but what he had to do. The last words he wrote that night were:

> Whatever happens now I owe my life to God, and will try to serve him in every way I can.[6]

Chapter 5

~

THE BEGINNING OF THE END
OF THE COLD WAR

A wise man turns chance into good fortune.
—Thomas Fuller, 1732

In spite of wounds that would have slowed down even a young man for a long time, Reagan soon had launched himself full tilt back into the work of a United States president. The intensity with which he pursued his mission was stronger than ever.

Reagan's first move was to take charge of how his administration would deal with the Soviet Union, looking ahead to the desirability of arms control. His second move was to drive ahead on getting his economic plans accepted by Congress, including the Democratic-controlled House.

The staff squabbling about the reply to Brezhnev's letter had stopped in its tracks the day Reagan was shot. Forty-four days had passed since Reagan had received the Brezhnev letter, and an answer was overdue. So on Saturday, April 18, while he was sitting in the White House solarium, Reagan decided to take matters into his own hands. He reached for a pen and began to write his own letter to Brezhnev.

Earlier, Reagan had talked to Haig about writing the letter, and recalled the secretary of state's reaction:

> When I told him I was thinking of writing a personal letter to Brezhnev, Al was reluctant to have me actually draft it. If I was going to send a letter, he said the State Department should compose it . . . As I was to learn over the next year, he didn't even want me as the president to be involved in setting foreign policy . . . He didn't want to carry out the president's foreign policy; he wanted to formulate it and carry it out himself.[1]

Evidently Haig had forgotten Reagan's words in the first meeting of the National Security Council: sitting next to Haig, Reagan had carefully said that while he wanted all their advice, he would make the final decisions. So now, further emboldened by his recent pledge to God, Reagan handwrote his own three-page letter, consciously ignoring the secretary of state. In his diary he noted:

> Wrote a draft of a letter to Brezhnev. Don't know whether I'll send it but enjoyed putting some thoughts down on paper.[2]

The draft was given to Richard Allen for comment and evaluation. The national security adviser had the handwritten draft typed, and convened a couple of meetings to get the views of specialists from the State Department, CIA, and NSC, including Walter Stoessel and Seymour Weiss from State, Robert Gates from CIA, and Richard Pipes. Pipes recalls the draft as "mawkish." "I could not believe my eyes . . . it was written in a Christian turn-the-other-cheek spirit, sympathetic to the point of apology, full of icky sentimentality . . . Weiss called it 'atrocious.' All of us agreed it should not be sent. We were unanimous that the President's sentiments, if at all, should be included in a paragraph or two of the formal reply."[3]

The next two days, Sunday and Monday, came and went, and there was still no official comment on the letter Reagan had drafted. On Tuesday, April 21, Reagan wrote, somewhat scornfully, in his diary:

My Dear Mr. Pres.

I regret and yet can understand the somewhat intemperate tone of your recent letter. After all we approach the problems confronting us from opposite philosophical points of view.

Is it possible that we have let ideology, political ~~philosophical~~ and governmental policies &c. philosophy keep us from considering the very real, every day problems of the people we represent?

*   *   *

A decade or so ago Mr. Pres. you and I met in San Clemente Calif. I was Gov. of Calif. at the time and you were concluding a series of meetings with Pres. Nixon. Those meetings had captured the imagination of all the world. Never had peace and good will among men seemed closer at hand.

When we met I asked if you were aware that the hopes and aspirations of millions & millions of people through out the world were dependent on the decisions that would be reached in your meetings.

You took my hand in both of yours and assured me that you were aware of that and that you were dedicated with all your heart & mind to fulfilling those hopes & dreams.

The people of the world still share that hope. Indeed the peoples of the world despite ~~the~~ differences in racial & ethnic origin have (very) much in common. They want the dignity of having some control over their individual destiny. They want to work at the craft or trade of their own choosing and to be fairly rewarded. They want to raise their families in peace with out harming any one or suffering harm them selves.

Govt. exists for their convenience not the other way round.

If they are incapable (AS SOME WOULD HAVE US BELIEVE) of self govt. then where in the world do we find people who are capable of governing others.

Excerpts from Reagan's April 18, 1981,
draft of a letter to Leonid Brezhnev.

> I should know today whether my letter to Brezhnev has passed inspection by the striped pants set.[4]

The next day Reagan got the verdict of the "striped pants set" in the State Department. They liked part of what he had written. In his diary on Wednesday night, April 22, Reagan wrote:

> Won part of the battle with the diplomats. They drafted the letter to Brezhnev along usual lines but included major portions of mine. We sent it back for a re-write including more of mine.[5]

What the people at State had actually done was to take the last third of Reagan's draft, which was somewhat innocuous, and attach it to the end of the State Department draft.

By the next day, Thursday, April 23, Reagan had decided enough was enough. He sat down with the letter from Secretary Haig that State wanted to send, and signed it. Then Reagan took the three-page draft he had written five days earlier and some of the light green stationery that is kept only for the president's use. Using the earlier draft as a guide, he began writing his own personal letter to Brezhnev. When it was finished, it was slightly longer, four pages, and a stronger, clearer version of his earlier draft.

Reagan then ordered that both letters—the typed one from Secretary Haig and his handwritten one—be sent to Brezhnev at the same time.

With that single decision Reagan overruled his cabinet and the White House staff, setting a precedent that was to occur often in his administration. The handwritten letter was purely a Reagan document, embodying his foreign policy.

This is what Reagan wrote:

> **My Dear Mr. President:**
> In writing the attached letter I am reminded of our meeting in San Clemente a decade or so ago. I was Governor of

California at the time and you were concluding a series of meetings with President Nixon. Those meetings had captured the imagination of all the world. Never had peace and good will among men seemed closer at hand.

When we met I asked if you were aware that the hopes and aspirations of millions and millions of people throughout the world were dependent on the decisions that would be reached in those meetings.

You took my hand in both of yours and assured me that you were aware of that and that you were dedicated with all your heart and soul and mind to fulfilling those hopes and dreams.

The people of the world still share that hope. Indeed the peoples of the world, despite differences in racial and ethnic origin, have very much in common. They want the dignity of having some control over their individual destiny. They want to work at the craft or trade of their own choosing and to be fairly rewarded. They want to raise their families in peace without harming anyone or suffering harm themselves. Government exists for their convenience, not the other way around.

If they are incapable, as some would have us believe, of self-government, then where among them do we find any who are capable of governing others?

Is it possible that we have permitted ideology, political and economic philosophies, and governmental policies to keep us from considering the very real, everyday problems of our peoples? Will the average Soviet family be better off or even aware that the Soviet Union has imposed a government of it's own choice on the people of Afghanistan? Is life better for the people of Cuba because the Cuban military dictate who shall govern the people of Angola?

It is often implied that such things have been made necessary because of territorial ambitions of the United States; that we have imperialistic designs, and thus constitute a threat to your own security and that of the newly emerging nations. Not only is there no evidence to support such a charge, there is solid evidence that the United States, when it could have dominated the world with no risk to itself, made no effort whatsoever to do so.

When World War II ended, the United States had the only undamaged industrial power in the world. Our military might was at it's peak, and we alone had the ultimate weapon, the nuclear weapon, with the unquestioned ability to deliver it anywhere in the world. If we had sought world domination then, who could have opposed us?

But the United States followed a different course, one unique in all the history of mankind. We used our power and wealth to rebuild the war-ravished economies of the world, including those of the nations who had been our enemies. May I say, there is absolutely no substance to charges that the United States is guilty of imperialism or attempts to impose it's will on other countries, by use of force.

Mr. President, should we not be concerned with eliminating the obstacles which prevent our people, those we represent, from achieving their most cherished goals? And isn't it possible some of those obstacles are born of govt. objectives which have little to do with the real needs and desires of our people?

It is in this spirit, in the spirit of helping the people of both our nations, that I have lifted the grain embargo. Perhaps this decision will contribute to creating the circumstances which will lead to the meaningful and constructive dialogue which will assist us in fulfilling our joint obligation of finding lasting peace.

Sincerely,
Ronald Reagan[6]

The tone of Reagan's letter and the issues it emphasized were significantly friendlier than the tough version sent by the experts in the State Department. But he did point out to the Soviet leader that government ideologies and policies had gotten in the way of allowing the people—those whom government is supposed to serve—"the dignity of having some control over their individual destiny." It was an implicit challenge to the legitimacy of their government, one that Reagan would express more strongly later when he called the Soviets the focus of evil in the modern world.

At the same time, Reagan was aware of the terrible losses the Soviets had endured in World War II and the lack of trust that lay between the two nations. So he appealed directly to the Soviet leaders, trying to convince them the United States carried no intention to harm them. Perhaps it was a naive approach; perhaps the Soviets scoffed at his words; perhaps they did not believe what he wrote. It would require many years and Reagan's reelection before there was a breakthrough.

Looking back, that letter that Reagan sent to Brezhnev in the spring of 1981 looks more and more like the beginning of the end of the Cold War, because it was with this letter that Reagan established his unique approach to the Soviet Union—the approach he would follow throughout his presidency.

Reagan knew he had a long way to go before he confronted the leaders of the Soviet Union about serious arms control. The U.S. economy was floundering, and unless he could persuade Congress to support his economic program, it would most likely not regain its vigor. And while Reagan had already begun to strengthen U.S. military power, he could not continue on that track until and unless a growing economy provided the necessary money.

So at 5:09 p.m. on April 22, he picked up the phone in the Oval Office and called Tip O'Neill, an old Irish Democrat from Massachusetts. What Reagan did was somewhat audacious: he asked to address a joint session of Congress. Reagan knew that the Speaker of the House could not deny such a request from a president who had just narrowly escaped an assassin's bullet. With that single phone call, Reagan created the best possible opportunity to drive home his economic program.[7]

On April 28, just seventeen days after Reagan left his hospital bed, he walked into the Capitol to address a joint session of Congress. In less than the space of a month the political atmosphere had changed dramatically. Democrats and Republicans alike stood and applauded as Reagan entered the hall. The national Gallup polls showed that Reagan's approval rating had jumped to 62.6 percent, a breathtaking number for a new president.[8] The polls clearly affected the members of the House and Senate. As O'Neill noted, the Congress is responsive to the people, "and the will of the people is to go along with the President."[9]

As Reagan spoke that night he knew he was being welcomed with special respect. He took full advantage of this, urging the Congress to approve his economic program.

As he spoke of his cherished economic program, he could sense that things had changed; there was now a very good chance that he would get what he wanted. That night he wrote in his diary:

Addressed a joint session of Cong. re the ec. pckg. I walked into an unbelievable ovation that went on for several minutes . . . the speech was interrupted 14 times (3 of them standing ovations). In the 3rd of those suddenly about 40 Democrats stood and applauded. Maybe we are going to make it. It took a lot of courage for them to do that and it sent a shiver down my spine.

Except for that all the applause came from the Repub. side. The Demos. just sit on their hands—except for the greeting.

The response from the public has been overwhelming.[10]

A few days later the House of Representatives voted on Reagan's spending proposals. As the May 18 issue of *Time* magazine described it, "Ronald Reagan's velvet steamroller smashed through the Democratic House of Representatives last week, flattening opposition to his radical plan to curtail federal spending . . . not a single Republican deserted his party, while 63 Democrats abandoned theirs. That gave Reagan a 77-vote margin in the 253–176 roll call."[11] Included in the budget resolution were not only Reagan's spending controls but also his defense increases.

On May 18, Reagan compromised on his tax proposal after Democrats demanded a reduction in the top rate from 70 percent to 50 percent. Reagan commented in his diary:

> I'll hail it as a great bipartisan solution. H--l! It's more than I thought we could get. I'm delighted to get the 70 down to 50. All we give up is the 1st year 10% beginning last Jan. to 5% beginning this Oct. Instead of 30% over 3 yrs. (36 mos.) it will be 25% over 27 months.[12]

More victories followed. On July 31, after a series of contentious congressional votes and a lengthy conference to iron out differences between the House and the Senate, the Omnibus Budget and Reconciliation Act of 1981, embodying changes in scores of programs, was passed in its final form. The Economic Recovery Tax Act of 1981 passed in the House 238–195 and in the Senate 89–11 on July 29, and in final form on August 4, 1981. Reagan's July 29 diary entry says:

> This on top of the budget victory is the greatest pol. win in half a century.[13]

Would Reagan have gotten his economic program and his defense buildup if he had not been shot? Probably not. Would he have been able to steadily rebuild U.S. military might if the economy had not revived strongly? Almost certainly not. With a weak military posture, would Reagan have been able to use his negotiating skills to convince the Soviets to join us and reduce the number of nuclear missiles on both sides? No, not a chance.

Ronald Reagan did not rise from the dead early in his first administration, but he might as well have. When he walked down the aisle in the Capitol that night to address the two houses of Congress, it was just a month since the day he had been shot by an assassin. The fact that he had recovered and could speak powerfully and smoothly about his economic policies seemed surreal. By all rights he should have died, but there he was, smiling and waving as he strode to the podium.

That night, the first eighty-eight days of Reagan's presidency—one-fourth of the first year of his first term—faded away into the history books. Suddenly, his economic program was alive, something that he and his staff had barely dared hope for. If his economic program worked the way he expected, Reagan would be able to sustain an increase in military spending, the next priority on his list.

It was a clear, simple idea: economic growth begat a potent military force, which begat a strong negotiating posture to confront the Soviet Union.

Chapter 6

~

GOING FOR ZERO

*Reagan's anti-nuclearism is one of the
best kept secrets of his political career, for
it fails to conform to conventional wisdom.*
—PAUL LETTOW, *RONALD REAGAN AND HIS QUEST TO
ABOLISH NUCLEAR WEAPONS*, 2005, PAGE xi

In 1980, when Reagan was elected president, the destruction
that could flow from a nuclear war could eradicate hundreds of
millions of people. Now Reagan had the power to try eliminating
all those nuclear weapons. And in 1981, with his economic policies
in place, he began working in earnest to try to stop what he called
an oncoming Armageddon.

On January 29, at Reagan's first meeting with the White House
press, he was asked about how he would handle the Soviet Union.
Reagan responded:

> We should start negotiating on the basis of trying to effect
> an actual reduction in the numbers of nuclear weapons. That
> would then be real strategic arms limitation.[1]

This may not sound radical today, but it signaled a sea change
in U.S. goals. Previous administrations had sought only to *slow* the

nuclear missile buildup. Reagan's aim—and his goal as long as he was president—was far more ambitious. He sought not to slow the arms race but to *reverse* it.

One of the reporters, Sam Donaldson of ABC News, asked a taunting question: "Do you think the Kremlin is bent on world domination that might lead to a continuation of the Cold War, or do you think that under other circumstances détente is possible?"

Reagan did not mince any words; he was clear about who our enemy was, but he intended to talk directly to the Soviet leaders, not ignore them.

> Well, so far détente's been a one-way street that the Soviet Union has used to pursue its own aims. . . . I know of no leader of the Soviet Union since the revolution, and including the present leadership, that has not more than once repeated . . . their determination that their goal must be the promotion of world revolution and a one-world Socialist or Communist state. . . .
>
> The only morality they recognize is what will further their cause, meaning they reserve unto themselves the right to commit any crime, to lie, to cheat. . . .
>
> We operate on a different set of standards. I think when you do business with them, even at a détente, you keep that in mind.[2]

Most of the press was stunned that Reagan would speak of the Soviets this way. As the months wore on, Reagan repeated again and again what he felt was necessary in order to conduct a negotiation in which the United States and the Soviet Union met on equal terms. His view was that with those conditions in place, progress could be made. Few people believed he would ever get such cooperation, including most of his national security staff. But he persevered, insisting that the Soviets must be willing to discuss reducing nuclear weapons if they wanted to negotiate with the United States. A month later, on February 24, 1981, a reporter asked Reagan what the chances were that he might "have a summit meeting with Brezhnev." Reagan was agreeable to negotiating with the Soviets—*if* they played with the new rules he was insisting on.

> I have repeatedly said that I am willing to negotiate if it's a legitimate negotiation aimed at verifiable reductions, in particular, the strategic nuclear weapons.[3]

Brezhnev never agreed to negotiating a verifiable reduction of the Soviets' strategic nuclear weapons.

On April 30, 1981, Reagan chaired the first meeting of the NSC since he had been shot by the would-be assassin. The meeting focused on the question of when to begin arms control negotiations with the Soviets. Should the United States begin negotiations before the modernization of its own outmoded nuclear weapons was well under way? Should it stipulate a "date certain" when it would negotiate with the Soviets? One group wanted to begin negotiations soon, as many of the European allies wanted. Another group questioned whether the United States should carefully study the issues before beginning negotiations. As Reagan listened to the debate, he would often interrupt and make a comment that usually settled the argument. On the issues of the modernization of our nuclear weapons, Reagan broke in and said:

> We all agree that we need positive movement on modernization before we go into the negotiations. If we do not, then the Soviets will drag their feet because of their large advantage in TNF [theater nuclear forces].[4]

Everyone in the meeting agreed.

On June 16, 1981, Reagan had his third major news conference, largely on the economy, in Room 450 of the Old Executive Office Building. His answers were broadcast live on both radio and television. About a third of the way in, a reporter asked: "What do

Reagan chairing a meeting in the Situation Room.

you think the proper role of the United States is in preventing the spread of nuclear weapons and nuclear weapons technology?"

Reagan replied:

> Well . . . we're opposed to the proliferation of nuclear weapons and do everything in our power to prevent it. . . . But I'm not only opposed to the proliferation of nuclear weapons, but, as I've said many times, I would like to enter into negotiations leading toward a definite, verifiable reduction of strategic nuclear weapons worldwide.[5]

On July 6, 1981, Reagan chaired another meeting of the NSC. The focus was on what should be done about the proposed trans-Siberian oil pipeline and the infusion of cash it would provide to the Soviet economy—and, in turn, what that would allow the Soviets to spend on their military. Richard Allen noted, "The items we will discuss today are of great importance . . . the decisions you make . . . will set the course of our East-West trade policy . . . and will be important in setting the course of our relations with the Soviet Union."

The general feeling was that the United States should not do anything to help the Soviet Union build a pipeline. Reagan had spent most of his time listening, but as the meeting was ending he likened the Soviet Union's statements to those of Hitler, showing clearly what the United States was up against:

> We are held by our Allies to be most rigid to maintain a stricter position. Our Allies note they have the Soviets next to them. Trade is more essential to them.
>
> But, how do we say to our own people that we must continue to sacrifice—and to our Allies—if we are not prepared to use all our weapons?
>
> Don't we seem guilty of hypocrisy—weak—if we are not prepared to take a stronger position? I for one don't think we are being harsh or rigid.
>
> The Soviets have spoken as plainly as Hitler did in "Mein Kampf." They have spoken [of] world domination—at what point do we dig in our heels?[6]

Despite Reagan's opposition to the pipeline, there was little or nothing the West could do to stop the Soviets from creating it. One action Reagan took to slow the Soviets, however, was a closely held secret, and only saw the light of day decades later.[7]

It all began on July 19, 1981, at the economic summit meeting in Ottawa, Canada. That Sunday President Reagan flew up to Ottawa and later in the day had a meeting with François Mitterrand, the president of the Republic of France. Mitterrand took Reagan aside and told him that French intelligence had recruited a KGB colonel named Vladimir I. Vetrov to spy on the Soviets. The spy's code name was Farewell, and the intelligence he provided had been given the name "Farewell Dossier." Mitterrand offered to share that intelligence with Reagan.

The KGB's files were "incredibly explicit. They set forth the extent of Soviet penetration into U.S. and other Western laboratories, factories, and government agencies. They made clear that the Soviets had been running their R&D on the back of the West for years. Given the massive transfer of technology in radars, computers, machine tools, and semiconductors from U.S. to USSR, the Pentagon had been in an arms race with itself."[8] The Soviets had established Directorate T, part of the KGB's First Chief Directorate, to acquire Western technology; Line X was its operating arm of KGB agents assigned to Western embassies and charged with collecting the information.

The NSC senior staff member to whom the Farewell Dossier was assigned was Dr. Gus Weiss. During the fall of 1981, Weiss was cleared to read all the thousands of documents and became intrigued.[9] Everyone else who had seen what the Soviets had been doing was outraged and began working on how to prevent it from happening in the future, but Weiss had a different idea: "Why not help the Soviets with their shopping? Now that we know what they want, we can help them get it."[10]

Pumping oil and gas in Siberia required a lot of technology, including complex computer and software systems—systems the Soviet Union would be likely to steal from the United States. Weiss's idea was to "fix" one of the United States' best such systems so that if anyone used it to control the pressure in a pipeline, it would blow up—and then let the Soviets steal the system. What would be more just than to have someone steal your technology and then have it explode when it was used? Weiss told CIA director Casey, and Casey asked Reagan if it would be okay to try it.

Reagan liked the idea immediately, and gave them orders to proceed.[11]

A KGB agent purchased one of the "fixed" systems in Canada and took it back to Moscow sometime in 1982. It was put to work in

Siberia, to make sure the pressure in the gas pipeline was just right. Then the "fix" kicked in and there was a tremendous explosion. "The result was the most monumental non-nuclear explosion and fire ever seen from space. . . . NORAD feared a missile liftoff from a place where no rockets were known to be based. . . . The Air Force chief of intelligence rated it at three kilotons, but . . . detected no electromagnetic pulse, characteristic of nuclear detonation."[12] Gus Weiss was the only person in the White House (except for Reagan) who knew what happened, and while he could not explain it to anyone, he did tell his colleagues not to worry.

As Reagan moved into the fall of 1981, he began to focus on the idea of wiping out a very specific group of missiles—the 750 Soviet nuclear missiles that were aimed at cities in Europe. The initiative came to be known as the "zero-zero" plan.

On October 13, 1981, Reagan chaired a NSC meeting—this one classified Top Secret—to discuss theater nuclear forces negotiations, set to begin in Geneva on November 30. The Reagan administration was already committed to the 1979 dual-track decision that the United States would provide NATO with weapons—108 Pershing II missiles and 464 ground-launched cruise missiles (GLCMs)—to counter the Soviet SS-20s, SS-4s, and SS-5s targeted especially on the cities of Western Europe, while at the same time seeking negotiations with the Soviets aimed at reducing nuclear weapons in Europe. Meanwhile many people were protesting the installation of Pershing IIs and GLCMs in Western Europe, and political leaders were under pressure to reverse their decisions to accept these weapons. It was a short meeting, only about forty minutes. But at the halfway mark, Weinberger introduced the concept that would lead to the zero-zero initiative:

> We need to assess the nature of our tasks brought on by the strength of Soviet programs. They have 750 SS-20 warheads now. The SS-20's are mobile, accurate, powerful, hard to find and to hit,

and they are targeted against all of Europe and against China and Japan. The U.S. has no counter. In this light, we might need to consider a bold plan, sweeping in nature, to capture world opinion.

If refused by the Soviets, they would take the blame for its rejection. If the Soviets agreed, we would achieve the balance that we've lost. Such a plan would be to propose a "zero option."[13]

What Weinberger was leading up to was an idea that had been floated in Europe almost a year earlier. The idea was simple: The United States would agree not to deploy any of these new missiles in Europe if the Soviets agreed to eliminate every one of their 750 missiles.

President Reagan was very interested in the zero option but cautious, and asked these questions:

> Do we really want a "zero option" for the battlefield? Don't we need these nuclear systems? Wouldn't it be bad for us to give them up since we need them to handle Soviet conventional superiority? . . . How will we verify an agreement? . . . Even if you could have inspections, who could really travel and verify in that vast country?[14]

Al Haig probably felt that Weinberger was intruding on his territory. The secretary of state denounced the idea, saying:

> The "zero-zero" will not be viewed as the President's initiative. It has already been proposed by the German Social Democrats and by [German] Foreign Minister Genscher in Moscow, and it is a subject of intense debate in Europe. There are also some serious problems with any "zero-zero" option. We should be looking for the hooker and must study this issue fully. What would happen in one or two years when it comes time to deploy, if we have a "zero-zero" option on the table? . . . the Europeans will surely reject any new deployments.[15]

Weinberger replied:

The Soviets will certainly reject an American "zero option" proposal. But whether they reject it or they accept it, they would be
set back on their heels. We would be left in good shape and would
be shown as the White Hats.

Reagan, distrustful of the Soviets, was still dubious:

Even if you could have inspections, who could really travel
and verify in that vast country?

William Casey answered:

With a zero ban, it would be easier.

Reagan continued:

Even then, the Soviet Union is a large country. Couldn't
they easily hide something in Siberia or somewhere else?

Edwin Meese suggested:

With a zero ban, we would have an easier indicator of whether or
not the Soviets were complying.[16]

Reagan took the idea under study, and no decision was made
that day in October.

On November 12, 1981, the NSC met again to discuss the issue
of zero-zero. In the interim, Reagan had thought about the zero
option and studied numerous papers on the issue that ended up
on his desk. After Richard Allen briefly introduced the meeting,
Reagan took over:

> I read the paper and those options. Negotiating history and my experience tell me that we should be choosing something between these two options. We should not be saying "zero" or nothing, and we should not be proposing two positions at once.
>
> We should, instead, simply go in and say that we are negotiating in good faith for the removal of these systems on both sides. We should ask the Soviet Union to share in this effort. We should not say this is what we would like to have, but we will settle for less.

And then Reagan gave a little lesson in negotiations to the eighteen advisers sitting in the Cabinet Room:

> One should ask for the moon, and when the other fellow offers green cheese, one can settle for something in between.[17]

Anyone who had ever worked closely with Reagan would have recognized that he had made up his mind, that he wanted to present the Soviets with a tough zero-zero option. It was clear that he would be telling the Soviets that if they did not begin to dismantle the SS-20s aimed at European cities, they would soon be facing hundreds of more powerful missiles in Europe aimed directly at Soviet cities.

Secretary Haig immediately objected to the zero option. "Asking for the moon, for zero," Haig said, "could be turned against us and to our disadvantage."[18] He continued to raise point after point why the zero option was a bad idea. Reagan patiently listened and then replied:

> I would describe the SS-20 system as being deployed at the rate of one per week and capable of destroying every population center in Europe.
>
> On our side, we are countering these with deployment of missiles able to reach deep into Russia.

It is my belief that we can begin negotiations with the hope that we can eliminate all of these missiles totally, verifiably, and globally.

Then, in good faith, we can with regard to other nuclear weapons, look to a realistic reduction.

This is not an all or nothing approach.

It is a hope in good faith negotiations; and we would be willing to match Soviet reductions.[19]

Secretary Haig continued to persist, somewhat annoyed that Reagan was not following the suggestions of his foreign policy chief. "Within 24 hours after you announced this," Haig argued, "the real question you would be asked in Europe is whether that is your only position."[20] The discussions continued as others— Secretary Weinberger and Eugene Rostow, the director of the Arms Control and Disarmament Agency—jumped in.

Reagan finally interrupted:

Right. We'll ask for dismantling and destruction of the specified land-missile systems, and we would be offering the negotiations in good faith on the other systems. . . .

We're not issuing an ultimatum, but are expressing a hope. We are not saying we could ask for more or settle for less. We are naming their and our missile systems and we are hopeful on the rest.[21]

Now Haig interrupted again. "I hope so," he exclaimed. "But we are risking the collapse of our position of its own weight. We must keep in mind Western unity."[22]

Reagan answered:

We should know here what figures we could accept if the Soviets make a counteroffer. . . .

Then, if the Soviets storm against our position, we can ask

> them: Well, what do you think? What is your number? If we
> know the minimum number we can live with, we can answer
> them.[23]

For the next ten or fifteen minutes the discussion went back and forth as Secretary Haig tried again and again to persuade the president and other cabinet members that the zero option was a badly flawed idea. At one point, in exasperation, Haig blurted out: "I'll be a pain in the butt. There is no way we can consult with the Allies on this position without trouble."

Finally, Reagan ran out of patience. He turned to Secretary Haig and said:

> Al, we're not delivering an ultimatum. We'll tell our Allies
> we're seeking the "zero" and that we're negotiating for as long
> as it takes in good faith; and we'll ask for their support.[24]

Weinberger backed up Reagan with this question: "Why would the Allies reject such a bold, dramatic proposal?"

Haig immediately replied: "It's not bold and it's not dramatic. It's been discussed in Europe for the last 12 months."

Well, someone had to be right, and Reagan had now had enough of the squabble between his key advisers. To put an end to the discussion, he asked:

> What shall I say about it in my speech?

Reagan was committed to speak on arms reduction and nuclear weapons to the National Press Club in six days. In asking for ideas for his speech from the men around the table in the Cabinet Room, Reagan was making it clear that he intended to announce his support for the "zero option, and not discuss limits on other missiles":

> Why clutter up the speech then? Its first effect with the Allies and Soviets is what counts. Let's leave it to the Soviets' SS-20's, 4's, and 5's against our Pershing II's and GLCMs [ground-launch cruise missiles].[25]

On Wednesday, November 18, 1981, as planned, Reagan addressed the National Press Club in Washington, D.C., a speech broadcast live on both radio and television. It was a strong speech on the danger of nuclear weapons and Reagan's desire to negotiate arms reduction with the Soviet Union.

One-fourth of Reagan's speech was devoted to reading the handwritten letter he had sent to Soviet president Leonid Brezhnev seven months earlier, on April 24. The letter was classified, but he wanted everyone to know its contents. The letter spelled out how he wanted to deal with the Soviets—not in great detail, but how Reagan felt in his heart.

The second major item in Reagan's speech was addressed directly to the Soviets—the zero-zero option. In Reagan's words:

> The United States is prepared to cancel its deployment of Pershing II and ground-launched cruise missiles if the Soviets will dismantle their SS-20, SS-4, and SS-5 missiles. This would be an historic step. With Soviet agreement, we could together substantially reduce the dread threat of nuclear war which hangs over the people of Europe.
>
> This, like the first footstep on the Moon, would be a giant step for mankind.[26]

Chapter 7

~

THE BOND WITH POPE
JOHN PAUL II

One of the first posts Reagan filled on taking office was that of envoy to the Vatican. He named a devout Catholic who was one of his friends—William A. Wilson. Many other positions were at least as important, but Reagan took a special interest in this one. Reagan knew that Pope John Paul II would be landing in Alaska to refuel on February 26, 1981, and he wanted Wilson to fly to Alaska and greet the Pope as Reagan's emissary.

On February 6, twenty days before the Pope's scheduled

refueling stop, Reagan discovered his plan had fallen apart. He described his anger in his diary that night:

> During day discovered my Ambassador appointments were processed by State Department. They take forever.
>
> I want Bill Wilson cleared by them before 26th so he can meet Pope in Alaska. Told Penn James to tell the guy at State that was advising him to get off his A-- & do it.[1]

The State Department cleared Bill Wilson in record time. He flew to Alaska, met with the Pope, and returned and reported back to President Reagan on February 28.

Reagan's acute interest in Pope John Paul II and Wilson's trip was not new. It went back to 1978, when John Paul II became the first non-Italian to be selected as Pope since the 1520s. Soon he was moving to distinguish himself as one of the most interesting Popes in history. His country, Poland, had suffered brutally for the past forty years—first under the Nazis and then under the yoke of the Soviets. He opposed Communism, not just because of its hostility to religion and its economics but because it was evil, preventing people from being free. Reagan was fascinated as he learned more about John Paul II, and he wrote two radio commentaries about the Pope's stunning visit to Poland in June 1979. Religion was a powerful force even among young people who had, Reagan noted, spent their entire lives under Communist atheism:

> For 40 years the Polish people have lived under first the Nazis and then the Soviets. . . . Now with the eyes of all the world on them they have looked past those menacing weapons and listened to the voice of one man who has told them there is a God and it is their inalienable right to freely worship that God.[2]

The Pope opposed the Marxist-oriented "liberation" theology supported by many of the Catholic clergy in Central America.

Reagan would later quote the Pope's words in a commencement address he gave at Notre Dame:

It was Pope John Paul II who warned in last year's encyclical on mercy and justice against certain economic theories that use the rhetoric of class struggle to justify injustice. He said, "In the name of an alleged justice the neighbor is sometimes destroyed, killed, deprived of liberty or stripped of fundamental human rights."[3]

Reagan saw in the Pope a man whom he believed thought as he himself did, a new Pope who—as the spiritual leader of almost a billion Roman Catholics worldwide—could be a main player on the same world stage Reagan was intent on joining.

This was a man Reagan would watch.

For the next year and a half—1979 to 1980—Reagan was fully dedicated to running his campaign for the presidency, but he never forgot this Pope and what he believed in: human rights, especially the right to worship freely. There is no evidence that Reagan contacted the Pope before becoming president, but that all changed soon after he took office.

What probably brought them together besides their mutual feelings about Communism, Poland, and human rights were the assassination attempts. Reagan was shot on March 30, 1981, and nearly died. On May 13, six weeks later, John Paul II was also shot by an assassin, and nearly died. Two people who would live to have such a massive impact on the world both came close to death at about the same time.

President Reagan was informed of the attempt on the Pope's life within hours of its occurrence. Deeply concerned and worried, he wrote this in his diary that night:

Word brought to us of the shooting of the Pope. Called Cardinal Cooke & Cardinal Krol—sent message to Vatican & prayed.[4]

As the months passed, Reagan and the Pope formed a bond on two issues: Poland and nuclear weapons. Both worked hard to rescue Poland from the clutches of the Soviet Union. The Pope was intensely concerned with Poland because it was his birthplace, his home, while Reagan had a special interest in Poland because the demands from its Solidarity labor union movement, formed in September 1980, were a potential crack in the Soviet empire. Both men shared a deep aversion to nuclear weapons. They would work to reduce them in the hope of one day eliminating them from the world.

By the end of 1981, the growing restlessness in Poland from its Solidarity movement had gotten dangerous enough for the Soviets to act. On December 12, 1981, Poland's puppet government, guided by the Soviets, declared martial law and began arresting thousands of the "troublemakers." President Reagan was among the first to know of this action from U.S. intelligence sources, and that night wrote in his diary:

> Word received that Poland has moved on Solidarity. Leaders have been arrested, union meetings & publications banned, martial law declared. Our intelligence is that it was engineered & ordered by the Soviets. If so, and I believe it is, the situation is really grave.[5]

For the next couple of days there were many calls on the situation in Poland. On Monday, December 14, President Reagan personally called the Pope to express his concern. By coincidence, later in the day a papal delegation visited Reagan to talk not only about Poland but also about saving the world from nuclear holocaust. John Paul II had sent these delegations from the Pontifical Academy of Science to four countries—the United States, the Soviet Union, Great Britain, and France—as well as to the United Nations, to explain their study of the devastating effect nuclear weapons could have on the world. It was only a fifteen-minute presentation, but their conclusions had a strong effect on Reagan, confirming the views he had held for a long time.

On Tuesday, December 15, 1981, while the implementation of martial law in Poland continued, President Reagan chaired a working lunch, classified Secret, with three top advisers to the Pope—his secretary of state, Agostino Cardinal Casaroli; the delegate to the United States, Pio Laghi; and his undersecretary for public affairs, Audrys Backis.

The lunch was held in the Map Room, a quiet room rarely seen by visitors to the White House. With Reagan were Vice President George Bush, James Baker, Al Haig, and William Wilson.[6]

The participants first discussed the Vatican and U.S. analyses of the situation in Poland. Casaroli spoke for the Pope. He and Reagan did almost all the talking. Early into the meeting Reagan began laying out some of his thoughts:

> We should take full propaganda advantage of the fact that what has sparked the imposition of martial law was the Solidarity demand that there be a national referendum on the government. This is a clear comment on the lack of popular support for the government. . . .
>
> I wonder if, in our emphasis on the impressive buildup of Soviet military power, we have failed to appreciate how tenuous may be the Soviet hold on people in its empire. . . .
>
> The Vatican and the Pope have a key role to play in events in Poland, and elsewhere in Eastern Europe. The Pope's visit to Poland showed the "terrible hunger" for God in Eastern Europe. I have heard reports of the fervor of the underground Church in the Soviet Union itself, stories of Bibles being distributed page-by-page among the believers.[7]

When Reagan finished, Cardinal Casaroli looked at Reagan and quietly expounded on the issues that concerned Pope John Paul II. They went far beyond freeing one European country. They were concerned with the world—and the Vatican saw President Reagan as someone who believed as they did and had the power and the will to help them make it happen.

Casaroli recalled that in 1963 an American diplomat in Budapest had told him that "the policy of the United States was to avoid a nuclear confrontation with the Soviet Union, but to work for small openings in the Iron Curtain, to plant the seeds of freedom." Casaroli continued: "Although times have changed, the same principle still applies. The time is not yet ripe for major change in Eastern Europe.

"I and others," said Casaroli, "consider the United States 'the sanctuary' for the future of the world. It is a big responsibility for a President, but you should know the world relies on your good judgment and wisdom."

President Reagan replied:

I hope I can live up to that challenge.[8]

Then Reagan changed the subject to nuclear war—the topic of the previous day's visit from the papal delegation. Reagan explained his position:

Currently the only way to deter nuclear war is to arm as strongly as the potential opponent.

However, this is not good enough. There could be miscalculations and accidents. It is necessary to reduce the number of forces on both sides.

The United States has made a start in Geneva, offering to dismantle one type of missile. I hope this start can be turned into wider moves towards arms reduction. I was struck by the Papal report's conclusion that in the event of a war there would be no way to care for the huge number of wounded.[9]

Cardinal Casaroli replied: "It is relatively simple to understand the horror of nuclear war. It is less easy to figure out how to keep it

from occurring. A credible military deterrent depends on a resolve to incur the horrors of that war if necessary. There should be
some better way."

Casaroli pointed out that another group of scientists was meeting that day with President Brezhnev of the Soviet Union to present to him the same report Reagan had received the day before.

Casaroli continued: "It is a challenge of our time to find the
wisdom to avoid nuclear war. . . . Because of the Vatican's position,
it has to rely not only on the United States, but also on the Soviet
Union for peace in the world."

Then Casaroli made the Vatican's deepest concerns clear:
"Some way is needed to break out of the arms spiral in which each
side wants a little cushion and this spurs the other side to further
escalate. Some way is needed to break that cycle, or to find a balance at a lower level."

Reagan responded to the challenge by spelling out more details of his policy for dealing with nuclear weapons:

> There is no miracle weapon available with which to deal
> with the Soviets, but we could threaten the Soviets with our
> ability to outbuild them, which the Soviets know we can do if
> we choose.
>
> Once we have established this, we could invite the Soviets
> to join us in lowering the level of weapons on both sides.[10]

That Reagan shared these thoughts with John Paul's represen-
tatives showed the depth of his trust in these men, for most of what
Reagan was telling them was his personal national security policy.
He would continue to employ those policies for the years to come.
He even introduced Eisenhower and the use of an "international
authority":

> If the superpowers were engaged in a serious process of re-
> ducing their armaments, the other nations of the world would
> feel obliged to join in.

SECRET

SECRET

THE WHITE HOUSE

WASHINGTON

MEMORANDUM OF CONVERSATION

SUBJECT: President's Working Lunch with Agostino
             Cardinal Casaroli

PARTICIPANTS: The President
               The Vice President
               Secretary of State Alexander M. Haig, Jr.
               President's Chief of Staff James Baker
               Acting Assistant to the President for
                   National Security Affairs James W. Nance
               President's Personal Envoy to the Vatican
                   William A. Wilson
               Acting Assistant Secretary of State for
                   European Affairs, H. Allen Holmes
               NSC Staff Member Dennis C. Blair

               Agostino Cardinal Casaroli, Vatican Secretary
                   of State
               Archbishop Pio Laghi, Apostolic Delegate to
                   the United States
               Monsignor Audrys Backis, Under Secretary for
                   Political Affairs

DATE, TIME   December 15, 1981, 12:45 p.m. to 2:15 p.m.
AND PLACE: The Map Room

After an exchange of pleasantries, Cardinal Casaroli observed
that, based on his conversations with Secretary of State
Haig, the U.S. and the Vatican analyses of the situation in
Poland had many points in common. (S)

Secretary Haig stated he had described two scenarios for
what had happened in Poland: Under the first, President
Jaruzelski had acted to prevent Soviet intervention, and
under the second he had acted as a result of Soviet pressure
to do so. (S)

Cardinal Casaroli stated that he believed that Jaruzelski
had acted both because of Soviet pressure and to prevent the
Soviets themselves from intervening. He believed that
without Soviet pressure Jaruzelski would not have imposed
martial law, but based on his personal knowledge of Jaruzelski,
Cardinal Casaroli felt that he was nationalist enough not to
want the Soviet Union to intervene directly. (S)

The President said that he found it hard to believe, as had
been announced, that Polish troops would actually shoot
Polish workers for labor violations. (C)

SECRET
Rev 12/15/11
NSC 1.13(a)

Reagan's secret meeting with representatives of the Pope, page 1.

The President said that the Vatican and the Pope had a key
role to play in events in Poland, and elsewhere in Eastern
Europe. The Pope's visit to Poland had showed the "terrible
hunger" for God in Eastern Europe. The President said he
had heard reports of the fervor of the underground Church in
the Soviet Union itself. He had heard stories of Bibles
being distributed page-by-page among the believers. (S)

Cardinal Casaroli acknowledged that there was a hunger for God
in specific groups in Eastern Europe, but that in general,
youth was "insensible" to God. Despite strong religious beliefs among certain minorities, young people in general were
apathetic. He told a story of the Pope's visit to Poland.
The Pope in Krakow was prepared to address a group of some
30,000 young people. Having been told that some of these had
prepared a demonstration, he put aside his prepared speech
and improvised remarks to exert a moderate influence on the
crowd. That night the youth held their demonstration in the
streets, and the Police had called a priest to tell the demonstrating youths to wait until the Pope left town. This illus-
trates that there are changes coming in Eastern Europe little
by little, but that the time is not ripe for real change in
Eastern Europe. He recalled the advice given to him in 1963
by an American diplomat in Budapest. He had said that the policy
of the United States was to avoid a nuclear confrontation with
the Soviet Union but to work for small openings in the Iron Curtain, to plant the seeds of freedom. Although times had changed
since 1963, the same principle still applied. The time was not
yet ripe for major change in Eastern Europe. (C)

Mr. Wilson pointed out that we will probably only know in retro-
spect what the time for real change actually was. (U)

Cardinal Casaroli stated that he and others considered the
United States "the sanctuary" for the future of the world.
It was a big responsibility for the President, but he should
know that the world relied on his good judgment and wisdom. (U)

The President replied that he hoped he could live up to this
challenge. He turned to the visit the day before by the
Papal delegation to deliver the study on nuclear war. He
stated that currently the only way to deter nuclear war was
to arm as strongly as the potential opponent. However, this
was not good enough. There could be miscalculations and
accidents. It was necessary to reduce the number of forces
on both sides. The United States had made a start in Geneva,
offering to dismantle one type of missile. It was hoped
that this start could be turned into wider moves towards
arms reduction. He stated that he had been struck by the
Papal report's conclusion that in the event of a war there
would be no way to care for the huge numbers of wounded. (U)

Reagan's secret meeting with representatives of the Pope, page 4.

> President Eisenhower, at a time when the United States had a marked nuclear advantage over the Soviet Union, offered to turn over all nuclear weapons to an international authority.
>
> The world would be different today if the Soviets had not refused to join in this offer.[11]

Casaroli replied: "It is an extremely difficult question, but one vital for the nations of the world to address and solve. The Vatican for its part cannot play a major role, but will provide the moral assistance that it can." Then he made a special offer in the Pope's name: "If an informal channel is needed to deal with the Soviet Union, one that would remain private, the Pope would be available to establish it."[12]

The whole lunch only took an hour, and Reagan and Casaroli talked so constantly it is difficult to see how they got any food. What began as a discussion of Poland soon turned into a careful examination of a much more serious issue: How to tame nuclear weapons. As with Poland, the Pope and Reagan seemed to be on the same page, but Reagan had made it clear that he believed the United States had to engage in an arms buildup to bring the Soviets to the bargaining table. The Pope would be silent in 1983 when it came time to introduce Pershing II and cruise missiles into Europe to counter the threat of Soviet missiles aimed at Europe. He would support the sanctions levied on Poland for imposing martial law, although he would later plead—successfully—for them to be lifted because they were hurting the Polish people. And he would cause extensive rewriting of the American bishops' 1983 letter on war and peace.

On Saturday, December 19, a week had passed since the government of Poland, under orders of the Soviets, had imposed martial law on the country. Reagan was convinced that the actions of Solidarity had forced the Soviets' hand. While this was a setback to the Polish people, it was also an opening to show the nature of the Soviets to the world.

Reagan knew the keen interest of the Vatican and the Pope in freeing Poland, and he had a strong hunch that the Soviets' hold on many of the countries in its empire was weakening. Reagan decided to take action that would hasten the collapse of the Soviet Union. He had no illusions that it would happen rapidly, but he was convinced that the Soviets' days were numbered. In the next five days Reagan held four National Security Council (NSC) meetings to discuss what should and could be done to alleviate the crisis in Poland.

On Monday, December 21, when the second meeting of the NSC on the Poland question was well along, Reagan interrupted and began to lay out how he wished to proceed. Reagan challenged the members of the council who were there that day—including George Bush, Al Haig, deputy secretary of state William P. Clark, Caspar Weinberger, deputy secretary of defense Frank Carlucci, William Casey, UN ambassador Jeane Kirkpatrick, Edwin Meese, and Richard Pipes. It was clear that Reagan had thought about what the United States should do to protect Poland from moves by the Soviet Union, and now he began to lay out the steps he thought were necessary:[13]

This is the first time in 60 years that we have had this kind of opportunity. There may not be another in our lifetime.

Can we afford not to go all out? I'm talking about a total quarantine of the Soviet Union. No détente! We know—and the world knows—that they are behind this. We have backed away so many times! After World War II we offered Poland the Marshall plan, they accepted, but the Soviets said no.

Let's look at the International Harvester license. Kirkland said in a conversation with him that our unions might refuse to load ships. How will we look if we say yes (let U.S. exports to the Soviet Union proceed) while our unions—our own "Solidarity"—won't load the ships?

I recognize that this is a great problem for International Harvester and for Caterpillar. It may mean thousands of layoffs. But can we allow a go-ahead (on these transactions)? Perhaps we can find a way to compensate the companies if we say no. Perhaps put the items in inventory and use them by some other means.

But can we do less now than tell our Allies, "This is big Casino!" There may never be another chance!

It is like the opening lines in our own Declaration of Independence. "When in the course of human events . . ." This is exactly what they [the Poles] are doing now.

One other thing in addition to the Marshall Plan. The Soviets have violated the Helsinki Accords since the day it was signed. They have made mockery of it. We are not going to pretend it is not so.

The room was quiet for a few moments. Then Bush spoke: "I have thought a lot about this problem over the weekend. I agree with the President that we have a real turning point." Everyone else in the room joined in and agreed with what Reagan had said.

But Reagan was not done. After a number of his advisers had commented, he took the platform once again, expanding on his vision:

Let me tell you what I have in mind.

We are the leaders of the Western world. We haven't been for years, several years, except in name, but we accept that role now.

I am talking about action that addresses the Allies, and solicits—not begs—them to join in a complete quarantine of the Soviet Union. Cancel all licenses. Tell the Allies that if they don't go along with us, we let them know, but not in a threatening fashion, that we may have to review our Alliances.

The Helsinki Accords have been violated constantly.

I am thinking back to 1938 when there was a great united effort opportunity. In a speech in Chicago, FDR asked the free world to join in a quarantine of Germany.

On that request, his brains were kicked out all over.

But I am also reminded of Warner Brothers action on its movie "Confession of a Nazi Spy." Interests that wanted to continue selling movies in Germany—even though the Holocaust had already started—offered to buy the film, including a profit for the makers, to prevent it from being shown (to protect their position in German markets).

But Warner Brothers refused to do it. The film was run and had as much impact as anything (in alerting world opinion).

If we show this kind of strength—and we have labor and the people with us; if we demand that Solidarity get its rights; if that happens—nothing will be done. But if not, then we invoke sanctions (against the Soviet Union) and those (of our allies) who do not go along with us will be boycotted, too, and will be considered to be against us.[14]

There were nineteen advisers in the Roosevelt Room, but only treasury secretary Donald Regan and Alexander Haig raised objections. They wanted to go slowly and alert the allies. Haig insisted on "warning the Soviets in an unequivocal way . . . we must decide that we are prepared to act."

Reagan listened and then answered:

That doesn't bother me at all.

If we don't take action now, three or four years from now we'll have another situation and we wonder, why didn't we go for it when we had the whole country with us?

I am tired of looking backward.[15]

Al Haig thought Reagan was making a terrible blunder, a dangerous one. With the meeting almost over, he tried one last time to get Reagan to change his mind:

Let me make no mistake. This is a matter of life and death for the Soviet Union.

They would go to war over this.[16]

Reagan did not argue with Haig; he just quietly ignored the threat of war with the Soviet Union that had been laid on the table. As Reagan got ready to leave the room, he looked at his national security advisers and joked:

Remember, everyone stock up on Vodka![17]

That Monday night, December 21, 1981, Reagan took out his personal diary and wrote about what he had just done.

Another non stop day with virtually no time between meetings.

Most important was NSC meeting re Poland. I took a stand that this may be the last chance in our lifetime to see a change in the Soviet Empire's colonial policy re Eastern Europe.

We should take a stand & tell them unless & until martial law is lifted in Poland, the prisoners released and negotiations resumed between Walesa (Solidarity) & the Polish govt. We would quarantine the Soviets & Poland with no trade, or communications across their borders. Also tell our NATO allies & others to join us in such sanctions or risk an estrangement from us. A TV speech is in the works.[18]

For the next two days, Reagan focused on the developing crisis in Poland. He sensed that the Soviet empire was beginning to develop cracks—small ones, to be sure, but the kind that might be widened. He was now convinced that what was happening in Poland was his first real opportunity to widen one of those cracks. This was his first chance to hurt the Soviet Union, and he was not about to let it pass him by.

On Tuesday, December 22, Reagan welcomed the Polish ambassador and his wife in the White House. Both had defected and asked for asylum in the United States because of what was being done to the Polish people by the Soviet Union. That night, after working with his key advisers, Reagan wrote in his diary that he was going to turn his Christmas message to America into a direct condemnation of the Soviet Union—and a helping hand to Poland:

> I go on TV tomorrow nite 3 networks. It's supposed to be a Christmas message but I intend to deliver a message to the Soviets & the Pols.
>
> We can't let this revolution against Communism fail without our offering a hand.
>
> We may never have an opportunity like this one in our lifetime.[19]

Reagan's personal diary, December 22, 1981.

The next morning, Reagan sent a personal letter, classified Top Secret, Sensitive SPECAT, to Leonid Brezhnev, president of the Supreme Soviet. Here are some excerpts:

> The recent events in Poland have filled the people of the United States and me with dismay. . . .
>
> The most elementary rights of the Polish people have been violated daily: massive arrests without any legal procedures; incarcerations of trade union leaders and intellectuals

in overcrowded jails and freezing detention camps; suspension of all rights of assembly and association; and, last but not least, brutal assault by security forces on citizens. . . .

The United States cannot accept suppression of the Polish peoples. . . . The United States will have no choice but to take concrete measures affecting the full range of our relationship. . . . As leaders of two great and powerful nations, we bear a mutual obligation to demonstrate wisdom, moderation and restraint.

Let me assure you that I am prepared to join in the process of helping to heal Poland's wounds and to meet its real needs—if you are prepared to reciprocate. . . . The alternative is not in the interests of anyone.[20]

That night at 9:00 p.m., Reagan addressed the United States from the Oval Office. In addition to celebrating Christmas, Reagan confronted the Soviet Union.

Here is some of what Reagan said. One of the first paragraphs was written by Reagan himself:

Some celebrate Christmas as the birthday of a great and good philosopher and teacher. Others of us believe in the divinity of the child born in Bethlehem, that he was and is the promised Prince of Peace. Yes, we've questioned why he who could perform miracles chose to come among us as a helpless babe, but maybe that was his first miracle, his first great lesson that we should learn to care for one another.

Then Reagan focused on the situation in Poland:

As I speak to you tonight, the fate of a proud and ancient nation hangs in the balance . . . this Christmas brings little joy to the courageous Polish people . . . The men who rule them and their totalitarian allies fear the very freedom that the Polish people cherish.

They have answered the stirrings of liberty with brute force, killings, mass arrests, and the setting up of concentration camps. . . . It is no coincidence that the martial law proclamations imposed in December by the Polish Government were being printed in the Soviet Union in September.

I have also sent a letter to President Brezhnev urging him to permit the restoration of basic human rights in Poland provided for in the Helsinki Final Act. In it, I informed him that if this repression continues, the United States will have no choice but to take further concrete political and economic measures affecting our relationship.

Let the light of millions of candles in American homes give notice that the light of freedom is not going to be extinguished.[21]

Earlier that same day, December 23, 1981, the fourth NSC meeting in less than a week had taken place. Reagan opened the meeting with this note:[22]

We've been in this room often lately. We need a wardrobe change.

Several of Reagan's advisers had raised their concerns about the upcoming speech. Some were worried about the criticism that would come from the newspapers; others believed that this kind of problem was best handled by the United Nations, and thought people would wonder why the United States was acting unilaterally.

Reagan sharply informed the dissenters in the NSC that he intended to tell the United Nations what he believed:

In my view, I am ready to take on the United Nations at any time. There is hardly a news service in the U.S. that doesn't have a coterie of apologists for the USSR.

There was UN refusal to get anything done there—they would just say, "see the situation isn't that bad (in Poland), and, see others have refused to go along." The U.S. has no support.

Let us save that for the inevitable moment when they will ask, "Why no UN?" We can reply that we didn't treat it there because the UN is impotent, and there is no point in sending it there. We want practical action.

By the end of 1981, a dozen or so letters had been exchanged between President Reagan and Pope John Paul II, a clear indication of the bond that was building between the two men. Some were sent by cable, but many were delivered directly. The letters from the Vatican were beautifully written on thick embossed paper; Reagan's letters were not quite as elegant, but just as clear and direct as the Pope's in spelling out his intentions. (Most of the Vatican's letters are classified and will not be declassified for fifty or more years.) By early 1982, many months before Reagan would meet the Pope in person, the tone of their relations had been set by these letters. Messages flowed back and forth between Reagan and the Pope, through diplomatic representatives, telephone calls, and letters, demonstrating the trust and mutual admiration that had sprung up between the two men.[23]

A few days after New Year's in 1982, Reagan sent one of these personal letters to John Paul II. It was a decisive letter, one that bound together the two men's "responsibilities to mankind," and in it Reagan acknowledged his horror of nuclear conflict and his commitment to preventing what could be the "last epidemic of mankind," and he pledged to take the first step toward removing the nuclear specter that haunts mankind.

This is the full text of President Reagan's letter to the Pope:

The White House
Washington
January 11, 1982

Your Holiness:

For the past several weeks we have consulted closely on the events in Poland by message, telephone and through our diplomatic representatives. I would like to respond in this letter to another joint concern, the prevention of nuclear war.

Your letter of November 25 and a Delegation from the Pontifical Academy of Science described eloquently your convictions about the nature of nuclear war and the necessity of preventing its outbreak. On December 15, Cardinal Casaroli and I had an excellent and thorough discussion of the subject which I am sure he has reported to you in detail.

I fully share your horror at the disastrous consequences of nuclear conflict, the "last epidemic of mankind." I am determined to prevent such a catastrophe.

Your words of encouragement were welcome as we begin our negotiations with the Soviet Union in Geneva. We hope that our proposal for the elimination of all intermediate-range nuclear missiles will be the first step in a disarmament process which will go far toward removing the spectre of fear which haunts mankind.

Finally, I would like to send you best wishes for the coming year.

May we both successfully carry out our responsibilities to mankind.

Sincerely,
RONALD REAGAN[24]

Chapter 8

~

THE NUCLEAR
ABOLITIONIST: 1982

I went through a period in college,
in the aftermath of World War I,
where I became a pacifist
and thought the whole thing was a frame-up.
—RONALD REAGAN, EUREKA COLLEGE, 1928–1932

The first record we have of Reagan's publicly expressing his desire to eliminate all nuclear weapons is on March 23, 1982. That day he traveled from the White House to New York City to address a thousand people at the National Conference of Christians and Jews, where Henry Kissinger presented him with the Gold Medal for Courageous Leadership in Government, Civil, and Human Affairs. Only Nancy Reagan, Ed Meese, deputy White House chief of staff Michael Deaver, and press secretary Larry Speakes made the journey with him.

But before Reagan spoke to his audience, he sat down with seven members of the editorial board of the *New York Post* for a long interview. Right at the end of the interview, one of the editors requested "permission to ask one small question." Speakes agreed: "Sure. Let's go ahead with one more quick one and then scoot out." It didn't work that way. The editor's question was a long and detailed one about the growing rearmament of the Soviet Union.

The question got Reagan's attention, and he explained how he now felt about the Soviet Union:

> They've deprived their people. They've lowered their standards of living just to continue with this massive buildup. And I must say they've been tremendously successful with it. They're—not only quantitatively but qualitatively—militarily they have been an industrial giant.
>
> This is one of the reasons why we can't retreat on what we're doing, because I believe we've come to the point that we must go at the matter of realistically reducing—

And then Reagan seemed to pause, as if he was pulling together all he had learned in his first year—especially the intelligence from the CIA—about the Soviets. He seemed to be thinking of what had to be done and, in the space of a few moments, he came to a conclusion and finished answering the editor's question:

> —if not totally eliminating the nuclear weapons—the threat to the world.[1]

Reagan's comment was stunning. If he was serious, with one comment he had carved out a new policy objective for the national security of the United States.

And Reagan was serious. From that day on, he was a bona fide abolitionist of nuclear weapons. He never saw that dream come true, but it came a long way.

Over his seven remaining years in the White House, Reagan referred again and again—more than 150 times—to the necessity of wiping out nuclear weapons, not just to protect the United States but to protect every other country in the world. He didn't just talk to a reporter or two. He talked to the country and the world, to joint sessions of the Congress, to the United Nations, and especially to the men in charge of the Soviet Union. He wanted all countries—especially the Soviet Union—to join the United States and reduce all their stockpiles of nuclear warheads.

At first no one took him seriously. Perhaps it was just too hard to accept the fact that a president of the United States honestly felt he had a chance to prevent billions of people from being killed or maimed by nuclear weapons. Even in the White House, precious few supported his new policy goal. His advisers, save one or two, just did not believe it was possible, that it was a waste of time to even think about it. But Reagan being Reagan, he quietly ignored them.

When Ronald Reagan was a student at Eureka College in Illinois between 1928 and 1932, he did more than major in economics and play college football. He was also a pacifist. Reagan did not remain a pacifist when World War II broke out, but readily admitted that he had felt differently in his early twenties:

> I went through a period in college, in the aftermath of World War I, where I became a pacifist and thought the whole thing was a frame-up.[2]

While he was a young man in college he had a discussion with a friend working with him in the kitchen of the girls' dormitory— one of them was washing and the other drying—about whether the United States would ever use the capabilities developed in World War I to bomb cities and thus civilians. Reagan was certain the United States would never do such a thing.[3] The story, slightly revised, found its way into his March 9, 1988, speech at Notre Dame, and a later speech, in which he did not indicate which side of the argument he had been on:

> Our class debated whether or not Americans—people who, to our way of thinking, stood for high moral standards—

would ever drop bombs from a plane on a city. And the class was about evenly divided. Half felt it might be necessary. The other felt that bombing civilians would always be beyond the pale of decency, totally unacceptable human conduct, no matter how heinous the enemy.

We believed that young men in America would refuse such an order. But a decade later, during World War II, few, if any, who had been in that room objected to our country's wholesale bombing of cities under the hard pressures of total war. Civilization's standards of acceptable conduct had changed.

It's hard to say they changed for the better.[4]

Ten years after he left Eureka College, Reagan got a personal taste of war during World War II. He was no longer a pacifist. He still abhorred war, but now he would fight if the cause was clear and just. In the weeks before he left Des Moines, Iowa, for Hollywood, he completed the work that would make him an officer in his cavalry reserve unit. He was called up and served in a unit making training films and editing film from the front lines. He left the military with the rank of captain, appalled by what he had witnessed. Perhaps he was most deeply affected by what he had seen as one of the first Americans who reviewed the films of the bodies in the German concentration camps.

By the time I got out of the Army Air Corps, all I wanted to do . . . was to rest up awhile, make love to my wife, and come up refreshed to a better job in an ideal world. (As it came out, I was disappointed in all these postwar ambitions.) . . .

I was a near-hopeless hemophilic liberal. I bled for "causes"; I had voted Democratic, following my father, in every election. I had followed FDR blindly, though with some misgivings. I was to continue voting Democratic through the 1948 election— Harry S. Truman. . . .

Like most of the soldiers who came back, I expected a world suddenly reformed. *I hoped and believed that the blood and death . . . of World War II would result in a regeneration of mankind . . .* and that the bird of happiness would rise out of the ashes and fly everywhere at once.

I was wrong. . . .

I discovered that the world was almost the same and perhaps a little worse. My first reaction was to take a vacation at Lake Arrowhead. There I could laze around and take time to figure things out. . . . The result of my weeks of freedom crystallized a determination in my mind.

I would work with the tools I had: My thoughts, my speaking abilities, my reputation as an actor.

I would try to bring about the regeneration of the world I believed should have automatically appeared.[5]

The vow that Reagan made to himself in September 1945 was one of the most grandiose promises of the century. Undoubtedly others have made similar statements, but very few, perhaps none, have come closer to accomplishing them. Reagan never fully got his dream, but he did have a vision that served him well.

After the war, Reagan was thirty-four years old, tall, handsome, soon to be divorced—and wealthy (he had just received a Warner Bros. contract for seven years worth over $20 million in today's dollars).[6]

The world waited for him.

A few months after American nuclear bombs leveled two Japanese cities, Reagan was asked to do a dramatic reading of a powerful poem that condemned the use of nuclear weaponry. The poem, written by Norman Corwin, was entitled "Set Your Clock at U-235." The dinner, held on December 10, 1945, was sponsored by a group called the Hollywood Independent Citizens Committee of the Arts, Sciences and Professions, which was reputed to support left-of-center causes.

The poem Reagan read that night warned of the dangers of nuclear weapons and suggested an international group to control them:

> *We are all in the zone of danger: we are in it together . . .*
> *The answers are in us together . . .*
> *Unless we work at it together, at a single earth.*[7]

Reagan must have done an excellent job reading that poem because he was asked to repeat his reading two days later. But Warner Bros. intervened with an argument about his contract, and Reagan was forced to pass up any further opportunities.

In 1950, Reagan was asked to write an article for one of the Hollywood magazines, where he laid out the essence of his religious views:

> I wouldn't attempt to describe what God is like, although I place my greatest faith in Him. I think the wonderful line in the Bible, which says God is love, comes as close as words can.
>
> I certainly don't expect to spend eternity on a cloud, but I do think there's something beyond the grave, that we were given souls for a reason, that if we live as the Bible tells us, a promise will be kept. I don't believe in hell. I can't believe that an all wise and loving Father would condemn any one of his children to eternal damnation. Nor do I believe that God can be blamed for all the tragedies in the world.
>
> The tragedy of war, for example.
>
> If we each lived according to the rule of the Bible, if we loved our neighbor and did unto others as we would have others do unto us, how could war ever be?
>
> The responsibility is in our hands alone.
>
> Our lives are in our hands. . . . I think God gave us certain control over our own destiny. He showed us by rules and by countless examples how to live happily and well.

I believe in prayer. . . . Now I go to a Protestant church, the Hollywood Beverly Christian Church—though not as regularly as I should. . . .

The late Franklin D. Roosevelt, while still a young man, was stricken with polio. There must have been moments when he desperately asked "Why did this happen to me?" But today we often wonder: Would he have been as great a man if it hadn't happened? . . . The struggle he went through and the patience he learned brought out the greatness which might otherwise have laid dormant within him.

For each of us is the sum total—in a way—of everything that happens in our daily lives . . . in spite of these great misfortunes, and in spite of all the suffering we see around us every day, I think of the poet who wrote:

God's in His Heaven,
All's right with the world.

And I feel within me that this is indeed the truth.[8]

The idea that human beings were responsible—that what people did made a difference—was also the point of a story he often told at the beginning of speeches to audiences around the country in the years before he became president. Of course, it also got a laugh. Here's a version of that story as he told it to the Future Farmers of America in 1986:

An old farmer had a piece of creekbottom land that had never been developed at all—it was all rocks and brush and all messed up. And he started in on it, clearing it—the underbrush, and hauling away the rocks, then cultivating the soil there. And he planted a garden—everything from vegetables on to corn, and it really became a garden spot. And he was pretty proud of what he'd done. So, one Sunday morning in church after the service he asked the preacher if he wouldn't stop by to have a look.

Well, the preacher arrived. And he took one look and he said, "Oh, this is wonderful." He said, "These are the biggest tomatoes I've ever seen. Praise the Lord." And he said, "Those green beans, that squash, those melons." He said, "The Lord really has blessed this place. And look at the height of that corn." He said, "God has really been good." And the old boy was listening to all this, and he was getting more and more fidgety and finally he blurted out, "Reverend, I wish you could have seen it when the Lord was doing it by himself." [Laughter]

I've always liked that joke because it makes a good point: God did give us this great and good land, but it's up to us to make it flourish and to preserve its freedom, to see it grow, and to keep it a nation of greatness.[9]

After 1945, as Reagan slowly made the political transition from Democrat to Republican, there is no record of him talking again of the immorality of nuclear weapons for twenty-two years. But at least twice along the long path to his becoming president, the dangers of nuclear weapons to the entire world made it into his speeches. On September 28, 1967, as the governor of California, he spoke to students and faculty at Eureka College. At one point he asserted:

We are the generation that exploded the atomic bomb and brought a permanent terror to the world.[10]

Then, nine years later, on August 19, 1976, after narrowly losing the presidential nomination to President Ford, he was asked to speak to the Republican National Convention for a few minutes. Out of nowhere, he electrified the delegates, and the rest of the nation, with these words:

> We live in a world in which the great powers have poised and aimed at each other horrible missiles of destruction, that can, in a matter of minutes, arrive in each other's country and destroy virtually the civilized world we live in.[11]

But no one was prepared when Reagan announced nearly fifteen years later that the best thing to do was get rid of all nuclear weapons. From the Soviets came a long silence. The people close to him, especially his national security advisers, seemed to humor him, assuming the notion would eventually go away. But it didn't.

On February 18, 1982, in a meeting in the Situation Room that lasted over an hour, Reagan had been briefed on the exact dimensions of the Soviet threat. He wrote in his diary:

> Had a briefing on Soviet Arms. It, was a sobering experience. There can be no argument against our re-arming when one sees the production complex they have established for the mfg. of every kind of weapon and war machine.
>
> Their sophistication is frightening.[12]

On April 16, 1982, the National Security Council met to consider a review of national security objectives ordered by the president. William Clark, the national security adviser, opened the discussion, noting, "The importance of this study is indeed great; it will guide not only budget decisions but also the national security for the balance of the century."[13]

Tom Reed, counselor to the NSC, summarized:

The threats we face and the nature of our objectives are such that we are at a time of greatest danger to our national security since World War II . . . we call for active measures to counter Soviet expansionism, to encourage the liberalizing tendencies in the Soviet bloc, and to force the Soviet Union to bear the brunt of its economic mismanagement.

The bottom line is that we are helping encourage the dissolution of the Soviet Empire.[14]

Reagan listened, and then informed the group about his own thinking:

I have always been of the view that the Soviets, if they think they are ready to engage us, will not need an excuse, but at the same time they will not engage us if they feel threatened. What we need is presence so that they know if they come in, they will have to confront the US. Can't we use our presence in Europe to obtain that effect?

You look at Russian history. Protecting the homeland has always been of paramount importance. If they know that we might respond to them by hitting them anywhere in the world, that's a strong deterrent.[15]

Reagan concluded:

We will do whatever is necessary to meet our objectives. A vigorous defense build-up will also be a great help at arms control talks. The Soviets do not believe that they can keep up with us.

If you compare Western Europe to the Soviet Union, you find that our Allies collectively have a greater population and higher GNP. Why should the Russians look ten feet tall and our Allies look like pygmies?[16]

A few days later, on April 21, 1982, the NSC met to discuss the U.S. negotiating position for the Strategic Arms Reduction Talks (START) with the Soviet Union.

The first negotiations between the two superpowers on their stocks of nuclear weapons had taken place in 1969 in Helsinki, Finland, and were known as the Strategic Arms Limitation Talks (SALT). SALT I was signed in 1972 by President Nixon and Leonid Brezhnev, and SALT II was signed by President Carter and Brezhnev in 1979 but was never ratified by the U.S. Senate. For many years Reagan argued that both the SALT agreements allowed the Soviet Union to significantly increase the number of its nuclear weapons.[17]

During the long, complicated discussion at that April 21 meeting, President Reagan ruled out any reference to the old SALT treaty:

> I agree that we should not have a negotiation position taking an approach linked to SALT. It's obvious that if we do, some will push us to ratify SALT II, which we think is lousy.
>
> Isn't one of the problems with limiting warheads that we cannot easily verify their numbers? This is really an important issue. . . . The land based missiles are certainly the most important of all. Are they difficult to verify?
>
> We have to reduce the first-strike sudden threat of the missiles. The bombers take 12 hours to arrive and are easier to spot. The submarines are not so accurate; and both the submarines and bombers can be attacked before they shoot their missiles.
>
> The ICBM [intercontinental ballistic missile] is different. The greatest psychological factor has to be an emphasis on the land-based missiles and their special threat.

Ambassador Edward Rowny responded, "You are absolutely right. These missiles are the most destabilizing weapons. SALT II allowed them to build and deploy more." Eugene Rostow agreed with Rowny: "That's right. They are the most destabilizing weapons." And Secretary Haig told Reagan, "Your decision on the

TOP SECRET

NATIONAL SECURITY COUNCIL MEETING

DATE, TIME AND PLACE:	Wednesday, April 21, 1982 The Cabinet Room -- 10:30-11:40 A.M.
SUBJECT:	Strategic Arms Reductions Talks (START)

PARTICIPANTS:

The President
The Vice President

State
Secretary Alexander M. Haig, Jr.
Mr. Richard Burt, Director, Politico/
Military Affairs

OSD
Secretary Caspar W. Weinberger
Under Secretary Fred C. Ikle

OMB
Associate Director William Schneider

CIA
Director William J. Casey

USUN
Ambassador Kenneth Adelman

JCS
General David C. Jones

ACDA
Director Eugene V. Rostow
Ambassador Edward L. Rowny

White House
Mr. Edwin Meese, III
Mr. James A. Baker, III
Mr. Michael K. Deaver
Judge William P. Clark
Mr. Robert C. McFarlane
Admiral John M. Poindexter
Mr. Richard G. Darman

The Vice President's Office
Admiral Daniel J. Murphy

NSC
Colonel Michael O. Wheeler
Mr. Sven Kraemer
Lt Col Robert Linhard

Minutes

Judge Clark: Mr. President, today we will beginning final preparations in the NSC process to develop the U.S. negotiating position
for START. There are divergent views on many of the complex
issues involved. That is healthy. We will begin today with a
presentation by Richard Burt (Department of State) on the START
interagency process thus far.

TOP SECRET

Minutes of the April 21, 1982, NSC meeting.

TOP SECRET

<u>The President</u>: I agree that we should not have a negotiattion position taking an approach linked to SALT. It's obvious that if we do, some will push us to ratify SALT II, which we think is lousy.

Isn't one of the problems with limiting warheads that we cannot easily verify their numbers? That is really an important issue.

* * *

<u>The President</u>: The land-based missiles are certainly the most important of all. Are they difficult to verify?

We have to reduce the first-strike sudden threat of the missiles. The bombers take 12 hours to arrive and are easier to spot. The submarines are not so accurate; and both the submarines and bombers can be attacked before they shoot their missiles. The ICBM is different. The greatest psychological factor has to be an emphasis on the land-based missiles and their special threat.

* * *

<u>The President</u>: It's too bad we cannot do in START what we did in INF, or what Ike (Eisenhower) proposed on all nuclear weapons. First, we need to restore the balance.

* * *

<u>The President</u>: How many Titan missile silos do we have (for M-X)?

* * *

<u>The President</u>: What about those SS-16's? Are they in Kamchatka? I am concerned about our West Coast and Alaska.

Excerpts from Reagan's statements and decisions
during the April 21, 1982, NSC meeting.

framework of our START position will probably be the most important of your Presidency."

Reagan wistfully ended the meeting on this note:

It's too bad we cannot do in START what we did in INF [intermediate-range nuclear force], or what Ike [Dwight D. Eisenhower] proposed on all nuclear weapons.

First, we need to restore the balance.[18]

Reagan was referring to a speech Eisenhower made to the United Nations on December 8, 1953, eleven months after taking office, in which he called for the elimination of all nuclear weapons in the world. His straightforward idea was "to take this weapon out of the hands of the soldier . . . and put it into the hands of those who will know how to strip its military casing and adapt it to the arts of peace."

Eisenhower could not persuade the Soviets to join him, and the nuclear arms race began. Now Reagan was clearly thinking of what might have been, and of how important it would be, even now, to rein in all these nuclear weapons.

But no member of Reagan's National Security Council responded to his passing thought. No one acknowledged his reference to the 1953 speech.

Later the same day, April 21, 1982, Reagan expressed his ideas—as he often did—in a personal letter, this one to a Miss Virginia Adams at the West Virginia School of Lay Ministry. He told her directly of his hopes:

We must reduce and hopefully eliminate nuclear weapons but we cannot do so unilaterally. The Soviet Union has the greatest offensive military power the world has ever seen.[19]

On May 9, 1982, President Reagan flew with his wife, Nancy, to Eureka College to give the commencement address, forty-five years after he graduated. Reagan had loved being a student in Eureka College, and loved even more to go back and speak. This was one of his main points to the students:

> My duty as President is to ensure that the ultimate nightmare never occurs, that the prairies and the cities and the people who inhabit them remain free and untouched by nuclear conflict.
>
> I wish more than anything there were a simple policy that would eliminate that nuclear danger.[20]

The next day, May 10, found him in Chicago, answering questions from students at Providence St. Mel High School. The press was there to take notes on what Reagan said. At the close of the forty-five-minute event, one student stood up and asked why "the United States had to have nuclear weapons instead of just relying on conventional weapons."

Reagan carefully answered the student's question in detail, and ended by saying:

> The ultimate goal that we could all dream of is the same one that's in Geneva now—getting rid of them forever. And, believe it or not, you can be proud of your country. Under President Eisenhower, a number of years ago . . . he offered to the Soviets and to the world to turn all such weapons over to an international body like the United Nations and take all of them away as a threat between nations.
>
> And the Soviet Union refused.
>
> So, we're going to try again.[21]

A little over a month later, on June 17, 1982, Reagan addressed the United Nations for the first time. That day he did not mention his dream of getting rid of all nuclear weapons, but he did severely criticize the Soviet Union. Reagan focused especially on the time the Soviets had had an opportunity to eliminate nuclear weapons and rejected it. Here are excerpts of that speech:

> In 1946, in what became known as the Baruch plan, the United States submitted a proposal for control of nuclear weapons and nuclear energy by an international authority. The Soviet Union rejected this plan. . . .
>
> During my recent audience with His Holiness Pope John Paul II, I gave him the pledge of the American people to do everything possible for peace and arms reduction. . . . We must serve mankind through genuine disarmament.
>
> With God's help we can secure life and freedom for generations to come.[22]

During the latter part of 1982, Reagan's high-powered national security staff began taking him seriously about his views on nuclear weapons. Some were aghast; others argued with him. No one seemed to encourage him. No one seemed to think he was right, except Pope John Paul II.

But before he could pursue his dream, Reagan had many other things to do—especially guiding his economic program through a bad recession and making one critical personnel change.

Al Haig had never accepted that President Reagan meant it when he'd said at the first meeting of the National Security Council in early 1981 that he would make the decisions. As time went on Haig became more difficult to work with. On June 25, 1982, he submitted his resignation, and Reagan accepted it. Haig announced that his reason for leaving was a fundamental disagreement on foreign policy, but as Reagan wrote that night in his personal diary:

> Actually the only disagreement was over whether I made policy or the Sec. of State did.[23]

Even before he'd accepted Haig's resignation, Reagan had called someone he highly respected, George Shultz, and asked him if he would become his next secretary of state. That same night Reagan wrote in his diary:

I'd called him and like the patriot he is he said "yes."[24]

Reagan's personal diary—an example of one day, June 25, 1982.

Shultz was sworn in on July 16, 1982, and soon became the key person at Reagan's side as he began his drive to convince the Soviet Union of the necessity of nuclear arms reduction.

Toward the end of 1982, the U.S. economy started to recover, George Shultz settled in as secretary of state, and there was also a major change in the Soviet Union: Brezhnev—who had resisted all of Reagan's attempts to engage him on the issue of nuclear arms— died on November 10, 1982. He was succeeded by Yuri Andropov, the former head of the KGB. Many doubted that the former head of the KGB would be an improvement over Brezhnev, but to Reagan at least it was someone new, someone he could try his negotiating skills on again.

Chapter 9

~

"STAR WARS"

*I want to be remembered as the president of the United States
who brought a sense and reality of peace and security.
I want to eliminate that awful fear that each of us feels
sometimes when we get up in the morning, knowing that
the world could be destroyed through a nuclear holocaust.*
—Ronald Reagan, 1983

In the fall of 1981 Reagan turned to one of his most treasured
priorities—how to defend the United States against a nuclear missile strike. But here Reagan had a new problem: he had no defensive missiles. Reagan was familiar with defensive missiles. In 1975,
when he was governor of California, he'd watched President
Nixon build a hundred defensive missiles in Grand Forks, North
Dakota, as part of the United States' planned Safeguard ABM program. But the system was deactivated not long after it was finished,
as the Democratic Senate and House, led by Senator Edward M.
Kennedy, had argued against Safeguard's effectiveness. As summarized in the *New York Times:*

> The first was the basic argument . . . that the Soviet Union could
> overwhelm the Safeguard system by throwing in warheads until all

the Safeguard missiles were exhausted and then start attacking the Minuteman intercontinental ballistic missiles.

The second argument was also made that it would have a destabilizing effect on the nuclear balance if it appeared that the United States was trying to get itself in a position where it could launch a strike against the Soviet Union, and then defend itself against any retaliatory Soviet strike.[1]

On July 31, 1979, Reagan traveled to the North American Aerospace Defense Command (NORAD) in Colorado. He was briefed on U.S. capabilities for detecting an incoming nuclear missile and warning the city that was its intended target. NORAD is buried deep inside a large mountain behind a massive steel door, but when General James Hill, the four-star general in charge, was asked what would happen if just one of the Soviets' most powerful missiles landed outside that huge steel door, he replied, "It would blow us away."[2]

Reagan knew before he went to NORAD that the United States could not stop a nuclear attack or even a single missile. But seeing NORAD and hearing the words of the general somehow made it more real. While flying back to California that night, he and Martin Anderson, who accompanied Reagan, talked about what they had seen. It was clear that Reagan was deep in thought. Very soon he would be running for president of the United States. There was a good chance he would win. And if he won, one day he might be confronted by the same dilemma that potentially faces every president.

If the president is alerted about incoming nuclear missiles, he has only two choices. If he chooses *not* to fire U.S. nuclear missiles at the enemy who launched the attack, then perhaps only one or two U.S. cities would be gone, and a million or more Americans. If the incoming missiles are aimed at the White House or the Capitol, it does get messier. But there is a second choice. The president can, if he wishes, unleash all U.S. nuclear missiles on the country responsible for the attack, of course killing many, many millions of innocent people.

As the discussion on the plane continued, Reagan grew quieter and more serious. Perhaps he was thinking about what he would do if he became president. He seemed frustrated, even though he knew there was no recourse, and finally said:

> We have spent all that money and have all that equipment, and there is nothing we can do to prevent a nuclear missile from hitting us. . . .
>
> The only option a president would have would be to press the button or do nothing.
>
> They're both bad.
>
> We should have some way of defending ourselves against nuclear missiles.[3]

He never mentioned it when he got home, even though he seemed deeply concerned. He simply waited until the time was ripe for doing something about it.

During the campaign in 1979, one document supporting missile defense was prepared for Reagan, but it was never used. The idea for missile defense was a major plank in the Republican platform of August 1980, but Reagan said nothing about it during the campaign. The reason was simple; he was known as a hawk by his political enemies, who misinterpreted—deliberately—any mention of nuclear weapons. But as president, Reagan began to take a more active interest in missile defense.

Missile defense was not high on the priorities of most politicians, even most of Reagan's policy advisers. Neither the Department of Defense nor the Department of State was especially keen on it. So a small White House group was established to investigate the current state of missile defense. What was the state of the technology? How much would it cost? The group was chaired by Ed Meese and included Martin Anderson, Richard Allen, and George (Jay) Keyworth, the president's science adviser.

The first meeting of this small White House group was on

September 14, 1981. Edward Teller, the well-known scientist, attended this meeting and strongly supported the idea of missile defense. On October 12 another meeting was held, and the small group was joined by General Daniel Graham and Karl Bendetsen, a supporter of Graham's "high frontier" concept and retired CEO of Champion International.

Almost three months later, on January 8, 1982, the group met in the afternoon with President Reagan in the Roosevelt Room. The topic was "strategic national security planning," another name for missile defense. Those attending were the president, Edwin Meese, William Clark, Martin Anderson, Jay Keyworth, Karl Bendetsen, William Wilson, and Joseph Coors, a longtime Reagan supporter. Reagan asked many questions about the technical feasibility and cost of missile defense, and was quite pleased with what he heard.[4]

The people close to Reagan knew he liked missile defense and that it would just be a matter of time until he did something about it. It had now been almost two and a half years since Reagan's NORAD briefing and his conclusion that the only hope lay in defensive missiles—missiles the United States did not have.

It would take another fifteen months before Reagan would be able to bring his "baby" to life. And very few people were informed when it did come to life.

In the months since he'd become president and had gingerly tried out his idea of eliminating nuclear weapons worldwide, Reagan had been confronted with objections. One was cheating on arms control treaties. Another was the rogue-state argument. "Sure," some people said, "it would be great to get rid of these weapons. But what if some madman saves one or two, or secretly builds some new ones? Then couldn't he or she blackmail us all? Or even kill us all?"

To Reagan, the answer to this dilemma was clear: the United States needed a missile defense system that would work. If all the nations who feared a madman breaking the nuclear-free boundary possessed such a system, they could easily blast an incoming nuclear missile out of the sky before it could hurt them. The Soviets already had crude defensive missiles. As noted previously, the United States had tried building its own defensive missile system but had dismantled it after congressional opposition.

Reagan saw two purposes for missile defense. The first and obvious one was to protect the United States from incoming nuclear missiles. The second purpose—a dream for the long-term future—was to create a defensive missile system that *every* nation would have one day when all nuclear weapons had been destroyed. The reason? Reagan worried that someone somewhere might cheat on a worldwide disarmament agreement and hang on to a nuclear missile or two for blackmail purposes. Missile defense would then be the world's insurance.

To our knowledge, others who supported missile defense wanted it simply to protect their own countries. They did not think of missile defense as the key to one day eliminating all nuclear weapons. Reagan did.

Reagan's idea, unique, as far as we know, was to marry the idea of missile defense with his vision of eliminating all nuclear missiles.

As Christmas 1982 drew to a close it became clear to Reagan that now was the time to strike. His economic program was beginning to show results. His effort to increase U.S. military power was humming along. The new secretary of state, George Shultz, was working very well with him. Meanwhile, the Soviet Union was struggling with its economy. Now was the time to try to make missile defense a reality. Reagan knew it was a long shot, requiring the United States' most talented scientists to invent what the country did not have, but he was determined to try.

On December 22, 1982, just three days before Christmas, the Joint Chiefs of Staff assembled in the Cabinet Room of the White House at 11:00 a.m. The chairman of the Joint Chiefs, General John Vessey, sat directly across from Reagan. The other four members of the Joint Chiefs, from the Army, the Marine Corps, the Navy, and the Air Force, flanked Vessey. A golden chandelier hung over the large oval table.

To the president's right, hanging on the wall over the fireplace, was a three-foot-high painting of Dwight D. Eisenhower, sternly gazing down on the generals in front of him. As the meeting began you could almost feel that Eisenhower would have approved of what Reagan was about to do; after all, Reagan had selected this portrait to hang in the Cabinet Room.

Sitting on Reagan's right were Vice President Bush, Edwin Meese, and William Clark. On his left were Cap Weinberger and James Baker. The meeting lasted for an hour and ten minutes, and as it wound down, Reagan began questioning the Joint Chiefs about missile defense.

Years later, Reagan would describe what he said to the Joint Chiefs that morning:

> I said, look, every weapon that's ever been created in the world has resulted in a defense, a defensive weapon, the sword and later the shield, and so forth.
>
> And I said, isn't it, with our technology, possible that we could produce a system that could hit those missiles as they came out of their silos—using space, whatever.
>
> Well, they kind of huddled for a minute, and then they came back and they said could you give us a couple of days on that?
>
> And I said yes.[5]

After the meeting was over, the generals drove back across the Potomac River to the Pentagon. One of them telephoned Clark and asked, "Did we just get instructions to take a hard look at missile defense?" The national security adviser assured the general that they had indeed been asked by President Reagan to investigate the idea.[6]

In Reagan's view, there were three levels of arms control policy. The first level was simply arms reductions. The greater the nuclear reduction, the higher Reagan's pleasure and satisfaction.

Level two focused on the zero-zero plan for intermediate-range nuclear forces in Europe. Not only was the plan important for Europe, but if it succeeded, it would stand as a proof of concept, a precedent showing that disarmament *could* be accomplished. As Reagan saw it, lifting the nuclear threat to Europe was the first step toward eliminating all nuclear weapons.

Reagan's third level—his overarching goal—was the total elimination of all nuclear weapons in the world. All the other aspects of arms control—reductions, zero-zero schemes—were subsidiary to the main game, elimination. He knew it was a long shot. In fact, he probably thought it would fail. But that was the way Reagan negotiated.

As 1983 dawned, Reagan was halfway through his first four-year term. A number of things were building up in Reagan's favor—the economy, defense increases, a new man as secretary of state, and another new leader in the Kremlin—and his desire to achieve serious arms reduction with the Soviet Union increased. One of the first meetings of the New Year was on January 13, 1983, with the National Security Planning Group (NSPG). The topic under discussion was the zero-zero plan in Europe. George Shultz started the discussion. "Zero is our objective," he said, "and we should never abandon zero-zero; it is the best conclusion, and it has great appeal."[7]

Countering the buildup of Soviet missiles aimed at Europe required NATO deployment of U.S.-built Pershing IIs and cruise missiles. As the discussion progressed on the number of missiles and warheads and the likely positions the Soviets might take, Reagan suggested:

Why not go along with an interim reduction of the forces, while continuing the negotiations for Zero-Zero? We can say we will start with a lower deployment of missiles and make it enough so they will still face Pershings targeted at Russia. . . . We should deploy on schedule.[8]

The other members of the group, one by one, expressed their approval as the discussion continued. Reagan then summed up where they were heading, saying:

> Well, I think we are all agreed that we want equality, Zero-Zero, and at some point, talk about reduced numbers as an interim step. The date to start is when we start to deploy.[9]

Then Reagan made a brief statement indicating that his vision of arms reduction was radically different from that of everyone else in the room:

> If they [the Soviets] want to talk about other systems such as aircraft and submarines and the like we can say that everything is negotiable, but we are talking first about the most destabilizing weapons.[10]

When Reagan said that "everything was negotiable," no one commented. But he seemed to be talking about *all* nuclear weapons—nuclear bombs carried in U.S. airplanes, and nuclear missiles in U.S. submarines.

Reagan also joked:

> I have gotten so interested in the negotiating position that perhaps I should trade jobs with Nitze.[11]

Paul Nitze was the main arms control negotiator, a highly respected professional. Reagan was only partially joking. He longed to get into the action directly.

The meeting was coming to an end when Reagan summed up what everyone had agreed to:

> Once we start deploying, the Soviets will understand. In the proposal, the Soviet's plan, if there are 1,046 warheads on

SS20s [the nuclear missiles of the Soviets], could we say that the Soviets can destroy every town in Europe of a particular size?

We could tell that to the placard carriers [the men and women who were protesting against deploying the missiles in Europe].

We will deploy. We will start with Zero.[12]

Later that night Reagan wrote in his personal diary:

An N.S.C. meeting re our arms negotiations—we'll stick with our zero option plan.

Found I was wishing I could do the negotiating with the Soviets—They can't be any tougher than Y. Frank Freeman & Harry Cohn [Hollywood executives during Reagan's Screen Actors Guild years].[13]

On N.S.S. meeting re—our arms negotiations—we'll stick with our zero option plan. Found I was wishing I could do the negotiating with the Soviets—They can't be any tougher than Y. Frank Freeman & Harry Cohn.

Reagan's personal diary, January 13, 1983.

Reagan's self-confidence was always muted, visible only to a very few who had known him for a long time. But that small slip, where he told the National Security Planning Group he wished he could take the place of Paul Nitze and negotiate directly with the Soviets, revealed his inner confidence.

With the arms reduction talks—concerning conventional weapons, zero-zero in Europe, and the large intercontinental nuclear missiles—beginning to move forward, Reagan returned to the other building block in his grand design: missile defense.

By February 11, 1983, the Joint Chiefs of Staff were ready to report back to Reagan on his request of December 22, and they joined him in the Cabinet Room at the White House for a luncheon meeting. It was a long meeting as White House meetings go, from 12:10 to 1:43. Only a small group was invited; besides the president, there were seven men from the Department of Defense—Secretary Weinberger, the deputy secretary, and the five generals. There were four from the White House—James Baker, Edwin Meese, Michael Deaver, and deputy assistant security adviser Robert McFarlane.[14]

The Defense Department did spend a lot of time discussing plans for the big MX nuclear missile, but they also told Reagan exactly what he had hoped for—that a missile defense was feasible and possible.

That night when Reagan sat down to write an entry in his diary, he was energized. He now had the key to his dream.

Winter is back—virtually a blizzard. Camp David is out—we're in for the weekend. . . .

An almost 2 hr. lunch with Joint Chiefs of staff. Most of time spent on MX and the commission etc.

Out of it came a super idea.

So far the only policy worldwide on nuclear weapons is to have a deterrent. What if we tell the world we want to protect our people, not avenge them; that we're going to embark on a program of research to come up with a defensive weapon that could make nuclear weapons obsolete?

I would call upon the scientific community to volunteer in bringing such a thing about.[15]

Fri. Feb. 11 Winter is back - with a blizzard. Camp David is out - we're in for the weekend. Started snowing last night. By noon we'd sent almost everyone home before they got snowed in.

George S. & George B. reported in to full N.S.C. planning group. Both trips were very successful. I think we're ahead of the game on the international scene.

An almost 2 hr. lunch with Joint Chiefs of staff. Most of time spent on MX & the commission etc. Out of it came a super idea. So far the only policy world wide on nuclear weapons is to have a deterrent. What if we tell the world we want to protect our people not avenge them; that we are going to embark on a program of research to come up with a defensive weapon that could make nuclear weapons obsolete? I would call upon the scientific community to volunteer in bringing such a thing about.

Reagan's personal diary, February 11, 1983, on page 120.

On the evening of March 7, Reagan sat down with his personal diary and laid out his plan:

> I'm going to take our case to the people only this time we are declassifying some of our reports on the Soviets and can tell the people a few frightening facts. The d--n media has propagandized our people against our defense plans more than the Russians have. We are still dangerously behind the Soviets & getting farther behind.[16]

On March 8, 1983, Reagan became more aggressive. At 8:40 that morning Caspar Weinberger presented him with the first copy of the 1983 edition of _Soviet Military Power_, an annual report on Soviet military forces and weaponry that the Department of Defense had decided to declassify in late 1981 to better inform the public. At ten o'clock he boarded a Marine helicopter for the trip to Andrews Air Force Base, where he climbed up the stairs of Air Force One and flew to Orlando, Florida. Later that day he addressed the forty-first annual convention of the National Association of Evangelicals with a powerful speech. Later he said:

I wanted to remind the Soviets we knew what they were up to.[17]

Here are a few paragraphs from that speech:

They [the Soviets] must be made to understand we will never compromise our principles and standards. We will never give away our freedom. We will never abandon our belief in God. And we will never stop searching for a genuine peace. . . .

Let us pray for the salvation of all of those who live in the totalitarian darkness. Pray they will discover the joy of knowing God. But until they do, let us be aware that while they preach the supremacy of the state, declare its omnipotence over individual man, and predict its eventual domination of all peoples on the Earth,

They are the focus of evil in the modern world.[18]

That phrase, "focus of evil in the modern world" represented the toughest statement Reagan—or any president—had ever made about the Soviets. And it was much stronger than the Soviets knew, for they assumed that some speechwriter had come up with the wording. Also, they focused on a later phrase in the speech that talked about "the aggressive impulses of an evil empire." The Soviets and the media latched onto the words "evil empire," and Reagan's speech became known worldwide as the "Evil Empire Speech."[19] The new leader in Moscow, Yuri Andropov, and other leaders were not amused by the words Reagan pinned on them. The Soviet newspapers denounced Reagan, saying he "exhibited pathological hatred of socialism and communism."

What no one knew is that the original draft had said "surely historians will see there the focus of evil in the modern world," thus postponing judgment to future observers. But Reagan carefully edited the speech draft by crossing out the words "surely historians will see there" and replacing them with his own words,

"They are," putting the emphasis on what he saw now. Today many recall the speech that called the Soviet Union an "evil empire." But that Reagan actually hit the Soviets much harder, saying, "They are the focus of evil in the modern world," has been largely forgotten by most of the rest of the world, though it is probably remembered by many Soviets.

There was one other Reagan edit to the speech that resulted in its most important words, in which he told the world he favored eliminating all nuclear weapons. As far as we know, no one paid much attention to those words, although the Soviets may have taken note. But now it was clear and in the open that Reagan favored the abolition of all nuclear weapons. Here is what he said:

> I ask you to resist the attempts of those who would have you withhold your support for our efforts, the administration's efforts, to keep America strong and free, while we negotiate real and verifiable reductions in the world's nuclear arsenals— and one day, with God's help, their total elimination.[20]

This marked the first time Reagan had spoken those words to a large audience. Maybe he was testing to see what the reaction would be, but he slipped it into the speech himself, without mentioning it to a soul. He apparently liked the reaction—or lack thereof—because two weeks later he would incorporate the idea into the second public bombshell he dropped in March 1983.

But before Reagan moved on to that explosive speech, he penned another bombshell, one that few people ever saw. These were Reagan's secret handwritten orders of March 19, in which he laid out modifications in his negotiating strategy on intermediate-range nuclear missiles aimed at the cities of Europe, but made clear that the ultimate objective remained Soviet destruction of all such missiles.

Reagan retired to the woods of Camp David, where he would

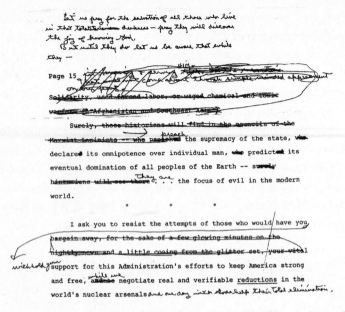

Excerpts of Reagan's handwritten changes on the "Evil Empire" speech, from pages 122 and 123.

have some quiet, and personally wrote out his zero-zero manifesto on his yellow legal-size paper. He then gave the document to William Clark with this instruction:

> Bill, please place this into the system.

Here are excerpts of Reagan's orders, which would in a few days be embodied in National Security Decision Directive 86, issued March 28, 1983:

> I believe we must announce our intention to offer an interim plan for reducing the number of I.N.F. [Intermediate-range Nuclear Force] missiles before the negotiations recess . . .

let me suggest that we tell our allies and our team that we intend to continue trying to persuade the Soviet representatives of the wisdom and mutual benefit of eliminating this entire family of weapons.

(Before they eliminate the family of man)

So our ultimate goal remains the same but we are willing to negotiate an equitable & verifiable interim reduction—when the sessions resume in June.

The Soviet team at one point indicated a willingness to reduce the number of S.S. 20's to 162 but at the same time predicated this on Nato remaining at zero. This of course would have left the situation virtually unchanged from what it is at present.

True they would have reduced their warheads from around 1300 to 486 but they would retain a monopoly on Intermediate-range missile targeted on the NATO nations who in turn would have no deterrent force at all. And this is what is at issue—both nations should have a deterrent NUCLEAR force or as we have urged—no such force at all in order to stabilize the situation on the continents of Europe and (?) Asia. . . .

If agreement can be reached as to the number of weapons we will begin our phased deployment on schedule up to the number agreed upon while the Soviet U. dismantles weapons down to meet us. If no agreement can be reached, we will have to continue deployment to the level necessary to provide a believable deterrent.[21]

On March 23, 1983, President Reagan gave another momentous speech. This one originally had been intended to be about the growing military power of the Soviets; the Defense Department had carefully studied the Soviets' infrastructure and prepared a draft of a speech explaining this ominous tide. Reagan liked the essence of the speech; he wanted the country to understand why the military

I. N. F. Negotiations

I believe we must announce our intention to offer an interim plan for reducing the number of I.N.F. missiles before the negotiations resume. I say this with one qualifier — have we discussed this with the people at the table — namely Paul Nitze? No one can have knowledge of the nuances and the flavor unless they've been present during the negotiations.

Having said that let me suggest that we tell our allies and our team that we intend to continue trying to persuade the Soviet representatives of the wisdom and mutual benefit of eliminating this entire family of weapons. (Before they eliminate the family of man)

So our ultimate goal remains the same but we are willing to negotiate an equitable & verifiable interim reduction — when the sessions resume in June.

The Soviet team at one point indicated a willingness to reduce the number of S.S.20's to 162 but at the same time predicated this on Nato remaining at zero. This of course would have left the situation virtually unchanged from what it is at present. True they would have reduced their war heads from around 1300 to 486 but they would retain a monopoly on intermediate range missiles targeted on the Nato nations who in turn would have no deterrent force at all. And this is what is at issue — both nations should have a deterrent force or as we have urged — no such force at all in order to stabilize the situation on the continents of Europe & [Asia] ?

We will finalize the details with regard to proposed numbers and means of verifiability as quickly as possible and after consultation with our allies present an interim plan to the Soviets prior to resuming negotiations in June. If agreement can be reached as to the number of weapons we will begin our phased deployment on schedule up to the number agreed upon while the Soviet U. dismantles weapons down to meet us. If no agreement can be reached we will have to continue deployment to the level necessary to provide a believable deterrent.

Reagan's handwritten zero-zero negotiating strategy.

buildup continued to be necessary. But he also decided it was the perfect vehicle to launch the idea of missile defense.

Reagan decided it was not necessary or wise to tell many people in advance about his insert. In particular, he did not inform the State Department, the Defense Department, or the CIA. He told William Clark what he wanted, and Clark appointed several staffers to help him craft the first insert draft.

On March 21, in the morning, just two days before the speech was scheduled, one of Clark's staff phoned Larry Eagleburger, the undersecretary of state, and leaked to him what Reagan was about to do. The word spread like a fire in dry grass. George Shultz was among the first to hear, and he quickly went to the White House to express his concern.[22]

Soon many staff members from State and Defense joined in sounding the alarm, some furious that the president might do something like this without asking their advice. But Reagan pretty well knew how they all felt already and remained convinced it was the right thing to do. The lack of agreement did not deter him from pressing on.

The two days before Reagan gave his speech were filled with turmoil, and a few words were changed, but the essence of what Reagan wanted in that insertion stayed.

At 8:02 on the night of March 23, Reagan, seated behind his desk in the Oval Office, began addressing the world. Here are the key excerpts from what became known as the "Star Wars" speech:

> My fellow Americans . . . I've reached a decision which offers a new hope for our children in the 21st century, a decision I'll tell you about in a few minutes.
>
> I've become more and more deeply convinced that the human spirit must be capable of rising above dealing with other nations and human beings by threatening their existence. . . .
>
> We're engaged right now in several negotiations with the

Soviet Union to bring about a mutual reduction of weapons. . . .

I'm totally committed to this course.

If the Soviet Union will join us in our effort to achieve major arms reduction, we will have succeeded in stabilizing the nuclear balance. Nevertheless, it will still be necessary to rely on the specter of retaliation, on mutual threat. And that's a sad commentary on the human condition.

Wouldn't it be better to save lives than to avenge them?

After careful consultation with my advisers, including the Joint Chiefs of Staff, I believe there is a way. Let me share with you a vision of the future which offers hope. It is that we embark on a program to counter the awesome Soviet missile threat with measures that are defensive. Let us turn to the very strengths in technology that spawned our great industrial base and that have given us the quality of life we enjoy today.

What if free people could live secure in the knowledge that their security did not rest upon the threat of instant U.S. retaliation to deter a Soviet attack, that we could intercept and destroy strategic ballistic missiles before they reach our own soil or that of our allies?

I know this is a formidable technical task, one that may not be accomplished before the end of this century. Yet, current technology has attained a level of sophistication where it's reasonable for us to begin this effort. It will take years, probably decades of effort on many fronts. There will be failures and setbacks, just as there will be successes and breakthroughs.

But isn't it worth every investment necessary to free the world from the threat of nuclear war?

We know it is. . . .

I clearly recognize that defensive systems have limitations and raise certain problems and ambiguities. . . . I call upon the scientific community in our country, those who gave us nuclear weapons, to turn their great talents now to the cause of mankind and world peace, to give us the means of rendering these nuclear weapons impotent and obsolete.

Tonight, consistent with our obligations of the ABM treaty . . . I am directing a comprehensive and intensive effort to define a long-term research and development program to begin to achieve our ultimate goal of eliminating the threat posed by strategic nuclear missiles.

This could pave the way for arms control measures to eliminate the weapons themselves. . . .

I believe we can do it. As we cross this threshold, I ask for your prayers and your support. Thank you, good night, and God bless you.[23]

Reagan wanted to get his message across to people, and also to get the attention of Yuri Andropov. He succeeded on both counts. The speech struck the political world like a thunderbolt. And Andropov was one of the first to respond, accusing Reagan of intensifying the arms race and claiming the United States had started down "an extremely dangerous path."

George Shultz summed it up like this:

It was a stunning and dramatic speech. It expressed a deep vision: we had painted ourselves into a corner with the concept of Mutual Assured Destruction, and the president proposed a way out. Its bottom line was honest: a research program aimed at finding out how to defend against the threat of strategic ballistic missiles.[24]

Reagan sat down that night with his diary and wrote his reaction to what he had wrought:

The big thing today was the 8 p.m. TV speech on all networks about the Nat. Security. We've been working on the speech for about 72 hours & right down to deadline. We had a group in for dinner at the White House. I didn't join them except before the dinner a few words of welcome. Nancy & I then dined early upstairs. The group included several former Secs. of State, Nat. Security Advisers, distinguished Nuclear scientists, the Chiefs of Staff etc.

I did the speech from the Oval office at 8 & then joined the party for coffee. I guess it was O.K.—they all praised it to the sky & seemed to think it would be a source of debate for some time to come. I did the bulk of the speech on why our arms build up was necessary & then finished with a call to the Science community to join me in research starting now to develop a defensive weapon that would render nuclear missiles obsolete.

I made no optimistic forecasts—said it might take 20 yrs. or more but we had to do it.

I felt good.[25]

On Tuesday, March 29, Reagan sat down with six reporters for a long interview. One of the questions on defensive missiles led to Reagan's announcing what can only be called a radical proposal.

Reagan was aware that any effective defensive missile system had a political Achilles' heel: If either the United States or the Soviet Union was successful in developing such a system before the other, that country would be invulnerable, and could launch a first strike that could not be answered. This was the basic worry the Soviets had about the missile defense Reagan intended to build.

So Reagan countered by offering to give the Soviets any successful defensive missile system the United States might build. As far as we know, no one suggested this idea to him.

Here is what he told the reporters in the Oval Office that day:

I am determined to continue doing everything I can to persuade them [the Soviets] that legitimate arms reduction is the only path to follow. To look down to an endless future with both of us sitting here with these horrible missiles aimed at each other and the only thing preventing a holocaust is just so long as no one pulls the trigger.

This is unthinkable. . . .

If a defensive weapon could be found and developed that would reduce the utility of these or maybe even make them obsolete, then whenever the time came, a President of the United States would be able to say, "Now, we have both the deterrent, the missiles—as we've had in the past—but now this other thing that has altered this." And he could follow any one of a number of courses. He could offer to give that same defensive weapon to them to prove to them that there was no longer any need for keeping these missiles.

Or with that defense, he could then say to them, "I am willing to do away with all my missiles. You do away with all of yours."[26]

Chapter 10

~

CLOSE TO NUCLEAR WAR: 1983

*I feel the Soviets are so defense minded, so paranoid
about being attacked, that without being in any way
soft on them, we ought to tell them no one here has
any intention of doing anything like that.*

What the h--l have they got that anyone would want?
—RONALD REAGAN, PERSONAL DIARY, NOVEMBER 18, 1983

As spring began to blossom in Washington in 1983, there were
still serious problems: the danger of Communism in Latin America, the war in Afghanistan, the troubles in Poland—all due to the
influence of the Soviet Union. The Soviet economy was hurting,
but it was still strong enough to build up more nuclear weapons
in their stockpile every year, and to pursue the dream of a Communist world. Of course, there were many more, relatively minor
problems throughout the world and in the United States—but
the major problem the United States faced remained the Soviet
Union. Reagan saw the danger, and an opening. If the United
States was ever going to convince the Soviet Union of its dangerous folly, now was the time. Nothing was guaranteed, but the odds
of success were swinging in Reagan's direction.

But there was one problem that Reagan had not bargained on.

The Soviet leaders were wary of Reagan's intentions and becoming increasingly nervous about his moves, perhaps thinking of what they would do in his shoes. They were used to having nations fear them, and they continued to build up the nuclear weapons that instilled that fear. But now Reagan was challenging them, making it clear that if they wanted to have an arms race, the United States would race—and beat them.

The Soviets found it difficult to believe that any country would deliberately build up its armed forces in order to persuade an enemy to join them in a sharp reduction of nuclear weapons so that neither party could destroy the other. They were much more inclined to believe that any enemy attempting to build up a superior force could have only one reason: first strike and domination. A Soviet intelligence officer, Oleg Gordievsky, who had been secretly recruited by the British, described Soviet intelligence during this time: "A closed political system dominated by men of weak intellect, with little understanding of the world and ideological blinders, is prone to self-indoctrination."[1]

Over the years Reagan had made it clear, repeatedly, that his main goal was a world at peace, a world free of the possibility of a nuclear strike. He abhorred the idea of a nuclear war; he didn't even like the idea of any country having nuclear missiles. He thought that every substantial reduction taken in nuclear weapons was a step toward a better world. He expressed these sentiments dozens of times during his political years, trying to drive home that this was his top priority.

It was a difficult point to make. How often can you tell people the world might be destroyed? Most find the concept unpleasant just to think about. Others simply refuse to even think about the possibility of being burned to a crisp. But that did not deter Reagan from pressing forward. In spite of all that Reagan had said— both before and after he was elected—nothing seemed to move the Soviets. Most worrisome was their continuing to build up their stockpiles of nuclear weapons, especially those carried on ICBMs. Between 1981 and 1983, they increased ICBM warheads by 1,016, or 17 percent, while the U.S. number declined slightly, by nine warheads.[2] Reagan was right to be nervous.

For two years, Reagan's attempts at dealing with Brezhnev had met with no success. Brezhnev was from the old school of the Soviet empire and was fairly contemptuous of Reagan. For instance, here is how Brezhnev responded after Reagan sent that first, friendly letter to him early in 1981:

> I got an icy reply from Brezhnev. He said he, too, was against making immediate plans for a summit, repudiated everything I'd said about the Soviet Union, blamed the United States for starting and perpetuating the Cold War, and then said we had no business telling the Soviets what they could or could not do anywhere in the world.
>
> So much for my first attempt at personal diplomacy.[3]

Now Reagan had to deal with someone who promised to be even more difficult: Yuri Andropov. Andropov, who took over the Soviet Union on November 12, 1982, was not a typical leader of a powerful nation. For fifteen years, he had been in charge of the KGB, perhaps the most ruthless and feared secret police and spying organization in the world. He was cold-blooded, smart, cruel, and capable of killing.

For the better part of his life Andropov and the KGB had aimed their sights at their main enemy, the United States. Their nickname for the United States was the "Main Adversary."[4] The Soviet leaders, especially Brezhnev and Andropov, considered Reagan a serious threat. After the first six months of his presidency had gone by, they were convinced they had been right. Christopher Andrew and Vasili Mitrokhin explain in their book, *The Sword and the Shield,* that:

In a secret speech to a major KGB conference in May 1981 a visibly ailing Brezhnev denounced Reagan's policies as a serious threat to world peace. He was followed up by Andropov, who was to succeed him as General Secretary eighteen months later. To the astonishment of most of the audience, the KGB chairman announced that, by decision of the Politburo, the KGB and GRU were, for the first time, to collaborate in a global intelligence operation, codenamed RYAN—a newly devised acronym for *Raketno-Yadernoye Napadenie* ("Nuclear Missile Attack").

RYAN's purpose was to collect intelligence on the presumed . . . plans of the Reagan administration to launch a nuclear first strike against the Soviet Union. . . . "Not since the Second World War," Andropov informed foreign residencies, "has the international situation been as explosive as it is now."[5]

The KGB agents stationed abroad who were responsible for implementing RYAN looked doggedly for any evidence that the United States was preparing a nuclear first strike. But, of course, they could not find any firm indications that such a first strike was being put together. When Andropov succeeded Brezhnev in November 1982 as general secretary, they still had not found any evidence. Undaunted, Andropov redoubled the RYAN effort, still convinced that Reagan intended to strike the Soviet Union. So it was no surprise that Andropov's rule brought no change in the Soviets' attitude toward Reagan and his policies.

Andropov opposed Reagan's plan to begin working on the Strategic Defense Initiative (SDI) and quickly denounced it, accusing Reagan of wanting "to disarm the Soviet Union in the face of the U.S. nuclear threat."[6] KGB headquarters interpreted "the announcement of the SDI ('Star Wars') program in March 1983 as part of the psychological preparation of the American people for nuclear attack."[7] Andropov was also flatly opposed to Reagan's offer not to install U.S. Pershing II nuclear missiles in Europe—aimed at the Soviet Union—if the Soviets removed all their nuclear missiles aimed at cities in Europe. Instead he demanded that Reagan refrain from installing any nuclear missiles in Europe.

In response to a Fourth of July message from Andropov, Reagan wrote a long letter, in his own hand, to Andropov on July 11, 1983, trying to assure Andropov that the United States was peaceful. Playing his loner card, Reagan invited the Soviet leader to engage in a secret exchange of letters:

> I appreciate very much your letter pledging an, "unbending commitment . . . to the cause of peace, the elimination of the nuclear threat" . . . could we not begin to approach these goals in the meetings now going on in Geneva?
>
> You and I share an enormous responsibility for the preservation of stability in the world. . . . Historically our predecessors have made better progress when communicating has been private and candid. If you wish to engage in such communication you will find me ready. I await your reply.[8]

Andropov, who was in poor health due to a kidney aliment, replied a few weeks later, on August 4, 1983. It was clear that he did not like the proposals put forward by Reagan, but the letter was cordial. He acknowledged "the assurance that the U.S. Government shared a devotion to the cause of peace and the elimination of the nuclear threat" and said that "the important thing of course is to begin to move forward on issues of limiting and reducing nuclear arms. It is a particularly urgent necessity to prevent a nuclear arms race in Europe . . . the results of which would be extremely serious."

Then he moved quickly to the main proposal Reagan had made, the zero-zero plan for Europe. "So long," said Andropov, "as the United States has not begun deploying its missiles in Europe, an agreement is still possible." Andropov ended his letter by telling Reagan that "I shall welcome a concrete, businesslike and candid exchange of opinion with you on these and other questions."[9]

July 11, 1983

Dear Gen. Secretary Andropov

I appreciate very much your letter pledging an "unbending commitment of the Soviet leadership and the people of the Soviet Union to the course of peace, the elimination of the nuclear threat and the development of relations based on mutual benefit and equality with all nations."

Let me assure you the government & the people of the United States are dedicated to, "the course of peace" and "the elimination of the nuclear threat". It goes without saying that we also seek relations with all nations based on "mutual benefit and equality." Our record since we were allied in W.W.II confirms that.

Mr. General Secretary could we not begin to approach these goals in the meetings now going on in Geneva? You and I share an enormous responsibility for the preservation of stability in the world. I believe we can fulfill that mandate but to do so will require a more active level of exchange than we have heretofore been able to establish. We have much to talk about with regard to the situation in Eastern Europe, South Asia, and particularly this hemisphere as well as in such areas as arms control, trade between our two countries and other ways in which we can expand east-west contacts.

Historically our predecessors have made better progress when communicating has been private and candid. If you wish to engage in such communication you will find me ready. I await your reply.

Sincerely
Ronald Reagan

Secret letter from Ronald Reagan to Yuri Andropov, July 11, 1983.

A few days later Reagan got an update on other Soviet defense activities:

> Had a briefing on the Soviets & Space. There is no question but that they are working (twice as hard as us) to come up with a military superiority in outer space.[10]

About three weeks later, on August 24, 1983, Reagan replied to his new pen pal in Russia:

> I can see that we both recognize the awesome responsibility history has placed on our shoulders to guide the two most powerful countries in the world in this difficult and dangerous period. . . .
>
> In my view, this central issue has three key aspects: first, the vital need for the world to move toward the principle of settling international disputes by peaceful means, without the use of threat of force; second, the urgent need to reduce stocks of weaponry, particularly the most destructive and destabilizing types; and third, the necessity of creating a sufficient level of trust and confidence between us to permit us to reach the first two objectives.

Reagan came to the end of this letter with this appeal:

> Mr. Chairman, I cannot exaggerate the importance of clarifying any misunderstanding which arises regarding the implementation of prior agreements. For nothing is so destructive of confidence as a perception by one party to an agreement that its provisions are being disregarded by the other.[11]

Andropov replied to Reagan three days later, on August 27, 1983. He rebuked Reagan, denouncing "the deployment of new American missiles" in Europe. His final words carried a soft threat:

"I would like to hope that . . . you personally will approach the resolution of the task we face with a sense of high responsibility for the fate of peace and international security."[12]

Four days later the Cold War atmosphere got much colder.

The night of September 1, a Korean civilian airliner carrying 269 passengers flew by accident into Soviet airspace. A Soviet military pilot, following orders, targeted the plane and shot it down. All 269 passengers, including some Americans, died as the plane dropped into the Sea of Japan. At first, the Soviets said nothing. But a Top Secret U.S.-Japan listening post picked up the "radio transmissions from a Soviet pilot as he visually inspected the plane, fired his missiles and reported to his headquarters in Russia, 'The target is destroyed.' "

Reagan declassified the radio intercept, and George Shultz announced the results to the world.[13] If Reagan had not overruled the intelligence agencies, which were reluctant to release the intercept, it is likely that no one ever would have known what happened, and the Soviets would not have been censured for killing those civilians.

Three weeks later, on September 25, 1983, a potentially much more serious error occurred. Lieutenant Colonel Stanislav Petrov, the duty officer of the Soviet warning system for a nuclear attack, was manning his station when the alarm suddenly went off. Soon it was indicating that the United States had launched five ICBM missiles at the Soviet Union. The colonel was supposed to initiate a counterattack immediately, setting off World War III. But his instinct said something was wrong. Why only five missiles? If the United States was launching a nuclear attack, surely it would have unleashed hundreds of missiles. So he waited.

Apparently a Soviet satellite misinterpreted sunlight glinting off clouds above a U.S. missile site and thought five missiles were being launched. Ground radar was checked, and eventually it was realized that the nuclear attack warning was false.[14]

Armageddon was averted. But it had been close—too close.

And things seemed to be getting worse. On September 28, 1983, the terminally ill Andropov issued a denunciation of American policy from his sickbed. He couched what he said in apocalyptic language, unparalleled since the early depths of the Cold War:

> Outrageous military psychosis . . . the Reagan administration, in its imperial ambitions, goes so far that one begins to doubt whether Washington has any brakes at all preventing it from crossing the point at which any sober-minded person must stop.[15]

The two cases—firing missiles at an airliner carrying 269 civilians, and getting a nuclear attack warning because the sun hit a satellite at just the right angle—indicated that the Soviets were a bit on edge. Andropov, in particular, seemed increasingly determined to see a plot that would have the United States trying to wipe out the Soviet Union with a first nuclear strike. He was not the only one who was coming to believe something that was not true, but at least Andropov had RYAN to report to him and tell him nothing was wrong. So far, in the fall of 1983, RYAN had not had any luck in finding plans for a first strike by the United States. But KGB agents were desperately looking for the slightest sign that the Americans would try to strike first. If they had found any evidence at all, then Andropov—who was by now dying of kidney failure, so sick that he had to work from a hospital room—would have had his satisfaction as he ordered a preventive nuclear strike to destroy the United States.

A month later, on November 2, 1983, the Defense Department conducted its annual test of U.S. nuclear weapons capability with a bit more enthusiasm than usual, and inadvertently made the Soviets even more tense. During this test the United States did not launch missiles or conduct any large troop movements; it merely checked the commands and the communications that would be used to launch nuclear missiles in case of war. The 1983 test was called "Able Archer" and improved the exercise so that it was more realistic than past mock nuclear weapons efforts had been.

Don Oberdorfer, in his book on the Cold War, *The Turn*, explained the seriousness of the war plans Able Archer was designed to test:

> The U.S. nuclear war plan, or Single Integrated Operational Plan (SIOP), on the Pentagon books at the time under orders signed by Reagan, called for the United States in full-scale war to use its nuclear arsenal against 50,000 Soviet targets, including 25,000 military targets, 15,000 industrial and economic targets and 5,000 targets associated with the Soviet leadership. If the Soviets fired back, as they were certain to do, it would be virtually a doomsday scenario. After being briefed on the war plan, Reagan considered it "a scenario for a sequence of events that could lead to the end of civilization as we knew it."[16]

The mock trials seemed to work fine. The Soviet Union and the other Warsaw Pact nations monitored all the exercises and noted that there seemed to be a sharp increase over previous years' tests in the volume of communications. The Soviets responded by placing "about a dozen nuclear-capable Soviet fighter aircraft stationed in forward bases in East Germany and Poland" on higher alert status.[17]

Looking back at those times, we all know now that Reagan had no designs to attack the Soviet Union. He was convinced that no superpower should ever start a nuclear war—although he was fully prepared to retaliate, rather than surrender, if the Soviets should ever make the mistake of attacking the United States. But what made the Soviets so nervous, so untrusting of Reagan, was that they could not understand why a powerful leader would spend a huge amount of money to build up his military might and then not use that new might for conquest. Further, they thought (as did many Americans) that to build up this military might and then destroy large parts of it to reduce nuclear weapons was a bit foolish, if not crazy.

Reagan was well aware what so many thought of him and his visions. But that did not deter him. He was fully informed about the growing fears of the Soviets and their terror of a preemptive nuclear strike by the United States. On November 18, 1983, after being briefed on what some of the Soviet leaders thought about Able Archer, he sat down and wrote in his personal diary:

> George Shultz & I had a talk mainly about setting up a little in house group of experts on the Soviet U. to help in setting up some channels. I feel the Soviets are so defense minded, so paranoid about being attacked that without being in any way soft on them we ought to tell them no one here has any intention of doing anything like that.
> What the h--l have they got that anyone would want?[18]

This led to a difficult choice.

Reagan knew that if he continued to move ahead with his plans, there was some risk, although small, that the Soviets—especially Yuri Andropov—might decide to strike first. If that should happen, Reagan felt he would have no choice but to unleash the United States' full nuclear might in return. Nearly everyone in the United States would die, albeit with the questionable satisfaction of knowing that the enemy would die as well. His other option was equally unpalatable: to stop putting the Soviets under pressure, accept them as they were, and simply hope that their stockpile of nuclear weapons would stop growing—and that Communism would not spread too fast and far in the world. Reagan went for the first choice. He said often that he did not want a war but he would not surrender to avoid one.

Ten months before, on January 13, 1983, in a Top Secret meeting of the National Security Planning Group, Reagan had ordered that the Pershing II ballistic missiles be deployed in West

Germany when they were ready. And when the missiles were ready to be deployed, Reagan reaffirmed the order. By November 23, 1983, the first Pershing II missiles were installed. Everyone waited to see what the Soviets would do.

While waiting for the Soviets' reaction, Reagan chaired an NSC meeting on November 30, 1983. The agenda was the progress on the Strategic Defense Initiative. This program had caused the most consternation for the Soviets, many of whom believed it was being built to allow the United States to strike them at will without worrying about a counterattack. Reagan did not flinch and pressed everyone to continue with SDI. After listening to George Shultz and Caspar Weinberger, Reagan said:

> I agree with Secretary Shultz that we are charting a new road. To take an optimistic view, if the U.S. is first to have both offense and defense, we could put the nuclear genie back into the bottle by volunteering to eliminate offensive weapons.
>
> The pessimistic view is that a meeting similar to this National Security Council is now underway in the Kremlin; if the Soviets get new defenses first, we can expect nuclear blackmail.
>
> Therefore, we do need to handle this initiative as carefully and sensibly as possible, but hope and pray we get there first and can make the offer the Soviets would never make. . . .
>
> The message to the Soviets is that if they want an arms race, the U.S. will not let them get ahead. Their choice is to break their backs to keep up or to agree to reductions. . . .
>
> We are not alone, and the Soviets really make this decision for us. How are we to face the day when they have both offensive weapons and an effective defense?[19]

As the Pershing II nuclear missiles were being installed in Germany, the Soviets thought about their predicament for two weeks—and then broke off communications with the United States negotiators, formally suspending all arms control negotiations in

Geneva. Reagan continued to site Pershing II missiles in Europe, and the Soviets left Geneva and went back to Moscow, taking their negotiation papers with them. Although they refused to talk to Reagan, Reagan continued to talk to them and especially to Andropov through the press and a personal letter.

The same day Andropov pulled the plug on arms reduction talks in Geneva, December 8, Reagan was leaving on a trip to Indianapolis, Indiana. It had been a busy morning. For an hour he had been in a special meeting with his national security staff, including the vice president, James Baker, Edwin Meese, Michael Deaver, and Robert McFarlane, to discuss the Soviets walking out of the negotiation talks in Geneva. At 11:30 a.m., Reagan sat down for a private talk with Caspar Weinberger, and then he had a one-hour lunch with his vice president. Later, as Reagan walked on the South Grounds, he stopped for three minutes to respond to the reporters who had been covering the strategic arms reduction talks:

It was just 30 years ago today, on December 8th, 1953, that President Dwight Eisenhower made a speech on this very subject of nuclear weapons.

And in that speech, he said, "To the making of these fateful decisions, the United States pledges before you . . . its determination to help solve the fearful atomic dilemma—to devote its entire heart and mind to find the way by which the miraculous inventiveness of man shall not be dedicated to his death, but consecrated to his life."

And this administration endorses this view completely, and this is what we are dedicated to.[20]

On December 9 Reagan chaired a special meeting of the NSPG on Soviet plans for a protracted nuclear war. There were only ten of his advisers in the meeting, and the meeting was not recorded by the NSC.[21] The vice president and Shultz did not attend. The main advisers were Weinberger, Casey, Meese, and McFarlane. Reagan noted in his diary that night the seriousness of what they had said:

> A sobering briefing on Soviet offensive power & plans for a protracted nuclear war. I wish some of our pacifist loud talkers could have access to this information. A preliminary budget review on Defense budget. Cap has pulled it down from $321 bil. to $305 bil. I have a hunch it will come out around $295 but we should ask for $305 because the Dems. will cut whatever we come in with.[22]

On December 14, 1983, a citizen sent a letter to Reagan, who responded, as he did frequently, and let off a little steam:

> Would it surprise you to know I share your horror of nuclear weapons and am convinced there must never be a nuclear war? . . . In recent years the Soviet Union has engaged in the biggest military build up in history both in conventional forces and in nuclear weapons. . . . My hope indeed my dream is that if we can once start down the road of reducing on both sides the number of missiles they will be convinced of the wisdom of eliminating all such weapons.[23]

A week later, Reagan gave an interview to representatives of the French newspaper *Le Figaro,* saying:

> I'm proposing that [research on strategic defense] in the interest of hopefully being able to eliminate those weapons. If we could succeed and bring about a realistic defensive weapon against them, then my next step would be to inform the Soviet Union that we had this and now we were prepared to join them in eliminating all such weapons in the world.[24]

And just before Christmas, on December 23, 1983, as tensions continued to be high, Reagan wrote another letter to Yuri Andropov trying to convince the Soviets he had no intention whatsoever of surprising them with a nuclear first strike:

> I continue to believe that despite the profound differences between our two nations, there are opportunities—indeed a necessity—for us to work together to prevent conflicts, to expand our dialogue, and to place our relationship on a more stable and constructive footing. Though we will be vigorous in protecting our interests . . . we do not seek to challenge the security of the Soviet Union and its people . . .

Then Reagan finished the four-page letter with these thoughts:

> While I am under no illusions as to the difficulty of the problems we now face, I nonetheless believe that serious and forthright exchanges could open up avenues to mutually beneficial arrangements. . . . You have pledged to me your commitment to peace and I have made a similar and heartfelt pledge.[25]

Not hearing from Andropov, Reagan continued to move ahead with his program. On Friday, January 13, 1984, there was an important meeting of the National Security Council. It was an unusually large meeting, with twenty-one participants. At stake was whether or not to modify Reagan's negotiating position at the Mutual and Balanced Force Reductions (MBFR) talks, given that the Soviets had walked out on the arms reductions talks in Geneva in all areas (conventional forces, INF, and START) and refused to give a date when they might return. There was considerable debate about which way to go, and Reagan would have to settle the disagreements. There were essentially three options:

- Stand firm on the present position
- Attempt to initial a treaty that addressed the question of parity and included a comprehensive verification package
- Initiate initial, asymmetrical reductions, followed by an eighteen-month freeze, then seek a comprehensive data agreement followed by reductions to parity

Reagan listened quietly to part of the discussion, and then interrupted to say:

> I do not want to be in the position of shifting if they gave nothing in return. On the other hand, if they have provided new movement, then it would be advisable for us to respond positively.[26]

The discussion continued for over an hour, with the key advisers doing the talking: Shultz, Weinberger, General Vessey, Gates, Kenneth Adelman of the U.S. Arms Control and Disarmament Agency, the MBFR negotiator Morton Abramowitz, and Meese.

When they had finished Reagan told the council his decision. He said there were four points he wanted everyone to follow. It was clear he was not changing his negotiating stance:

- We have received sufficient movement from the Soviets in their proposals to warrant a response from the West.
- We will not make a proposal simply to bring the Soviets back to the negotiating table.
- We will respond to the Soviet proposals, but not before they have agreed to set a date for the resumption of the talks.
- We have something concrete in hand that demonstrates Western responsiveness and flexibility to discuss with our Allies. Following Allied agreement, we would be prepared to table a new proposal at the resumption of the Mutual and Balanced Force Reduction (MBFR) negotiations.[27]

That night, before Reagan went to bed, he wrote a few sentences in his personal diary:

> An NSC meeting on our approach to Soviets re arms negotiations. We've notified them of our report to Congress on their violation of various treaties & agreements.
>
> They do just plain cheat.[28]

Three days later, on the morning of January 16, Reagan gave a major address on United States–Soviet Union relations. His speech was directly aimed at the Soviets. He was keenly aware that some men in the Politburo, led by Andropov, were still sensing a nuclear threat that was not there, and he was determined to convince them of his peaceful intentions. It was one of the most important speeches Reagan ever gave. If it had not been done carefully and correctly, he could have set off a Soviet nuclear strike. Here are the key excerpts from that January 1984 speech:

> During these first days of 1984, I would like to share with you and the people of the world my thoughts on a subject of great importance to the cause of peace—relations between the United States and the Soviet Union. . . . We live in a time of challenges to peace, but also of opportunities to peace.
>
> Our economy is now in the midst of the best recovery since the sixties. Our defenses are being rebuilt, our alliances are solid, and our commitment to defend our values has never been more clear.
>
> This may be the reason that we've been hearing such strident rhetoric from the Kremlin recently. These harsh words have led some to speak of heightened uncertainty and an increased danger of conflict. This is understandable but profoundly mistaken. . . .
>
> I have openly expressed my view of the Soviet system. I don't know why this should come as a surprise to Soviet Leaders . . .

this doesn't mean that we can't deal with each other . . . they cling to the fantasy of a Communist triumph over democracy. The fact that neither of us likes the other system is no reason to refuse to talk. Living in the nuclear age makes it imperative that we do talk. In our approach to negotiations, reducing the risk of war, and especially nuclear war, is priority number one. A nuclear conflict could well be mankind's last. . . .

Indeed, *I support a zero option for all nuclear arms.*

As I've said before, my dream is to see the day when nuclear weapons will be banished from the face of the Earth. . . .

Whenever the Soviet Union is ready to do likewise, we'll meet them halfway. . . . People want to raise their children in a world without fear and without war. . . . If the Soviet Government wants peace, then there will be peace.[29]

Reagan was pleased with the speech. In his diary that night he reviewed what he had intended:

The press, especially TV is now trying to explain the speech as political, etc. . . . the speech was carefully crafted by all of us to counter Soviet propaganda that we are not sincere in wanting arms reduction or peace.

It was low key & held the door open to the Soviets if they mean what they say about having peace to walk in.[30]

As the days went by there was no response from the leaders of the Soviet Union. On January 25, 1984, Reagan gave the annual State of the Union message to a joint session of the Congress. Unperturbed by the silence from the Soviet Union, he continued to hammer home his argument. In fact, in one whole section of the speech he directly addressed the people of the Soviet Union. Some who heard his speech jumped to the conclusion that Reagan was afraid of the Soviets and was trying to placate them. It was not so.

> Tonight, I want to speak to the people of the Soviet Union, to tell them it's true that our governments have had serious differences, but our sons and daughters have never fought each other in war. And if we Americans have our way, they never will.
>
> People of the Soviet Union, there is only one sane policy, for your country and mine, to preserve our civilization in this modern age: A nuclear war cannot be won and must never be fought. The only value in our two nations possessing nuclear weapons is to make sure they will never be used.
>
> But then would it not be better to do away with them entirely? People of the Soviet, President Dwight Eisenhower, who fought by your side in World War II, said the essential struggle "is not merely man against man or nation against nation. It is man against war."
>
> Americans are people of peace. If your government wants peace, there will be peace.[31]

Reagan was trying to calm the Soviet leaders in hopes of preventing a first strike. But had they struck, he was committed to counterattacking. Much as he abhorred the idea of all-out nuclear war, he would press the "button" before he died—and the Soviets knew that he would, because he had told them. In an interview on July 25, 1989, after leaving office, Reagan was asked: "Will you just sit here and accept the missiles, will you launch a retaliatory attack? How do you deal with that?" And Reagan answered:

> But, yes, our reply, and I—this had to be, that if ever the word came, that they had pushed the button, yes, we had to set all of ours in motion.

And one more question was asked: "Do you think the Russians understood this clearly?" and Reagan said:

I have a hunch they did, yes, because I made it very plain to him—what we were gonna take and what we weren't going to take.[32]

Chapter 11

~

REAGAN WINS
REELECTION: 1984

It is no doubt a good thing
to conquer on the field of battle,
but it needs greater wisdom and
greater skill to make use of victory.
—POLYBIUS, 125 B.C.

In the first days of 1984, Reagan's main goal—persuading the Soviets to join the United States in a significant reduction of nuclear weapons—was stalled, going nowhere. Two years of work with Leonid Brezhnev and then one year with Yuri Andropov had yielded little. And efforts had hit a low point in December, when Andropov suspended all arms negotiations.

Strobe Talbott, one of the top observers of U.S.-Soviet relations, wrote a book in 1984 called *Deadly Gambits: The Reagan Administration and the Stalemate in Nuclear Arms Control.* The book's last sentence read: "The Reagan revolution in arms control was over." While in hindsight Talbott's book turned out to be spectacularly wrongheaded, it neatly encapsulates the thoughts of many in 1984.

And now Reagan faced yet another challenge: reelection. His chances of winning a tough campaign were probably no more than fifty-fifty. He was now seventy-three years old. His wife, Nancy, argued that he had had enough, that it was time to leave, to retire in California and spend time with his family. But there were many tasks Reagan yearned to finish, especially negotiating with the Soviet Union.

Some things were going well for Reagan. The economy was roaring back, and military strength was growing by leaps and bounds. As Reagan weighed the successes and failures of his administration in early 1984, he had already made the difficult choice to run for reelection.

Reagan had been a tenacious man all his life. He was not about to walk away from the difficulties of the presidency—especially his vision of drastically reducing the number of nuclear missiles on both sides of the Cold War. On Friday, January 27, just two days after he had given his well-received State of the Union message, he wrote in his diary that he had decided to run, although he had told only two people:

Campaign time is coming closer even though I have not actually said the words to anyone (except [daughter] Maureen & Nancy) that I'll run.[1]

Reagan's official announcement to run for reelection was made on Sunday, January 29, 1984. Afterward he noted in his diary:

The response has been terrific—calls, wires etc. running 10 to 1 in our favor.[2]

When Reagan made the decision to run for reelection, he was committing himself (if he got reelected) to five more years on the most demanding of jobs. He would be seventy-seven years old when he left Washington and returned to California. But he seemed to be driven. He believed that God had spared his life for a purpose after he survived the assassin's bullet in 1981—and perhaps that purpose was to dispel the cloud of nuclear fear.

A few weeks after Reagan had announced his intent to run again, he got a letter from an old friend praising his January 25 State of the Union address and his decision to run. In his reply, Reagan explained a little of how he felt:

> I thank you for your generous words about the speech. I have to tell you I've faced a lot of audiences, as you know, but that "joint session" does make for a slight case of nerves before and after. . . . I'm glad, too, that you approve my decision about running. Wasn't it Lincoln who said, "having put the hand to the plow, it's no time to turn back"?[3]

On February 7 Reagan flew to his ranch in California, where he could have privacy and rest. The ranch, with its small adobe house sitting a mile high on a plateau that had a view of the Pacific Ocean on one side and mountains on the others, was, in his mind, as close to Heaven as you could get on Earth.

Two days after he settled in on the ranch, on February 9, 1984, Reagan received word that his bête noire, Yuri Andropov, had died.

The next day, February 10, he sent a message to the Politburo expressing his condolences and stressing his desire for dialogue with the Soviets no matter who the new general secretary would be.

While he waited for the Soviets to select Andropov's successor—a process that could take days, as the Politburo wrangled over which of its members to appoint—Reagan decided to address the Soviets and the United States.

On February 11, while he was still at Rancho del Cielo, Reagan gave a radio address to the nation on U.S.-Soviet relations:

> I'd like to speak to you about a subject always on the minds of Americans, but of particular interest today in the view of the

> death of Soviet leader Yuri Andropov: our relations with the
> Soviet Union. . . .
>
> We know that our relationship is not what we would like it
> to be. . . . What is needed now is for both sides to sit down and
> find ways of solving some of the problems that divide us. . . .
>
> We have fought side by side in the victory over Nazi Ger-
> many . . . our sons and daughters have never fought each
> other. We must make sure they never do.
>
> Avoiding war and reducing arms is a starting point in our
> relationship with the Soviet Union. . . . If the Soviet Govern-
> ment wants peace, then there will be peace.[4]

When Andropov passed away, a new era began in the Soviet
Union. The old, brutal leadership, starting with Stalin and going
through Brezhnev and Andropov, was at an end.

When the dust of Andropov's death cleared, the Politburo finally
made its decision. Konstantin Chernenko, who had been Leonid
Brezhnev's deputy for almost thirty years and had been passed over
in favor of Andropov in November 1982, was selected as the new
leader of the Soviet Union on February 13, 1984. Because of his long
association with Brezhnev, it was expected that Chernenko would
continue in his footsteps, a throwback to the old Soviet leaders. But
Vice President George H. W. Bush's report on meeting Chernenko
at Andropov's funeral led Reagan to write in his diary:

> I have a gut feeling I'd like to talk to him about our prob-
> lems man to man & see if I could convince him there would be
> a material benefit to the Soviets if they'd join the family of na-
> tions. . . . I have our team considering an invitation to him to
> be my guest at the opening of the Olympics.[5]

Reagan would continue to express his inclination to meet with
Chernenko in his diary—in March and even as late as June 14.[6]
But Chernenko had a serious problem: his health.

When Chernenko was named the general secretary by the Politburo he was, for all purposes, an invalid. He was only seventy-two years old, one year younger than Reagan, but he was seriously ill with emphysema, so debilitating—however well he managed at Andropov's funeral—that he could not give a speech or hold a salute for a military parade. He was utterly dependent on the other members of the Politburo. Andrei Gromyko was essentially in charge of foreign policy. Mikhail Gorbachev would often run Politburo meetings. The other members of the Politburo apparently worked as a group, providing Chernenko with suggestions on what to do.[7]

Chernenko's dependence on the Politburo was confirmed on June 26 when France's François Mitterrand told Reagan of his trip to Moscow and meeting with Chernenko. Reagan wrote in his diary of Mitterrand's conclusions:

> Chernenko gives evidence of not being well & doesn't say a word without a script in front of him. He [Mitterrand] believes the Politburo is kind of a collective in charge.[8]

It is difficult to know how deeply Chernenko was involved in the decisions made while he was general secretary.

The day after Chernenko was chosen, on February 14, 1984, Reagan sent him a letter, classified Secret, stressing what he would like to do and what he would not do:

> In the months ahead, we will be ready to discuss with you the entire agenda of issues in which our two nations have an interest. . . . We will be interested in whatever ideas and proposals you may have to put forth. . . . We also believe that we need to return to the negotiating table. . . .
>
> Let me conclude by seeking to lay to rest some misunderstandings . . . we do not seek to challenge the security of the Soviet Union and its people.[9]

Nine days later, a letter from Chernenko was sent to Reagan. It basically reaffirmed the arguments that had been made earlier by Brezhnev and Andropov. But in the last paragraph he did go on to say:

> *A turn toward even and good relations between our two countries has been and continues to be our desire.*[10]

Over the next five months, a half dozen similar letters went back and forth between Reagan and Chernenko. Much was discussed on paper, but little changed. The Soviets still declined to come back to the negotiating table, and the stalemate continued.

Meanwhile, Reagan was forced to spend more and more time on his campaign, although he continued to make an effort to reassure the Soviets that the United States was not thinking about a nuclear first strike. More important, he kept steady pressure on them, telling them again and again they should come to the table to discuss how to reduce nuclear weapons—and someday get rid of them all. But the Soviets weren't moving.

In the summer of 1983, the national polls taken by Gallup had shown Reagan ten points behind his likely opponent, Walter Mondale. By Christmas of 1983 Reagan was running even with Mondale. And by February 1984, Reagan had pulled ahead of Mondale by nine points—a gain of almost twenty points since the summer of 1983.[11] It was beginning to look like Reagan had a good chance of winning in the fall.

On March 27, 1984, Reagan called a meeting of the National Security Planning Group to discuss the current status of arms control negotiations and consider how to respond to a March 19, 1984, letter from Chernenko.

It was a small meeting of top people. The secretaries of defense and state each presented their views, as did the director of the Arms Control and Disarmament Agency, the chairman of the

Joint Chiefs of Staff, the director of the CIA, and Reagan's two top negotiators, Rowny and Nitze. No one thought it would be possible to make much progress in an election year, but Shultz was more in favor of trying than Weinberger, who was concerned about the appearance of concessions. Reagan listened intently to his advisers for close to an hour. Then he took charge.[12]

We are all not as far apart as it might seem. There is no question that the Soviet Union is trying to make us look non-cooperative. I believe the Soviets want to avoid the onus for having walked out of Geneva. In my answer to the letter from Chernenko, we should recognize that we have opposite views on who is threatened.

We should cite their quotations that are threatening to us; we should cite their build-up. Then we could cite the fact that in the 1940's, we proposed to do away with all these systems and they said no. Nineteen times since then, we have tried to reach agreements, for example, Eisenhower's open sky proposal.

We can't go on negotiating with ourselves. We can't be supplicants crawling. We can't look like failures.

I've read the papers and made some notes. Let me share them with you. They want to avoid the onus of walking out, therefore, it is unlikely that they will give us anything in START and INF right now. We want an agreement, but we want a good agreement. I do not intend to make unilateral concessions to get them back to the table. . . .

If there are some things that are good, then we shouldn't ignore them simply because they are a part of SALT II. For example, having a launcher limit isn't wrong, so long as it is matched by warhead and throw-weight limits. In short, we need a position which takes part of their approach and melds it with ours so that they have a fig leaf for coming off their position. . . .

> George (Shultz), I want you to be our public spokesman
> on arms control. Leaks and gratuitous backgrounders have got
> to stop. . . .
>
> Anyone have any disagreements?

No one did.

Reagan and Chernenko continued to exchange letters, but little happened as the election approached, with the Soviets waiting to see whether Reagan or Mondale would win. During this time Reagan continued to learn of Chernenko's weak grip as leader:

> We were to learn that to a large extent Chernenko was not
> as much in control of the Communist Party or the Politburo as
> Brezhnev or even Andropov, but shared it as spokesman for a
> kind of consensus leadership at the top of the hierarchy. . . .
> Chernenko was ill and might not live long. When he appeared
> in public, he seldom said anything without a script. Another
> old hard-liner from the Stalin era, Andrei Gromyko, was calling the shots on Soviet foreign relations.[13]

In late July and early August, Reagan spent two weeks at his beloved ranch in California. While he was on vacation he took the time to think about what he should do next with the Soviet Union. It was now becoming clear to him that the key to progress lay with Gromyko.

At about the same time that Reagan was coming to that conclusion, George Shultz was meeting with President Reagan on other business but asked for some private time. It was August 13, 1984. Shultz told Reagan that he had picked up word from two sources that Gromyko might like to be invited to the White House when he made his next pilgrimage to the United States to visit the United Nations. He hadn't been invited since 1979, when the Soviet Union invaded Afghanistan.

Reagan recalled in his diary:

> We looked at the Soviets from several directions. I approved asking Gromyko to the White House if he comes, as he usually does, to New York for the U.N. General Assembly opening. I have a feeling we'll get nowhere with arms reductions while they are suspicious of our motives as we are of theirs. I believe we need a meeting to see if we can't make them understand we have no designs on them but think they have designs on us. If we could once clear the air maybe reducing arms wouldn't look so impossible to them.[14]

Ten days after deciding to invite Gromyko to the White House, Reagan flew to the Republican National Convention in Dallas to receive his party's nomination. Here are some excerpts of Reagan's address at the convention that year:

> The greatest challenge of all is to reduce the risk of nuclear war, by reducing the levels of nuclear arms.
>
> I have addressed parliaments, have spoken to parliaments in Europe and Asia during these last 3½ years, declaring that a nuclear war cannot be won and must never be fought. And those words, in those assemblies, were greeted with spontaneous applause.
>
> There are only two nations who by their agreement can rid the world of those doomsday weapons—the United States of America and the Soviet Union. For the sake of our children and the safety of this Earth, we ask the Soviets—who have walked out of our negotiations—to join us in reducing and, yes, ridding the Earth of this awful threat.[15]

The hall stayed silent for a moment as Reagan finished, and then the audience burst into wild applause.

A couple of weeks after the convention, on September 6, 1984, Reagan was interviewed by two reporters from the *Sunday Times* of

London. The men and women of Europe were beginning to take a keen interest in Reagan. If he did get reelected, what would he do? One of the reporters asked: *"If* you get reelected—not when, *if*— what's going to be your major priority on the international scene? I think that's what people in Europe—" Reagan cut him off and answered, naming the same priority he had been espousing for several years:

> On the international scene? Well, it has to be peace.
>
> And it has to be reduced arms, particularly in the strategic field. I have to believe that if we can persuade the Soviet Union to join in reducing those weapons, that perhaps we can all see the wisdom of not only reducing but eliminating.
>
> I don't think the world should have to live with this threat hanging over them it. . . . The weapons are capable of destroy- ing mankind and civilization.[16]

September 1984 was a busy time. Reagan was scheduled to ad- dress the United Nations on September 24; Gromyko was address- ing the United Nations on September 27, and then meeting with Reagan in the White House on September 28.

Reagan's speech marked the third time he had addressed the General Assembly of the United Nations. Gromyko and other So- viets in the audience listened intently as he spoke:

> In a few minutes, I will turn to the menace of conflict on a worldwide scale and discuss the status of negotiations between the United States and the Soviet Union. . . . We need to find ways to reduce—and eventually to eliminate—the threat and use of force in solving international disputes. . . .
>
> Today, to the great end of lifting the dread of nuclear war from the peoples of the Earth, I invite the leaders of the world to join in a new beginning.[17]

With U.S.-Soviet negotiations still at a stalemate, Gromyko's speech the next day must have sent a chill of excitement up the spine of those who caught the meaning of what he said. For buried amid a great deal of anti-U.S. rhetoric lay these words:

> *The Soviet Union and the states of the socialist community are concentrating their efforts on achieving the key objective: that of preventing a nuclear catastrophe.*
>
> *For if the destructive potential which has now been accumulated in the world were unleashed, the human race could well become extinct. To prevent this is a task of overriding importance.*
>
> *Our country strove for a ban on nuclear weapons, both before it possessed them and after it had developed these weapons. The U.S.S.R. continues to favor immediate measures to reduce and ultimately to eliminate nuclear weapons totally. This is the goal of a comprehensive set of initiatives put forward by the Soviet Union.*[18]

One can argue about the history of the Soviets' desire for a ban on nuclear weapons, but there could be no doubt about the thinking of the Soviet leaders at this point in time. Their main spokesman, their foreign minister, was now saying exactly what President Reagan had been saying for several years. And it was very unlikely that Gromyko's words had not been cleared carefully with Chernenko, Gorbachev, and other key members of the Politburo in Moscow. Most probably, Gromyko's words represented the thinking of the majority of the Politburo. Yes, they were only words, and few heard them in the midst of the strident rhetoric. But this was the first time an influential Soviet leader had proposed such heresy.

For whatever reasons—whether it was the economic difficulties the Soviets were having compared to the vibrant U.S. economy, concerns about the massive military might that Reagan was acquiring, or the likelihood that Reagan would be reelected and would be with the Soviets for another four years—the stated policy objectives of the two superpowers were now essentially the same. And if the Soviet Union was really willing to back up those words, there was suddenly a chance that the two nations could make significant progress in their negotiations.

The Soviets had not yet blinked completely, but one eye had shut a little. There was a possible change in the wind—although, of course, that all depended on whether Reagan would be reelected.

Reagan's meeting with Gromyko the next day, on September 28, 1984, was crucially important. This was Reagan's highest-level meeting to date with one of the leaders of the Soviet Union. He had never sat down with Leonid Brezhnev or Yuri Andropov. Given Chernenko's health and Gromyko's position, this meeting was the closest Reagan could come to a Soviet leader.

For the meeting, the National Security Council and the State Department had provided Reagan with a number of briefing books, filled with facts and suggestions. On Monday morning, a few days before Gromyko was expected, Reagan telephoned the secretary of state and asked him to come to the White House. When Shultz joined him in the Oval Office, Shultz recalls that Reagan said:

> George, I've looked over your talking points, and they are very good.
>
> But I've been thinking about this all weekend up at Camp David, and I've written my own talking points, and I'm very satisfied with them.
>
> You can look them over if you want.[19]

Reagan decided to trust his own instincts for this, the most important moment in nearly four years of nuclear arms negotiations. As Reagan had done before, he was following his own course, not the one his advisers set for him.

The 991 words on four legal-sized yellow pages that Reagan wrote for his discussion with Gromyko—words Gromyko eventually took back to the Politburo in Moscow—would prove to be one of the turning points of the Cold War.[20] Each phrase of the document is significant, but must be taken in the context of the whole in order to understand how Reagan worked. Here is what Reagan said:

> There are differences between our two political & economic systems and I don't think either one of us will change. But we do have to live in the world together and we do have some things in common. We are both superpowers as viewed by the rest of the world and the rest of the world knows that the fate of all mankind is in our hands: that a war between us could literally wipe out all humankind.
>
> Mr. Minister the United States will never start such a war. Now you may say you have nothing but my word for that but I ask you to look at the record. When World War II ended—a war in which we were allies, we were the only nation whose industry was intact—not ravaged by war. Our military strength was at its greatest & we alone had the ultimate weapon, the nuclear bomb.
>
> We could have dictated to the world. We didn't. Instead we set out to help not only our allies but also our erstwhile enemies to rebuild their economies & their industrial strength.
>
> At the same we dismantled our military and today have only ⅔ as many nuclear weapons as we had in 1967. We have in these last several years removed 1000 nuclear weapons from Europe & will have removed another 1400 by 1988. During these same years—since the Salt I agreement was signed the Soviet Union has added 6000 warheads, 3800 of those since the signing of Salt II. Since 1972 we have built only 2 systems—you have built 31.
>
> Yes we are rebuilding our depleted strength now because your own massive military buildup, the greatest in world

history, is far beyond any defense needs and we feel it is a threat to us. From Lenin through Brezhnev your leaders & others high in your government have repeatedly proclaimed their dedication to world revolution & the eventual one world communist state. There were missiles in Cuba, continued expansion in South East Asia & Africa as well as in Latin America.

Let me make it clear. I'm citing some of the reasons why we feel you are a threat to our security and why we are determined to acquire sufficient strength to deter hostile action against us by you. We are not out to achieve superiority but we do not intend to become vulnerable to an attack or to an ultimatum in which our choice would be surrender or die.

Now you have expressed a belief that we are the aggressor and while I've already listed some reasons why we don't think there is any substance for such a belief, let me take that a step further. We are well aware of the great losses you suffered in World War II. We know also that history records invasions of Russia going back over the centuries. Can we not take steps to clear the air of these suspicions? Would not arms reductions be an easy problem to solve if we could prove to each other that neither of us has any aggressive intent?

We both know that other countries have turned to nuclear weapons and more are quietly working to achieve that goal. The danger of such proliferation is the possibility of accidental war brought on by neither of us but triggering a conflict that could ultimately involve us both. But what if we who have the power to destroy the world should join in saving it? If we can reach agreement on reducing and ultimately eliminating these weapons, we could persuade the rest of the world to join us in doing away with all such weapons.

We have shown each other that we can make some progress on bilateral issues. We have come to agreement on several matters beneficial to us both. Maybe one of the things

Mr. Minister I've looked forward to this meeting and wish it could have taken place 3 or 4 years ago. I very much want to hear your views but if you don't mind I'd like to begin by expressing a few thoughts of my own, hoping that I can persuade you that I don't eat my young.

There are differences between our 2 peol. & ec. systems and I don't think either one of us will change. But we do have to live in the world together and we do have some things in common. We are both super-powers as viewed by the rest of the world and the rest of the world knows that the fate of all mankind is in our hands: that a war between us could literally wipe out all human kind.

Mr. Minister I tell you with all sincerity the U.S. will never start such a war. Now you may say you have nothing but my word for that but I ask you to look at the record. When W.W. II ended — a war in which we were allies, we were the only nation whose industry was intact — not ravaged by war. Our military strength was at it's greatest & we alone had the ultimate weapon, the nuclear bomb.

We could have dictated to the world. We didn't. Instead we set out to help not only our allies but our erstwhile enemies to rebuild their economies & their industrial strength. At the same time We dismantled our military and today have only 2/3 as many nuclear weapons as we had in 1967. We have in these last several years removed 1000 nuclear weapons from Europe & will have removed another 1400 by 1988. — (INSERT 1)

Yes we are rebuilding our depleted strength now because your own massive militar buildup, the greatest in world history, is far beyond any defense needs and we feel it is a threat to us. From Lenin through Brezhnev your leaders & others high in your govt. have repeatedly proclaimed their dedication to world

First page of Reagan's own talking points for his historic meeting with Gromyko.

we should consider with regard to arms negotiations is the presence of senior levels in addition to the technicians. Another idea is a back channel which allows us to explore problems and solutions and to exchange ideas informally without commitments. We are ready to begin such a process with you & Ambassador Dobrynin if you think such an idea has merit.

Mr. Minister, I know you feel we are invading your sovereignty when we get into the area of human rights. I hope you've noticed that we would prefer quiet diplomacy on this subject, but let me point out why we are concerned. Ours is a nation of immigrants. We are made up of the bloodlines of all the world, and our people retain a loyalty to the countries of their origin. A man does not forget his mother because he has taken a wife. We also have a governmental system responsive to public opinion. It is easier for us to arrive at agreements with you if segments of our society are not upset by what they feel is a violation of human rights in the land of their ancestry. May I point to your handling of the matter of the Pentecostal familys in our embassy. We have not, nor will we indicate in any way that this was anything other than a generous action by your government. Your handling of that matter made such things as the grain agreement easier for us to achieve.

I know some of your colleagues with less knowledge of our system than you have possibly think an American President can simply make decisions & they become policy or law. We have an elaborate system of checks & balances which as you know makes a President's life not quite that simple.

Mr. Minister the people of both our countries if asked would, I know, say peace was their greatest desire.

If we really are worthy of being their leaders shouldn't we provide them with what they want above all else.

And have we any right to lead if that is impossible for us to deliver?[21]

After a meeting of about three hours between Reagan, a few key advisers, and Gromyko's party, Reagan arranged a private moment with the Soviet leader. George Shultz reported:

> As we were about to leave for lunch, the president took Gromyko aside and had him stay back in the Oval Office, where the two of them conversed in English without interpreters. The president later told me that in their private conversation he had been struck by Gromyko's description of the two superpowers sitting on top of ever-rising stockpiles of nuclear weapons and by Gromyko's statement that the Soviet Union wished to reduce the size of those piles. "My dream," Reagan had told him, "is for a world where there are no nuclear weapons."[22]

What was said at the brief private meeting between Reagan and Gromyko was confirmed eleven years later by Anatoly Dobrynin, the Soviet ambassador:

> The president [Reagan] emphatically told him [Gromyko], as if this was a big secret, that his personal dream was a "world without nuclear arms." Gromyko answered that nuclear disarmament was "the question of all questions." Both agreed that the ultimate goal should be the complete elimination of nuclear weapons. And that was about all there was to the private meeting.[23]

As Reagan walked out to the group outside the Oval Office he must have been pleased by the progress made that day. There was now a small crack in the Soviets' reluctance to negotiate reducing nuclear weapons. Reagan realized that he had to be patient—and, most importantly, that he had to get reelected in six weeks—if he was ever going to realize any part of his vision.

When Gromyko and Reagan left the Oval Office they walked together through the long colonnade that leads to the main mansion of the White House and were greeted by Nancy Reagan at the reception for lunch. Gromyko devoted much of his attention to her, and at one point he took her aside and murmured, "Does your husband believe in peace?"

Nancy replied, "Yes, of course."

"Then whisper 'peace' in your husband's ear every night," Gromyko said.[24]

"I will, and I'll also whisper it in your ear," she said. And with that Nancy leaned over with a smile and said softly, "Peace."

Nancy's quick thinking and sophisticated repartee greatly impressed Gromyko. He got such a "kick out of this exchange [he] recounted it to the Politburo, with great animation."[25]

After Gromyko left the White House in the afternoon, he wrote a brief statement for the Soviet news agency, TASS, on what had transpired when he met Reagan. Near the end of the statement Gromyko summed it up:

> The President spoke in favor of more frequent meetings between representatives of the two sides—at high, middle or other levels.
>
> As such, if combined with the necessary content of negotiations and if, as well, constructive goals are set, namely,
>
> **An end to the arms race, the reduction of nuclear arms, so as to ultimately bring about its complete elimination,**
>
> And removal of dangerous international tensions, all this would certainly help to straighten out the state of affairs both in the world as a whole and in the field of bilateral relations between the two powers. . . .
>
> The Soviet Union will continue to judge the real intentions of the American side by its practical deeds. The future will show whether or not Washington is going to correct its line of policy.[26]

The Soviets still had their suspicions, but clearly they now had more trust in Reagan than they'd had before the visit. Gromyko had now alluded three times—once in his speech to the United

Nations on September 27, a second time when he met privately with Reagan, and then with the statement for TASS—about reducing nuclear stockpiles and ultimately eliminating all nuclear missiles.

It was true that those three statements barely compared to Reagan's long insistence on these issues—he'd been pushing his vision in one form or another for three and a half years now, mentioning it in speeches or to reporters eighty-seven times—but Reagan knew it was a start. And so when Gromyko left and flew back to Moscow, there was a lot riding on Reagan's reelection.

On October 1, 1984, three days after his meeting with Gromyko, Reagan addressed the Economic Club of Detroit. The last question asked was, "Mr. President, what was it like to meet Mr. Gromyko? Were your talks constructive?" Reagan replied:

> I don't know whether we could become friends, or whether that's important, but I think the talk was very constructive. . . . We don't like their system; they don't like ours. We're not out to change their system, and they better not try to change ours. But we are the two superpowers, and between us we could, if we got careless,
>
> We could destroy the world.
>
> But by the same token, if we decide to stand together on some issues that should be of interest to both of us, namely, reduction and hopefully elimination of nuclear weapons,
>
> We can save the world. . . .
>
> We are ready to join with them in approaching this principal problem of runaway armaments in the world.[27]

Reagan almost certainly knew that what he was saying in a major speech just three days after meeting with Gromyko, and just weeks before the U.S. election, would be listened to avidly by those men in the Politburo in Moscow. And he was driving home a powerful theme that he thought would get the attention of the Soviet leaders—the two countries could destroy the world or save it.

With the election only five weeks away, Walter Mondale was gaining on Reagan in the polls. In the first debate on October 7 in Louisville, Kentucky, Reagan did not do as well as expected. The debate was focused almost exclusively on domestic issues, and many of Reagan's staff—especially those who knew little of his intense interest in reduction of nuclear weapons—had burdened him with superfluous, detailed papers that he gamely tried to master.

Only once did Reagan ignore his "helpers" and shift over to something he really liked:

> I said that we would become respected in the world once again and that we would refurbish our national defense to the place that we could deal on the world scene and then seek disarmament, reduction of arms, and, hopefully, an elimination of nuclear weapons. We have done that.[28]

But in a sea of domestic issues, Reagan's statement just sailed into the air and was not even touched by the newspapers the next day. Reagan lost the debate and acknowledged it to himself in his personal diary:

> Sat. another rehearsal—the whole crew at Camp D. An afternoon ride & lots of cramming . . . I have to say I lost. I guess I'd crammed so hard on facts & figures in view of the absolutely dishonest things he's been saying in the campaign, I guess I flattened out. Anyway I didn't feel good about myself. And yet he was never able to rebut any of the facts I presented & kept repeating things that are absolute falsehoods. But the press has been calling him the winner for 2 days now.[29]

Consequently the race tightened up even more and Mondale was soon only six points behind Reagan.

A few days later, on October 18, Reagan flew to New York City for the Al Smith dinner, a traditional forum for presidential candidates. Henry Kissinger dropped by Reagan's hotel room before dinner, and Reagan wrote in his diary that night:

> We had a good session. He [Kissinger] feels my firmness about the Soviets has worked & that if I'm elected they'll want to get together on arms talks.[30]

That was just the tonic that Reagan needed.

The final and decisive debate took place on Sunday night, October 21, in the Kansas City Convention Center. Millions of Americans would be watching, many of whom had not yet decided how to cast their votes. This debate focused on foreign policy, and Reagan had very clear ideas of what should be done. As the debate progressed, Reagan was unexpectedly asked about his age by one of the panelists, Henry Trewhitt, the diplomatic correspondent for the *Baltimore Sun*:

Mr. President . . . You already are the oldest President in history. And some of your staff say you were tired after your most recent encounter with Mr. Mondale. I recall yet that President Kennedy had to go for days on end with very little sleep during the Cuban missile crisis. It there any doubt in your mind that you would be able to function in such circumstances?

Across America, 67.3 million people held their breaths. If Reagan stuttered through his answer, he would be history. If he ignored the question, he would still be history. He was in the reporter's trap.

But Reagan had an ace up his sleeve. He leaned forward, looked over at Mondale, and said:

Not at all, Mr. Trewhitt, and I want you to know that also I will not make age an issue of this campaign. I am not going to exploit, for political purposes, my opponent's youth and inexperience.

Then he smiled broadly, looked up, and said:

I might add, Mr. Trewhitt, I might add that it was Seneca or it was Cicero, I don't know which, that said, "If it was not for the elders correcting the mistakes of the young, there would be no state."[31]

There was silence for a moment. Then appreciative laughter swept the hall and most likely every home in America watching the television screen. Trewhitt looked stunned and said, "Mr. President, I'd like to head for the fence and try to catch that one before it goes over." Trewhitt's question and Reagan's answer might not have had much to do with foreign policy, but they destroyed any chance Walter Mondale might have had to be the next president of the United States. Even Mondale could not resist laughing while his hopes of becoming president melted away.

As the debate continued, the questions became more serious. At one point Marvin Kalb, chief diplomatic correspondent for NBC, asked in a condescending tone:

Mr. President, when you made that proposal, the so-called Star Wars proposal, you said, if I'm not mistaken, that you would share this very super-sophisticated technology with the Soviet Union. After all of the distrust over the years, sir, that you have expressed towards the Soviet Union, do you really expect anyone to take seriously that offer that you would share the best of America's technology in this weapons area with our principal adversary?

Reagan smiled a bit and answered:

Why not? What if we did—and I hope we can; we're still researching—what if we come up with a weapon that renders those missiles obsolete? There has never been a weapon invented in the history of man that has not led to a defensive, a counter weapon.

But suppose we came up with that? Now, some people have said, "Ah, that would make war imminent, because they would think that we could launch a first strike because we could defend against the enemy."

But why not do what I have offered to do, and asked the Soviet Union to do? Say, "Look, here's what we can do. We'll even give it to you.

"Now, will you sit down with us and once and for all get rid, all of us, of these nuclear weapons and free mankind from that threat?"

I think that would be the greatest use of a defensive weapon . . . "Here's what we can do. Now, if you're willing to join us in getting rid of all the nuclear weapons in the world, then we'll give you this one, so that we would both know that no one can cheat. . . ." I think the world will be better off. . . .

I have said that it seems to me that this could be a logical step in what is my ultimate goal, my ultimate dream, and that is the elimination of nuclear weapons in the world.[32]

Reagan rose dramatically in the polls after the second debate. It is difficult to know exactly how important his views on reducing nuclear missiles and missile defense were, but it seemed clear that a lot of people who listened liked what he said.

On November 6, 1984, the American people reelected Reagan by one of the largest margins in American history. Reagan won forty-nine out of fifty states. Only Minnesota went for Mondale, and then only by a small percentage. More than 54 million voters, the highest tally thus far in U.S. history, voted for Reagan. Reagan's position had changed dramatically. Instead of being a lame duck with declining political power, he now had four more years to pursue his priorities.

With Reagan back in office and the U.S. economy and military strength growing, the Soviet Union could not intimidate the United States. Moreover, the Soviets had problems of their own. Their economy was weak and growing weaker—and the United States knew it and was doing everything it could to let them bear the burden themselves. Finally, the Soviets were temporarily without a real leader, with the sickly Chernenko functioning only as a placeholder.

Reagan just basked in his new situation—and waited.

Chapter 12

~

REAGAN'S NEGOTIATING STRATEGY

The old order changeth,
Yielding place to new.
—ALFRED TENNYSON, 1869

Reagan did not have to wait long.

When he was reelected, the Soviet leaders swung into action. First there was a flood of warm letters. One of the letters, sent on Wednesday, November 7, was from the Presidium of the Supreme Soviet of the USSR, the highest organ of state power in the Soviet Union. They addressed Reagan as "Esteemed Mr. President." In the text of the letter, after giving Reagan their congratulations on winning reelection, the Soviet leaders continued, "It is to be hoped that the coming years will be marked by a turn for the better in relations between our countries . . . the Soviet Union is prepared for joint work to rectify Soviet-American relations on the basis of equality and respect for legitimate interests of each other, remove the threat of war, and radically improve the international situation."[1]

The day before the election, Secretary of State George Shultz suggested Reagan write a letter to Chernenko after Reagan won (people around Reagan were very sure he was going to win). Shultz suggested that Reagan take this opportunity to set forth a comprehensive, concrete agenda for U.S.-Soviet relations for the next four years.[2]

Reagan apparently liked the idea, but instead of sending a letter, he sent an oral message to Chernenko in Moscow. Chernenko answered without delay, with this oral reply on Thursday, November 8, 1984:

> *Thank you for the oral message. . . . I and my colleagues in the Soviet leadership come out firmly for reversing the present unfavorable trends . . . in Soviet-American relations. We take note of your statement about the possibility and necessity of establishing more stable and constructive relations between our two countries for the long term. . . . For our part, we are prepared to search on this path for solutions to the problems that stand before the Soviet Union and the USA, above all the task of eliminating the nuclear threat.[3]*

At the end of his first term President Reagan had one of the most powerful group of advisers ever put together in the White House. They were smart, tough, and precise. They did not always agree with Reagan, but their suggestions—even when they differed from Reagan's decisions—were valued highly. But after he won reelection, some of the internal squabbling started to get out of hand.

Shultz had gradually become Reagan's closest adviser and often took positions that Reagan liked but were not shared by others. Ever since Shultz had become secretary of state in 1982, the number of personal meetings between him and Reagan had steadily increased. By 1984 Shultz was having more than fifty personal meetings a year with Reagan. Some of the staff resented it, but as Reagan spent more and more time negotiating with the Soviet leaders, he relied more and more on Shultz to carry out his plans.[4]

The infighting between Shultz and two of his fellow advisers—
Cap Weinberger, the secretary of defense, and Bill Casey, the director of the CIA—finally escalated to the point where Reagan had to
step in. After meeting with Shultz on November 13, he decided
what he had to do. He did not like it, but he knew that he had to
rein in two of his most trusted advisers. Here are his diary notes:

> A long meeting with Secretary Shultz. We have trouble. Cap
> [Weinberger] and Bill Casey have views contrary to George's
> on South America, the Middle East & our arms negotiations.
> It's so out of hand George sounds like he wants out.
> I can't let that happen.
> Actually George is carrying out my policy.
> I'm going to meet with Cap & Bill & lay it out to them.
> Won't be fun but has to be done.[5]

On Friday, November 16, he decided when he would take
action:

> Tomorrow morning I'm meeting with Cap W. & Bill Casey
> to iron out (if I can) some difficulties involving George S.[6]

The three men sat down in the Oval Office at 10:30 a.m. on
November 17. We don't know what was said during the hour-long
meeting—but Shultz did not resign, and Weinberger and Casey
acquiesced to Reagan's demands.

KONSTANTIN CHERNENKO WRITES TO REAGAN

On November 17, 1984, just eleven days after Reagan won reelection, Chernenko sent him a letter agreeing to open up new
arms reduction negotiations, including negotiations on nuclear
weapons. Chernenko also agreed to open negotiations on strategic

and medium-range missiles, as well as weapons in outer space. Here are key excerpts from this historic document:

> We propose that the Soviet Union and the United States of America enter into new negotiations with the objective of reaching mutually acceptable agreements on the whole range of questions concerning nuclear and space weapons. . . . There is an organic, and I would say, objective relationship between these issues and it is precisely in this way that they should be treated at the negotiations we are proposing.
>
> In other words, such negotiations must encompass both the issue of non-militarization of space and the questions of strategic nuclear arms and medium-range nuclear systems. In all these directions we are prepared to seek most radical solutions which would allow movement towards a complete ban and eventually liquidation of nuclear arms. . . .
>
> In order to settle these matters, we propose that A. A. Gromyko and George Shultz meet, let's say in the first half of January 1985. We would be prepared for this purpose to receive the Secretary of State in Moscow, or such a meeting could be arranged in a third country as may be agreed by the sides.[7]

The Soviets had now agreed to negotiations on every nuclear issue that Reagan had been talking about since he took office. They had agreed, in principle, to reduce their stockpile of nuclear missiles.

Of course, the details would still need to be worked out, and that wouldn't be easy. But although no one said it out loud, in getting them to come back to the table on his terms, Reagan had won.

Between the two superpowers, the United States and the Soviets now had more than sixty-two thousand nuclear warheads in their stockpiles. Many of these nuclear missiles were a hundred times more powerful than the atomic bomb that leveled Hiroshima in 1945.

How much of this arsenal each side was willing to give up, and what other conditions each demanded, would determine whether the ice of the Cold War thickened or began to crack. But both Reagan and Shultz had long and deep backgrounds in the skills of negotiation, and they made a formidable pair.

Reagan quickly sat down with Shultz to discuss Chernenko's letter. The two men agreed that they should continue to push for the goal Reagan had been aiming for since March 1982. In his personal diary on November 28 Reagan wrote:

> We [Reagan and Shultz] agree that since Chernenko has talked as I have of total elimination of nuclear weapons that should be our goal in the negotiations.[8]

The next few weeks were busy ones for Reagan as he and his advisers held four meetings to prepare for the upcoming nuclear negotiations. Even though Chernenko was in poor health, it was assumed that he would be alive, and the United States' strategies were all directed toward him.

THE CIA WEIGHS IN: SOVIET STRATEGY AND THE STATUS OF SOVIET FORCES

The November 30 NSPG meeting was a time for the president to listen, and what he heard was chilling:

> CIA Director Casey introduced Mr. Doug George [the CIA's senior specialist on arms control issues], noting that Mr. George's presentation had been developed along with Larry Gershwin [CIA analyst]. . . . The presentation described the Soviet approach to arms control talks, taking into account military considerations, arms control policy, political considerations, and economic considerations.[9]

George's presentation noted that Soviet offensive systems included twenty-five hundred strategic nuclear delivery vehicles, or SNDVs. Many of them were ICBMs, which carried multiple warheads and were mobile, traveling on rail or road. He also reported that the Soviets were continuing to build up their ICBMs, including their European deployments, even as they diversified their offensive forces with bombers and air-launched cruise missiles. Their "hot" production lines would enable them to go beyond the limits of the SALT II agreement.

The Soviets had a near monopoly in strategic defense. They were upgrading their ABM system around Moscow and a vigorous research program was under way for deployment of a widespread ABM system in the 1990s. The Soviets also had their own ASAT (anti-satellite) interceptor and their own SDI program.

The one bright spot in the briefing was that the Soviets couldn't keep up with U.S. developments in computers and therefore feared that, should the United States enter the strategic defense race in earnest, they could not compete with U.S. technology.

The main Soviet objectives for negotiations, the CIA concluded, were to protect the gains they had made and put political pressures on the United States and its allies to slow down U.S. defense spending and technological development, to stop or delay INF deployments in Europe, and to stop SDI with an ASAT moratorium. Soviet economic problems were unlikely, in the CIA's view, to cause them to limit their strategic programs—or to forgo developing the capabilities to go beyond existing agreements in both offense and defense.[10]

Reagan had a question:

I wonder whether or not deterrence would be enhanced if we made it clear to the Soviet Union that we might launch-under-attack. But I wonder whether we have the warning capacity to be certain that we would have warning and that we would not be caught by surprise.[11]

The response from Reagan's NSC brain trust was that launch-on-attack was not practical given current capacities. The ability SDI would provide to implement such a policy in the future made SDI look "very good indeed" in Casey's view.

In his diary that night, Reagan summed up the guidance he had given the meeting participants:

> I made it plain there must be no granting of concessions (one sided) to try & soften up the Soviets.[12]

The NSPG met again on Wednesday, December 5, for the second of the four critical meetings focused on the negotiations. Reagan began by stating his personal views on what the negotiations with the Soviets should contain:

> We and the Soviet Union may be coming together more than many people realize.
>
> We have never believed that we would find ourselves at war with Russia except to defend ourselves against attack. We have to look at defense measures just the way the Soviet Union does. We have to look at civil defense and air defense and ABM. The Moscow subway is significant to their civil defense.
>
> Everything they have says that they are looking at a first-strike because it is they, not we, who have built up both offensive and defensive systems.
>
> We could build on the Soviet preoccupation with protecting the homeland by making clear that we have no intention of starting a nuclear war. It is our view that they may want to make war on us. We have no objection to their having defenses, but we have to look at defenses for ourselves, and we need to look at reducing and ultimately eliminating nuclear weapons.
>
> Relative to the goal of eliminating nuclear weapons, an initial reduction of 1,000 is meaningless. Both sides have indicated

that they would like to get rid of nuclear weapons entirely, but they are afraid of SDI. We must show them how defenses are not threatening.

The Soviet Union is ahead of us in ASAT capability. We should first talk about getting rid of these offensive arms like this F-15 ASAT.

We must make it clear that we are not seeking advantage, only defense.[13]

Reagan continued, driving home how he felt about the Soviet leaders:

It would be silly if we go into these talks without being realistic. There is a quotation which is attributed to Brezhnev in Prague, namely, that the Soviet Union has gained a great deal from détente and that therefore, in 1985, the Soviet Union should have its way around the world.

I doubt that they had in mind Pearl Harbor but rather expected that they believe that they would be so powerful that they could coerce us into achieving their objectives peacefully. . . .

It is important to link research on SDI to making nuclear weapons obsolete.

We are behind in ASAT, which is the ability to knock down satellites, but we are willing to negotiate the end of ASAT because they are offensive weapons. SDI is a non-nuclear defensive system.

I still wonder whether or not we could give them the technology. . . .

SDI gives us a great deal of leverage on the Soviet Union.[14]

On December 7, Reagan sent a long letter to Chernenko, classified Secret/Supersensitive, agreeing to the negotiations Chernenko had proposed in his November 17 letter, and suggesting some ideas for the first meeting in Geneva, Switzerland. Here are some key excerpts from the three-page letter Reagan sent:

> Our two countries have now announced the beginning of new negotiations on the whole range of questions concerning nuclear and outer space weapons, as you proposed in your letter of November 17 . . .
>
> First, we agree on the objective of eventually liquidating nuclear arms, as you put it. . . .
>
> George Shultz will go to Geneva prepared to negotiate a mutual understanding on the subjects and objectives of follow-on negotiations. . . .
>
> In closing, let me state as strongly as I can my personal commitment to make the results we have agreed to seek as productive, as concrete and as beneficial as possible. I intend to give my personal attention to the arms control negotiations that our Foreign Ministers will seek to launch in Geneva.[15]

Later that evening in his diary, Reagan expressed some of his misgivings as he began this crucial adventure:

> We're facing a closer to home problem which has to do with the upcoming talks with the Soviets re arms reductions. We're convinced they want above all to negotiate away our right to seek a defensive weapon against ballistic missiles.
>
> They fear our technology. I believe such a defense could render nuclear weapons obsolete & thus we could rid the world of that threat.
>
> Question is will they use that to break off the talks & blame us?[16]

We're facing a down to home problem which has to do with the upcoming talks with the Soviets re-arms reductions. We're convinced they want above all to negotiate away our right to seek a defensive weapon against ballistic missiles. They fear our technology. I believe such a defense could render nuclear weapons obsolete & thus we could rid the world of that threat. Question is will they use that to break off the talks & blame us?

Reagan's personal diary, December 7, 1984, on page 185.

On December 10, the NSPG met again, this time to go over the details Reagan's negotiators would have to master before sitting down across from the Soviets. But Reagan took the opportunity to remind everyone at the table—whether they agreed with him or not—that his goal was the elimination of all nuclear weapons in the world:

> Chernenko and Gromyko quoted my words supporting the goal of the ultimate elimination of nuclear weapons. . . .

After considerable discussion, Reagan commented:

> We need talks which can eliminate suspicions, and I am willing to admit that the Soviet Union is suspicious of us. . . .
> Life in the U.S. is too good for anyone to consider starting a war and [Reagan's tone becomes humorous] I hope life doesn't get so boring in Russia that they would consider starting a war.

As the meeting drew to a close Reagan turned to Shultz and said:

> I want to make sure that you have the Brezhnev quotation from Prague where he said that because of détente, by 1985 the Soviet Union would have their way in the world. They were wrong.[17]

The 1973 Brezhnev quotation Reagan referred to was one he had cited before, in a radio commentary he wrote and taped on March 23, 1977. He quoted Brezhnev as saying:

"We are achieving with détente what our predecessors have been unable to achieve using the mailed fist. We have been able to accomplish more in a short time with détente than was done for years pursuing a confrontation policy with NATO. Trust us comrades, for by 1985, as a consequence of what we are now achieving with détente, we will have achieved most of our objectives in Western Europe. We will have consolidated our position. We will have improved our economy. . . . A decisive shift in the correlation of forces will be such that come 1985, we will be able to extend our will wherever we need to."[18]

The NSPG's final preparatory meeting took place on December 17. It was to be a discussion of the exact content of the Geneva talks—to include START, INF, Space and the relationship between offense and defense. The meeting was opened by the national security adviser, who gave a long, detailed rundown of all the possibilities. Reagan interrupted McFarlane to say:

SDI is the main target of the Soviet Union in Geneva.

They are coming to the table to get at SDI. We need to stay with our SDI research program no matter what. International control for world protection might be possible at some point with SDI. SDI would help alleviate the dangers associated with the impossible job of verification.

Someone like Qadhafi could develop nuclear weapons and perhaps smuggle them into the United States. We would need a wide range of measures to handle the threat of a covert nuclear weapon. People now understand how to build nuclear weapons and that you cannot make mankind unlearn what it already knows.

Look at the test flight recently of an SS-X-24 with ten warheads. I emphasize that there is no price on SDI, and we must be frank with the Soviet Union on the need to go down the path toward defense, to eliminate nuclear weapons, but clearly we are not going to give up SDI.[19]

Shultz and Weinberger joined the discussion, and for the rest of the meeting, Reagan and these two men dominated what was said. Again, Reagan interjected to focus on SDI:

We must stress that in a context of the Soviets' having already said that they want to give up nuclear weapons, if they walk-out of Geneva because of SDI, we can emphasize that they are not serious. We must be prepared to make clear to the American people that this is a system which does not kill people; that it would free the world from the threat of nuclear weapons.

SDI is important in dealing with the problem of verification. SDI could be put in international hands to protect the whole world. The Soviet Union will have difficulty walking out when we have made a sound case. . . .

I have been reading about the phenomenon of nuclear winter, and about the volcano Timbora[20] which erupted in 1816, creating a cloud which created winter conditions—snow and ice—around much of the world there was no summer. Nuclear winter ought to encourage reductions. . . .

I have been talking with a number of experts who are critical of SDI, and they all seem to think that it is a nuclear weapon. We need to explain to them that it is not a nuclear system we seek. . . .

Turning to Secretary Shultz, Reagan said:

We should get the Soviet Union to agree to work towards the elimination of nuclear weapons, and then throw this commitment back at them if they stand in the way of strategic defenses. . . . I desire to get this process of reductions going . . . the Soviet Union had been continuing to build up their forces. . . .

> We need to emphasize the idea of elimination of nuclear weapons and in the end, the zero option for INF would be a great step in that direction. . . .
>
> Whatever we do, we must be resolved among ourselves that SDI is not the price for reductions. . . .

In his diary that night Reagan reiterated his suspicions about Soviet goals for the negotiations:

> We had a N.S.P.G. meeting again on our negotiating posture in the upcoming meeting with Gromyko & the arms talks. I believe the Soviets have agreed to the talks only to head off our research on a strategic defense against nuclear weapons.
>
> I stand firm we cannot retreat on that, no matter what they offer.[21]

We had our NSPG meeting again on our negotiating posture in the upcoming meeting with Gromyko & the arms talks. I believe the Soviets have agreed to the talks only to head off our research on a strategic defense against nuc. weapons. I stand firm we cannot retreat on that no matter what they offer.

Reagan's personal diary, December 17, 1984.

The following night, on December 18, Reagan recorded in his diary even stronger suspicions about what the Soviets might do in the days ahead:

> More & more I'm thinking the Soviets are preparing to walk out on the talks if we won't give up research on the strategic defense system.
>
> I hope I'm wrong.[22]

GORBACHEV JOINS GROMYKO AND CHERNENKO

As President Reagan and his negotiation experts in Washington wound up their plans for Geneva, some interesting events were taking place in Moscow and London.

Mikhail Gorbachev, a protégé of Yuri Andropov, was taking a more prominent position in the Kremlin. For some time he had been in charge of agriculture in the Soviet Union, but in May 1984 he had been appointed the ideological secretary, an important role in the Politburo. The post had been held by Andropov in 1983 and was considered a step up in the competition to become the next general secretary. At fifty-three, Gorbachev was young for a Soviet leader, and in 1984 few knew much about him. Those who did considered him to be intelligent, full of energy, and ambitious.

On December 17, 1984, Gorbachev flew to London as the head of a delegation from the Supreme Soviet, the first important overseas mission he had undertaken. Gorbachev spoke at a luncheon hosted by Sir Geoffrey Howe, the British foreign secretary. His topic was the forthcoming series of arms reduction talks with the United States. Although much of what Gorbachev said that day mirrored Gromyko's words at the United Nations almost three months earlier, as well as what Chernenko had written in his November letter to Reagan, it was still striking news to the British and other countries throughout the world when Gorbachev said:

> *The Soviet Union is prepared . . . to advance toward the complete prohibition and eventual elimination of nuclear weapons.*[23]

Now, as he was getting ready for the resumption of the arms control talks in Geneva, Reagan could say that the three most powerful men in the Kremlin—Chernenko, Gromyko, and Gorbachev—all agreed with his vision.

But there was a catch.

Gorbachev asked for something in return for his support of Reagan's position. As Reagan suspected, the Soviets were most concerned about "Star Wars." They simply could not abide the idea of the United States getting defensive missiles that would make their huge stockpile of nuclear weapons obsolete. Reagan had seriously offered to share the missile defense system with them, but the Soviet leaders did not believe him.

In his speech Gorbachev made this point very clear when he said:

> *I would like to stress that in present circumstances it is especially important to avert the transfer of the arms race to outer space. If it is not done it would be unreal to hope to stop the nuclear arms race.*[24]

Gorbachev had more up his sleeve when he flew to London. He also talked personally to the prime minister, Margaret Thatcher, about "Star Wars." Gorbachev knew she was very close to President Reagan and had many questions herself about SDI. He also knew she was going to the United States in four days and expected to have a private talk with Reagan at Camp David.

While Prime Minister Thatcher was flying across the Atlantic to Washington, Reagan was examining a new letter, classified Secret/Sensitive, that had just come from Chernenko, dated December 20, 1984. After the usual opening pleasantries about the upcoming negotiations, Chernenko echoed Gorbachev's recent one-two punch. He began by accepting the idea that Reagan had been championing for three years—"liquidate nuclear weapons, completely and everywhere." Chernenko wrote:

> *Recently you have spoken on more than one occasion, also in your letters of November 16th and December 7th and earlier in your conversation with Andrei A. Gromyko, in favor of moving along the road leading eventually to the liquidation of nuclear weapons, completely and everywhere. We, of course, welcome that.*

> *The Soviet Union, as is known, as far back as the dawn of the nu-*
> *clear age came out for prohibiting and liquidating such weapons. We*
> *also made specific proposals as to how it could be achieved. At that time,*
> *given the good will on the part of the US, it would have been, of course,*
> *much easier than it is now to resolve the task of liquidating nuclear*
> *weapons. But even today it is not yet too late to start practical movement*
> *towards this noble objective.*

But then the other shoe dropped:

> *In my letter to you of November 17 I noted the objective fact that the*
> *key link in this whole chain is the question of strike space weapons, and*
> *to be more precise, the question of neither side having such weapons. To*
> *be quite frank: emergence and deployment of strike space systems would*
> *make it impossible to conduct serious negotiations on the limitation and*
> *reduction of strategic arms.*[25]

On December 21, some reporters asked a few questions of President Reagan, who, with Nancy, was accepting an eight-foot-square Christmas card from the citizens of Johnstown, Pennsylvania. Just as the Reagans were getting ready to leave, one reporter asked: "How do you feel about the fact that both Mitterrand and Thatcher are concerned about 'Star Wars'?" Reagan, knowing that Thatcher would be talking to him at Camp David the next morning, replied:

Well, I'll get them to understand what it is, too. Today the only defensive weapon we have is to threaten that if they kill millions of our people, we'll kill millions of theirs.

I don't think there's any morality in that at all. We're trying to look for something that will make those weapons obsolete, and they can be eliminated once and for all.[26]

The Reagans then headed for Camp David, where they got ready to meet Margaret Thatcher the next day. That night the Reagans relaxed, watched a movie, and went to bed early. Saturday morning, Thatcher was flown to Camp David and by 10:40 a.m. was in the Aspen Lodge for a private meeting, classified Secret, with Reagan.

Thatcher and Reagan had known each other since 1975, when Reagan was in England and met privately with her not long after she became leader of Britain's Conservative Party. They had quickly become good friends.

But on this visit she had some serious business to attend to. After congratulating Reagan on his landslide win at the polls, she began talking about her recent meeting with Gorbachev. She insisted Gorbachev was "an unusual Russian in that he was much less constrained, more charming, open to discussion and debate, did not stick to prepared notes. His wife was equally charming." It was clear Thatcher was deeply impressed, even though she had spent only a few hours with him. However, she did note that she often says to herself "the more charming the adversary, the more dangerous."

As their discussion moved to the upcoming negotiations, Reagan noted:

> Our goal is to reduce, and eventually eliminate nuclear weapons. Chernenko now claims that this is also a Soviet goal. . . . Gromyko has told me that we cannot continue to sit on two mountains of weapons.[27]

Thatcher replied that she had a special interest in learning more details about the SDI program. Gorbachev had told her:

> *Tell your friend, President Reagan, not to go ahead with space weapons.*

Thatcher delivered the message.

Reagan ignored Gorbachev's demand, but Thatcher continued, "If you develop SDI, the Russians would either develop their own, or more probably, develop new offensive systems superior to SDI."

Reagan realized he had been handed a Soviet threat. He ignored it and noticed it was time for Thatcher and him to join the others at Laurel Lodge for lunch. After the dozen guests had settled in their seats, Thatcher stood up to talk, and soon it was clear that she wished to speak further about Gorbachev and SDI. As it turned out, in the three hours she was there, it seemed that her main mission was to get Reagan to kill SDI.

Thatcher began:

Gorbachev has spent an inordinate amount of time on SDI, and he has asked me to tell the President to stop the militarization of outer space . . . the Soviets clearly fear U.S. technological prowess. However, Gorbachev suggests that the Soviets would either develop their own strategic defense system or add additional offensive systems.

We do not want our objective of increased security to result in increased Soviet nuclear weapons. Nuclear weapons have served not only to prevent a nuclear war, but they have also given us forty years of unprecedented peace in Europe. It would be unwise to abandon a deterrence system that has prevented both nuclear and conventional war. Moreover, if we ever reach the stage of abolishing all nuclear weapons, this would make conventional, biological, or chemical war more likely. Hitler won the race for the rocket; the United States won the race for the nuclear bomb.

These comments reflect concerns. We have some real worries, especially about SDI's impact on deterrence. The wretched press has tried to make out that we have major differences. This is simply not true, but we do feel it is unwise to conclude where we will go on SDI . . . personally I have some doubts . . . Even if an SDI system proved 95 percent successful—a significant success rate—over 60 million people would still die from those weapons that got through. . . . We must emphasize that SDI is only a research program.

Reagan tried once again to calm her concerns:

We cannot and should not, however, have to go on living under the threat of nuclear destruction. We must eliminate the threat posed by strategic nuclear weapons. My ultimate goal is to eliminate nuclear weapons . . . we also know that in a nuclear war there would be no winners.[28]

Thatcher had more to say:

I don't wish to debate strategic theory. Some claim SDI would be an incentive for the Soviets to produce more offensive systems and could encourage the Soviets to launch a preemptive first strike. From our point of view, deterrence remains our fundamental objective. And like you, we are fearful of the Soviets finding an excuse to walk out of the Geneva talks. . . . SDI, as I understand it, seems to suggest inherent United States superiority. I am not convinced of the need to deploy such a system, particularly if it could eventually be knocked out by other technological advances.

Thatcher did not change her mind, but as she left, she reiterated her desire for a technical briefing in London on SDI.

The events of the last week had shown Reagan that he had the attention of the Soviets—in spades. In one week Gorbachev had demonstrated his cunning by ingratiating himself with Prime Minister Thatcher, delivering a clear message about what the Soviets feared the most—"Star Wars"—and arranging to have that message delivered to President Reagan by someone Reagan trusted, in his Camp David hideaway. At the same time, Chernenko had played the same hand with his long, ingratiating letter that ulti-mately sent the same message: no SDI.

For their part, the Soviets were in an increasingly desperate situation. Besides the country's poor economic performance, their leader, Chernenko, apparently was sinking fast, his health sliding away. Two men were increasingly in charge of Soviet foreign af-fairs—Gromyko and now Gorbachev.

Chernenko had indicated that arms reduction negotiations would resume, but there was still the overhanging problem that the key leaders of the Soviet Union were either aged, dead, or dying. What was needed were new leaders to match the new think-ing. As the New Year of 1985 broke, there was some movement to begin implementing the "new thinking" of the Soviet Politburo. While the Soviets sorted out this difficulty, Reagan continued his drumbeat calling for the reduction of nuclear weapons and their eventual elimination.

On January 5, 1985, George Shultz, with his negotiating team, flew to Geneva to meet with Gromyko to set up the ground rules for the negotiations. After two days of discussion they had reached agreement, and the new talks were set to begin on March 12, 1985—fifteen months from when the Soviets had walked out. Shultz sensed from the discussions that "we had come to a turning point" in the relations of the two countries.[29]

When Shultz returned on January 9, Reagan held a major press conference broadcast live on nationwide radio and television. Rea-gan emphasized once again what he had been advocating for years:

> Our objective in these talks will be the reduction of nu-clear arms and the strengthening of strategic stability. Our ulti-mate goal, of course, is the complete elimination of nuclear weapons. . . .
>
> I would like to also point out that because they themselves [the Soviets] have expressed the desire to totally eliminate nu-clear weapons. . . .

> We're searching for a weapon that might destroy nuclear weapons, not be nuclear itself—destroy weapons, not people. And if we come up with such a thing, then is a time to turn to the world, to our allies, possibly even our adversaries, and say, "Look, we now have this."
>
> And if we haven't by this time eliminated nuclear weapons entirely, this could be a big contribution factor to bringing that about.[30]

On January 17, Reagan sat down with two reporters, Ann Devroy and Johanna Neuman, of *USA Today*. Toward the end of their questions one of the reporters asked why SDI was so important in the nuclear arms negotiations that were about to begin. Reagan explained, in depth, why he felt it was necessary:

> Suppose we could succeed in getting down to the point of elimination of nuclear weapons.
>
> But we know how to make nuclear weapons, and if down someplace in the future [someone were to make nuclear weapons] . . . who would know that they were doing it?
>
> But, if in the meantime, our technology has made it plain that there is a defense against such things, then you have guarded against that ever happening in the future.

Perhaps more telling was Reagan's annoyed retort when, at the end of the interview, he was asked how much influence Nancy had on his policies.

> May I voice a frustration?
>
> It's not only my wife, it's everyone—this picture that is being created that I sit at the desk and wait to see who's going to grab this arm and pull me this way or grab this one and pull me that way.
>
> You know something? I'm too old and stubborn to put

> up with that. I make up my mind. I do listen for counsel and ad-
> vice. I want to get expertise from people that are expert in vari-
> ous fields. But I haven't changed my views since I've been here.
>
> And with Nancy, yes, we've been married for 30-odd years,
> and of course we talk, and of course she has opinions. And I lis-
> ten to her opinions. And sometimes we argue about them, and
> I don't listen. . . . Like any other human beings, we don't al-
> ways see eye to eye on something. . . . But it doesn't make any
> dents in the marriage.

Delighted, the reporters thanked him for the lively retort. We can only hope the Soviet leaders read about who pulled Reagan's "strings."[31]

Four days later, on January 21, 1985, Reagan gave one of his most important speeches, his Second Inaugural Address, drafted in his own hand. Here are the excerpts of what Reagan said about nuclear weapons:

> We seek the total elimination one day of nuclear weapons
> from the face of the Earth. . . . Is there either logic or morality
> in believing that if one side threatens to kill tens of millions of
> our people our only recourse is to threaten killing tens of mil-
> lions of theirs?
>
> I have approved a research program to find, if we can, a se-
> curity shield that will destroy nuclear missiles before they reach
> their target. . . . It would render nuclear weapons obsolete.
>
> We will meet with the Soviets, hoping that we can agree on
> a way to rid the world of the threat of nuclear destruction.[32]

On February 6, as Reagan's political power continued to grow and the Soviets moved toward his way of thinking, Reagan deliv-ered his State of the Union address. One sentence described the most important issue in his mind:

> All of us have no greater dream than to see the day when nuclear weapons are banned from this Earth forever.[33]

In Moscow, on February 23, 1985, General Secretary Konstantin Chernenko addressed the Twenty-seventh Congress of the Communist Party of the Soviet Union on some of the new thinking that was going to take place in the Kremlin. In fact, Chernenko himself did not speak that day, although it was stated that he had prepared the text of the speech that was read out at the meeting.

Here are some excerpts from Chernenko's statement, as published by *Pravda*:

> *Comrades, we, the generation of today, are first and foremost duty bound to prevent a new world conflagration, to save life on earth. . . .*
>
> *Comrades, the core of our foreign policy today is, of course, the struggle for terminating the arms race imposed by imperialism, for averting the threat of a world nuclear war.*
>
> *We are at the threshold of new negotiations with the United States.*
>
> *First: We do not strive to acquire any unilateral advantages over the United States . . . or for military superiority over them. We do not need it, as we have no intention of either threatening them or imposing our will on them, but want to live in peace. . . .*
>
> *Second: We want termination . . . of the arms race. . . .*
>
> *Third: We want a real reduction of the arms stockpiles, destruction of a substantial portion of them by way of a beginning, and not the development of increasingly new weapon systems. . . .*
>
> *Our ultimate objective here is the complete elimination of nuclear weapons everywhere on this planet, the complete removal of the threat of nuclear war.*
>
> *Now history poses . . . the question of mankind's future . . . the enormous significance that a binding agreement between the nuclear powers could . . . prevent the outbreak of nuclear war.[34]*

Soon Secretary Shultz sent a copy of the speech to John Poindexter, now the national security adviser, and instructed him to show President Reagan the "arms control section." After Reagan read it, he wrote this note in the upper left corner of the speech:

> Very interesting—now all they have to do is indicate how fast they are willing to go in destroying weapons. RR[35]

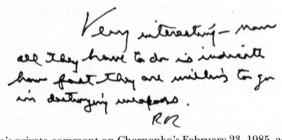

Reagan's private comment on Chernenko's February 23, 1985, address to the Communist Party of the Soviet Union.

The mood in Reagan's administration was now cautiously optimistic. The Soviets were at least claiming to understand what President Reagan had been saying about nuclear weapons for the past four years—the Soviet political consensus had swung around 180 degrees, until they were talking much like Reagan. Because the government of the Soviet Union was not democratic, effecting such a change in their policies was extremely difficult. Nothing less than a majority vote on the fifteen-man Politburo—perhaps even in some cases a unanimous vote—could lead to change.

Although, as president of the United States, Reagan was constrained in ways the Soviet leaders were not, in some ways he held far *more* power than his Soviet counterpart—as Reagan had shown in the preceding months. Reagan had not asked for a vote about starting to research the Strategic Defense Initiative. Reagan had not needed anyone's permission to start talking about reducing the nuclear weapons of both superpowers, with the eventual goal of total abolition. For none of his initiatives had he needed to ask for a vote of the Cabinet or even the National Security Council—although eventually he would need Congress's power of the purse.

Reagan had demonstrated his greater political power in seizing the initiative in the Cold War. He had decided the direction and strategy of U.S. policy, and now, finally, had also succeeded in getting the Soviets to accept his vision.

On March 4, 1985, Reagan chaired a National Security Council meeting in the Cabinet Room. Every one of his twenty-three top arms negotiators were there. They were discussing the various options for dealing with the Soviets. Reagan spent twenty minutes with the group, and in his diary that night wrote what he had suggested to them:

> It's a very complicated business. I urged one decision on them—that we open the talks with a concession.
> Surprise!
> Since they [the Soviets] have publicly stated they want to see nuclear weapons eliminated entirely, I told our people to open by saying we would accept their goal.[36]

In an interview later that afternoon with reporters from *Newsweek* magazine, Reagan expressed these views:

> They themselves have voiced it. We're going to Geneva and both Gromyko and Chernenko—maybe others, I don't know about them. But at least these two on several occasions lately have said that their purpose, their goal is the total elimination of nuclear weapons.
> Now, we'll accept that goal and strive with them to meet that goal.[37]

As the hands on the clock ticked closer to the Geneva meeting, things began to warm up. On March 7, 1985—just five days before the talks were scheduled to begin—Reagan was visited by five Soviet leaders for a meeting that lasted a little over an hour. Reagan described their visit in his diary that night:

> Big event was meeting with Politburo member (Soviet) [Vladimir] Shcherbitsky. He had Ambassador Dobrynin & a couple of others with him. I had George Shultz, Bud [Robert C. McFarlane], Don Regan & a couple of others with me.
>
> He & I went round & round. His was the usual diatribe that we are the destabilizing force, threatening them. It was almost a repeat of the Gromyko debate except that we got right down to arguing.
>
> I think he'll go home knowing that we are ready for negotiations but we d--n well aren't going to let our guard down or hold still while they continue to build up their offensive forces.[38]

The next day, on March 8, President Reagan met with ambassadors Max Kampelman, John Tower, and Maynard Glitman. These were the men who would be attending the first meeting of the Nuclear and Space Arms Negotiations (as the United States had proposed renaming them) with the Soviet Union. Shultz, Weinberger, and McFarlane were also present. Reagan told his team:

> The challenge of statesmanship is to have the vision to dream of a better, safer world and the courage, persistence, and patience to turn that dream into reality. Since the dawn of the nuclear era, all God's children have lived with the fear of nuclear war and the danger of nuclear devastation.
>
> Our moral imperative is to work with all our power for that day when the children of the world can grow up without the fear of nuclear war.

So, today we reaffirm that vision: a world dedicated to the elimination of nuclear weapons.[39]

On March 12, 1985, the hard work would begin. The issues were complex and difficult and required intelligent, reasonable men and women to sort them out, but once the two superpowers began to negotiate—assuming both sides were serious—much of the tension of a possible nuclear war would fade away. The fears of 1983 seemed like a bad dream as the negotiators from Moscow and Washington prepared to sit down together.

Suddenly, just when it seemed as though all was in place, things abruptly changed.

The first problem—albeit one that would not play a role for a long time to come—was with President Reagan. On the afternoon of March 8, after he had said good-bye to his negotiating team headed for Geneva, he went to the Bethesda Naval Hospital for his annual checkup. He seemed to be in excellent health, especially for a seventy-four-year-old. But the check on his colon turned up "a polyp specimen" that needed a biopsy.[40] It was a portent of future problems.

The president spent the next two days at Camp David, delighted his overall health was so good and very pleased with the upcoming negotiations in Geneva.

When he returned to Washington, everything seemed just perfect. But on Sunday, March 10, with negotiations set to begin in forty-eight hours, General Secretary Chernenko—showing uncanny timing—died. Reagan got the news in a phone call on the morning of March 11:

Awakened at 4 A.M. to be told Chernenko is dead. My mind turned to whether I should attend the funeral. My gut instinct said no. Got to the office at 9. George Shultz had some arguments that I should—He lost. I don't think his heart was really in it. George Bush is in Geneva. He'll go and George Shultz will join him leaving tonight.

Word has been received that Gorbachev has been named head man in the Soviet.[41]

As Gorbachev took leadership of the Politburo, there was much ahead for him to deal with. He was probably well up to date concerning the negotiations with the United States. But his nation was besieged by other problems—namely, a sinking economy and a shortage of money to maintain military power, to say nothing of the personal politics within the Politburo.

And on Tuesday, the negotiating teams for the United States and the Soviet Union returned to the arms negotiating table for the first time in nearly a year and a half—with the Soviets now reporting to a new general secretary.

Chapter 13

~

THE ASCENT OF
GORBACHEV: 1985

*Gromyko, then Foreign Minister, carried the day with
a nominating speech for Gorbachev . . .
he coined the now celebrated remark,
"This man has a nice smile, but he has iron teeth."*
—GEORGE J. CHURCH, *TIME*, JANUARY 4, 1988

As the years roll by, it becomes difficult to remember what the Soviet Union was like in the winter of 1985. Yes, the Soviets had agreed to come back to the negotiating table with the United States after the dangerous low point in relations in 1983. But they remained a hugely powerful dictatorship, controlled by die-hard Communists in the Politburo who ruled their country with an iron fist. Their stockpile of nuclear weapons now significantly exceeded that of the United States, and continued to grow every year.

In that winter of 1985, Soviet citizens still lived in a country that was much like a prison. (An estimated half a million Jews who wished to leave for religious reasons were refused visas to emigrate.) And the Soviets continued to spread their Communist ideology and weapons throughout the world, not least in some Central American countries on the doorstep of the United States.

They remained involved in the war with Afghanistan that they had started in 1979. They were still the country Reagan had called "the focus of evil in the modern world."[1]

And as Soviet negotiators returned to the table at the pleasure of their new general secretary, Reagan's challenge remained the same. He had to convince them to agree to a sharp reduction in the number of nuclear weapons on each side.

The Soviets knew that Reagan was building up the power of the United States' total military forces—land, sea, and air. And they were doing the same, especially with nuclear weapons. Reagan's plan was to make the United States so strong that no one would even think of trying to intimidate it, but he also was serious that, once the Soviets agreed to negotiate as equals, he would be happy to reduce our weapons, especially the nuclear ones.

The basic problem Reagan had in convincing the Soviets of his intentions was that what he was doing was unique: heads of state in large countries did not typically build up their military strength so they could take it down or destroy it. But Reagan was not a typical head of state, and he meant to do what he had promised. The trouble was that the Soviets simply did not believe him, as was also the case with many Americans and other people around the world. They thought he was building power for the same reason everyone else did.

Now Reagan's job was to convince the Soviets he was serious, and get them to join him in his plan—and in doing so, he had to deal with a new counterpart, Mikhail Gorbachev.

As all this was going on, Reagan was losing some of his best staff in the White House. James Baker, his chief of staff, was going to Treasury; Edwin Meese, his counselor, was becoming the attorney general; Michael Deaver, deputy chief of staff, was entering private life. George Shultz, his secretary of state, was staying and would continue to be Reagan's key adviser as he dealt with the Soviets. Cap Weinberger, his secretary of defense, remained and did an excellent job of building up the nation's military strength, and

Bill Casey stayed on at CIA—but neither of these two fully supported Reagan's strategies for negotiating with the Soviets.

As Mikhail Gorbachev took power, all anyone knew for sure about the new leader was that he was much younger and much healthier than the three general secretaries who had gone before him during the four years that Reagan had been president. As the protégé of Yuri Andropov, the former head of the KGB for fifteen years, and a close friend of Andrei Gromyko, the foreign secretary, it would not be surprising if he was a tough, smart Communist like them. His friends on the Politburo said of him, "He has a nice smile, but he has iron teeth."

Yet soon the media were writing stories about how young and charming Gorbachev was, how smart and quick, how reasonable. Even Margaret Thatcher had been impressed. But Reagan remained cautious.

A few days after the announcement of Gorbachev's appointment, Reagan held a press conference with members of the Magazine Publishers Association. One of the publishers asked Reagan, "Secretary Gorbachev is of a different generation . . . perhaps more pragmatic and worldly and less theological. . . . Do you have any reason to believe that he is fundamentally different from his immediate predecessors?"

Reagan had no hope that Gorbachev would be a "nice" Soviet, but on the other hand, he believed that with enough continual pressure, like the demands and criticisms he had been heaping on the Soviets during the past four years, Gorbachev would see that it was in the interests of the Soviets to change their spots. So Reagan replied:

> Well, I don't think there's any evidence that he is less dominated by their system and their philosophy than any of the others.
>
> But it isn't true that I don't trust anyone under 70. [Laughter]

> What is most evident . . . is that the Soviet Union is in a different frame of mind than they've been in the past: That they are back at the negotiating table on arms reductions because they recognize a hard, cold fact, and that is that the United States isn't going to unilaterally disarm in the face of their military buildup . . . they have to compete with us . . . they, I believe, are really going to try and, with us, negotiate a reduction of armaments.
>
> That has never been done before . . . this is the first time that they, themselves, have said they would like to see the elimination of nuclear weapons.[2]

As Reagan confronted the Soviet Union, now with a new leader who was relatively young and in good health, he continued to use the same pressures he had applied during the past four years. First and foremost, when talking to the press or giving a speech broadcast in the United States and around the world, he spelled out the bad things the Soviets were involved in, asking and demanding they change their ways. Second, he worked to open communications with his counterpart—writing to Gorbachev, carefully reading the letters Gorbachev sent back to him, and responding with his own long, detailed missives. Third, Reagan kept a careful eye on his advisers, chairing many meetings of the National Security Council and the National Security Planning Group, and shaping the policies they would use in their negotiations with the Soviets.

The day that Mikhail Gorbachev assumed his new responsibilities, March 11, Reagan immediately sent him a letter, classified Secret/Sensitive, congratulating him. The letter included these points:

> I am sure you are aware that American interest in progress on humanitarian issues remains as strong as ever. . . .
>
> Most significantly, the negotiations we have agreed to begin in Geneva provide us with a genuine chance to make progress

toward our common ultimate goal of eliminating nuclear weapons. . . .

You can be assured of my personal commitment to work with you and the rest of the Soviet leadership in serious negotiations. In that spirit, I would like to invite you to visit me in Washington.[3]

Gorbachev replied two weeks later, on March 24. His letter, classified Secret, was businesslike and not hostile. Perhaps the most important point he made came about halfway through the letter:

The Soviet leadership is convinced that our two countries have one common interest uniting them beyond any doubt: not to let things come to the outbreak of nuclear war which would inevitably have catastrophic consequences for both sides.

Toward the end of his letter Gorbachev said:

I hope, Mr. President, that you will feel from this letter that the Soviet leadership, including myself personally, intends to act vigorously to find common ways to improving relations between our countries.[4]

On March 25, Secretary Shultz sent a memorandum, classified Secret/Sensitive/Eyes Only for the President, to President Reagan pointing out parts of the Gorbachev letter that he thought should be read carefully: "I draw your attention in particular to the final paragraphs of the letter, in which Gorbachev says he has a 'positive attitude' to the idea of holding a summit. He indicates that it would not be necessary to sign documents at such a meeting."[5]

It would be about eight months before Reagan and Gorbachev would meet in Geneva for their first summit. Gromyko approached Shultz about the timing in May, proposing a November summit in a European city. Discussions continued in June, and on July 1 the Soviet Union agreed to a summit in Geneva on November 19 and 20. The announcement was made by both countries on July 3, the

Soviets also announcing that foreign minister Gromyko had been kicked upstairs to the office of president of the USSR and Eduard Shevardnadze was replacing him.[6]

While the top priority of both sides was the nuclear weapons summit, they were also under many other pressures. Gorbachev would have his hands full for at least six months as he gradually took control of the Soviet Union. Reagan was equally busy with the many issues he was dealing with.

During this time Reagan and Gorbachev exchanged a dozen letters, discussing the complicated issues that lay before them. The letters between the leaders were detailed and frank, as each leader used them to take the measure of the other. The first letters were relatively quiet, but they became more serious as the two men locked heads over the Soviets' bête noir: Reagan's Strategic Defense Initiative.

For the past two years, the Soviets had made it very clear they were increasingly upset about SDI. Under Andropov, they'd feared that SDI indicated the United States was getting ready for a first strike against the Soviet Union. Then—initially under Chernenko, now under Gorbachev—those fears had become more generalized ones about the militarization of space as a new arena in the arms race, one in which the United States could take a tremendous lead over the Soviet Union.

Reagan fired off the first tough letter, classified Secret/Sensitive, on April 30, seven weeks after Gorbachev was in his new job. He did not mince words and directly challenged Gorbachev:

> I was struck by the characterization of our Strategic Defense Initiative which you made during your meeting with Speaker O'Neill's delegation—that this research program has an offensive purpose for an attack on the Soviet Union. I can assure you that you are profoundly mistaken on this point. The truth is precisely the opposite. . . .
>
> I note that Foreign Minister Gromyko told the United Nations General Assembly in 1962 that anti-missile defenses could

be the key to a successful agreement reducing offensive missiles. They would, he said then, "guard against the eventuality . . . of someone deciding to violate the treaty and conceal missiles or combat aircraft" . . . Not only have you deployed an operational ABM system, but you have upgraded it and you are pursuing an active research program . . .

Finally, let me turn to an issue of great importance to me and to all Americans . . . we believe strongly that strict observance of the Universal Declaration of Human Rights and of the Helsinki Final Act is an important element of our bilateral relationship. . . .

I have written you in candor. I believe that our heavy responsibilities require us to communicate directly and without guile. . . . I hope you will give me your frank view of these questions and call to my attention any others which you consider require our personal involvement.[7]

It was six weeks before Gorbachev replied to Reagan's letter. His June 10, 1985, letter, classified Secret/Sensitive, was also ten pages long and a clear example of how difficult the negotiations would be. He was just as tough and direct as Reagan when it came to what the Soviets wanted from the negotiations:

> I noted the intention expressed in your letter of April 30 to share thoughts in our correspondence with complete frankness. This is also my attitude. . . .
>
> Now turning to major problems. . . . It is not an accident that all agreements reached on the subject of arms limitations became possible only because the sides adhered in working them out to the principle of equality and equal security. . . . But as soon as the U.S. departed from that principle, the process of the arms limitation and reduction was ruptured. Regrettably this remains to be the case at present, too.
>
> It is the Soviet Union that is surrounded by American military bases stuffed also by nuclear weapons, rather than the U.S.—by Soviet

bases. Try to look at the situation through our eyes, then it will become clear. . . . With regard to third countries, we impose neither our ideology, nor our social system on anybody. And do not ascribe to us what does not exist. . . .

There is also another aspect of the program of "strategic defense," which remains as if in a shadow for the broad public. But not for responsible leaders and military experts. They talk in Washington about the development of a large-scale ABM system, but in fact a new strategic offensive weapon is being developed to be deployed in space. And it is a weapon no less dangerous by its capabilities than nuclear weapons.

What difference does it make, what will be used in a first disarming strike—ballistic missiles or lasers. If there is a difference, it is that it will be possible to carry out the first strike by new systems practically instantly. . . .

In matters affecting the heart of national security, neither side can or will rely on assurances of good intentions. Any weapon system is evaluated by its capabilities, but not by public statements regarding its mission. All facts unambiguously indicate that the U.S. embarks upon the path of developing attack space weapons capable of performing purely offensive missions. And we shall not ignore that.

I must say this frankly . . . The persistent refusal of the American side to stop the arms race cannot but put in question the intentions of the U.S. . . .

However, there should be no misunderstanding concerning the fact that we do not intend and will not conduct any negotiations relating to human rights in the Soviet Union. We, as any other sovereign state, regarded and will regard these questions in accordance with our existing laws and regulations. . . .

In conclusion, I would like to confirm my positive attitude to a personal meeting with you. I understand that you feel the same way.[8]

In a second, shorter letter, classified Secret/Sensitive, sent on June 22 (five pages), Gorbachev continued in the same vein, making it crystal clear that the Soviets wished to negotiate, but did not wish to give up their hard-won nuclear superiority. He once again brought up the issue of Reagan's Strategic Defense Initiative, this time making a threat:

> The "star wars" program—I must tell you this, Mr. President—already at this stage is seriously undermining stability. We strongly advise you to halt this sharply destabilizing and dangerous program while things have not gone too far.
>
> If the situation in this area is not corrected, we shall have no choice but to take steps required by our security and that of our allies.[9]

Even as the date for the superpower summit in Geneva was set, it was becoming very clear that while both parties wished to negotiate, they were many miles apart. The stalemate stood for three months, during which time there were no letters between Reagan and Gorbachev.

Meanwhile, a cancerous tumor was found in Reagan's colon, and on July 13 he underwent major surgery. He was in the hospital for a week, and on August 11, after taking care of some business, he left for his ranch in California for three weeks of recuperation. But by early September he was back at work in the White House and resuming preparations for the November summit.

On September 9, 1985, Reagan was interviewed by representatives of college radio stations. Toward the end one of the students asked, "Mr. President, what specific goal would you most like to accomplish during the remainder of your administration—but realize that you will be unable to?" Reagan's careful answer provides some insight about how he felt about the upcoming meeting with Gorbachev at Geneva:

> First of all, with the arms talks—maybe it might be impossible. I don't know. But I would like to see the end of nuclear weapons.
>
> I would like to envision the Soviet Union and the United

States agreeing, and then verifiably eliminating those weapons, and then being able to turn to lesser nations, or other nations that maybe have some, and saying, "Look, we've done this now. Come on, get in line. You do it, too. Let's rid the world of this nightmare and this threat."[10]

A few days later, on September 12, a new letter, classified Secret/Sensitive, came in for Reagan from Gorbachev. The Soviet leader had not changed his mind on any of the key issues they had been discussing, but the tone was less confrontational. On the first page of the nine-page letter, Gorbachev wrote:

> The differences between our two countries are not minor, and our approach to many fundamental issues are different. All this is true. But at the same time the reality is such that our nations have to coexist whether we like each other or not. If things ever come to a military confrontation, it would be catastrophic for our countries, and for the world as a whole.
>
> Judging by what you have said, Mr. President, you also regard a military conflict between the USSR and the USA as inadmissible.
>
> On several occasions we have explicitly expressed our view on the American program of developing space attack weapons and a large-scale anti-ballistic missile system. . . . I stress once again—the implementation of this program will not solve the problem of nuclear arms, it will only aggravate it, and have the most negative consequences for the whole process of the limitation and reduction of nuclear arms.
>
> In the final analysis the outcome of these talks will be decisive in determining whether we shall succeed in stopping the arms race and eliminating nuclear weapons in general.
>
> I want to propose to you the following formula—the two sides agree to a complete ban on space attack weapons, and a truly radical reduction, say by 50 percent, of their corresponding nuclear arms.[11]

That the Soviets were proposing a massive reduction in large intercontinental nuclear missiles was, in one sense, a major step forward—and exactly what Reagan had been advocating for years. But, of course, the proposal was tied to an attack on the other half of Reagan's vision, which they continued to characterize as a "space attack weapon."

On Friday, September 20, Reagan spent an hour in the morning on security briefings and discussion of the Strategic Defense Initiative and then chaired a meeting of the National Security Council to discuss strategy for the upcoming summit. Besides Casey and Shultz, he had before him virtually all of his key advisers—Vice President Bush, James Baker, Fred Ikle from the Department of Defense, Edwin Meese, Robert Gates, John Wickman from the Joint Chiefs of Staff, Donald Regan, Robert McFarlane, and Jack Matlock of the NSC.[12]

Toward the end of the meeting, President Reagan returned to one of his special interests, the issue of human rights:

How best to handle human rights?

In studying our successes and failures in the past, I noted that quiet diplomacy had produced substantive results. However, when the glare of publicity was brought on these negotiations, the Soviets quickly hardened their position. I think that we might speak privately to the Soviets and indicate that we were prepared to cooperate on this issue. In particular, we would not publicize their concessions if they complied fully with the Helsinki Agreement. . . .

The success of one quiet arrangement, whereby we had rescinded the grain embargo,[13] with the result that there were some happy people now living in the West. That one was worked quietly through Ambassador Dobrynin.

Vice President Bush agreed:

Human rights will be one of the most divisive issues on the agenda. In my meeting with Georgy Arbatov it was clear that the

Soviets will either seek to avoid discussion or launch a concerted counterattack on us. However, many of these problems could be resolved along the lines the President suggested; that is, through quiet agreements by high-level diplomats working privately.

At the end of the NSC session President Reagan expressed some additional thoughts about the Soviets:

> The Soviets traditionally only make agreements where they see clear advantages. I agree with the Secretary of State that the most acute problem facing the Soviets at this time is the state of their economy. The question is how far Gorbachev will be prepared to go because of this. We must be prepared to seize any opening presented to us.
>
> In this regard, Richard Nixon's recent statement was entirely a propos. The former President pointed out: "We *want* peace. They *need* peace."[14] Thus the Soviets will have some motivation to reach agreement.

Secretary Weinberger "concurred that the Soviets will perceive a need for reducing their arms burden," but suggested that "only at a later date will they be persuaded to move in this direction." President Reagan ended the meeting by agreeing with Weinberger and returning to the issue of SDI:

> I believe SDI may very well be our most important leverage.
> I am prepared, once any of our SDI programs proved out, to then announce to the world that integrating these weapons in our respective arsenals would put international relations on a more stable footing.
> In fact, this could even lead to a complete elimination of nuclear weapons.
> We must be prepared to tell the world that we are ready to

consult and negotiate on integrating these weapons into a new defense philosophy, and to state openly that we are ready to internationalize these systems.[15]

The U.S.-Soviet summit in Geneva now lay only six weeks away, and as it drew near it was clear that SDI would be the major bone of contention. Gorbachev was seeming to promise that unless the United States kept SDI in the laboratory, the summit would be a failure.

Reagan was puzzled. The missile defense he wanted had no nuclear warheads and was designed solely to intercept incoming nuclear missiles. It was designed to save people, not kill them.

Even more puzzling was that the Soviet Union had many of their own defensive missiles, with powerful nuclear warheads. Yet the Soviets were insistent that the United States not build any of its own, even though the United States' missiles would be non-nuclear.

Both the Soviet Union and the United States had signed the Anti-Ballistic Missile treaty in 1972, agreeing not to "deploy ABM systems for the defense of the territory of its country." Each country could have one system (as of 1974) to defend its capital or an ICBM missile site.

In 1975, the United States had shut down its Grand Forks, North Dakota, missile defense site only a few days after installing a hundred missiles there. Yet the Soviet Union kept its nuclear-tipped defensive missiles deployed around Moscow and continued to upgrade them. On October 13, 1982, the CIA published a National Intelligence Estimate, titled "Soviet Ballistic Missiles Defense." They summarized the extensive research of the Soviets, which employed ten thousand workers, and warned that missile defense could be extended beyond Moscow. So Soviet resistance to Reagan's SDI program seemed the height of hypocrisy.

Although Reagan and his advisers were well informed about the Soviet Union's anti-ballistic-missile efforts, there had been little public discussion about them.

To counter this, the State Department and the Defense Department produced a thirteen-page document entitled "Soviet Strategic Defense Programs." Signed by Secretary Shultz and Secretary Weinberger, it said:

> Soviet efforts in most phases of strategic defense have long been far more extensive than those of the United States. The USSR has major passive defense programs. . . . Soviet activities in strategic defenses include the expansion of the world's only operational Anti-Ballistic (ABM) system around Moscow.

This operating ABM system around Moscow had GALOSH interceptors that could strike an incoming nuclear missile. The interceptors had "nuclear-armed, ground-based missiles designed to intercept warheads in space shortly before they reenter the Earth's atmosphere."[16]

On October 7, Reagan chaired an NSPG meeting discussing Soviet strategic defenses. In his personal diary that night he summarized what he had been told:

> We had an NSPG meeting to hear a briefing on the Soviet Unions progress in defensive weapons against nuclear missiles. They are raising h--l about our research & they've been at it for 20 yrs. & we're just starting.[17]

Although the two superpowers were tantalizingly close to agreeing on a treaty that would do away with thousands of nuclear missiles, the seemingly irrational Soviet resistance to Reagan's "Star Wars" might make it all fall apart.

Chapter 14

~

"STAR WARS" IN MOSCOW

Who speaks not truly, lies.
—SHAKESPEARE, *KING JOHN*

On October 12, 1985—with five weeks to go before the Geneva Summit—President Reagan addressed the nation from his cabin at Camp David, and began to show the nation the absurdity of the Soviets' negotiating position on SDI:

> Last week our State and Defense Departments released the most comprehensive report yet on the strategic defense program of the Soviet Union. . . . The Soviets refuse to admit they have any strategic defense program at all.
>
> This is not only deception, its dangerous deception, for without a full picture of what is going on, the people of the world cannot know what they need to know to keep the peace.
>
> Let me give you just a few details about Soviet strategic defense programs. . . . The Soviet Union today [1985] has the world's only operational antiballistic missile system. . . . But that's not all. The Soviets have for a long time been doing advanced research on their version of SDI. They don't talk about that.
>
> All they say about SDI is that the United States shouldn't

> have it, but as many as 10,000 Soviet scientists and engineers
> are believed to be working on research related to SDI. . . .
>
> We welcome the day when the Soviet Union can shoot
> down any incoming missile, so long as the United States can
> shoot down any incoming missile, too.[1]

What Reagan was doing sailed over the heads of the media.
But he knew that millions of Americans were listening to his reasons for missile defense, and that in laying the groundwork of public support for his vision he was making it more difficult for the
Soviets to argue against him.

On October 22, in the morning, Reagan attended another
meeting of the NSPG on arms reduction. That night, he summed
up the discussion and his views on what the United States should
be doing:

> Then an N.S.P.G. meeting on how we reply to the Soviets
> arms proposals. We're still working on that.
>
> My own idea is that we undermine their propaganda plan
> by offering a counter proposal which stresses our acceptance
> of some of their figures—such as a 50% cut in weapons & a
> total of 6,000 warheads etc.
>
> Those are pretty much like what we've already proposed.[2]

Over the weekend, on November 2–3, Reagan went up to Camp
David alone, rode his horse under gray and threatening skies, and
in his spare time called two former presidents—Richard Nixon,
with whom he spoke frequently, and Gerald Ford—to see if they
had any counsel for his upcoming meeting with Gorbachev. He
wrote in his diary:

> Over the weekend I called Nixon & Ford to get suggestions
> they might have on the Summit. Dick had a h--l of a good idea
> on the arms negotiations.

> We probably won't have them settled by the time the Summit ends. His suggestion is that we state what we have agreed on, that we will continue negotiating on the other points & as a token of our resolve to achieve results we each take 1000 missiles out of the silos & store them for a set time. If we can't come to a reduction agreement we put them back in the silos.
>
> Back to the W.H.[3]

On Tuesday, November 5, President Reagan got to watch a movie very unlike the ones he used to make in Hollywood:

> N.S.C. meeting was a movie. We saw a demonstration of our new Bomber, one of the greatest advances in aircraft in years & years.
>
> It's of course most hush hush—I should call it what it is—a fighter bomber.[4]

On Saturday afternoon, November 9, Reagan drove over to the Voice of America offices to make a special address to the Soviet people, although his words would also be carried throughout the United States and in fifty other countries. His purpose was to tell them directly what he intended to do at the summit in Geneva. In the past the Soviets had jammed the frequencies so that the Soviet citizens could not hear broadcasts from America. But this time, according to monitors in the American embassy in Moscow, two and possibly three frequencies were clearly audible and probably not jammed. According to the U.S. consulate in Leningrad, one Russian-language frequency was loud and clear. Shortwave signals throughout the Soviet Union, for those who had a shortwave receiver, were clear.

So, at least for that one day, Reagan's speech found a little crack in the Iron Curtain. Here are excerpts of what he said:

> Americans are a peace-loving people. We do not threaten your nation and never will. The American people are tolerant,

slow to anger, but staunch in defense of their liberties. . . . We joined together to defeat the common enemy of fascism. . . . Even before we entered World War II, America was supplying massive quantities of food and equipment to those fighting the Nazis. . . . I remember President Roosevelt's praise for the Russian people's heroism. How can any of us alive then forget that terrible year of 1941 when the Nazis were repulsed at the gates of Moscow? . . .

Americans fought for 4 years on all fronts. . . . Some are buried on Soviet soil. . . . [W]e had made war on a vicious ideology, not on a people. And we demonstrated our desire for peace by rapidly demobilizing. At the end of 1945, we had an armed force of almost 12 million men. By 1948 we had reduced that number to less than 1½ million.

We were the only country with nuclear weapons. We proposed giving those weapons up altogether to an international authority so that no country would have such destructive power at its disposal. What a pity this idea was not accepted.

I believe our two nations, and those others that have nuclear weapons, should come together and agree on how, gradually, to eliminate offensive nuclear weapons, as we make our defensive system available to all. . . .

We must live together in peace.[5]

On November 12, President Reagan got some very good news from Dick Wirthlin, his chief pollster and political strategist; his approval rating was at 65 percent.[6] Wirthlin was especially admired by Reagan because his polls were accurate and relayed bad news as well as good.

On Wednesday, November 13, 1985, Reagan called a meeting to inform his cabinet of his plans for the Geneva summit. In addition, he had long talks with George Shultz, Caspar Weinberger, and William Casey. That night he noted in his diary that:

> Bill Casey brought in 3 of his experts on the Soviet U. Their presentations on the people of Russia were great & confirmed things I had heard from unconfirmed sources.
>
> The Soviet U. is an economic basket case & among other things there is a rapidly spreading turn by the people to religion.[7]

The information Reagan was now receiving from the CIA confirmed what he had long suspected. In 1963 he had written a speech in which he declared that the Soviet Union's Communist economy could not last. Now, more than twenty years later, it was looking like his prediction, shared at the time by very few experts, was coming true. And the idea of religion spreading in the Soviet Union was so against Communist ideology that it was hard to believe. Yet a few people Reagan had talked to in the past five years had told him just that—and now it seemed that they were right. Altogether, Reagan was going to Geneva with a much stronger case against the Soviets than anyone knew.

In the days just before Reagan headed for Geneva, he took an unusual step, writing out a memorandum to himself by hand. In it Reagan summarized what he knew about Gorbachev—what he was like, how he would act, what he would do. The memo is also chock-full of the strategy Reagan intended to apply in his negotiations with Gorbachev. Some of that strategy is not surprising; some is. Here is the complete text of the memo Reagan wrote himself:[8]

> I believe Gorbachev is a highly intelligent leader totally dedicated to traditional Soviet goals. He will be a formidable negotiator and will try to make Soviet foreign and military policy more effective.
>
> He is (as are all Soviet General Secretaries) dependent on the Soviet-Communist hierarchy and will be out to prove to them his strength and dedication to Soviet traditional goals.

If he really seeks an arms control agreement, it will only be because he wants to reduce the burden of defense spending that is stagnating the Soviet economy. This could contribute to his opposition to our SDI. He doesn't want to face the cost of competing with us. But another major reason is because the USSR's military planning differs from ours. We generalize and plan in a kind of defensive pattern—how must we be able to cope with various contingencies worldwide. On the other hand they would like to win by being so much better prepared we could be faced with a surrender or die ultimatum. Thus any new move on our part, such as SDI forces them to revamp, and change their plan at great cost.

He doesn't want to undertake any new adventures but will be stubborn and tough about holding what he has. His major goal will continue to be weaning our European friends away from us. That means making us look like the threat to peace while he appears to be a reasonable man of peace out to reduce tensions between us. But if he has to make a choice, then he will opt for demonstrating to his own hierarchy that he is a strong leader.

In the world of P.R. we are faced with two domestic elements. One argues that no agreement with the Soviets is worth the time, trouble or paper it's written on so we should dig in our heels and say "nyet" to any concession. On the other side are those so hungry for an agreement of any kind that they would advise major concessions because a successful Summit requires that.

My own view is that any agreement must be in the longterm interest of the United States and our allies. We'll sign no other kind. In a way, the Summit will be viewed generally as a success because we've met, shaken hands and been civil to each other. It can also be a success if we fail to arrive at an arms agreement because I stubbornly held out for what I believe was right for our country.

What are some of their needs and priorities? Well, I believe they hunger for some trade and technology transfers. There is no question but that we have a tremendous advantage on that front. Well, I happen to think that trade is for us a major bargaining chip. We shouldn't give it away. But how about just hanging back until we get some of the things we want instead of giving consideration up front to what they want?

On another important subject for discussion and even negotiation, I'm sorry we are somewhat publicly on record about human rights. Front page stories that we are banging away at them on their human rights abuses will get us some cheers from the bleachers but it won't help those who are being abused. Indeed, it could wind up hurting them.

Let me quote a remark by Richard Nixon, talking about the 1972 Summit. He had been importuned by Jewish leaders before going to Moscow that he should get agreement on liberalizing Jewish immigration before making any agreements on trade, arms control or whatever. Here are his own words: "I did not follow this advice. After we had reached agreement on arms control and trade and other items they wanted, I took Brezhnev aside and told him that in order to get Congressional approval for those agreements which require it, it would be very helpful if we could act positively on the Jewish emigration front. An indication of the success of this policy is that in 1968, the year before I took office, only 600 Jews were allowed to emigrate. In 1972 after our Summit meeting, the number rose to 35,000. In 1973, the Jackson-Vanik Amendment was passed which made Jewish emigration a public condition for most favored nations treatment. That year, the number of Jews allowed to emigrate was cut in half and today the number is down to a trickle."[9]

Then he added a line pertinent to our upcoming Summit. He expressed optimism that I might accomplish what he did in 1972, but only if I didn't force Gorbachev to eat crow and embarrass him publicly. We must always remember our main goal and his need to show his strength to the Soviet gang back in the Kremlin. Let's not limit the area where he can do that to those things that have to do with aggression outside the Soviet Union.

To those who believe Arms Control must be the goal as an end in itself with no connection to regional issues, let us ask if Salt I in 1972 wasn't possible because the year before tensions in Central Europe were eased by the Berlin agreement? Conversely did Salt II fail of ratification on it's own or did the invasion of Afghanistan have something to do with it?

They should be told in the coming meeting that Congressional approval on trade or arms control or whatever else they want will be difficult if not impossible to get if they continue to support their clients in Southeast Asia, the Middle East and Latin America.

Those who think the Summit can be made to look successful if we get agreements on cultural exchanges, the consulate we want, fishing and trade matters are dealing with window dressing. Yes they can be useful but they must be viewed as just trimming for the main events which are the security issues like arms control, the regional areas of conflict and the prevalent suspicion and hostility between us. Indeed those trimmings could be harmful when used by some as evidence that all our concerns about national security were no longer pertinent. The target of their self-generated euphoria would, of course, be defense spending.

So let me add here; another of our goals probably stated to Gorbachev in private should be that failure to come to a solid, verifiable arms reduction agreement will leave no alternative except an arms race and there is no way we will allow them to win such a race.

Let us agree this is the first of meetings to follow. That in itself will give an aura of success. We will have set up a process to avoid war in settling our differences in the future. Maybe we should settle on early 1987 as the next meeting time and maybe we should discuss offering that it be in Moscow. He can come back here in 1988.

With regard to a communiqué that is more language than substance—a frank statement of where we agreed and where we disagree—is something for us to discuss.

But let there be no talk of winners and losers. Even if we think we won, to say so would set us back in view of their inherent inferiority complex.

Reagan felt ready to take on Gorbachev, but he could not resist adding two more lines:

And so we take leave of historic Geneva, and I get the h--l out of there and head for the ranch.

Happy Thanksgiving Comrades!

Between the lines of this memo lies Reagan's approach to negotiation, lessons he had learned the hard way as he sat across the bargaining table from the executives who ran the Hollywood studios. After he left office, Reagan recorded some of those ground rules:

You're unlikely to ever get *all* you want;

You'll probably get more of what you want if you don't issue ultimatums and leave your adversary room to maneuver;

You shouldn't back your adversary into a corner, embarrass him, or humiliate him;

And sometimes the easiest way to get some things done is for the top people to do them alone and in private.[10]

Reagan had one more piece of business to attend to before he headed off to Geneva. For months he had been discussing and explaining his plans for the summit with the media, both at home and abroad; with his negotiation staff; and with Congress. Now it was time to talk directly to the American people. Here are two excerpts from the speech he made to the nation on November 14:

In 36 hours I will be leaving for Geneva for the first meeting between an American President and a Soviet leader in 6 years. I know that you and the people of the world are looking forward to that meeting with great interest, so tonight I want to share with you my hopes and tell you why I am going to Geneva.

My mission, stated simply—is a mission for peace.

When we meet in Geneva, our agenda will seek not just to avoid war, but to strengthen peace. . . . We should seek to reduce the suspicions and mistrust that have led us to acquire mountains of strategic weapons. Since the dawn of the nuclear age, every American President has sought to limit and end the dangerous competition in nuclear arms.

I have no higher priority than to finally realize that dream. . . . [W]e go to Geneva with the sober realization that nuclear weapons pose the greatest threat in human history to the survival of the human race, that the arms race must be stopped.[11]

Chapter 15

~

THE GENEVA
"FIRESIDE" SUMMIT

A Chinese philosopher, Sun Tzu, 2,500 years ago, said,
"Winning a hundred victories, in a hundred battles
is not the acme of skill.
To subdue the enemy without fighting
is the acme of skill."
—RONALD REAGAN, MAY 27, 1981

Reagan's arrival in Switzerland marked another major turning point for the United States and the Soviet Union. This was the day he had worked toward for five years: the first summit between the two superpowers' leaders in six years. Everyone in the world seemed to be watching as the two men prepared to speak. For the first time in so long, there was hope that these two great powers might improve their relationship and erase the threat of a nuclear war.

And yet . . . the two countries had been on hostile terms since World War II. Neither liked the other's philosophy. Reagan's status outside of the United States was questionable; many foreigners looked on him as someone who was itching to go to war. His adversary, Gorbachev, was largely an unknown quantity. Yes, they had both agreed on paper and in their speeches that they wanted better relations. But in practice, they disagreed on so many issues. With all this arrayed against them, was it possible that real change would arise from this historic meeting?

The Geneva summit took place primarily in the Château Fleur d'Eau, one of the most impressive estates in Europe. As Reagan described it in his autobiography:

> We looked out from our bedroom at the long gray expanse of Lake Geneva. There were patches of snow along the edge of the lake and in the garden of the magnificent lakeside eighteenth-century residence that had been loaned to us for a few days.[1]

In his diary, Reagan wrote a prayer:

> Lord, I hope I'm ready & not over trained.[2]

On Tuesday, November 19, at 10:20 a.m., Reagan joined Gorbachev for their first meeting, held in a small room in the luxurious Swiss mansion. They sat around a small round table and began to talk for the first time, joined only by two interpreters and the note takers who carefully wrote down each man's words.

There was no staff sitting with them and nudging them with advice, no reporters barking questions, no television cameras trained on every move. No, for now at least the two prizefighters left their trainers behind as they stepped in the ring for the fight's first round, weeks of training and preparation and coaching falling into the past to leave each man alone with his adversary. And what happened in this first sparring match would have a major impact on the world.

Their first private meeting had been scheduled to last for twenty minutes. But that allotted time quickly passed, and still the two had not come out. When forty minutes had gone by, Don Regan, the chief of staff, got antsy and dispatched an assistant, Jim

Kuhn, to tell Reagan that his "meeting needed to end." When Kuhn refused, Regan said, "What about the schedule?" Kuhn still refused to interrupt the meeting.

The clock kept ticking. By the time Reagan and Gorbachev had spent an hour together, Don Regan and Bud McFarlane were pulling their hair out, watching their carefully laid plans for the day's agenda dissolve as the Soviet and American teams sat idle. Another ten minutes passed, and McFarlane suggested that Kuhn ask Shultz what to do. Kuhn reluctantly found Shultz in another room with Foreign Minister Shevardnadze and explained their problem. Shultz looked up and in a "voice booming around the room" said clearly to Kuhn, "If you're stupid enough to walk into that room and break up the meeting between those two leaders, then you don't deserve the job you have." Kuhn returned to Regan and McFarlane and reported that Shultz "just ripped my neck off in front of Shevardnadze. Leave the president alone. Nobody goes in."[3]

Finally, Reagan and Gorbachev emerged, smiling, an hour later.

What Reagan and Gorbachev said was written down that day in 1985, but for years the records remained classified, and no one, save a few archivists and some intelligence people with a need-to-know classification, could read them. Now those records have been opened, and we can finally see just how important their private meetings were in determining the course of the negotiations. (Note: In quoting these conversations, we've made slight changes to the record so that each man's words are rendered in the first person.)

EXCERPTS FROM REAGAN AND GORBACHEV'S FIRST ONE-ON-ONE MEETING—70 MINUTES

Reagan began the meeting by emphasizing what the two men had in common—their simple upbringings, the enormous responsibility each now held in his hands, and their common hope for peace:

THE WHITE HOUSE

WASHINGTON

MEMORANDUM OF CONVERSATION

REAGAN-GORBACHEV MEETINGS IN GENEVA
November, 1985

First Private Meeting

DATE: November 19, 1985

TIME: 10:20 - 11:20 A.M.

PLACE: Maison Fleur d'Eau,
             Geneva, Switzerland

PARTICIPANTS:

United States

President Ronald Reagan
Dimitri Zarechnak, Interpreter

Union of Soviet Socialist Republics

Mikhail Gorbachev, General Secretary, Central Committee,
     Communist Party of the Soviet Union
Yuri D. Uspensky, Interpreter

*   *   *   *   *   *   *

After the official photographers and the rest of the staff
left the room, President Reagan began the conversation by
telling the General Secretary that the two of them could really
talk now. The President indicated that he approached this
meeting with a very deep feeling and hoped that both of them
could realize its importance and the unique situation that they
were in.

The President indicated that both he and the General
Secretary had come from similar beginnings which were quite
different from their current positions. He, Reagan, was born
and began his life in a small farming community, and now the two
of them were here with the fate of the world in their hands, so
to speak. The U.S. and the Soviet Union were the two greatest

F96-087 #37

BY dlb NARA DATE 5/15/00

First page of Memorandum of Conversation of Reagan
and Gorbachev's first private meeting at the Geneva Summit.

> The two of us can really talk now. . . . I am approaching this meeting with a very deep feeling, and hope that both of us realize its importance and the unique situation that we are in.
>
> Both of us come from similar beginnings, which were quite different from our current positions. I was born and began my life in a small farming community, and now the two of us are here with the fate of the world in our hands. The United States and the Soviet Union are the two greatest countries on Earth, the superpowers. They are the only ones who can start World War III, but also the only two countries that could bring peace to the world.

Then he moved on to address the suspicions and mistrust that had characterized the two countries' relations:

> We will talk about many things, including arms, in the main meeting but I wonder if the primary aim between us should not be eliminating the suspicions which each side has of the other. The resolution of other questions would follow naturally after that. To talk about arms, while such suspicions exist, is an empty exercise, as both of us are defensive at the various negotiations because of these suspicions.
>
> Countries do not mistrust each other because of arms, but rather countries build up their arms because of the mistrust between them.
>
> I hope that in our meetings both of us can get at the source of the suspicions which exist. The Soviet Union does not approve of the U.S. system of government, and the U.S. does not approve of the Soviet system, and each could follow its own way, but with peaceful competition.[4]

Gorbachev in turn emphasized his wish to improve relations with the United States, and stressed that the Soviet Union held no enmity toward the U.S. government or its people.

I would like to return to the beginning, and thank you for receiving me. I agree with you that this meeting is important in itself and I am glad that it is taking place. . . . I would like to avail myself of the opportunity which such a private meeting affords. . . .

The main conclusion I have come to, is that I was convinced that I and you could not ignore each other. Nothing good would happen if the two sides took a different approach. But I was convinced that I could begin to change our relations for the better. This is my main theme. . . .

In the Soviet Union, it is considered that serious measures ought to be undertaken to improve U.S.-Soviet relations. . . . I am convinced that there is not only the fear of mutual destruction . . . but a realistic evaluation shows that the U.S. and the Soviet Union could cooperate, and they have done so in the past. . . .

Sometimes there have been squalls in the bilateral relationship which have been severe, perhaps extremely so, but I can definitely state that in the USSR there is no enmity toward the United States or its people . . . the leadership of the Soviet Union recognize the role of the United States in the world, and wish it no harm.

In reply, Reagan returned to the importance of communication, and to his theme of addressing the mistrust between the countries:

There is no question but that the Soviet and American peoples have many things in common. . . . Unfortunately, it is not people but governments that create arms.

I know something about the Soviet Union and its concern about war because of the suffering . . . the fact that 20 million people have been lost . . . People do not like war. Americans hate war. . . .

People do not get into trouble when they talk to each other, but rather when they talk about each other. There has been too much of the latter on both sides, and not enough of talking to each other.

> In the meeting ... the sides could explain why there is mistrust between them, and could make a beginning to try to eliminate this mistrust.

Gorbachev then underlined his desire for peace between the two superpowers, while turning the conversation to other countries:

> *If our two sides reached a substantive agreement in Geneva, which would increase people's hope and would not destroy their view of the future with respect to the question of war and peace, this would be a great accomplishment.*
>
> *There are many problems in the world, involving capitalist countries and socialist countries, not to mention third world countries. . . .*
>
> *There is hunger, illiteracy and disease, causing a great deal of turmoil. We need to take a new political approach to these issues in order to resolve them. This is the base for my approach to foreign policy, as well as that of my colleagues.*

Reagan, of course, parried by pointing out that the Marxist desire to "help" other countries is often tied with the desire to spread socialism:

> I agree that the two countries could mutually help the developing countries, but one of the things that creates mistrust ... [is] the Marxist idea of helping socialist revolutions throughout the world. . . . The United States and USSR could help them to improve their standard of living.
>
> The United States has a very firm belief that people in all countries have the right of self-determination and the right to choose their own form of government.

Gorbachev defended Marxist revolutions, nimbly comparing them to the American and French revolutions:

> *There have been those who considered that the American Revolution should have been crushed. The same applies to the French Revolution and to the Soviet Revolution. . . . The Soviet Union does not consider that a way of life could be imposed if a society were not ready for it. . . . All these things which happen in the world have their national roots.*

The conversation then turned to smaller matters, with Gorbachev sharing Russian geological data predicting an earthquake in California and Nevada. Reagan replied at length to say that the United States was familiar with such predictions, and that a major earthquake was long overdue.

When Reagan and Gorbachev finally left the room, each seemed pleased. They had done no more than feel each other out, chess players probing each other's defenses, but each seemed to find in the other a worthy opponent.

The day's schedule called for two plenary sessions with lunch in between. The first plenary lasted a little over an hour, lunch two hours, and the second plenary another hour. Then, toward the end of the second session, Reagan asked Gorbachev if he would like to take a walk—just the two of them. Gorbachev accepted immediately.

SECOND ONE-ON-ONE MEETING—65 MINUTES

Soon the two leaders had bundled up in their coats and scarves and headed out the door. They were free to talk privately, and they seemed to beam with enjoyment as they headed down the grounds to a small boathouse next to the lake.

The trip to the boathouse did not happen by accident. When Reagan and Nancy first arrived in Geneva they'd taken a walk and explored the grounds. Upon seeing the small house by the lake, with its fireplace and warm atmosphere, Reagan knew he had found what he was looking for—a quiet, private place to talk directly to Gorbachev. Reagan then asked the staff to check out the house and inform the Soviets about it. So when he and Gorbachev took their walk they both knew where they were going.

On their way down to the little house they did not talk about anything of substance, chatting instead about some of the movies Reagan had made in the 1940s. Gorbachev even mentioned that he had recently watched one of Reagan's best movies, *Kings Row,* and had liked it very much.

Five minutes after leaving the session, the two men and their interpreters were cozily ensconced in the boathouse, while hundreds of reporters and staff members stood outside in the cold wondering what they were up to.

Once they were both seated in front of the fire and the door of the boathouse was shut, President Reagan handed some papers on arms reductions to Gorbachev and suggested:

> Here are some documents that might contain the seed of something the two of us could agree on. I have one copy for you done in Russian.

Gorbachev took the documents and devoted a few minutes to carefully reading them. Then he made it clear that some of the large nuclear weapons could be sharply reduced, but he was still against SDI.

> *Some of the issues dealt with do contain some substance that merit serious discussion. . . .*
> *I do have some questions to ask on space weapons.*

Reagan replied:

> The material set forth in these papers I just gave you should be viewed as a seed for possible instructions to the arms negotiators of both sides.

Gorbachev quickly agreed to a huge 50 percent reduction in strategic nuclear weapons—and then made it clear such a reduction would be dependent on killing SDI.

> *With reference to paragraph 1 of the first paper, concerning 50 percent reduction in strategic offensive arms—this is acceptable. . . .*
>
> *However . . . arms reductions must be viewed in their interrelationship with space weapons.*
>
> *That idea was agreed upon in Geneva in January [1985].*

Reagan refused to see SDI as part of the arms race, and attempted to defuse the issue by again offering to share a working SDI system with the Soviets:

> I do not see these defensive weapons as constituting a part of the arms race . . . when such arms were developed they would be shared with everyone involved in nuclear weapons.

Gorbachev, ignoring Reagan's last remark, released a salvo of questions, none of which dealt with the main issue. First, he said, the intermediate-range nuclear force proposal required further clarification. Second, it had not been made clear which weapons were to be covered, particularly British and French missiles. Also, what about cruise missiles launched from aircraft? Aircraft carriers? What about the precise meaning of research and testing under the ABM treaty? And finally, the broad interpretation of ABM needed further clarification.

Reagan ignored all the questions except one, the interpretation of the ABM Treaty, and made a slight jab regarding countries that might try to acquire a first-strike capability:

> We do indeed have more than one interpretation of the ABM Treaty . . . testing would be included . . . just to have a

laboratory theory would not be enough . . . They would be shared by all.

The worst thing that I can imagine is for any one country to acquire a first-strike capability.

Gorbachev instantly responded that Reagan did not trust him:

> The Soviet Union has declared for all the world to hear, and is now declaring to the United States as well, that the Soviet Union would not be the first to use nuclear weapons.
>
> However, I know that the United States does not believe me.

To which Reagan replied:

You and I may not always be here.

Gorbachev then moved from their personal relationship to the mistrust between the two countries:

> When I spoke of not being believed I meant that the United States did not believe the Soviet Union's statement I just mentioned. In that case, why should the Soviet Union believe your statement about sharing results of the research in question.

Reagan explained how such an agreement would work:

Because the negotiators of both sides could set down in a specific agreement that both governments had agreed not to retain a monopoly of defensive weapons, an agreement that you and I would sign. Our two countries are not alone in the world.

There are others, such as Qadhafi [president of Libya], for example, and people of that kind, who would not at all be averse to dropping a nuclear weapon on the White House. I believe in the idea of both our governments agreeing that both conduct relevant research, and that both share the results of such research. If one country produced a defensive shield before the other, it would make it available to all.

Gorbachev replied with emotion. He did not share Reagan's logic, and seemed to be afraid of the United States going into space with a defensive missile:

> *If the two sides were indeed searching for a way to halt the arms race and to begin to deal seriously with disarmament, then what would be the purpose of deploying a weapon that is as yet unknown and unpredictable?*
>
> *Where is the logic of starting an arms race in a new sphere?*
>
> *It must clearly be understood that verification of such weapons would be totally unreliable because of their maneuverability and mobility even if they were classified as defensive.*
>
> *If the goal is to get rid of nuclear weapons, why start an arms race in another sphere?*

Reagan, a bit emotional himself, argued that this was a no-lose proposition for the Soviet Union:

Remember, these are not weapons that kill people or destroy cities. These are weapons that destroy nuclear missiles.

If there were agreement that there would be no need for nuclear missiles, then one might agree that there would also be no need for defenses against them. But I would urge you to remember that we are talking about something that is not yet known. And, if it were known, it would still be years away.

Why then should we sit here in the meanwhile with mountains of weapons on each side?

Gorbachev proposed a joint announcement to stop any research or testing of what he called "space weapons," and then move on to 50 percent reduction of offensive nuclear weapons.

> *I suggest we announce to the world that President Reagan and General Secretary Gorbachev have declared firmly in official statements that both countries will refrain from research, development, testing and deployment of space weapons . . . [and] begin the process of 50 percent reductions in offensive arms.*

Reagan asked if Gorbachev was serious about opening both countries' laboratories:

> Do you have in mind that Soviet laboratories would be open to visits by our experts, and that their experts would be free to visit our laboratories?

Gorbachev agreed:

> *The Soviet Union would agree to open its laboratories provided they were used for the purpose of verifying how the agreement on banning and non-use of space weapons was being complied with.*

Reagan returned to the main issue, the Soviets' strange resistance to SDI:

> I do not know why you keep on speaking of space weapons . . . we certainly had no intention of putting something into space that would threaten people on Earth.
>
> Some years ago, there had been some talk about putting nuclear missiles into orbit in space, weapons that could be dropped on any point on Earth. This is not what we are talking about . . . [W]e should go forward to rid the world of the

threat of nuclear weapons, [with] a shield that would protect our countries should there be an unforeseeable return to nuclear missiles.

Now, as the meeting drew to a close, Gorbachev reiterated his opposition to SDI and made a veiled threat:

> *I want to repeat something I had said at the plenary meeting. I pointed out that the Soviet Government had really carefully considered everything that has been said by you with regard to your Strategic Defense Initiative, especially all your arguments in favor of it . . . [A]s a political leader, I can not possibly agree with you with regard to this concept.*
>
> *Let me assure you that this is not the result of some merely capricious attitude. I am not saying this for some sort of petty reasons.*
>
> *I have to conclude that if the Soviet Union were . . . dragged into this new dimension of the arms race, the other side would be bound to lose confidence and would seek to counter your SDI in any possible way—including by increasing the numbers of its offensive arms. . . .*
>
> *You should certainly realize that the great majority of people throughout the world, including scientists, are extremely concerned over the development of space weapons. . . . [I]t is clear that strategic defense would only be useful after a first strike by the side deploying such defense.*
>
> *This is a very serious problem today, and I ask you to reflect on it seriously.*
>
> *The Soviet Union has no desire to harm you as President—or to harm the United States as a country.*
>
> *I firmly believe it is necessary to do all in my power to prevent this from happening.*

Reagan refused to budge, but tried to end the meeting on a conciliatory note:

Well, I think we have used up a considerable amount of time at this meeting. . . . I recognize that both of us have made some strong statements, and it will be difficult for either of us to reverse direction. However, it seems to me that in the idea of ultimately sharing the results of research there is something that might be of interest to both of us.

The people of the United States overwhelmingly want this defense. They look at the sky and think what might happen if missiles suddenly appear and blow up everything in our country.

We believe that the idea of having a defense against nuclear missiles involves a great deal of faith and belief. When I say we, I mean most of mankind.

Gorbachev stuck to his position as well, again couching his resistance in terms of dire possible consequences should "space weapons" be launched:

> *Missiles are not yet flying, and whether or not they will fly depends on how you and I conduct our respective policies. But if your strategic defense initiative is actually implemented, then layer after layer of offensive weapons, Soviet as well as U.S. weapons, would appear in outer space, and only God himself would know what they are. God provides information only very selectively and rarely.*
>
> *I urge you to recognize the true signal I am conveying to you as President, and to the United States Administration as a whole, that the Soviet Union does indeed wish to establish a new relationship with the United States, and deliver our two nations from the increasing fear of nuclear weapons.*
>
> *The Soviet Union has conducted a deep analysis of the entire situation, and has come to the conclusion that it is necessary precisely now to proceed on the basis of the actual situation. Later it will be too late. . . . Please do not regard this as weakness on the part of me and the Soviet leadership.*[5]

The boathouse meeting, which began at 3:55 p.m., ended forty-nine minutes later, at 4:44 p.m. As President Reagan and Secretary Gorbachev walked back to the château—their words now unrecorded by note takers—they came to a surprising agreement. Later Reagan explained what happened:

> When we made the agreement, standing out in the parking lot in Geneva, which is where he and I made it all by ourselves, he had opened the subject by saying that there were things he'd like to show me in the Soviet Union. And knowing he had never visited our country, I said, "Well, there are some things I'd like to have you see." So, I said, "Why don't we have the 1986 summit in the United States, and I'm hereby inviting you."
>
> And he said, "I accept."
>
> And he said, "And there are things, as I say, that I would like you to see in the Soviet Union. And then we could make the '87 summit in the Soviet Union."
>
> And I said, "I accept."
>
> And we went in to our respective teams and told them that. And I think they were astonished, because they thought it was going to take a lot of debating and arguing and hassling to get agreement on future summits.[6]

Indeed, Reagan's advisers were stunned that afternoon when he told them he had worked out two more summits. For some time the advisers had been trying to figure out how to get one "rematch" with the Soviets, and now they had two. Reagan just smiled; he did like to get ahead of his advisers now and then, and seems to have discovered that his counterpart enjoyed doing the same.

Later Reagan recalled another private conversation with Gorbachev—one that probably also took place during that walk back to the Château Fleur d'Eau. Essentially it was a threat—a good-natured threat to be sure, but nonetheless a warning—that if Gorbachev seriously tried to win an arms race with the United

States, Reagan would do everything in his power to ensure he would lose:

> I said to him . . . it's not enough, you and I, engaged in dealings here trying to reduce the weaponry that we have. Why don't we start trying to reduce what causes the mistrust between us?
>
> I will tell you now. We can continue to disarm or we can continue the arms race. And I'll tell you now, you can't win the arms race. There is no way. There's no way that we're going to allow you to maintain supremacy, or anyone else, over the United States of America. . . .
>
> In the destroying of nuclear weapons—this is going to have to be tied to the conventional [weapons], because they [the Soviets] had superiority, and the only thing we had to respond to that superiority was nuclear. We weren't going to sit here, and join them in a nuclear disarmament at the expense of leaving them with a 10 to 1 advantage in tanks and artillery.[7]

In an important sense, the Geneva summit ended that day at 4:44 when Reagan and Gorbachev's meeting ended. There were other lunches, dinners, and meetings, to be sure, but the key elements were in the hands of the two men making the decisions, and the pattern had been set: going forward, it would be a matter of what the two men together could work out.

For now, they remained at an impasse—they both liked the idea of slashing their large intercontinental nuclear missiles by 50 percent; they both liked the idea of wiping out most of the missiles in Europe (with the exception of those in France and England) or aimed at European cities—but remained 180 degrees apart when it came to Reagan's Strategic Defense Initiative.

Yet both had discovered something priceless. They had found that they could talk to each other, argue, and even agree every now and then. They had gained each other's respect and knew that they could work together.

The Soviets learned one thing about Reagan that Gorbachev would seriously take into consideration the next time they met. Serge Tarasenko, the note taker for Gorbachev during the plenary meetings, watched Reagan closely and was surprised at what he saw. He expected an old man, a man who would be slow and deliberate. Instead, in his broken English, he described Reagan this way:

> *Suddenly he flare up, crisp, engaged.*
>
> *When you touch raw nerve, Reagan's flare will fill the room. He feel something close to his heart, he is like lion!*
>
> *When lion see antelope on the horizon, he is not interested, he go to sleep.*
>
> *Ten feet away, too much, leave it.*
>
> *Eight feet, the lion suddenly comes to life!!* [8]

Chapter 16

~

THE PRIORITY
OF HUMAN RIGHTS

If we cannot secure all our rights,
let us secure what we can.
—THOMAS JEFFERSON, MARCH 1789

On the last day of the Geneva summit, Reagan surprised Gorbachev.

It was November 20, 1985, and there was just one more private meeting between them scheduled, this one at the Soviet mission. It was planned as a fifteen-minute morning tête-à-tête, a time to talk further about nuclear weapons and perhaps have a cup of coffee. After Reagan arrived at the Soviet mission and the photo opportunities finished, Gorbachev and Reagan sat in a small room next to the main meeting room, while the rest of the delegation waited.

The one-on-one lasted not fifteen minutes but a little over an hour.

The three thousand reporters from around the world and the high-powered staff probably assumed that Gorbachev and Reagan were talking about nuclear weapons. Instead, Reagan took charge and began asking Gorbachev about human rights in the Soviet Union, pressing Gorbachev on why Soviet citizens were forbidden to leave the country at will, particularly those who had religious reasons.

Reagan's main concern during the past few years had seemed to be the reduction of nuclear missiles, and maybe their elimination. And after five years of work, he was finally at the table with the Soviets, discussing just that. But now he seemed to suddenly be revealing another, secret agenda, choosing to use this last private talk with the Soviet leader to press him on human rights.

Reagan cared deeply about the plight of individual people and families; he always had, and there are anecdotes galore about real people in real situations whom he reached out to help in whatever way he could. But his even more fundamental concern was the plight of people who were prevented from joining their loved ones in another country, worshiping as they wished, or choosing their own work. As he expressed it in his April 24, 1981, letter to Leonid Brezhnev:

> People want the dignity of having some control over their individual destiny.... Government exists for their convenience, not the other way around.[1]

When Reagan drafted this his staff found it sentimental, but it expressed the core of his philosophical views about government and human rights. It went to the heart of the difference between totalitarian governments and governments that were chosen by and served their people. A country could reduce or even eliminate its nuclear weapons, but that would not mean that its citizens were free. It could still be evil.

Reagan's June 2, 1952, commencement address, more than thirty-three years before at William Woods College in Fulton, Missouri, reveals the foundations of his commitment to human rights:

> America is less of a place than an idea.... It is nothing but the inherent love of freedom in each one of us.... It is simply

the idea, the basis of this country and of our religion, the idea of the dignity of man, the idea that deep within the heart of each one of us is something so God-like and precious that no individual or group has a right to impose his or its will upon the people, that no group can decide for the people what is good for the people so well as they can decide for themselves.[2]

And as early as May 15, 1967, not long after he became governor of California, Reagan talked about tyrannical governments' refusal to let their citizens travel. He was involved in a debate with Robert Kennedy, broadcast worldwide by satellite, one of the first experiments with such technology. A listener asked about a treaty the United States had signed with the Soviet Union, and Reagan answered:

I think that there were things that we could have asked in return. I think it would be very admirable, if the Berlin Wall, which was built in direct contravention to a treaty, should disappear. I think that this would be a step toward peace, and towards self-determination for all the peoples. We don't want the Berlin Wall knocked down so that it's easier to get at the throats of the East Germans.

We just think that a wall that is put up to confine people, and keep them within their own country instead of allowing them the freedom of world travel, has to be somehow wrong.[3]

It was a powerful statement. Richard Reeves, who was covering Kennedy as a reporter for the *New York Times,* later said that "Reagan just cleaned his clock"; as Kennedy was walking out of the studio, Reeves heard Kennedy say, "Who the hell's idea was this? Don't get me alone with this guy again."[4]

On January 20, 1975, Reagan, again a private citizen after eight years as governor of California, established a syndicated radio program. The program was a three-minute radio commentary every day of the week. Broadcasting nationwide to an estimated twenty million listeners a week, he wrote in his own hand thirty-one commentaries on human rights in the Soviet Union, Cuba, South Africa, and Poland. It was curious that few people in politics seemed to know about his steadfast interest in human rights when so many had listened to such commentaries.

In one of these commentaries, taped for distribution on October 2, 1979, more than a year before he became president, Reagan wrote about the plight of seven Pentecostals persecuted for trying to emigrate from the Soviet Union. They had sought refuge in the U.S. embassy in Moscow, and had been living there since June 29, 1978. Other members of the group had been imprisoned, found insane, and tortured, a scandalized Reagan reported, just for wanting to emigrate.[5]

Another of his essays, on June 29, 1979, was about a Russian author, Vladimir Bukovsky, who had spent half his adult life in Soviet prison camps and mental hospitals. Bukovsky argued that dissidents were speaking out openly in demand of rights supposedly guaranteed by the Soviet constitution—and that they were greatly encouraged by Western broadcasts reporting their hunger strikes and protests. Reagan concluded:

> Let our State Department take heed—a little less détente with the politbureau, and more encouragement to the dissenters might be worth a lot of armored divisions.[6]

In 1978, Reagan was traveling in Europe with Richard Allen, who would become his first national security adviser. They visited the Berlin Wall in East Germany. When Reagan walked over to the wall, he was struck by the overpowering brutality of it. He reached out and touched it, then turned to Allen and said simply:

> This wall should be torn down.

Bukovsky

Is something going on behind the Iron Curtain that we've been ignoring and does it offer hope for all mankind? * I'll be right back.

Vladimir Bukovsky is a 37 yr. old refugee from the Soviet U. who spent half his [ADULT] life in prison camps and infamous Soviet mental hospitals (call them torture chambers) before finding sanctuary in this country. In 1976 he was exiled from Russia in exchange for the Chilean Communist leader Luis Corvalán.

He has written a book, "To Build a Castle — My Life as a Dissenter".

*   *   *

But here is where his book is important to us. — In the 40's when Stalin was burying mils. & mils. of Soviet citizens in the torture camps of Siberia there was no word in our press about this. The victims lived in total hopelessness because there seemed to be no awareness of their plight. He makes it plain that beginning in the 60's when the "West" began to realize it's future was some how tied to what was going on in Soviet prisons the prisoners lived with hope & determination to continue dissenting & resisting. Guards would tell them that Radio Liberty & the BBC had carried stories of their hunger strikes & protests & thus they were encouraged to carry on.

Let our state dept. take heed — a little less detente with the politbureau and more encouragement to the dissenters might be worth a lot of armored divisions.
     This is RR. Thanks for listening.

Reagan's June 29, 1979, radio commentary on Soviet dissenters and the U.S. State Department.

During his presidency, Reagan continued to press the Soviets on human rights. On October 13, 1981, as a meeting on theater nuclear force negotiations was beginning, Reagan postponed the discussion to ask Secretary Haig:

> I want to touch upon another matter first in the area of Soviet human rights. What is the situation now with Professor [Woodford] McClellan's Russian wife, who is not being allowed to emigrate?
>
> What about the Soviet religion group [Pentecostals] in the basement of our Embassy in Moscow?
>
> What about Shcharanskiy? Would some quiet diplomacy help?
>
> These should not be part of our TNF negotiations, but is there any way we could indicate to the Soviets that we would be happier in any negotiations if there were progress with these cases?

Haig reported that he had raised these cases with Gromyko, but Gromyko had not budged. Reagan wanted to make sure the issue wasn't dropped:

> Let's keep track of this.[7]

On May 9, 1982, at his alma mater, Eureka College, Reagan gave a speech that clearly laid out what he believed made the Soviets tick—why they must have more than land, money, and nuclear weapons if they were to continue their quest to dominate the world—and how he wanted to change it:

> The Soviet Union is a huge empire ruled by an elite that holds all power and all privilege, and they hold it tightly because, as we've seen in Poland, they fear what might happen if even the smallest amount of control slips from their grasp.

They fear the infectiousness of even a little freedom. . . . [D]espite its signature of the Helsinki agreements on human rights, the Soviet Union has not relaxed its hold on its own people.[8]

On June 8, 1982, addressing a joint session of the British Parliament, Reagan gave his best-known speech on human rights:

I have discussed . . . the elements of Western policies toward the Soviet Union to safeguard our interests and protect the peace. What I am describing now is a plan, and a hope, for the long term—the march of freedom and democracy which will leave Marxism-Leninism on the ash-heap of history, as it has left other tyrannies which stifle the freedom and muzzle the self-expression of the people.

Of all the millions of refugees we've seen in the modern world, their flight is always away from, not toward the Communist world. . . . [O]ur military forces face east to prevent a possible invasion [from the Soviets]. On the other side of the line, the Soviet forces also face east to prevent their people from leaving.

Then Reagan reached back to the Old Testament's book of Exodus:

Since the exodus from Egypt, historians have written of those who sacrificed and struggle for freedom.

In that address to the British Parliament, Reagan went on to discuss the lack of human rights in the Soviet Union and how the West might help:

In the Communist world as well, man's instinctive desire for freedom and self-determination surface again and again.

To be sure, there are grim reminders of how brutally the police state attempted to snuff out this quest for self-rule—1953 in East Germany, 1956 in Hungary, 1968 in Czechoslovakia, 1981 in Poland. But the struggle continues in Poland. And we know that there are even those who strive and suffer for freedom within the confines of the Soviet Union itself.

How we conduct ourselves here in the Western democracies will determine whether this trend continues. . . . If the rest of this century is to witness the gradual growth of freedom and democratic ideas, we must take action to assist the campaign for democracy.

Some argue that we should encourage democratic change in right-wing dictatorships, but not in Communist regimes. Well—to accept this preposterous notion is to invite the argument that once countries achieve a nuclear capability, they should be allowed an undisturbed reign of terror over their own citizens. We reject this course. . . .

While we must be cautious about forcing the pace of change, we must not hesitate to declare our ultimate objective and to take concrete action to move toward them. We must be staunch in our conviction that freedom is not the sole prerogative of a lucky few, but the inalienable and universal right of all human beings.

So states the United Nations Universal Declaration of Human Rights.[9]

So on November 20, 1985, when Reagan spoke to Gorbachev at that third private meeting in Geneva, he was talking with the weight of forty years of political conviction.

But Reagan may also have had good strategic reasons for discussing human rights. As Reagan's speech to Parliament hinted, a look around the world shows that the only "successful" totalitarian countries are those that do not let their people leave. Imagine how long it would take for a major part of such a country's population to flee if its leader were to suddenly throw open the prison gates.

Perhaps, then, if one could really convince the leaders of a totalitarian country that they should allow their citizens to leave at will, the result might be more powerful than bombs and tanks.

REAGAN'S THIRD ONE-ON-ONE MEETING WITH GORBACHEV—70 MINUTES

Reagan began by emphasizing—as was his negotiating style—the benefits to the Soviets should they agree to human rights concessions.

> I want to talk with you privately about a subject which I know that the Soviet side considers to be interference in its internal affairs.
>
> I want to stress that I do not want to interfere in the internal affairs of the Soviet Union, but I do want to speak with you about human rights.
>
> In the United States system of government many of the things that we would hope to accomplish with the Soviet Union would require the support of the Congress, which, in turn, is influenced by the people of the country. I could get such support if some things were done in the area of human rights. In the United States, as you know, we have people from all over the world. Many of them retain a pride in their heritage, with regard to the countries where their parents and ancestors came from.
>
> Religious groups in the United States tend to influence Congress through lobby groups. An example of strong attachment to religious celebration occurred in the United States on St. Patrick's Day. This is a special holiday for the Irish, and my father came from Ireland. Other groups in the United States,

such as Ukrainian Americans, Lithuanian Americans and Polish Americans have their organizations, customs and holidays.

I do not wish to raise this issue in the main meeting.

I am also not asking to get your agreement to publicly announce actions which could be taken to deal with difficulties in this area, such as emigration. The recent release of several men and women who were allowed to join their spouses have made a big impact on the people in the United States.

But I wish to be frank—the question then arose, why not the rest?

An example of such an issue is the desire of Soviet Jews to emigrate to Israel. There is a large Jewish community in the United States, which has an influence on Congress.

If you can resolve some of these issues on your own, I would never boast that the Soviet side had given in to the United States. We would express our appreciation for what was done, and there would be no hint that this was done as a result of United States efforts.

But the fact that something was done would make it easier for me to do the type of things which our two countries could do together, such as in the area of trade, for which I need Congressional support.

Let me give you an example of this type of approach. In 1981, during my first year in office, the Soviet Government was eager to have a new long-term grain agreement with the United States, after the imposition of the grain embargo by my predecessor. I sat down with the Soviet Ambassador [Anatoly Dobrynin], and spoke with him about human rights concerns, citing the specific example of the Pentecostalists who had been living for five years in the basement of the Moscow Embassy.[10]

If they had left the Embassy they would have been taken by the police. They had come to the Embassy because they had gotten into trouble after having asked for permission to emigrate. I told the ambassador that I would not speak publicly about this, but there would be a better chance to have a grain agreement, since there was opposition in the United States to such an agreement, if something were done to free those people. Shortly after that, they left the Embassy and emigrated to the United States.

I never told anyone that I had done this. Those people were gratefully received in the United States, and they did not even know that I had spoken on their behalf. A short time later, the long-term grain agreement was concluded without difficulties in Congress, and this agreement is in place today.

This is the type of thing I am seeking here, and that is why I did not wish to raise these issues in the full meeting, not to make it appear that I was trying to interfere in the internal affairs of the Soviet Union. It would make it easier for us to do the types of things that we could do together, if I were not constantly reminded about the restrictions imposed on Soviet people, the refusal to permit them to practice their religion, etc.

I will not tell anyone that I have raised this issue with you.

Gorbachev listened attentively and received Reagan's plea seriously, indicating that he would, once again, look into the matter carefully. But he defended the Soviets' behavior.

> I considered that at some stage of U.S.-Soviet relations, the issue of human rights was being used for political purposes, not only by representatives of various political organizations which were anti-Soviet, but, and this came as a surprise—also by officials of the U.S. Administration, including the President.
>
> The Soviet side does not understand this.
>
> You mentioned why and how you had come to be involved in these issues. In all sincerity the Soviet Union is in favor of broader contacts, exchange of people—scientists, cultural representatives, all types of people—with the United States. We feel that this is necessary. I thought that you had said the same. The two countries depend on each other

today and would in the future. We should get to know each other better and create a good atmosphere.

The Soviet people have no enmity for the American people. The Soviet people have a positive attitude toward the people of the United States. If we work at this on the basis of non-interference in the internal affairs of the other country, the Soviet side would be ready to broaden its contacts with the United States.

It is truly interested in doing so. But what we need first is an atmosphere of good will between the countries. This is the fundamental question. . . .

People from the United States travel to the Soviet Union and vice versa. People in the U.S. have relatives in the USSR, and they come to visit the places of their origin, such as the Ukraine, the Baltic states, and so on. The Soviet Union welcomes this and is open to such visits. There are no difficulties in this regard. Lately, there has been an increase in contacts between representatives of religious groups. The Soviet side was in favor of this. There were marriages between U.S. and Soviet citizens. This was a very natural and understandable thing, and there are no objections to this. Since the group of U.S. Senators that had met with me before this meeting in Geneva had mentioned these issues, I had looked into them.

During the past five years more than 400 marriages have taken place, and out of these, only ten people have not been permitted to emigrate. The only obstacle to emigration is involvement of the person in question with state secrets.

In this case, the state has a specific responsibility, but it tries to let time pass, to let the individual do different kind of work so that his knowledge becomes outdated. His case is then returned to, and he is released.

Within the past five years restrictions have been placed only on ten of 420 to 450 people. But these were Soviet regulations, and the Soviet side asked that they be respected. This was one example.

You have mentioned Jews. The fate of Jewish people was of concern to the Soviet government. There are many Jews in the Soviet Union, as there are in the United States (which has the greatest number) and in other countries. After what the Fascists have done to the Jews, the Soviet Union has done everything it could to give them special attention, and it has not regretted doing so. Since many Jewish families had been separated, difficulties existed because of this, and the Soviet side tried to examine such cases. But such issues are mixed in with discussion of the situation of the Jews in the Soviet Union in general, this is not right. Then the Soviet side objects and furnishes data to back up what it says. This has been the Soviet Union's approach to all cases, including in its discussions with the United States. The Soviet Union is willing to look at specific cases, but when these things are used for political aims, they would be rebuffed. Specific cases would be examined quietly, in a humane way.

When a U.S. Congressional delegation visited the USSR at the invitation of the Supreme Soviet, the two bodies had agreed to establish a permanent group to examine such issues, and the Soviet side was in favor of this, but would not permit this issue to be used for political aims.

Reagan responded with specific examples of Soviet denial of human rights, but he also offered a way for Gorbachev to save face:

With regard to Jews and other religious groups, there are restrictions in the Soviet Union on their ability to practice their religion, e.g., Jews are not permitted to teach Hebrew. In the United States, in addition to attending the usual schools, Jewish families send their children to their own schools to study their ancient language. Perhaps some people would not think of emigrating from the Soviet Union if they were allowed to practice their religion.

With regard to other questions, the two countries have signed the Helsinki accords which assure certain freedoms, such as family reunification and the right to emigrate. However, our two countries are big ones, with very large bureaucracies. It is not possible for you or me to know everything that goes on at the lower levels, where people could make decisions which were contrary to the desires of the leadership.

You mentioned that only ten people had not been permitted to rejoin their spouses. But I have a much larger list of cases of separate families.

I want to give you one other example of a case in this category. I know of a piano player, a young man in the Soviet Union who wished to emigrate to Israel. Not only was he denied such permission, but he was also denied permission to play the piano with major orchestras, and his records could no longer be sold in stores. His career was destroyed as a result of the fact that he wished to emigrate. The bureaucracy can do many things of which you were not aware. This man had a wife and a small child. Apparently, he and his wife had been told that they could emigrate, but the baby would have to remain. Since the child was only one year old, they certainly could not have left him behind, so they did not emigrate.

Gorbachev made the point that if the general atmosphere between the United States and the Soviet Union improved, some of the human rights issues could be quickly resolved. But he also made it clear that if the question of human rights was used for political purposes, the Soviet side would rebuff any attempt:

> I would like to ask you about the following. For the Soviet leadership and for everyone in Soviet society it is clear whose side you are on in the area of human rights. You always speak of the lack of human rights in socialist countries. In other countries there is democracy and everything is okay. Since people are aware of the rights situation in the Soviet Union and in other countries, and can compare the situation, why are you taking this point of view? If other people said this, this might be understandable, but you always say that there is a clear distinction, namely, that there are no rights in socialist countries, but they are in bloom in the democracies. This causes consternation.
>
> At the level of me and you, one should be responsible and call things by their proper names, no matter where they occur. If things are

painted only in black and white, this would only inflame the distrust be-tween the countries. I think it would be better to take steps to improve the general atmosphere of our relationship, and the specific humanitarian issues could quickly be resolved.

The Soviet Union is prepared to resolve them. But if questions of human rights are used for political purposes, the Soviet side will rebuff such attempts.

I repeat, the Soviet Union is ready to examine specific cases, espe-cially those mentioned by you.

Reagan quickly assured Gorbachev of his intentions:

I was trying to clearly indicate that if such changes oc-curred, I would not indicate that I was the one that had per-suaded you to do this.

I realize that both of us have concerns about our political image, namely, that we do not want to have it seem that we were giving in to outside influences.

I wish to assure you that you would have no such problems with me. What happens is that various groups in the United States have relatives and families in other countries, and they get information from these people. Then organizations deliver this to me and demand that their grievances be resolved with regard to people in the Soviet Union. These things make their way into the press, and I can not do anything about that since the United States has a free press.

I am trying to say that we could work better together if such issues did not appear on the front pages, but rather if I spoke with you about these things confidentially.

Gorbachev finally closed the meeting on a cordial note:

I'm glad that we have had such a one-to-one talk, and that this has let us get to know each other better, and this is important. When the two

*of us communicate, especially about the larger political issues, we will
know what the other one looks like, and the image of the other person
will be present when decisions are made.*[11]

Yet as the discussion proceeded, it was clear that Gorbachev
was not happy about the questions being raised by Reagan. When
the two leaders left the small room after seventy minutes, George
Shultz noticed that "they were not smiling. The atmosphere had
been highly charged . . . The exchange had been intense."[12]

But Reagan was pleased. The night of November 20, 1985, he
summed up his observations on human rights in his personal diary:

> The last day of the Summit & this time Mr. G. was host. We
> went to the Soviet mission & he took me into a small room with
> interpreters.
>
> This was my chance to have at human rights.
>
> I explained that I wasn't telling him how to run his coun-
> try—I was asking for his help; that I had a better chance of get-
> ting support at home for things we'd agreed to if he would ease
> some of the restrictions on emigration, etc.
>
> I told him I'd never mention what he was doing out loud
> but he'd find that I could better meet some of his requests for
> trade, etc. He argued back sort of indicating that he thought
> they treated their people better than we did ours. He quoted
> statements made by some of the feminist extremists to prove
> we were unkind to women.
>
> I fought back—only time will tell if I made any headway.[13]

Did these and other probes by Reagan have anything to do
with the changes that would sweep the Soviet Union? There's no
direct evidence, but the circumstantial case is strong that Reagan's
pressure sped up the process.

When Reagan returned to the United States from the Geneva
talks, Marine One whisked him directly to the U.S. Capitol. With

*Reagan's personal diary for November 20, 1985, on his
human rights efforts to Gorbachev at the Geneva Summit.*

little sleep, Reagan walked into the House chamber and was
greeted by a cheering joint session of the Congress. He did not
seem tired as he told them about his journey:

> It's great to be home. . . . In the past few days . . . we spent
> over 15 hours in various meetings . . . approximately 5 of those
> hours were talks between Mr. Gorbachev and myself—just one-
> on-one . . . That was the best part—our fireside summit. . . .
>
> I can't claim that we had a meeting of the minds on such
> fundamentals as ideology or national purpose, but we under-
> stand each other better, and that's a key to peace. I gained a
> better perspective. I feel he did, too.
>
> We discussed nuclear arms and how to reduce them. I ex-
> plained our proposals for equitable, verifiable, and deep re-
> ductions. . . . We have a long way to go, but we're still heading
> in the right direction. . . .
>
> Mr. Gorbachev insisted that we might use a strategic de-
> fense system to put offensive weapons into space and establish

nuclear superiority. I made it clear that SDI has nothing to do with offensive weapons. . . .

We discussed human rights. We Americans believe that history teaches no clearer lesson than this: Those countries which respect the rights of their own people tend, inevitably, to respect the rights of their neighbors. Human rights, therefore, is not an abstract moral issue.

It is a peace issue.[14]

In their joint statement of November 21, 1985, on the summit meeting, Reagan and Gorbachev "agreed that a nuclear war cannot be won and must never be fought."[15]

Chapter 17

~

GORBACHEV'S GAMBIT

The best-laid schemes o' mice and men,
Gang aft a-gley,
And lea'e us nought but grief and pain,
For promised joy.
—ROBERT BURNS, "TO A MOUSE," 1785

Much had been accomplished at the Geneva summit, but Reagan and Gorbachev had miles to go before they could reach an agreement. They had agreed to have at least two more summits—one in the United States and one in the Soviet Union. Although they had not signed any papers, they had agreed to Reagan's proposals to reduce 50 percent of their large, strategic offensive nuclear arms and to eventually eliminate the intermediate-range missiles aimed at countries in Europe. Yet they remained at an impasse on SDI and on emigration rights for Soviet citizens. Each man was much happier that he had taken the other's measure at the summit, but their prospects for a signed treaty did not look promising.

For about two months things were pretty quiet and friendly. Reagan and Gorbachev exchanged two letters each. One of Reagan's was handwritten and five pages; one that Gorbachev sent was handwritten and fourteen pages. They swapped Christmas speeches to each other's countries, something that had never been done before.

Then it happened. Without a word to Reagan, on January 15, 1986, Mikhail Gorbachev announced to the world that the Soviet Union had a new, breathtaking plan to eliminate all nuclear weapons everywhere on Earth. The first copy was sent to Reagan the night before the speech, without the courtesy of letting him know it was coming. The plan was clearly the result of a lot of thinking, probably begun well before the summit in Geneva.

It had the looks of a maneuver by which Gorbachev was seeking to gain an advantage after the standstill at Geneva. The Soviets now publicly promised the world what Reagan had dreamed about: they would agree to getting rid of every nuclear weapon in the world— *if* Reagan agreed to give up the Strategic Defense Initiative and keep it in a laboratory, where, without testing, it would die.

The Soviet plan was seemingly bolder and more comprehensive than the U.S. plan that had been discussed two months before in Geneva. Here are some excerpts of Gorbachev's statement about the Soviet arms control proposal:

> The Soviet Union is proposing a step-by-step and consistent process of ridding the Earth of nuclear weapons . . . within the next 15 years, before the end of this century . . .
>
> Within the next 5–8 years the U.S.S.R. and the U.S.A. will reduce by one half the nuclear arms that can reach each other's territory . . . each side will retain no more than 6,000 warheads. It stands to reason that such a reduction is possible only if the U.S.S.R. and the U.S.A. mutually renounce the development, testing, and deployment of strike weapons. . . . [T]he first stage of nuclear disarmament should concern the Soviet Union and the United States because it is up to them to set an example for the other nuclear powers to follow . . .
>
> Stage two: At this stage, which should start no later than 1990 and last for 5–7 years . . . the U.S.S.R. and the U.S.A. will go on with the reduction agreed upon during the first stage and also carry out further measures designed to eliminate their medium-range nuclear weapons. . . .

Following the completion . . . of the 50 percent reduction in the relevant arms of the U.S.S.R. and the U.S.A. in the second stage . . . All nuclear powers eliminate their tactical nuclear arms. . . . At this stage the Soviet-American accord on the prohibition of space strike weapons would have to become multilateral. . . . All nuclear powers would stop nuclear weapons tests.

Stage three will begin no later than 1995 . . . the elimination of all remaining nuclear weapons will be completed. By the end of 1999 there will be no nuclear weapons on the Earth. . . . The Soviet Union calls upon all peoples and states and, naturally, above all nuclear states, to support the program of eliminating nuclear weapons before the year 2000. . . .

Mankind is at a crucial stage of the new Space Age. . . . We are against weapons in space. . . . Our material and intellectual capabilities make it possible for the Soviet Union to develop any weapon if we are compelled to do this. . . . It is our profound conviction that we should approach the third millennium, not with the "Star Wars" program but . . . peaceful exploration of space by all mankind.[1]

At first glance Gorbachev's nuclear weapons proposal was striking. Newspapers all over the world picked up the basic theme, which was simply "Let's get rid of all nuclear weapons in the world by the year 2000—less than 15 years away." It sounded great, and raised many hopes in many nations: Gorbachev had accepted the essence of Reagan's demand for nuclear arms reductions. The stated goal of the Soviets' new plan was the same as Reagan's—the elimination of all the nuclear weapons in the entire world. On paper, at least, the Soviets had capitulated, adopting Reagan's key demands.

They agreed to eventually destroy 50 percent of their large nuclear missile warheads, while the United States did the same. They agreed—in the 1990s—to take down their intermediate nuclear missiles aimed at the cities of Europe, even as the United States removed the missiles provided to NATO to target cities in the Soviet

Union. There remained a question of the nuclear missiles of France and England, but the broad agreement, the bedrock on which both sides agreed, was there.

On closer examination, however, the proposal left Europe vulnerable to Soviet missiles even as it eliminated U.S. ballistic missiles. Furthermore, a large part of what the Soviets proposed would occur only after Reagan, and perhaps Gorbachev, had left office or died. By that time, many things could have changed—Reagan would have been gone from the White House, with twelve years still to go in the Soviet plan. Gorbachev would last a bit longer than Reagan; after an attempted Soviet coup in 1991, he resigned on December 25, 1991, nine years before the plan was supposed to be complete.

Moreover, the plan depended totally on the word of the Soviets, that they would live up to everything they had promised.

And most important, the Soviets—in spite of the fact they had been working on their own "Star Wars" for twenty years—remained firmly opposed to the idea of the United States building its own. Everything the Soviets promised held only if the United States renounced "the development, testing and deployment of space-strike weapons," meaning SDI.[2] The deadlock on human rights remained as well; Gorbachev was convinced that other countries' concern with human rights violated the sovereignty of the Soviet Union, while Reagan had made it clear that the Soviet Union violated basic human rights and that the Soviets should let their people leave anytime they wished.

The new Soviet plan proved just how desperate the Soviets were to stop Reagan's Strategic Defense Initiative—they would destroy a large number of their largest missiles, destroy all the intermediate missiles aimed at European cities, stop testing weapons, and even give up making yearly increases in their stockpiles of nuclear warheads, so long as Reagan gave up SDI. The main goal of the Soviet plan, then, was not to eliminate nuclear weapons but to block the United States from developing missile defense. Gorbachev and the Soviets knew how badly Reagan wanted to get rid of nuclear weapons, so they were tempting him.

On January 15, when Reagan was first notified of Gorbachev's statement, he was surprised: three weeks earlier Gorbachev had written to Reagan that he valued the private nature of their confidential correspondence. And while Reagan was pleased with many parts of Gorbachev's statement, he knew that it was propaganda.

While many of Reagan's advisers thought that Gorbachev's statement should be ignored, Reagan disagreed. That night in his personal diary he wrote:

A long meeting with George Shultz & John Poindexter on . . . our response to a letter from Gorbachev who surprisingly is calling for an arms reduction plan which will rid the world of nuclear weapons by year 2000. Of course he has a couple of zingers in there which we'll have to work around.

But at the very least it is a h--l of a propaganda move. We'd be hard put to explain how we could turn it down.[3]

In a written statement Reagan pointed out that he had called for the total abolition of nuclear weapons at the Japanese Diet in 1983.[4] The next day Reagan talked briefly to the press and said that Gorbachev's plan was:

Different from the things that we have heard in the past from leaders in the Soviet Union. It's just about the first time that anyone has ever proposed actually eliminating nuclear weapons. We're very grateful for the offer. We're studying it with great care, and it is going to depend now on what takes place in Geneva.[5]

Over the next two weeks President Reagan and his chief advisers carefully studied the statement from the Soviet Union. On

February 3, 1986, President Reagan chaired an NSPG meeting, classified Top Secret, to discuss Gorbachev's plan.

There were three different options on the table that the advisers carefully discussed. Reagan listened to the debate and then, with about ten minutes to go, took the floor. This was one of his most important steps in the nuclear negotiations, and he did not want to accuse the Soviets of propaganda, as some of his advisers did.

Instead, Reagan spelled out his vision of U.S. strategy:

I agree with the general thrust of the conversation. I do not believe there is any need for U.S. movement in all three negotiating areas. I do agree that in reality "the ball is still in their court"—but there is a danger in attacking the Soviet generalization as only propaganda.

Then the public perceives the issue as: Who really wants to reduce? We need to *make the Soviets* expose the fact that they are not really serious about reductions negotiations. The U.S. should go to the negotiations, point out that the Soviets have made a general, overall offer, and agree on the overall aims of the process.

We should emphasize that what the U.S. seeks now is a *practical* way forward: a way to achieve verification in a concrete agreement, even if such involves a proposal we have already made. The U.S. should emphasize the point that we are trying to find a practical way to move forward in implementing the agreed eventual goals.

The United States does *not* give up SDI.

We should point out that SDI is not for the U.S. alone. We seek a mutual shift from sole reliance on offensive weapons to an offense-defense mix. We should remember the principle of sharing SDI at the deployment stage. All speakers here today agreed on the overall goal of SDI.

As we continue to develop SDI we need to find a way for SDI to be a protector for all—perhaps the concept of a "common trigger," where some international group, perhaps the UN, could deploy SDI against anyone who threatened use of nuclear weapons. Every state could use this guarantee. . . . We do not have all the answers. When research reveals the practicality of SDI, then we might want to mutually decide what to do.

There is no one [here] who wants to curtail SDI. But at the same time, there is no guarantee we know how to make SDI work yet. . . . The U.S. needs to be careful that our position is not propaganda. If it were, the Soviets would be quick to label it such, and negate the value of our position.

President Reagan ended the meeting by focusing on details of plans for eliminating the Soviet missiles aimed at Europe:

It is clear that we need to work in INF for total elimination of those systems. If the Soviets try to keep some SS-20s in Asia, perhaps we could counter by putting Pershing II and GLCM systems in Alaska, where they could reach Soviet systems in Asia.

The Soviets must know that if there is not complete elimination of INF, we will not eliminate our INF. There should be verifiable measures for destroying INF under an agreement.[6]

Later that night, Reagan wrote in his diary of his decision to treat the Soviets' propaganda play as a serious expression of their goals—despite what some of his advisers thought:

Then it was N.S.P.G. time in the situation room re Gorbachev's proposal to eliminate nuclear arms. Some wanted to tag it a publicity stunt.

I said no.

Let's say we share their overall goals & now want to work out the details. If it is a publicity stunt this will be revealed by them. I also propose that we announce we are going forward with SDI but if research reveals a defense against missiles is possible we'll work out how it can be used to protect the whole world, not just us.[7]

[Reagan's handwritten diary entry — facsimile reproduction]

Reagan's personal diary for February 3, 1986.

Over the next three weeks, on February 16 and February 22, Reagan sent two more letters to Gorbachev—one a frank, tough seven-page letter that attempted to clarify the actions of the Soviets, and the other making it clear that the United States approved of the Soviets' "new thinking" but reminding him that the United States had advocated those ideas for years.

In Reagan's February 16 letter, he hit Gorbachev hard on Soviet hypocrisy regarding "space strike weapons":

In the spirit of candor which is essential . . . I would add another point. You speak often of "space strike weapons," and your representatives have defined these as weapons which can strike targets in space from earth and its atmosphere, and weapons in space which can strike targets in space or on Earth.

I must ask, "What country has such weapons?"

The answer is, only one:

The Soviet Union.

Your ABM system deployed around Moscow can strike targets beyond the atmosphere and has been tested in that mode.

Your co-orbital, anti-satellite weapon is designed to destroy satellites. Furthermore, the Soviet Union began research in defenses utilizing directed energy before the United States did and seems well along in research.

I do not point this out in reproach or suggest that these activities are in violation of agreements. But if we were to follow your logic to the effect that what you call "space strike weapons" would only be developed by a country planning a first strike, what would we think?

We see the Soviet Union devoting enormous resources to defensive systems, in an effort which antedates by many years our own effort, and we see a Soviet Union which has built up its counterforce weapons in numbers far greater than our own. If the only reason to develop defensive weapons is to make a disarming first strike possible, then clearly we should be even more concerned than we have been.

We are concerned, and deeply so.[8]

There was no answer at all from Gorbachev.

On February 22 Reagan sent another letter to Gorbachev discussing the January 14 Soviet plan. Reagan was still somewhat bemused by the audacity of the proposal, fully aware that it could be a publicity stunt but fully committed to treating it seriously—no matter what his expert advisers thought. Here are some excerpts from the letter that make it crystal clear that the United States is fully aware that the Soviets have copied the U.S. idea—and that the United States likes it:

Dear Mr. General Secretary:

The elimination of nuclear weapons has been an American goal for decades, from our proposals at the dawn of the nuclear age to my vision of a nuclear-free world made possible through the reliance of our countries on defense rather than on the threat of nuclear retaliation.

In a 1983 speech to the Japanese Diet and on many subsequent occasions, I have advocated the abolition of nuclear weapons. I have done so because I believe this is an objective which reflects the deep yearning of people everywhere, and provides a vision to guide our efforts in the years ahead. . . .

It is in this spirit that I have studied with great care your letter of January 14 . . . and your subsequent statements on the prospects for progress in arms control. I believe they represent a significant and positive step forward. I am encouraged that you have suggested steps leading toward a world free from nuclear weapons . . .

Sincerely,
Ronald Reagan[9]

A couple of months went by with no response from Gorbachev. It was very quiet. On March 17, Reagan wrote to an old friend, Colonel Barney Oldfield, who had sent him a letter with some comments on the Soviets. Part of what Reagan said in return was:

How right you were. Some of that cautious wording about Soviet shenanigans way back then made no sense at all. I'm still hoping we can get them to make at least a first step on the road to reducing nuclear weapons but not by giving up SDI.

I think General Secretary Gorbachev has gotten the idea, but maybe doesn't know how to get off the limb he's on.[10]

While Reagan waited for Gorbachev to respond, another issue had come to a head. The question, Reagan recalled:

Was whether to continue abiding by terms of the SALT II treaty despite repeated Soviet cheating on its restrictions?

We knew of dozens of violations of the SALT and ABM treaties, including the Krasnoyarsk radar, which we knew incontrovertibly was intended for use in an antimissile defense.[11]

On March 25, President Reagan chaired a meeting of the NSPG focused on the U.S. policy of following "restraint in the face of the continued pattern of Soviet noncompliance with arms control agreements."[12]

Reagan wrote that night in his diary about the decision he made:

> We had an NSPG meeting on whether to continue observing the SALT II restraints in view of Soviet violations. State Dept. put up an argument to continue doing so. Others, including Cap [Weinberger] want to give it up.
>
> I'm inclined to vote for replacing that informal agreement with our arms reduction proposal now in Geneva. Tell the Soviets we can have a real reduction in weapons or an arms race—but we're not going to sit by & watch them keep on fudging.[13]

It was quiet for another week, and then on April 2, four months after the Geneva summit, Gorbachev finally sent a letter to Reagan. It was as if he had, until then, been waiting for Reagan to give in, hoping the president would accept the terms he was offering.

The main thrust of Gorbachev's letter was his desire to have another private tête-à-tête with Reagan—soon. Like so many powerful people upon first meeting Reagan, he seemed sure he could easily get the best of Reagan if he could just talk to him, though he was puzzled by the fact that all others had failed. These were the key excerpts in Gorbachev's new letter:

> *More than four months have passed since the Geneva meeting. We ask ourselves: what is the reason for things not going the way they, it would seem, should have gone? Where is the real turn for the better? We, within the Soviet leadership, regarded the Geneva meeting as a call for translating understandings of principle reached there into specific actions . . . we have put forward a wide-ranging and concrete program. . . .*
>
> *It was the desire that we work together in the cessation of nuclear tests, and set a good example to all nuclear powers that motivated my*

recent proposal for both of us to meet specifically on this issue at one of
the European capitals. . . .

> *I repeat, what is meant here is a specific, single-purpose meeting.*
> *Such a meeting, of course, would not be a substitute for the new major*
> *meeting that we agreed upon in Geneva. . . . Given the mutual will it*
> *would be also possible to ascertain other possibilities for agreement in the*
> *context of the forthcoming meeting both in the area of space and nuclear*
> *arms. . . . To be sure, we also have things to discuss as far as regional*
> *matters are considered.[14]*

For over a week Reagan weighed the letter from Gorbachev.
On April 11, he replied:

> It is clear that both of us are concerned about the relative
> lack of progress. . . . While I agree that it is very important, it is
> hard for me to understand that the basis for a meeting on our
> level, devoted solely to this issue, when it has been impossible
> to arrange for our representatives to discuss it. . . . [W]e should
> be able to arrange the meeting we agreed on in Geneva, as
> soon and as easily, as we could arrange a one-purpose meeting
> in Europe.
>
> Wouldn't it be better to treat this issue first at a lower
> level . . . ?[15]

Both sides now seemed to be jockeying for advantage. Gorbachev had hinted for a mini-summit somewhere in Europe, and
he wanted it before the promised summit in Washington, D.C.
Reagan was hesitant, preferring lower-level discussions first.

On April 16, Reagan chaired a NSPC meeting, classified Top
Secret, in which discussion continued as to how to handle SALT II.
The Soviets continued to violate the unsigned treaty, while the
United States upheld it. They were building new radar in Krasno-
yarsk, developing a new ICBM, and using encryption in their mis-
siles. The decision confronting President Reagan was whether or

not to continue observing the SALT treaties or break with them. Reagan had never liked either SALT I or SALT II, and it was now clear that while he was willing to go along with parts of SALT II, he had no intention of following it to the letter. He began by asking:

> What if we finesse SALT II by saying that our goal is some specific other limit? . . . Modernization must be seen as modernization, not as a build up. I'm willing to bring the number of missiles down if the Soviets will reduce. We can come down to any equal levels if they join us. . . .
>
> We need to say to people that both sides are modernizing, not engaging in an arms race. The Soviets are ahead in modernization, we are not. This isn't a race to achieve numerical superiority. The end result is no increase in total numbers.[16]

CHERNOBYL

On the morning of April 26, 1986, a large explosion rocked the Chernobyl nuclear power plant in Pripyat, Ukraine. It was the worst nuclear accident in history.

Soon the fallout from the accident had drifted over the western part of the Soviet Union and then on to other countries—in Eastern Europe, Western Europe, northern Europe, Scandinavia, and eastern North America. Especially large amounts of radioactive contamination fell on Ukraine, Belarus, and Russia. Thousands would eventually die from some form of cancer linked to this fallout.

As the radioactive debris floated across the Soviet Union and Europe, the accident stood as a stark reminder to Soviet leaders (and to people all over the world) of just how incredibly powerful a nuclear explosion could be, for the Chernobyl explosion, as bad as it was, was tiny compared to the power of even one of the tens of thousands of nuclear weapons the superpowers had stockpiled.

Yet as the Soviets scrambled to control the spread of the lethal radiation and evacuate citizens from affected areas, the Geneva summit and arms reduction seemed to fade away.

On May 23, Reagan sent a long letter, classified Secret/Sensitive, to Gorbachev. It had been six weeks since his last letter. He opened by offering U.S. aid in dealing with the explosion's aftermath and expressed his admiration for the courage of the Soviet people's response to the tragedy. Then Reagan returned to the question of nuclear arms reduction, asking Gorbachev when the Soviets would respond to U.S. proposals:

> In the absence of a response to our proposal, I have sought to communicate to you in our private correspondence. . . .
>
> I described to Secretary Dobrynin, for example, our readiness to reach agreement by the next summit on key elements of treaties to reduce strategic nuclear forces and eliminate intermediate range nuclear missiles, as well as on methods to remove both the threat of an effective first strike from either side and the use of space for basing weapons of mass destruction. . . . We have lost a full six months in dealing with the issues which most merit our personal attention. Let us not lose it for lack of effort.[17]

A week later, Gorbachev replied:

> *It is quite obvious that there is a practical need to begin establishing without delay an international system for the safe development of nuclear energy. . . . A total of 152 accidents at atomic power stations involving the release of radioactivity have been recorded throughout the world. . . .*
>
> *The lessons learned from this accident should benefit all mankind. What occurred at Chernobyl served as a serious reminder of the terrible forces contained in the energy of the atom. If an accident at a peaceful nuclear power plant turned into a disaster, one can imagine the tragic*

consequences for all mankind that would result from the use of nuclear weapons, which exist precisely for the purpose of destruction and annihilation.

The nuclear-space age requires new political thinking and new policies from the leaders of all countries. . . . Both these tasks—the safeguarding of the peaceful use of nuclear energy, and freeing our planet from nuclear weapons—require broad international interaction. . . . We call upon you to contribute to this important cause, on which depends the preservation of human civilization.[18]

For the rest of the summer and on into September there was very little of substance from the Soviets. Perhaps they were occupied with their own problems—dealing with the Chernobyl accident and the warning of nuclear destruction it symbolized. Too, the Soviet economy was failing, while the country continued to stockpile more nuclear weapons than it could ever use. By 1986 the Soviets had accumulated an astonishing 45,000 nuclear weapons in their arsenal, while the United States had only 24,401—still enough to devastate the Soviet Union several times over.[19] On top of the USSR's domestic issues, the U.S. military's new strength combined with the country's rapidly growing economy was making it even more formidable as an opponent. Add to that the possibility that the United States could figure out how to make "Star Wars" work, making it a truly invincible opponent, and Gorbachev was in trouble.

On the American side, Reagan was quite busy. During that three-and-a-half-month period of relative silence from the Soviets, he conducted five meetings of the NSC and NSPG devoted to nuclear arms reduction.

On June 6, Reagan chaired a small NSPG meeting. George Shultz began the meeting by outlining "the overall state of the relationship, concluding that the Soviets are at a fork in the road where they can either choose to wait out the President—gambling that Congress will cut the defense budget—or go for the agreement that will allow them to reduce their military spending on the premise that Ronald Reagan is their best hope for selling an agreement to the American public."

Toward the end of the meeting President Reagan outlined a possible plan that might meet the demands of the Soviets while preserving his Strategic Defense Initiative. He observed:

> Gorbachev has an internal dilemma, heightened by Chernobyl—we need to reach an agreement which does not make him look like he gave up everything.
>
> We cannot give away SDI, but we can make clear we do not seek a first-strike capability. . . . In this way, both sides would see SDI not as a threat, but as a defense against a madman.[20]

The next meeting of the NSPG, on June 12, was a general discussion of changes to the arms control strategy.

> We do not want a first-strike capability, but the Soviets probably will not believe us.
>
> The Soviets have economic problems, and Gorbachev has his own internal problems with the hardliners. Further, Chernobyl has altered Gorbachev's outlook on the danger of nuclear war.
>
> The time is right for something dramatic. We should go for zero ballistic missiles, agree to go forward with research permitted by the ABM treaty, invite the other side to witness testing when we come to that. No deployment of SDI until we eliminate ballistic missiles. Agree to share SDI with the world.
>
> The ABM treaty issue is okay, since research is permitted—we need an agreement to cover what we do when we are ready to test, providing for joint observers or something like that. The issue of the timing of the period of deployment and how deployment is linked to elimination of nuclear weapons need to be negotiated.[21]

By the end of June, Reagan was becoming concerned that nuclear arms reduction negotiations had stalled. It was now well over eight months since he and Gorbachev had sat down together, and there'd been little from Gorbachev save his consistent attempts to convince Reagan to abandon SDI.

Meanwhile, Reagan's time was running out: in just two years the politics of electing a new president would be going ahead full steam, and in twenty-seven months there would be a new president.

At an NSPG meeting on July 1, Reagan reviewed the SDI program. Toward the end of the meeting he made the following points:

> SDI is a strategic necessity and a crucial part of our three part response to the Soviet strategic threat:
>
> (1) modernizing our retaliatory forces,
> (2) negotiating deep, equitable and verifiable reductions of nuclear weapons and
> (3) taking steps now to provide future options for the possible introduction of strategic defenses.[22]

Then at a July 15 NSPG meeting, Weinberger made the case for continuing nuclear testing. As part of the arms reduction negotiations with the Soviets, Gorbachev had implored the United States to stop testing nuclear weapons. So far the United States had resisted. As Weinberger put it, "There is a military and technological necessity to test; since we depend on nuclear weapons for security, we must make certain they work."

Reagan agreed, and ended the meeting by quoting Thomas Jefferson:

> Jefferson observed that if the people have the facts the people won't make a mistake. Right now, the people don't have the facts on nuclear testing. We should give them to them.[23]

Gorbachev seemed to be stalling, perhaps hoping that Reagan would change his mind about SDI. But Reagan had no intention of shifting his view. Instead, Reagan brought together his key advisers, crafted a new version of his arms reduction proposals that might be accepted by Gorbachev, and then—on July 25—sent Gorbachev a frank, detailed seven-page letter in the hope of restarting the negotiation process. As Reagan recalled it later:

> In late July, I sent a sweeping new arms reduction proposal to Gorbachev based on ideas that had been developed during weeks of debate within the administration.
>
> During the discussion in which the proposals were hammered out, some of our arms control and State Department experts wanted me to hint to the Soviets that we might be willing to trade the SDI for greater Soviet concessions on offensive weapons. . . .
>
> I was committed to the search for an alternative to the MAD policy and said it as emphatically and as often as I could, privately and publicly: *The SDI is not a bargaining chip.*[24]

Behind the scenes, Reagan was arguing with some of his arms control and State Department staff who thought he should trade off SDI for more concessions on nuclear weapons. But Reagan held firm, and if his staff could not budge him, it was doubtful that Gorbachev could.

Here are excerpts from the letter Reagan sent Gorbachev on July 25:

> I have taken careful note of the proposals your negotiators made during the recent round in Geneva. . . . We both agree that neither side should deploy systems of strategic defense simply to augment and enhance its offensive capability. . . . [W]e would be prepared immediately to conclude an agreement incorporating the following limits:

Both sides would confine themselves for five years, through 1991, to a program of research, development and testing, which is permitted by the ABM Treaty . . . we would be prepared to sign a treaty now which would require the party that decides to proceed to deploy an advanced strategic defense system to share the benefits of such a system with the other providing there is mutual agreement to eliminate the offensive ballistic missiles. . . .

I would also be prepared to have our representatives discuss additional assurances that would further ban deployment in space of advanced weapons capable of inflicting mass destruction on the surface of the Earth. . . .

In the area of strategic offensive nuclear forces . . . I remain firmly committed to our agreement to seek the immediate implementation of the principle of a fifty percent reduction. . . .

At the same time, we could deal with the question of intermediate-range nuclear missiles by agreeing on the goal of eliminating this entire class of . . . missiles world-wide. . . .

The overall aim should be the elimination of all nuclear weapons. . . . I hope that we can move rapidly toward that "decisive turn" in relations between our countries which we both agree is overdue.[25]

The essence of what Reagan was proposing was, in his mind, an approach that would both calm the fears of Gorbachev and other Soviets and allow SDI to move ahead. Yet the Soviets, after analyzing Reagan's letter, were not happy.

On September 15, 1986, Gorbachev replied to Reagan with a letter delivered in person by Soviet foreign minister Eduard Shevardnadze. In it Gorbachev accused Reagan of fanning the flames, threatened the United States if it went forward with the new plans, and requested a private meeting in the very near future:

A massive hostile campaign has been launched against our country, which has been taken up at the higher levels of the United States administration and Congress. It is as if a pretext was deliberately sought to aggravate Soviet-American relations and increase tension. . . .

We witness attempts to justify the development of space weapons, and their testing. . . . It is, of course, fully understood that we will not agree to that. We see here a bypass route to securing military superiority. I trust, Mr. President, you recall our discussion of this subject in Geneva . . . should the United States rush with weapons into space, we would not help it. We would do our utmost to devalue such efforts and make them futile. You may rest assured that we have every means to achieve this and, should the need arise, we shall use those means. . . .

Upon reflection and after having given thought to your last letter I have come to the conclusion that the negotiations need a major impetus. . . . They will lead nowhere unless you and I intervene personally. I am convinced that we shall be able to find solutions. . . . This is exactly what the entire world is expecting from a second meeting between the leaders of the Soviet Union and the United States.

That is why an idea has come to my mind to suggest to you, Mr. President, that, in the very near future and setting aside all other matters, we have a quick one-on-one meeting, let us say in Iceland or in London, maybe just for one day, to engage in a strictly confidential, private and frank discussion (possibly with only our foreign ministers present). The discussion—which would not be a detailed one, for its purpose and significance would be to demonstrate political will—would result in instructions to our respective agencies to draft agreements on two or three very specific questions, which you and I could sign during my visit to the United States.[26]

Reagan tentatively agreed to meet Gorbachev, but he told the Soviets that he would not go until they had released American journalist Nicholas Daniloff, whom the KGB had recently arrested in Moscow on charges of espionage. Reagan was certain Daniloff was not a spy.

That night he wrote in his diary:

The General Secretary wants a meeting between him and me in London or Iceland—I opt for Iceland.

This would be preparatory to a Summit. I'm agreeable to that but made it plain we wanted Daniloff returned to us before anything took place. I let the F.M. [Shevardnadze] know I was angry & that I resented their charges that Daniloff was a spy after I had personally given my word that he wasn't.

I gave him a little run down on the difference between our 2 systems & told him they couldn't understand the importance we place on the individual because they don't have such a feeling.

I enjoyed being angry.[27]

The Soviets gave in to Reagan's demand ten days later. Reagan wrote in his diary the morning of September 29:

Didn't sleep at all well last night—I need my roommate. [Nancy had been out of town.] . . . George Shultz has won the day. Mr. and Mrs. Daniloff will be on their way home before the morning is over. That will be announced. . . .

Then I'll announce a meeting with Gorbachev in Iceland October 10, 11, 12.[28]

Chapter 18

~

SOVIET STRATEGY
AT REYKJAVIK: 1986

Reykjavik left me an even greater optimist . . .
I would not by any means call Reykjavik
a failure . . . now we are talking
about reduction and elimination.
—MIKHAIL GORBACHEV TO THE POLITBURO,
OCTOBER 14, 1986

On September 30, 1986, Reagan stepped into the White House Briefing Room and told the assembled reporters that there would finally be a second Soviet-American summit—and that it would take place in Iceland in just eleven days.

> I am pleased to announce that General Secretary Gorbachev and I will meet October 11th and 12th in Reykjavik, Iceland. The meeting was proposed by General Secretary Gorbachev, and I've accepted.[1]

The summit was an unusual meeting—prepared very quickly and designed to be informal, with each taking only a few advisers. Their two foreign ministers would be the only ones allowed to sit in on their talks. Kenneth Adelman, the adviser from the U.S.

Reagan and Gorbachev enjoy each other's company at Reykjavik.

Arms Control and Disarmament Agency who was traveling with Reagan, summed it up:

> It was a hasty acceptance of a hasty offer for a hasty meeting. . . . It was strange. It was strange of Gorbachev to propose the meeting then. . . . Strange of him to propose it at the close of such a nasty letter [September 15]. Strange to propose it in a week or ten days' time. Strange to propose it in London or Reykjavik rather than in Washington, where he and Reagan had already agreed to meet. And strange to have a summit in order to prepare a summit.
>
> The dangers were there right from the start.[2]

For there was no evidence that Gorbachev had changed his mind in the slightest—above all else, he, and certainly the Politburo in Moscow, wanted to stop SDI. Reagan remained convinced that it was wise not only to build SDI but also to supply it to every country in the world at cost. These positions had not changed since before the Geneva summit, when Reagan had written in his diary:

> George Shultz called from Moscow on scramble phone—7 more hours of talk—4 of them with Gorbachev. Apparently not much progress. Gorbachev is adamant we must cave in on SDI.
>
> Well, this will be a case of "an irresistible force meeting an immovable object."

Reagan boarded Air Force One, landed in Reykjavik, and headed for the home of the U.S. ambassador in Iceland, while Gorbachev settled down in a luxurious, 367-foot ship, the *Georg Ots*, anchored in Reykjavik Harbor. The weather was abysmal—the icy wind, driving rain and sleet, mere five hours of daylight, long black nights, and the angry Atlantic all made it a wonderful place to stay inside—but Reagan and Gorbachev both seemed to like it. And despite the fact that they remained at loggerheads on SDI, each seemed to believe that he could change the other fellow's mind.

For his part, Reagan was confident that Gorbachev would eventually understand the wisdom of SDI. After all, from the U.S. perspective, the argument for SDI was a powerful one, considering the Soviet buildup. The Soviets had had anti-satellite weapons since 1971,[3] their own strategic defense system in operation since 1972, and the Krasnoyarsk radar station in Siberia since 1983 (it had been built under Andropov, in violation of the ABM treaty). This and other radars "assist in the early warning of cruise missile and bomber attacks and enhance air defense electronic warfare capabilities."[4] And, of course, the most serious threat was the large and rapidly growing Soviet stockpile of nuclear weapons.

The Soviet Union and the United States together held over 98 percent of the nuclear stockpile in the world as of 1986. Both parties already had enough to destroy each other many times over, but the Soviets had many more with which to play intimidation games.

The Soviets had had a 36 percent advantage in numbers of warheads when Reagan became president; while the U.S. number had held relatively steady in the past five years, the Soviet stockpile had reached an all-time high. Indeed, few people seemed to notice that while Reagan was struggling with Brezhnev, Andropov, Chernenko, and now Gorbachev, the Soviets had somehow managed to manufacture almost 15,000 bright new nuclear weapons. In the months between the Geneva summit and Reykjavik alone, the Soviets had added 5,803 nuclear weapons, the largest increase of any one year. Since 1980, the Soviets had added both intermediate-range weapons targeted on Western Europe and strategic weapons—1,523 new ICBM warheads, 758 sea-launched missiles, and 580 nuclear warheads carried on long-range bombers.[5]

The more Reagan learned from U.S. generals and intelligence experts, and in light of the Soviets' blatant violations of treaties, the more necessary SDI seemed. The Soviets, for their part, were having great difficulties with their economy and were still dealing with the havoc raised by Chernobyl, while the growth of the U.S. economy and its buildup in military power left them nervous.

So as the strange summit began, it seemed unlikely that the two adversaries could come to any agreement.

FIRST MEETING: OCTOBER 11, 10:40–11:30 A.M.[6]

When Gorbachev and Reagan came out that morning they were alone, save for their translators and note takers. Their first, informal meeting was taken up with preliminaries. Reagan laid out his agenda for the summit:

> It seems to me that we have an entire series of problems which were left without adequate discussion at our meeting in Geneva. . . . I am referring to the problem of intermediate range weapons, space, and agreements on ABM defenses. . . . The world is impatiently awaiting an answer from us. . . .

We really will have to talk about human rights. . . . I already told you in Geneva, and I repeat it now, that human rights, and specifically questions of exit from the Soviet Union, are ever present in appeals to me.

Gorbachev agreed to address human rights, but made his priorities clear:

We will still talk about human rights. But now I would like to . . . go on to specific problems of arms control and disarmament, including strategic arms, medium-range missiles, the ABM Treaty and the cessation of nuclear testing.

Reagan agreed:

I agree that these problems [human rights] become secondary in importance as compared with the problems of nuclear arms . . . the entire world awaits their decision from us.

And then the two men discussed the unique responsibility each held:

Gorbachev: The meeting is a testimony to our responsibility . . . the world really does depend on our two countries.

Reagan: I believe our situation to be unique. Here we are, the two of us, sitting together in a room, and we may resolve the question of whether there will be peace or war in the world.

Gorbachev: You and I cannot allow the upcoming meeting to fail in this sense. It would be a very serious blow. . . . This would be a scandalous outcome, with consequences which would be difficult to predict. . . . But now, if you do not object, we will invite Mr. Shultz and E. A. Shevardnadze.

SECOND MEETING: OCTOBER 11, 11:30 A.M.–12:30 P.M.[7]

Shultz and Shevardnadze then took their seats at the small table and the real discussion began—although over the two days of the summit, Reagan and Gorbachev would do 95 percent of the talking.

> *Gorbachev: I will begin the presentation of our proposals. . . . [T]he principle question of international policy of the two countries is the . . . elimination of nuclear weapons as our mutual goal . . . nuclear war is inadmissible and impossible. . . .*
>
> *Our approach was presented in my announcement of 15 January 1986. . . . We expect that the USA will act in the same manner . . . not one of the parties should strive to achieve military supremacy over the other. . . .*
>
> *I would like to confirm now that the Soviet leadership is interested specifically in deep, 50 percent, reduction in SOA [strategic offensive arms] . . .*
>
> *We propose the complete elimination of USSR and USA missiles . . . in Europe. We are agreeing to great concession . . . a great new step we are now taking . . . we are ready to resolve the question also of missiles with a range of less than 1,000 km. We are ready to freeze their numbers. . . .*
>
> *The third question consists of the problem of ABM defense and banning nuclear testing. . . . Developments and testing in the sphere of SDI would be allowed within the confines of laboratories, with prohibition of outside-of-laboratory testing of means intended for space-based destruction of objects in space and on Earth. . . .*
>
> *It is expedient to agree on the full and final prohibition of nuclear testing. . . .*
>
> *This, Mr. President, is the packet of our proposals. . . .*

Reagan: We are very encouraged. . . . I also notice certain divergences in our position as concerns strategic and intermediate-range missiles. For example . . . our position also requires the reduction of Soviet missiles in Asia. . . .

I would like to draw a line to the ABM Treaty . . . we are proposing to you . . . to sign an agreement which would replace the ABM Treaty. This agreement would provide for both sides to conduct research in the sphere of defensive arms. . . . If we were the first to reach this boundary, then we would invite you to observe the testing of such systems. And if the tests showed . . . a defensive system, then this agreement would obligate us to share this system with the other side.

We propose to protect ourselves once and for all against the rebirth of strategic arms in the world. . . .

Gorbachev: First of all . . . I ask you to give them [our proposals] proper attention and to express your reaction later. . . .

We do not understand this. . . . About SDI. You need not worry. We have gotten to the bottom of this question, and if the USA created a three-level system of ABM defense, we will find an answer. We are not concerned by . . . the creations of new types of weapons which would destabilize the strategic situation in the world. If that is the goal of the USA, then we can still understand its position. . . .

But if it wants stronger security for its people,

And for the entire world,

Then its position contradicts that goal and is directly dangerous.

THIRD MEETING: OCTOBER 11, 3:30–5:40 P.M.[8]

Reagan, having examined the Soviets' written proposal, opened the meeting:

Reagan: You handed over a document for our examination . . . reducing ballistic missiles warheads is the central objective. . . . We have agreed on the idea of a 50 percent reduction. . . .

We are ready to accept establishment of a ceiling for bombers . . . we can accept establishment of an overall limit of 350 units for the number of bombers. . . .

As far as your proposal on intermediate-range missiles is concerned. I am disappointed with it. . . . I have to say that I will not accept an agreement that would include a ban on our Pershing missiles. The only thing that can be discussed is . . . the quantity of Pershing missiles and ground-launched cruise missiles. We cannot agree to having ballistic missiles in your forces and none in ours.

Finally let's put the issue of the treaty's period of effectiveness to rest. . . . We already have an agreement prohibiting deployment of mass destruction weapons in space. . . . Second, you voiced the concern that the United States might obtain a possibility for carrying out a first strike, and then avoid retaliation owing to defense. . . . [W]e do not have the capability for carrying out a first strike—and that is not our goal. . . .

We are ready to share our accomplishments in strategic defense. . . .

Regarding the issue of nuclear testing . . . nuclear testing will be limited and ultimately terminated in coordination with reduction and ultimate elimination of nuclear weapons. . . .

Let's now take a step toward agreement. . . . My decisions regarding the SALT-I and SALT-II treaties[9] were adopted because of the Soviet Union's failure to comply with these treaties. . . . Construction of a radar station in Krasnoyarsk is especially significant among the violations. . . .

I propose that we instruct a group of experts to meet today at 8 o'clock this evening and discuss all of the issues . . . do you agree to hold a meeting this evening at the expert level?

Gorbachev: We'll talk about it. . . . [T]he next issue. Do I understand correctly that the U.S. President no longer likes the zero opinion he proposed regarding medium-range missiles?

> **Reagan:** No, I like it very much, but only with a global resolution. . . . If the zero is on a global scale, then this would be fabulous. . . .

Gorbachev then asked a series of questions. His first concern was the nuclear weapons in South Korea. Shultz tried to answer but was cut off.

> **Gorbachev:** *I would like to hear the President's opinion. . . . If a solution is found for Asia, will you agree to the zero option in Europe?*

> **Reagan:** Yes.

Then Gorbachev changed tack:

> **Gorbachev:** *Now about something else . . . I am referring to the open-ended ABM Treaty . . . it is very important for both sides to be certain that no one will create weapons during this time that would undermine stability and parity . . . when someone is doing something behind your back during the reductions, a dangerous situation is created . . . logic requires that we strengthen the ABM Treaty.*
>
> *In the meantime your SDI will be limited to laboratory research.*

> **Reagan:** Let me return to the ABM Treaty. We are convinced that you violated this treaty by your actions in the area of anti-ballistic missile defense and construction of facilities contrary to the treaty. As far as SDI is concerned, I feel certain that this is the best possibility for ensuring peace in our century. . . . We propose writing it into the treaty that we will share with you the defensive weapons we are able to create.

> **Gorbachev** [ignoring everything Reagan said]: *Let's agree on this: We will accept your proposal for a meeting of experts at 8 o'clock this evening. . . .*

Now that we are discussing specific stages in nuclear arms reduction, we'll be fighting for verification, something that we need three times more than the USA.

Reagan: Listen, we are two civilized countries, two civilized peoples. When I was growing up—that was before your time—countries had rules of warfare. . . . But now . . . both countries have terrible missiles aimed at each other that can annihilate countless numbers of people, and primarily non-combatants—women, children.

The sole defense against this possibility is the threat that we also are in a position to carry out such mass extermination. This is an uncivilized situation.

I think that the world will become much more civilized if we, the two great powers . . . create defensive systems . . . I think that we would then be able to look proudly into the eyes of the entire world.

Gorbachev: I would prefer to reply in a less philosophical spirit. . . . Meeting the USA's position half-way, we are ready to agree with the proposal for laboratory research, which will allow you to see whether you need a full-scale . . . anti-ballistic missile system . . . During this entire time, you and I will still be left with huge nuclear arsenals . . . and no terrorist or madman will be able to do anything. . . .

Reagan: We have absolutely no desire to eliminate the ABM Treaty. This treaty is defensive, but you capitalize on its provisions to create a powerful defensive potential. We did not do this.

All we can say to the Americans is this: If the other side destroys us, we will destroy it. . . .

We propose supplementing the ABM Treaty with provisions on specific defensive weapons being created not for a first strike . . . We want this to be available to all the world.

Gorbachev: We will not deploy SDI. We have another concept.

Reagan: A couple of words in conclusion. You said that you don't need SDI, but then we would be able to carry out our programs in parallel, and if you find that you have something a little better, then perhaps you could share it with us.

Gorbachev: Excuse me, Mr. President, but I do not take your idea of sharing SDI seriously.

Reagan: If I thought that SDI could not be shared, I would have rejected it myself.

FOURTH MEETING: OCTOBER 12, 10:00 A.M.–1:35 P.M.[10]

The groups reconvened on the second day for the summit's last planned meeting. Both Reagan's and Gorbachev's support staffs had been up all night, trying to get all the details settled. They'd made some minor changes on zero-zero negotiations for Europe, and for the first time the Soviets had agreed to accept human rights as a standard agenda item. But nothing had budged on the main issue, SDI.

Now Reagan tried again to sell Gorbachev on the merits of U.S. SDI, while Gorbachev parried. Soon the conversation became heated.

Reagan: We have differences, we recognize that. The sides were not able to reach agreement. I am convinced that I cannot retreat from the policy I have declared in the field of space and defensive weapons.

I simply cannot do it.

Gorbachev: We have made major concessions to the United States. . . . We expect the same of the United States. . . . You and your people think that we have a greater interest in nuclear disarmament than the United States does, that if you put a little pressure on the Soviet Union it will raise its hand and surrender. That is a dangerous mistake. It is not going to happen. . . .

I have been waiting for you to start making concessions to me. On both the first and the second problems I was the one who made the concessions. Now I am testing you on the third question—the question of antimissile defense. . . .

I will tell you directly: We will fight harder for control than the United States does. . . . We will not agree to reduce strategic arms and intermediate-range missiles without confidence that the other side is fulfilling its obligations strictly. . . . You, Mr. President, must agree that if we are going to reduce nuclear weapons we have to be confident that the United States is not doing anything behind the back of the USSR . . . we do not touch the SDI program within the framework of the laboratory experiments . . .

Reagan: The United States never violated the ABM Treaty . . . but the Soviet side did. . . . Understand me, I cannot retreat from positions, renounce what I promised our people. I am serious about sharing this technology with the Soviet Union . . . if everyone has it then no one will be able to threaten anyone else.

Gorbachev: *We are giving him [the President] this opportunity to show that his idea is alive, that we are not burying it, that the United States can continue laboratory work on SDI, but cannot go beyond the framework of research.*

Reagan: I am not sure of that. And anyway, damn it, what kind of agreement are you defending? . . . But even when we destroy these missiles we must have a defense against others. The genie is already out of the bottle. Offensive weapons can be built again. Therefore I propose creating protection for the world, for future generations when you and I will no longer be here. . . .

I understand that you do not trust us, just as we do not trust you. . . . Long ago Karl Marx and Lenin both said that for the success of socialism it must be victorious throughout the world . . . the only morality is that which is in keeping with socialism. I must say that all the leaders of your country—except you, you still have not said such a thing . . . maybe you have not managed to express your views on this yet?

Gorbachev: So you are talking about Marx and Lenin again. Many people have already tried to bring down the founders of this well-known line of social thought. . . . I advise you not to waste time on this.

I see now that you do not want to meet us half-way on the issue of the ABM Treaty, which is absolutely essential in conditions where we are undertaking large reductions in nuclear arms. . . . So I see that the possibilities of agreeing are exhausted . . .

Perhaps you will report this to Congress, and we will report to the Politburo and the Supreme Soviet.

Reagan: I thought that we had agreement on the 50-percent reduction and on intermediate-range missiles. . . . How could it not be? How can we go away from here with nothing?

Gorbachev: Unfortunately, we in fact can.

Reagan: One more thing. I cannot return home and say nothing to our farmers on the issue that is so important to them. Why didn't you fulfill your obligation relative to grain purchases from us?

Gorbachev: It is very simple. You can tell them that the money with which the Russians could have bought grain ended up in the United States and Saudi Arabia because of the sharp drop in oil prices. So the

United States already has this money. . . . We know who began this
process of cutting oil prices, and whose interests it is in.

Maybe, if the President does not object. We will declare a break for
1–2 hours and during that time—possibly—our ministers will try to
propose something. I think that we can slow down a little. After all, we
do not want everything to end with a façade. . . . It is exceptionally im-
portant to reaffirm the ABM Treaty.

Then we can substantiate the risk that we are taking in questions
of strategic weapons and intermediate-range missiles. And so, if the
President does not object, we will take a break until 1500 hours.

FIFTH MEETING: OCTOBER 12, 3:25–4:30 P.M.[11]

This fifth and final meeting was unexpected. The summit was over,
the planes were warmed up, and everyone was ready to fly home.
But both Reagan and Gorbachev were frustrated and disappointed
by the morning's jousting and hoped that one last try would lead
to some sort of result.

Some of Reagan's staff were confident that Gorbachev was
using the two-hour break after the morning's meeting to call the
Politburo for clearance. At one point during their break, Reagan
threw up his hands and said:

> Why is he so against SDI?

Kenneth Adelman, the director of the U.S. Arms Control and
Disarmament Agency, who was in the room, spoke up:

> For two reasons. First, they have invested massive resources in
> their own SDI program over the past fifteen years, far more than
> we have. They've found there's something to it. The "something"
> there is to it can be done better by us than by them, since SDI plays
> into our strength—high tech, rather than their strength, brute mil-
> itary force.

Second, SDI represents a strategic end run. Rather than matching their new missiles with our new missiles—their SS-24 with our MX, their SS-25 with our Midgetman—SDI discounts the importance of these missiles together.[12]

When both sides returned to the table, Gorbachev plunged right in with a new proposal:[13]

> **Gorbachev:** *Concerning the ABM Treaty . . . Our formula is as follows:*
>
> *The USSR and the U.S. would pledge not to exercise their right to withdraw from the unlimited ABM Treaty for 10 years. . . . Testing of all space components of ABM defense in space shall be prohibited—except for laboratory research and testing.*
>
> *During the first five years . . . the strategic offensive weapons of the two sides shall be reduced by 50 percent.*
>
> *During the following five years . . . the remaining 50 percent of the two sides' offensive weapons shall be reduced.*
>
> *In this way, by the end of 1996 all the strategic offensive weapons of the USSR and the U.S. will have been eliminated.*

The key to this "new" idea from Gorbachev lay in the word *weapons*, meaning not just missiles but anything with nuclear capability—submarines, bombers, satellite killers in space, and so on. Moreover, while the reductions were equal, the final results would not be; since the Soviets were starting out with more missiles, they would end up with many more after taking out 50 percent. The first 50 percent would not kick in for five years—if indeed it kicked in at all, for in 1991 Reagan would have been out of office for three years, and only God knew where Gorbachev would be. (Actually, he would be stripped of his office in 1991.) And then would begin that second five-year period, during which time the Soviets were promising that the superpowers would eliminate *all* nuclear weapons. Meanwhile, of course, American SDI would never have been taken out of the laboratory.

The idea of eliminating all weapons quickly was patently rather absurd; Reagan was never going to strip the United States of that defense, and certainly neither was the Soviet Union. It was a ploy, and as soon as Reagan understood what Gorbachev was selling, the idea was dismissed. Instead, he returned to the more reasonable focus of ballistic missiles.

> **Reagan:** Our position offers a somewhat different formulation. . . . The two sides agree to limit themselves to research, development, and testing permitted by the ABM Treaty for the period of five years until 1991 inclusive, during which time a 50-percent reduction in strategic nuclear arsenals will be carried out.
>
> After that, both sides will continue to reduce the remaining offensive ballistic missiles at the same rate with the aim of completely eliminating offensive ballistic missiles by the end of the second five-year period. . . . At the end of this period, the two sides should have the right to deploy defensive systems.

> *Gorbachev: What we are talking about primarily is the renunciation of testing any space components of ABM defense in space—that is, refraining from any steps which would in effect pave the way to the deployment of such systems. . . . We are not undermining your idea of SDI. . . . We are only placing the system in the framework of laboratory research.*

Reagan, of course, knew that limiting SDI to the laboratory was tantamount to destroying it—it was the equivalent of building a new kind of airplane and then not flying it to see if it would work.

Reagan: I just don't understand why you object so much to SDI. . . . We want right now to provide for the possibility of defense in case, 10 years from now, when we no longer have missiles, someone should decide to re-create nuclear missiles. . . . And anyway, if you are so resolutely committed to the necessity of strengthening the ABM Treaty, what are we to make of the Krasnoyarsk Radar Station?

Gorbachev: [ignoring Reagan's question about Krasnoyarsk] *I still wish you would carefully examine our proposal. It encompasses elements of both your and our proposals. If it is acceptable, I am ready to sign it.*

Reagan: I know I won't live to be a hundred if I have to live in fear of these damned missiles.

Gorbachev: *You wouldn't have to give up SDI because laboratory research and testing would not be prohibited. . . . Anyway, I am categorically against any situation where our meeting results in one winner and one loser.*

Reagan: It looks like we're not getting anywhere. But I simply cannot understand why you object on the basis of fears of what will happen in ten and a half years, when there will be no ballistic missiles. Perhaps we ought to take another look at what we disagree about?

Gorbachev: *We already agreed on a 50-percent reduction of all strategic weapons in the course of the first five years. It would be logical for the remaining 50-percent to be eliminated in the following five years. The weapons to be eliminated would include all components of the triad— missiles, including heavy missiles, submarine missiles, and bombers. That would be fair.*

SIXTH MEETING: OCTOBER 12, 5:00–6:30 P.M.[14]

After a half-hour break, both sides sat down one last time.

> **Reagan:** Here is the final option which we can offer:
>
> The USSR and the U.S. pledge for the period of 10 years not . . . to withdraw from the unlimited ABM Treaty . . . while at the same time continuing research, development, and testing permitted by the ABM Treaty. . . .
>
> The first five years (until 1991 inclusive), will be a 50-percent reduction in the two sides' strategic offensive weapons.
>
> In the course of the following five years of that period, the remaining offensive ballistic missiles will be reduced . . . by the end of 1996 the USSR and the U.S. will have completely eliminated all offensive ballistic missiles.
>
> At the end of the 10-year period, each side may deploy *defensive systems.* . . .

> **Gorbachev:** *What I'm asking is, did you omit the mention of laboratories deliberately or not?*

> **Reagan:** Yes, it was deliberate. What's the matter?

> **Gorbachev:** *The first half of the formula talks about . . . strategic offensive weapons . . . but in the second part . . . it mentions offensive ballistic missiles. . . . Why this difference in approach?*

> **Reagan:** We were told during the break that the Soviet side would like a special mention of offensive strategic missiles. That's why we included that formula. . . . In the second part, however, we talked about ballistic missiles, in the belief that that's what you want.

> **Gorbachev:** *There is some kind of confusion here . . . in the following five years the remaining 50-percent of strategic offensive weapons must be eliminated.*

Reagan: Is that the only thing you object to? . . . It will have to be sorted out. . . . Evidently we have simply misunderstood you. But if that's what you want, all right.

Shultz: We need to be careful here. When we talk of eliminating all strategic offensive weapons, it does not refer to short-range ballistic missiles. . . . That's why I propose that we write that by the end of 1996 all strategic offensive weapons and all offensive ballistic missiles are to be eliminated.

Reagan: Let me ask this: Do we have in mind—and I think it would be very good—that by the end of the two five-year periods all nuclear explosive devices would be eliminated—including bombs, battlefield systems, cruise missiles, submarine weapons, intermediate-range systems, and so on?

Gorbachev: We could say that—list all those weapons.

Shultz: Then let's do it.

Reagan: If we agree that by the end of the 10-year period all nuclear weapons are to be eliminated, we can turn this agreement over to our delegations in Geneva so that they can prepare a treaty which you can sign during your visit to the United States.

But then the issue of SDI again raised its head:

Gorbachev: Well, all right. Here we have a chance for an agreement. What I am seriously concerned about is another factor. . . . We don't understand, then, why the American side does not agree to having research, development, and testing be restricted to the confines of the laboratory . . . which means that we cannot remove the mention of laboratories from our text . . . The question of laboratories is of fundamental importance.

Reagan: I do not agree that strict interpretation of the ABM Treaty means restricting the testing of ABM components solely to laboratories. . . . Our aim is to safeguard ourselves from a revival of missiles after they have been destroyed, in order to make a kind of gas mask against nuclear missiles. . . . And I have also spoken of the danger of nuclear maniacs.

Gorbachev: Yes, I've heard all about gas masks and maniacs— probably ten times already. But it still does not convince me.

Reagan: In any case, the world would welcome it if we could undertake to reduce nuclear weapons and not make this issue a stumbling block. We are asking not to give up SDI. . . .

Gorbachev: Such a stipulation will not prohibit research, development, and testing, including the kind that relates to space weapons. . . . We are talking about an agreement that is supposed to strengthen peace, instead of subjecting it to new dangers.

Reagan: I'm not demanding the right to deploy ABMs in space, I'm only talking about research permitted by the ABM Treaty. . . . We have differing interpretations of the ABM Treaty, that's a fact.

Gorbachev: We are . . . seeing to it that SDI testing takes place only in the laboratory. We cannot go along with allowing it to come out in the atmosphere or into space. That is unacceptable to us. It is a question of principle.

Reagan: I cannot go along with restrictions on the plan as you demand.

Gorbachev: In regard to laboratories. Is that your final position? If so, we can end our meeting at this point.

Reagan: Yes it is.

Gorbachev: You must understand me. To us the laboratory issue is not a matter of stubbornness or hardheadedness. . . . It is all too serious. . . . [T]he American side is pushing us to agree to give them the right to create space weapons. That is unacceptable to us.

Reagan: I can't go along with that. . . . In my country . . . I have a lot of critics who wield great influence. . . . They will accuse me of breaking my promise to the people of the United States regarding SDI. . . .

Gorbachev: You are now addressing me in a trusting manner. If we sign a package . . . you will become, without exaggeration, a great president. . . .

If not, then let's part at this point and forget about Reykjavik. . . .

I firmly believed that we could come to an agreement. Otherwise . . . I would not have come here in the name of the Soviet leadership. . . . [I]f we manage to achieve deep reductions and the destruction of nuclear weapons, all of your critics will not dare open their mouths. . . . The American side has essentially not made any concessions, not a single major step to meet us halfway. . . .

Reagan: I want to say one thing to you as one political leader to another. . . . I ask you as a political leader to take one step. . . . Let me say frankly that if I give you what you ask it will definitely hurt me badly at home.

Gorbachev: All right, then, let's end it here. What you propose is something we cannot go along with. I've said all I can.

Reagan: Are you really going to turn down a historic opportunity for agreement for the sake of one word in the text?

Gorbachev: You say that it's just a matter of one word. But it's not a matter of a word, it's a matter of principle. . . . We cannot agree to a situation in which you are expanding your SDI, and going into space. . . . If I go back to Moscow and say that . . . we have given the United States the right to test SDI in space . . . they will call me a fool and irresponsible leader. . . . It is a question that touches upon the interests of our people.

Reagan: After our meeting in Geneva I was convinced that you and I . . . understood each other very well. But now, when I have asked you a personal favor which would have enormous influence on our future relations, you have refused me.

Gorbachev: I can't understand how you can ask the USSR to agree to grant the U.S. the right . . . to test a space ABM system in space . . . at the same time we were destroying our offensive nuclear potential.

Reagan: I simply don't understand how you can think that I want to gain some special military advantage. After all, it's you, with your actions, who are violating the ABM Treaty. Yet we are not telling you to eliminate what you have. We're not setting that condition and we will not even mention it outside this room. . . .

For this reason I want to ask you once more to change your viewpoint—to do it as a favor to me, so that we can go to the people as peacemakers.

Gorbachev: We cannot go along with what you propose. If you will agree to banning tests in space, we will sign the document in two minutes. . . . We are not to blame. . . . I have done everything I could. . . .

Reagan: It's too bad we have to part this way. We were so close to an agreement.

I think you didn't want to achieve an agreement anyway. I'm very sorry.

> *Gorbachev: I am also very sorry it's happened this way. I wanted an agreement and did everything I could, if not more.*

Reagan: I don't know when we'll ever have another chance like this and whether we will meet soon.

> *Gorbachev: I don't either.*

WHAT HAPPENED?

It is striking that the Soviets seemed to easily agree on such huge issues as destroying 50 percent of their nuclear missiles and taking down all the missiles aimed at the European countries, yet refused to blink on SDI.

Reagan saw in SDI an innocent non-nuclear defensive missile system, an insurance policy for the world he dreamed of where only the occasional dangerous rogue would have a nuclear weapon.

The Soviets, clearly, saw things differently.

First, the Kremlin feared the United States would gain superiority with a powerful defensive system. And while the Americans remained naked on missile defenses, the Soviets would steadily improve their own defenses, in violation of the ABM treaty.

Second, the Soviets were developing space weapons, such as the anti-satellite weapon that could destroy U.S. satellites, thus blinding many of our weapons. If the Soviets could keep American SDI penned up in a laboratory, they would have a great advantage in missile defenses and space weapons. In other words, the Soviets wanted their superiority in this arena guaranteed—they wanted to make sure that the United States did not create or use any space weapons, while, of course, the Soviets could use theirs.

Moreover, there were two other major issues at play that the Soviets carefully did not talk about—their blatant disregard for the ABM treaty and the massive increase in their strategic nuclear stockpile. They refused to admit that the Krasnoyarsk radar facility existed, and while Gorbachev had been talking about abolishing nuclear weapons, he had in fact been adding to his stockpile (7,569 new Soviet nuclear missiles for the years 1985 and 1986, against only 44 added by the United States during that time).

Looking back on those two days in Iceland with all this in mind, Gorbachev's insistence on locking U.S. SDI away in a laboratory become less puzzling.

A few years after the Reykjavik summit Reagan explained some of what he thought had happened:

At Reykjavik, my hope for a nuclear-free world soared briefly, then fell during one of the longest, most disappointing—and ultimately angriest—days of my presidency. . . . For a day and a half, Gorbachev and I made progress on arms reduction that even now seems breathtaking. On the first day he accepted in principle our zero-zero proposal for the elimination of nuclear missiles in Europe, and my proposal, made the previous July, for the elimination of *all* ballistic missiles over ten years.

As the day wore on, I began to wonder whether the Chernobyl accident . . . was behind Gorbachev's new eagerness to discuss abolishing nuclear weapons. . . . I wondered: Has Chernobyl made Gorbachev think about the effects of a missile with ten nuclear warheads?

He and I had at it all afternoon. I proposed that in the first phase of our plan to eliminate our nuclear weapons each of us would scrap fifty percent of our missiles. . . . At the end of a long day, George Shultz suggested that we give the notes we had made during the meeting to our teams so they could put in writing what had been agreed to and what sticking points remained. . . . George and I were very excited. . . .

George and I couldn't believe what was happening. We were getting amazing agreements. As the day went on I felt something momentous was occurring.

As evening approached, I thought to myself: Look what we have accomplished—we have negotiated the most massive weapons reductions in history. I thought we were in complete agreement and were going to achieve something remarkable.

Then Gorbachev threw us a curve. With a smile on his face, he said: "This all depends, of course, on you giving up SDI." I couldn't believe it and blew my top. There is no way we are going to give up research to find a defense weapon against nuclear missiles. It had been the Strategic Defense Initiative that had brought the Soviet Union to Geneva and Reykjavik. I wasn't going to renege on my promises to the American people.

We knew from intelligence information that the Soviets were secretly researching a missile defense system similar to the SDI; their technology was inferior to ours, but if we stopped work on the SDI and they continued work on their system, it meant we might wake up one morning to learn they alone had a defense against missiles.

We couldn't afford that. The SDI was an insurance policy to guarantee that the Soviets kept the commitments Gorbachev and I were making at Reykjavik. We had had enough experience with Soviet treaty violations to know that kind of insurance was necessary. . . .

From the American vantage point, I said, it looks as if the Soviets didn't want us to proceed with the SDI because the United States was ahead in this technology and they were trying to catch up. . . .

I realized he had brought me to Iceland with one purpose: To kill the Strategic Defense Initiative. He must have known from the beginning he was going to bring it up at the last minute.

In my diary that night I wrote: He wanted language that would have killed SDI. The price was high but I wouldn't sell, and that's how the day ended.[15]

In the days after Reykjavik, a storm of newspaper, magazine, radio, and television coverage ensued, all with the same message about the mini-summit's failure.

The mass media worked with what they had, and so, as could be expected, the result was that they reported a disaster. Millions of copies of *Time* magazine carried a garish cover picturing the unhappy leaders under the headline "NO DEAL—Star Wars Sinks the Summit."[16] A *New York Times* editorial said:

> If the President's purpose at the Reykjavik summit . . . was finally to cash in, and for great arms control gains, he failed . . . the package failed and with it, the summit. . . . [T]he balance of terror remains . . . [N]ot only did the talks fail to bring . . . progress; they failed to set a date for the real summit.[17]

The *Washington Post* began with:

> The Iceland summit appears to have ended very unhappily . . . there can be no disguising the aura of collapse and bleak prospect that hangs over the Soviet-American scene now . . . no agreements, no summit plans, no "impulse" imparted to arms control negotiations, no steps reported in human rights . . . [Reagan played] high-stakes poker, and comes home empty-handed and having to explain why.[18]

However, as calmer heads began to understand the deeper meaning of what really happened in Reykjavik, the despair slowly faded away. That process began with Reagan and Gorbachev.

Within a few hours of the Reykjavik summit, Gorbachev held a long conference with the press. After making clear his disappointment, he did have some strong words that most of the reporting worldwide failed to emphasize:

> *Let us not panic. This is not the end of contact with the United States. . . . Let Americans think. We are waiting. We are not withdraw-*

ing our proposals. . . . The meeting was important and promising . . .
a step in a difficult dialogue.[19]

My impression is that we can deal with President Reagan. This
does not end contacts with the Reagan administration. They are con-
tinuing. This is not the end of international relations.[20]

The very next day, Reagan addressed the United States from
the Oval Office on what had happened in Iceland, emphasizing
the fact that more than nuclear weapons had been discussed:

> I want to take a few moments tonight to share with you,
> what took place in these discussions. The implications of these
> talks are enormous and only just beginning to be understood.
> We proposed the most sweeping and generous arms control
> proposal in history. . . .
>
> The General Secretary wanted wording that, in effect,
> would have kept us from developing the SDI for the entire 10
> years. In effect, he was killing SDI. And unless I agreed, all that
> work toward eliminating nuclear weapons would go down the
> drain—cancelled. I told him I had pledged to the American
> people that I would not trade away SDI. . . .
>
> I'm still optimistic that a way will be found. The door is
> open, and the opportunity to begin eliminating the nuclear
> threat is within reach. . . .
>
> But I also made it plain, once again, that an improvement
> of the human condition within the Soviet Union is indispens-
> able for an improvement in bilateral relations with the United
> States. For a government that will break faith with its own peo-
> ple cannot be trusted to keep faith with foreign powers. . . .
> When it comes to human rights and judging Soviet intentions,
> we're all from Missouri—you got to show us.[21]

Meanwhile, on the other side of the world, Gorbachev gave a report in Moscow. His chief foreign policy aide, Anatoly Chernyaev,

kept a personal diary that gives part of Gorbachev's view of the Reykjavik summit as he told it to the Politburo:

> *Beginning with speculation about who got the better of whom . . . But that was not our purpose in going there. Our initiative had a more important objective. The Geneva talks had reached a dead end. We felt the need for a significant breakthrough. . . .*
>
> *It turned out that on the first and second points of our platform—on strategic arms and medium-range missiles—we got to the point of having our ministers start preparing draft agreements. This experience alone was very beneficial.*
>
> *We understand the president's problems. He is not free in his decisions. And we did not dramatize the fact that the SDI and ABM problems stood in the way of Reykjavik being a complete success. We thought: Let the president consider what happened, let him consult with the Congress.*
>
> *Maybe another attempt will be necessary to breach the distance that separates us. We can wait—and we're not rescinding the proposals we advanced in Reykjavik. . . .*
>
> *We shouldn't get desperate . . . Reykjavik left me an even greater optimist . . . I would not by any means call Reykjavik a failure . . .*
>
> *The Americans stubbornly sought to drag us back to that with which our delegates at the Geneva talks have been struggling for so long. We wanted to give a real and practical expression to our agreement at the Geneva Summit. In other words, to give a real impetus to the process of nuclear disarmament. Indeed, before we were talking about limitations on nuclear arms. Now we are talking about their reduction and elimination.*
>
> *And thus, about the need to thwart any attempts at gaining superiority. That is why the central point of the summit was the problem of observing the ABM treaty. The American stance at Reykjavik showed that they have not given up the goal of gaining an advantage here. . . .*
>
> *But we still haven't lost hope. We planned Reykjavik as an event that would create significant opportunities for everyone to figure out*

where things really stand—for the Europeans, for the Americans, and for ourselves.[22]

Some of Gorbachev's remarks reflect a rather patronizing view of Reagan—yet by now he knew that he could not cajole or bully his counterpart. Reagan had learned the same thing about Gorbachev. Neither would give in until he felt it advantageous to do so. When that happened—when one man quit—if the winner was wise, he would not crow about his victory.

Instead he would move on to the next crisis.

Chapter 19

~

THE IRAN-CONTRA
CONTROVERSY

It was a mistake.
—RONALD REAGAN, MARCH 4, 1987

Reagan was now almost seventy-six years old and had a little over two years left in his term of office. If he couldn't accomplish his dream of arms reduction soon, it wouldn't happen at all. So, as November 1986 approached, he was preparing to make another push at the Soviets.

Then things began to unravel.

First, on November 4, 1986, the Democrats took control of the Senate. To be sure, Reagan had had to contend with a heavily Democratic House of Representatives for the first six years of his presidency, and they had proved to be an obstacle. But the Republican-controlled Senate had saved this from becoming an insurmountable political problem. But once all the votes from the 1986 election were in, the Democrats had gone from a six-senator disadvantage to a ten-senator advantage. The Democrats were suddenly in full control of Congress. The aftermath of the Reykjavik summit certainly hadn't helped the Republican cause in the midterm elections; newspapers and television all over the world were calling it a failure.

The day after Reykjavik the *Washington Post* interviewed one of the top pollsters for the Democrats, Patrick Caddell. His analysis was that while "the reaction in the first 48 hours would likely back the President, disappointment and disagreement with his Iceland decision could eventually 'mean 2 or 3 points in six or seven races'— perhaps enough to swing control of the Senate."[1] Caddell was right.

And now a more serious problem emerged, something that would take much of Reagan's time for several months. At first it was called the "Iran scandal," but the press quickly turned to calling it the "Iran-Contra scandal."

On November 3, 1986—the day before Election Day—an article had appeared in a small Lebanese newspaper, *Al Shiraa*. The story made the explosive claim that Bud McFarlane, the former national security adviser to Reagan, had traveled to Iran in May 1986 on an official mission. According to the piece, McFarlane had offered Iran powerful missiles and other military equipment for use in its war with Iraq, on condition that Hezbollah fighters in Lebanon release Western hostages. It claimed that McFarlane had taken with him a Bible and a cake shaped like a key to symbolize the opening of a new relationship between the United States and Iran.

The story sounded far-fetched, and its source was, and remains, unknown. But soon it was clear that it was true: the Iranians had received arms from the Pentagon through a Rube Goldberg exchange in which the Israelis took anti-tank rockets from their stockpile and sold them to Iran, and then the United States, in turn, sold the Israelis enough rockets to replenish their stockpile.

Months earlier, on January 7, 1986, Reagan had written of the plan in his diary. Ostensibly, the United States was not trading arms for hostages, but others saw it as doing just that. Here is how Reagan explained what was being done:

> The other issue is a highly secret convoluted process that sees Israel freeing some 20 Hizballahs who aren't really guilty of any blood letting. At the same time they sell Iran some

"Tow" anti-tank weapons. We in turn sell Israel replacements & the Hizballah free our 5 hostages. Iran also pledges there will be no more kidnappings.

We sit quietly by & never reveal how we got them back.[2]

With the plan now public knowledge, the Reagan administration faced a serious problem—Iran was supposedly one of our enemies, and shipping it weapons was in circumvention of U.S. law.

Lots of questions were asked, but answers were rare. Why would the United States swap rockets for hostages? Why would Israel want to help the Americans? Why was the United States helping Iran in its war with Iraq? Reagan's press conference of November 19 only added to the confusion.

Then, three weeks after the *Al Shiraa* article, the scandal really exploded.

Attorney General Meese's investigation of the arms-for-hostages deal revealed that the men who had dreamed up the idea had had an even cuter twist. First, the United States shipped rockets to Israel. Then Israel shipped the rockets to Iran and exacted an exorbitant price for them. Next the Israelis turned some of the excess money over to the Americans, who were now free to give it to anti-Communist freedom fighters in Nicaragua, El Salvador, and elsewhere in Latin America—the Contras. This effectively circumvented Congress's rulings about funding the Contras.

Now President Reagan had a new scandal on his hands. As soon as he heard what was going on, he called for a meeting of the National Security Planning Group. At a meeting convened at 10:15 a.m. on Tuesday, November 25, 1986, Reagan asked Meese to brief the top advisers on this new, explosive find. The participants in the meeting were George Bush, George Shultz, Caspar Weinberger, James Baker, William Casey, and Don Regan. The meeting only lasted fifty-four minutes, but that was more than enough to tell Reagan that something was seriously wrong.

Someone had had enough authority to command tons of

powerful weapons, sell them to Iran, and then use the money they had made to support the Contras in Central America—without telling the president. Not only was it against the law, it was also contemptuous of the president. Reagan knew he had to move fast and find out what was going on. This was happening on his watch, and if he did not get to the bottom of it, he would be blamed for what had happened.

When he left the National Security Planning Group meeting he headed directly to the Cabinet Room, where he spent the next thirty-seven minutes telling ten leaders of the House and Senate what he knew. He answered their questions, then left and walked outside to meet the press, to whom he laid out everything he knew and explained the next steps he would take. Here are the excerpts of what Reagan said at noon on November 25, 1986:

> Last Friday, after becoming concerned . . . with the implementation of my policy toward Iran, I directed the Attorney General to undertake a review. . . . [H]is preliminary findings . . . led me to conclude that I was not fully informed on the nature of one of the activities undertaken in connection with this initiative. This action raises serious questions. . . .
>
> Determination of the full details of this action will require further review and investigation by the Department of Justice. Looking to the future, I will appoint a Special Review Board. . . . I anticipate receiving the reports . . . at the earliest possible date. . . .
>
> Vice Admiral John Poindexter has asked to be relieved of his assignment as Assistant to the President for National Security Affairs and to return to . . . the Navy. Lieutenant Colonel Oliver North [Deputy Director of Political-Military Affairs] has been relieved of his duties on the National Security Council staff.
>
> I am deeply troubled that the implementation of a policy aimed at resolving a truly tragic situation in the Middle East

has resulted in such controversy. . . . I believe our policy goals toward Iran were well founded. However . . . in one aspect, implementation of that policy was seriously flawed. While I cannot reverse what has happened, I'm initiating steps . . . to assure that the implementation of all future foreign and national security policy initiatives will proceed only in accordance with my authorization.[3]

Many found it difficult to believe that the president had been unaware of what was being done. The Democrats, now in full control of the Congress, initiated their own investigations. In 1974, a different kind of scandal had grown so large that it forced President Nixon to quit. Now the Democrats were moving to determine whether or not Reagan deserved the same treatment.

On Tuesday, December 2, Reagan addressed the American people. Here are some excerpts from his speech:

Good afternoon. Since the outset of the controversy . . . relating to Iran, I've done everything in my power to make all the facts concerning this matter known to the American people. . . . I've pledged to get to the bottom of this matter . . .

The morning, Attorney General Meese advised me . . . that his investigation had turned up reasonable grounds to believe that further investigation . . . would be appropriate. . . . I immediately urged him to apply to the court here in Washington for the appointment of an independent counsel. . . . If illegal acts were undertaken, those who did so will be brought to justice . . . we will cooperate fully with these inquiries. . . .

In closing, I want to state again that it is my policy to oppose terrorism throughout the world, to punish those who support it, and to make common cause with those who seek to suppress it. . . .

The American people—you—will be the final arbiters of

this controversy. You will have all the facts and will be able to judge for yourselves. . . . Thank you, and God bless you.[4]

The scandal thundered along for at least four months, taking up much of the Reagan administration's attention. As the inquiry swept along, more and more curious things were uncovered; indeed, articles and books are still being written on the intricacies of Iran-Contra. In the final analysis, millions of dollars could not be accounted for—maybe the money went to the Contras, maybe it didn't.

The Iran-Contra scandal eventually faded away into a footnote in history, but a mystery still remains. Many of the people involved—John Poindexter, Bud McFarlane, and others from Iran, Israel, and Saudi Arabia—held important positions. But none seemed to have enough clout to make it all happen. Only one person, William Casey, the director of the CIA, seemed to be in a position that would allow him to run such a rogue operation.

Once Reagan had fired Poindexter and North and laid everything he knew on the table, the investigation moved rapidly ahead, and it soon became clear that Casey was the main suspect. He had testified incompletely and incoherently to the Congress already, and was scheduled to testify again on December 16, 1986—just three weeks after Reagan had made his first announcement on the matter.

And then, on December 15, Casey was stricken with two seizures in his office. Three days later doctors found that he had a cancerous brain tumor—in medical terms, a B-cell lymphoma of the large-cell type.[5] It was tragic, as Casey had been in charge of Reagan's presidential campaign in 1980 and served brilliantly as the head of the CIA. Because of his condition, Casey could not testify before the Congress. He was operated on and eventually died on May 7, 1987. Whatever he knew died with him.

At least one person who was deeply involved in trying to understand the scandal, George Shultz, concluded: "Casey, the street fighter, had clearly been driving this catastrophic effort."[6] Shultz had worked with Casey for over five years, sometimes closely. Later, he admitted he "wondered whether Casey's brain tumor had affected his judgment and behavior—and, if so, to what degree and for how long."[7]

As Reagan struggled with the scandal, it began to dawn on him that some of his most trusted advisers, especially in the national security area, had kept him in the dark on some critical issues and/or lied to him. He had been convinced that his actions to get American hostages back and to improve relations with Iran had been the right thing to do, but it was beginning to look as if he had been deceived.

Looking back at the scandal, the smartest thing Reagan did was to order that everything be opened up for scrutiny. If he had not done so—if he had done what politicians usually do and tried to cover it up—he almost certainly would have been hounded out of office. But he survived and with the assistance of his advisers, especially Secretary Shultz and Secretary Weinberger—who had fought any arms sales to Iran from the beginning—he recovered and went on to pursue his top priority.

In the weeks after Casey's death, the Reagan administration remained in flux. The special review board and the independent counsel were still at work, and there were major changes in the White House staff, as the top men in the National Security Council and the CIA either fell ill or were fired. One of them, Bud McFarlane, apparently tried to commit suicide on February 9, 1987, and ended up in Bethesda Naval Hospital.[8]

But Reagan soon picked up where he had left off. As the investigations moved ahead, he returned to his top priorities—persuading the Soviet Union to agree to nuclear arms reduction and to let its people emigrate. On January 1, 1987, using the Voice of America, he spoke to the people of the Soviet Union:

In 1986 the United States and Soviet Union took major steps toward lasting peace.... This fall, Mr. Gorbachev and I met again in Reykjavik, Iceland. ...

Yes, a great deal of work remains ... on the ultimate goal of eliminating all nuclear weapons. We agreed that as a start, we could eliminate all but a small number of U.S. and Soviet intermediate-range nuclear missiles. We also agreed to cut in half the number of strategic arms over a 5-year period. ...

The American people believe that God gave sacred rights to every man, woman and child on Earth—rights that include the right to speak and worship freely, and the right of each of us to build a better future for ourselves and our families. ... [L]et us remember that respect for those rights, for the freedom and dignity of individuals, is also the bedrock on which any true and enduring peace between our countries must be built. ... We welcome progress in this area as much as we welcome it in the effort to secure nuclear arms reduction.[9]

As 1987 began, it had been well over three months since Reagan and Gorbachev had last communicated, but Reagan was confident the Soviets would pick up where they had left off in Reykjavik, and he began to review his arms control strategy, principally with regard to SDI.

On February 3, 1987, Reagan chaired an NSPG meeting to go over the SDI program. Shultz and Weinberger led the discussion, as they usually did on SDI. Frank Carlucci now took John Poindexter's place as national security adviser, and General Colin Powell became his deputy, replacing another member who had been fired.[10] The acting director of the CIA was now Robert Gates, the former deputy for William Casey.

The meeting began with an announcement that Gates was unable to attend but had sent an important statement about the progress the Soviet Union was making in their own efforts to con-

struct an anti-ballistic missile system. The report stated that the Soviet Union was:

1. Continuing work on its own ABM system
2. Working on a new generation of both offensive and defensive
   systems
3. Pressing forward toward significant heavy lift capacity

It did not come as a surprise to hear that the Soviets were
working on ABM, something they'd been doing for fifteen years.
Reagan listened to the long discussion about how to proceed with
SDI testing and deployment and then, toward the end of the meeting, said:

> Why couldn't we just go ahead [and restructure the SDI
> program] without making any announcement? We could let
> others bring up any problems, and we could respond to
> them.
>
> We could, and should point out that we are not going as far
> as the Soviets have gone "under" the ABM Treaty. We may have
> only 5 years to prepare, since the Soviets are already installing
> battle management radars.
>
> If the Soviets press on with both their offensive and defen-
> sive improvements, we will be hurting.
>
> Why should we go to Congress?—just do it.[11]

Carlucci then pointed out that Reagan had "already issued an
NSDD [national security decision directive] which made commitments." NSDD 192, issued October 11, 1985, discussed the U.S. interpretation of the ABM Treaty and SDI. Reagan picked up a copy
of NSDD 192 and read portions of it aloud:

> I think it is a good position, well stated, and has stood the test
> of time. Moreover, it permits me to move as I have suggested. . . .

The whole story is in this NSDD. It covers the Soviet violations. It explains that I evaluated the price involved in my decision. It sets the criteria that "as long as the program receives adequate support." It's all laid out.

The NSDD makes it clear that my decision not to restructure the program in 1985 was temporary. But that I clearly retained the right to move to the broader interpretation when needed . . . we do need to effectively work this issue with the Congress.[12]

A week later, on February 10, Reagan followed up with another NSPG meeting. This one was devoted to arms control and SDI. The new national security adviser, Carlucci, began the meeting by stressing "the importance of security following these meetings. He noted that notes were taken by the NSC staff . . . and that meeting participants could come and review the notes as needed after the meeting. However, he asked that all notes taken by others at the meeting be left in the Situation Room."[13]

Early in the meeting President Reagan stepped in and said:

To ensure that the Soviets understood that we were not interested in a 1st strike capability, I put on the table at Reykjavik the idea of making an agreement in advance that we would share the benefits of SDI.

I made the point that it had to be an agreement in advance, so that it was clear to all that they agreed we could go forward with our effort.

Since then, I've had another thought.

Now, the Soviets want an agreement, but are determined to force us to give up SDI. How about looking at going forward with deployment—but of an international SDI, and international defense against any ballistic missile. . . .

This approach would take SDI out of the bargain. This

done, I can see no reason why we could not move forward with reductions.[14]

Reagan's idea was not welcomed. Kenneth Adelman objected: "We should not have this associated with the UN. If placed there, it would be a real loser. We can't forget that nuclear weapons are needed to deter war in Central Europe . . . we should not associate this idea with the elimination of all nuclear weapons."[15]

Caspar Weinberger was also unhappy with Reagan's new idea, saying: "We don't have to make such a trade! We should show them that it is in their interest, too, to seek offensive force reductions. If we bargain about how much SDI we will give up, we simply set ourselves up for a fall."[16]

Reagan ignored their criticism and said:

I want to return to the idea that I just suggested.

From the very first, we made it clear that we were prepared for and argued that we should share the benefits of the SDI program for the benefit of all. Our public diplomacy themes have stressed that:

- We want to deploy SDI and render ballistic missiles obsolete, effectively eliminating them;
- We don't intend to simply deploy more defense over our offensive capability; and
- We have offered to share the benefits.

The idea I have fits perfectly with these themes.

We can make it clear that we intend to go forward, with no restraints, based upon an agreement in advance that we will seek a system that is designed to hit *any* missile.

An international group can be established to monitor what we are doing. With such an agreement on defense, then we can press forward with offensive reductions.[17]

TOP SECRET

MEETING OF THE
NATIONAL SECURITY PLANNING GROUP
February 10, 1987

SUBJECT: Arms Control & SDI

MINUTES

ATTENDEES:

The President	Mr Robert Gates
The Vice President	Mr James Miller
Mr. Craig Fuller	Mr Kenneth Adelman
Secretary Shultz	Mr Donald T. Regan
Ambassador Nitze	Mr Will Ball
Ambassador Rowny	Mr Frank C. Carlucci
Secretary Weinberger	Gen Colin Powell
Admiral Crowe	Col Robert Linhard

REFERENCE DOCUMENTS:

Tab A -- Meeting Attendance List (U)
Tab B -- Meeting Agenda and Meeting Memorandum (S)
Tab C -- Mr. Carlucci's Prepared Talking Points (S)
Tab D -- Descriptions of Criteria Options Distributed at NSPG (S)
Tab E -- ACSG Paper Serving as Basis for Discussion (S/GRIP)

The meeting opened at 11:00 am in the Situation Room. Mr.
CARLUCCI stressed the importance of security following these
meetings. Ee noted that notes were taken by the NSC staff, in
this case by Bob Linhard, and that meeting participants could
come and review the notes as needed after the meeting. However,
he asked that all notes taken by others at the meeting be left in
the Situation Room.

Mr. CARLUCCI then began the agenda (Tab B) and framed the
first issue for discussion using the talking points attached at
Tab C.

After this introduction, the following discussion ensued.
(N.B. These notes reflect the thrust of the remarks made. And
while the notetaker did try to capture the speakers words as
closely as possible, these should not be considered verbatim
notes.)

TOP SECRET

Minutes of the February 10, 1987, NSPG meeting.

THE PRESIDENT: To ensure that the Soviets understood that we were
not interested in a 1st strike capability, I put on the
table at Reykjavik the idea of making an agreement in
advance that we would share the benefits of SDI. I made the
point that it had to be an agreement in advance, so that it
was clear to all that they agreed we could go forward with
our efforts.

Since then, I've had another thought. Now, the Soviets
want an agreement, but are determined to force us to give up
SDI. How about looking at going forward with deployment,
but of an international SDI, and international defense
against _any_ ballistic missile.

THE PRESIDENT: This approach would take SDI out of the bargain.
This done, I can see no reason why we could not move forward
with reductions.

*   *   *

THE PRESIDENT: I want to return to the idea that I just
suggested.

From the very first, we made it clear that we were
prepared for and argued that we should share the benefits of
the SDI program for the benefit of all. Our public
diplomacy themes have stressed that:
-- we want to deploy SDI and render ballistic
missiles obsolete, effectively eliminating them;
-- we don't intend to simply deploy more defense over
our offensive capability; and
-- we have offered to share the benefits.

The idea I have fits perfectly with these themes. We
can make it clear that we intend to go forward, with no
restraints, based upon an agreement in advance that we will
seek a system that is designed to hit _any_ missile. An
international group can be established to monitor what we
are doing.

With such an agreement on defense, then we can press
forward with offensive reductions.

Reagan's statements during the February 10, 1987, NSPG meeting.

Weinberger changed his mind after listening to Reagan and said: "This would certainly put us in a high moral position. And, if the USSR does not agree, we could still go ahead. We would not wait to obtain Soviet agreement, would we?"

President Reagan said:

> Hell no! We would press forward.[18]

As the meeting drew to a close and other advisers continued to dismiss the idea, Reagan made one last statement:

> If we were to approach the SDI program along the lines I have suggested in this meeting [an advance agreement on international sharing] then I would love to see Congress try to cut the funds for SDI.[19]

That night, Reagan's entry in his personal diary clearly explained what he had in mind when he'd talked to the NSPG earlier that day:

> NSC was about SDI & the ABM Treaty—getting ready for NSPG meeting at 11 A.M. The problem is how to continue arms reduction dialog with the Soviets & at same time eliminate any compromise on SDI.
>
> I have proposed a plan to seek an agreement that we will— when & if SDI is ready for deployment—put it in hands of an international force as a defense against any & all nuclear missiles from wherever they are launched in the World.[20]

By the end of February almost four months had passed since the Iran-Contra scandal had emerged. Finally, on February 26, 1987, the special review board appointed by Reagan—known informally as the "Tower board"—submitted its findings. Six days later, on March 4, 1987, Reagan addressed the nation:

For the past 3 months, I've been silent on the revelations about Iran. . . . I've paid a price for my silence in terms of your trust and confidence. But I've had to wait, as you have, for the complete story. . . . I'm often accused of being an optimist, and it's true I had to hunt pretty hard to find any good news in the Board's report. As you know, it's well-stocked with criticisms . . . but I was very relieved to read that sentence:

"The Board is convinced that the President does indeed want the full story to be told."

The Board's report. It's findings are honest, convincing, and highly critical; and I accept them. . . . Let me say I take full responsibility for my own actions and for those of my administration. As angry as I may be about activities undertaken without my knowledge, I am still accountable for those activities . . . as personally distasteful as I find secret bank accounts and diverted funds—well, as the Navy would say, this happened on my watch. . . .

A few months ago I told the American people I did not trade arms for hostages. My heart and my best intentions still tell me that's true, but the facts and the evidence tell me it is not. . . . [W]hat began as a strategic opening to Iran deteriorated . . . into trading arms for hostages. This runs counter to my own beliefs. . . .

It was a mistake.

I undertook the original Iran initiative in order to develop relations with those who might assume leadership in a post-Khomeini government. . . . I asked so many questions about the hostages welfare that I didn't ask enough about the specifics of the total Iran plan . . .

Now . . . the transfer of funds to the Nicaraguan *contras*. The Tower board wasn't able to find out what happened to this money . . . the facts here will be left to the continuing investigations of the court-appointed Independent Counsel and the two congressional investigating committees. . . . I didn't know about any diversion of funds to the contras. But as President, I cannot escape responsibility. . . .

What happens when you make a mistake is this: You take your knocks, you learn your lesson, and then you move on. That's the healthiest way to deal with a problem . . . but the business of our country and our people must proceed. I've gotten this message from Republicans and Democrats in Congress, from allies around the world, and . . . even from the Soviets. And . . . I've heard the message from you, the American people.

You know, by the time you reach my age, you've made plenty of mistakes. And if you've lived your life properly—so, you learn. You put things in perspective. You pull your energies together. You change. You go forward. . . .

I have a great deal that I want to accomplish with you and for you over the next 2 years. And the Lord willing, that's exactly what I intend to do. Good night and God bless you.[21]

In his autobiography *An American Life,* published about three years later, Reagan wrote of the scandal:

The cloud that descended over my credibility during the Iran-Contra affair undoubtedly affected the fate of some of my legislative goals during my last two years in office. With the Democrats controlling both houses of Congress, it's hard to say how much more we might have accomplished if the crisis hadn't occurred, but clearly it had some impact. . . . [T]o this day I still believe that the Iran initiative was *not* an effort to swap arms for hostages. But I know it may not look that way to some people. . . .

Because I was so concerned with getting the hostages home, I may not have asked enough questions about how the Iranian initiative was being conducted. I trusted our people to obey the law. . . . I did not know, during those first days following the discovery of the "smoking gun" memo, that North and others at the NSC had spent hours shredding documents. Nor did I have any idea of the full magnitude of how I had been misled. . . . I subsequently learned that North had allegedly claimed that he met with me often in the Oval Office and at Camp David, and that we spoke on the phone frequently . . . none of those things were true. The truth is—as he testified before Congress—that I hardly know him. . . .

The Tower Board . . . told us that Oliver North appeared to have diverted millions of dollars in "residual" income from the weapons sales to keep the Contras equipped and alive. I've seen speculation that the diversion amounted to as much as $8 million or $12 million . . . to this day, after all the trials and ten months of congressional investigation, there are still many details we do not know about the transfer of those weapons and the exchange of money for them. . . .

Because of his illness and subsequent death, I never had a chance to learn from Bill Casey what he knew about Iran-Contra. Probably only John Poindexter and Oliver North know all the answers. . . . If I could do it over again, I would bring both of them into the Oval Office and say:

"Okay, John and Ollie, level with me. Tell me what really happened and what it is that you have been hiding from me. Tell me everything."

If I had done that, at least I wouldn't be sitting here, writing this book, still ignorant of some of the things that went on during the Iran-Contra affair.[22]

Chapter 20

~

GORBACHEV CAVES
FIRST: 1987

Buried was the bloody hatchet;
Buried was the dreadful war-club;
Buried were all warlike weapons,
And the war-cry was forgotten,
Then was peace among the nations.
—H. W. LONGFELLOW, *HIAWATHA*

On Saturday, February 28, 1987, after six years of negotiation by Reagan, almost two years under Gorbachev's rule, and two days after the Tower board reported that Reagan had not known of the funds diversion to the Contras, the Soviets caved.

On that day, Gorbachev put out an open statement declaring "that Moscow was now ready to conclude a separate agreement with the U.S. on medium-range missiles in Europe.... 'We are putting our proposals on the table of negotiations with the U.S. in Geneva.' "[1] Finally the Soviets were agreeing to a reduction in intermediate-range nuclear forces *without* tying such a reduction to any conditions on American SDI. There was no letter or call to Reagan in advance; he was informed like the rest of the world.

Here is how Reagan responded to the Soviet announcement:

Having long sought progress in this area, I welcome the statement by Soviet General Secretary Gorbachev on Saturday that the Soviet Union will no longer insist on linking agreement on reductions in INF to agreements in other negotiations. . . .[2]

I've never felt more optimistic about the prospects for success in this area than I do today. And that's because this past week we've had a major breakthrough . . . the Soviets have at last agreed to negotiate a global reduction in the number of U.S. and Soviet longer range intermediate nuclear force, or as we call them, INF missiles.

The arms reductions agreement that, as a result of the Soviet statement, is now within reach derived from my "zero option" proposal of 1981. That proposal calls for eliminating all INF missiles. . . .

The Soviets have dropped their demand that we abandon our Strategic Defense Initiative as a precondition to an agreement on INF, and I welcome these developments.[3]

As well he might, for he had just achieved a major breakthrough with the Soviets, the result of years of hard work and diplomacy. After five months of silence from Gorbachev—he hadn't communicated with Reagan since the Reykjavik summit—the Russian leader's resistance to SDI had suddenly crumbled. The Russians had waved a white flag, made the key concession that would open the way to a comprehensive new arms treaty. The dam had been broken.

On Friday, March 6, 1987, after talking to many advisers, Reagan had lunch with his senior negotiators—Max Kampelman, Maynard Glitman, and Ron Lehman—to discuss INF. After lunch he presented a statement to the press:

The level, intensity, and seriousness of the effort in Geneva have brought us closer to significant reductions in nuclear arms. As you know, the Soviet Union has recently offered to move ahead with an agreement to cut longer range INF missiles. This is something the United States and our allies have long urged. This week, at my direction, the American delegation in Geneva proposed a draft treaty incorporating the understandings which General Secretary Gorbachev and I reached on this subject at Reykjavik. . . .

I am determined to maintain the momentum we have generated. For that reason, Secretary of State Shultz will go to Moscow to meet with Foreign Minister Shevardnadze. The Soviet Government has agreed that this visit will take place from April 13–16. These talks will provide a good opportunity to review the entirety of our relationship—including regional conflicts, human rights, and bilateral issues.[4]

Reagan was elated, but he was not about to celebrate in public until the treaty was signed. Here is what he wrote in his diary on March 6:

Then a working lunch with Max Kampelman & Ron Lehman & Mike Glitman. We brought them home from Geneva to talk about the Soviets & the proposal to go zero, zero, on INF forces in Europe.

It looks good but we mustn't get too carried away until we see how far they'll go on verification.[5]

Shultz had been sent to Moscow to determine how serious the Soviets were about their proposal, but the trip almost didn't happen. Congress was up in arms about recent concerns that the security of the U.S. embassy in Moscow had been badly compromised, and many did not think it was wise for Shultz to go to Moscow at that time. In fact, as he got ready to leave on April 11, seventy U.S. senators voted against sending him. Twenty abstained, leaving only ten in favor of the trip. But Reagan ignored the Senate's resolution. It turned out to be the right decision.

When Shultz arrived in Moscow on Monday, April 13, 1987, he first met with Foreign Minister Shevardnadze and discussed a range of items: human rights, bilateral issues, regional problems, and arms control.[6] The next day, on Tuesday, he went to the Kremlin for a meeting with Gorbachev. With Shultz were three of Reagan's senior advisers: Paul Nitze, Roz Ridgway, and Jack Matlock. Gorbachev was joined by Eduard Shevardnadze, Anatoly Dobrynin, and Yuri Dubinin. There was a spirited discussion, which lasted four and a half hours.

By the end of the meeting, Shultz admitted he was exhausted. "But," he said, "I was also exhilarated. The meeting had been tremendously productive." He worked through the night, and at 12:35 a.m. Moscow time, he called Reagan at Rancho del Cielo in California. Here is how Shultz later summarized their conversation:

> I told him that I had "consolidated all of the concessions we had achieved at Reykjavik on INF and START and had made great progress on short-range INF missiles." The President asked about likely reactions among our allies. "Some Europeans want zero," I said, "some want a number. I think they'll have a hard time arguing for something other than zero.
>
> "It's not peaches and cream. It's been a rough day. Gorbachev talked about a summit with content: an INF agreement, a Threshold Test Ban Treaty, and some overall points on START and space if these come out of negotiations. He talked about fall to the end of the year . . .
>
> "The Soviet Union *is* changing, and the strong policies you've kept in place—and the pressure—have made a real difference."[7]

Why, then, did Gorbachev suddenly agree to virtually all of Reagan's conditions? After all, their meetings in Geneva and Reykjavik had ended on a bad note, and in the intervening months Reagan's power had only weakened, with Democrats taking the Senate, the Iran-Contra scandal, turnover in important cabinet positions, and a new presidential election approaching. On the face of things, it seemed that it made more sense for Gorbachev to dig in his heels and wait for a new president, one who'd be willing to cut him a better deal.

The answer is that Gorbachev's hand was forced by the other pressures bearing down on the Soviet Union. That these pressures were growing was no coincidence; they had, in fact, been a major part of Reagan's strategy for dealing with the USSR. While Reagan did not want a war with the Soviet Union, he did want to defeat it, and he had a plan for doing so. (When asked about his view of the Cold War, he famously told Richard Allen, "Well, we win and they lose.")

The first time he'd hinted at such a strategy had been way back in 1963—long before he ran for his first political office, even before he supported Barry Goldwater in 1964. Even then, Reagan's intuition had told him that the Soviet economy was a house of cards. In his speech titled "Are Liberals Really Liberal?" he wrote:

> In an all out race our system is stronger, and eventually the enemy gives up the race as a hopeless cause.
>
> Then a noble nation, believing in peace, extends the hand of friendship and says there is room in the world for both of us.[8]

And when he became president, Reagan did everything he could, within reason, to undermine the Soviet economy, to make sure the Soviets gave up the race. That eventual economic collapse was, of course, what finally caused the death of the Soviet Union.

Reagan's approach to undermining the Soviets was simple. Access to Western capital markets was made more difficult, while export controls on sensitive technology were tightened. And some of the technology that the Soviets were able to buy illegally or steal was out of date or booby-trapped. (This was thanks, in part, to the 1981 French intelligence embodied in the Farewell Dossier.)

In 1984 and 1985 the network of KGB agents assigned to collect Western technology was uncovered and the agents were expelled from the countries where they were assigned. That was a serious blow to the Soviet economy. For many years, they had depended heavily on being able to buy technology surreptitiously or steal it. Acquiring technology had been a major part of their economy since 1917 and had been documented by many scholars over the years.[9] Yet although the Soviets' way of "shopping" was widely known, it wasn't until Reagan became president that there was a serious attack mounted on their ability to do so. In turn, this tightening of the screws quickly put the Soviets—whose scientific and technological base was probably ten to fifteen years behind that of the West—at a serious disadvantage in the arms race.

The Soviet economy also relied to a large extent on natural resources whose sale abroad could bring in hard currency. They sold some gold, diamonds, gas, and timber, but the main resource here was oil.

In 1973, the price of a barrel of oil had increased dramatically thanks to the Arab oil embargo, the first demonstration of the power of the Organization of Petroleum Exporting Counties (OPEC). The Iranian revolution in 1979 brought another oil crisis, and as Reagan took office in 1981, the price of oil was over $40 a barrel. These high prices were a bonanza for the Soviet Union, and over the next few years, though the price of oil slid down to $30 a barrel, the Soviets received billions of dollars in oil money that kept their sinking economy afloat, allowed them to support their client states, and let them continue pouring money into their military.

But Reagan, the CIA, and others who shared his views were working to reduce the flow of oil money. And in 1981, when the Saudi Arabians—the most powerful arbiters of oil prices—approached the Reagan administration for an important favor, Reagan made sure they got what they needed.

The Saudis, nervous about the Iran-Iraq war, petitioned the United States for all sorts of military hardware, especially planes.

In particular, they wanted Airborne Warning and Control Systems (AWACS). AWACS was a modified commercial jetliner that functioned as a powerful flying radar system, able to detect and track other airplanes in a 175,000-square-mile area—in short, an early warning system. The Saudis wanted to buy five AWACS jets and eight KE-3 refueling aircraft to use with them. The Israelis and their allies in the Congress fought the sale, but Reagan pushed it through, and five years later, the promised aircraft were delivered.

There is no record that there was a quid pro quo to Reagan for the sale of the AWACS planes, but the Saudis were appreciative and they showed it. They helped with Reagan's problems in Latin America, giving the Contras $1 million a month. And in August 1985 the Saudis decided to no longer function as the swing oil producer, keeping the oil supply artificially low and the price artificially high. They began pumping.

It could all be coincidence, but the price of a barrel of oil, which had stabilized at about $30, started to fall right after the U.S.-USSR Geneva summit in November 1985. By March 1986, the worldwide price of oil had fallen to $13 a barrel. And there it stayed, fluctuating from $12 to $15 for the rest of 1986. It was a devastating drop for the economy of the Soviet Union.

When Gorbachev and Reagan met in Reykjavik, Iceland, on October 11–12, the Soviet Union had been losing billions of dollars of hard currency. They could not pay for everything they had ordered. Gorbachev says in his memoirs, published in 1996, that "a sharp drop in oil prices cost the Soviet Union nearly half of its hard currency earnings," forcing the Soviets to cut supplies of oil to Eastern Europe and their purchases of grain from the United States.[10] As Gorbachev told Reagan at Reykjavik: "It is very simple. You can tell them that the money with which the Russians could have bought grain ended up in the United States and Saudi Arabia because of the sharp drop in oil prices."[11]

There is no official record that Saudi Arabia's decision had anything to do with its relationship with Reagan, but the circumstantial evidence is strong. Gorbachev clearly believed that Reagan engineered this attack on the Soviet economy, and it is wholly consistent with everything else Reagan had been doing. Regardless of the Saudi dealings, one truth remains clear: Reagan may not have fired any shots at the Soviets in the Cold War, but he surely attacked the Soviet economy. Yes, their economy might eventually have crashed of its own weight, but Reagan sped up the process.

So by early April of 1987, with the Iran-Contra scandal fading away and Reagan's political capital returning, with the U.S. economy booming and its military at peak strength, the Soviets found themselves under increasing stress, short of the technology and hard currency they needed to keep up. Thanks in part to Reagan's strategy, the Soviets were in a dilemma, their dreams of taking over the world drifting away. The new leaders, led by Gorbachev, were beginning to realize that much change was needed to rescue their economy. In effect, the Soviets had given up trying to conquer the world and accepted the inevitable. The Cold War was close to being over. The Soviets were now focused on rescuing their country, and Reagan, keeping his word, would never crow that the United States had "won" the Cold War.

Now it would just take time to file off the rough edges, sign the treaties, shake the Soviets' hands, and say, as Ronald Reagan wrote in 1963:

There is room in the world for both of us.[12]

Chapter 21

~

TREATY SIGNING IN WASHINGTON

There is no limit
to what a man can do or where he can go
if he doesn't mind
who gets the credit.
—Sign on Reagan's desk in the Oval Office

In April 1987, Reagan was keenly aware that he did not have much time left. In about sixteen months, the presidential campaign would nullify any of his new policies. And while Shultz's meeting in Moscow had been a success and the essentials of arms reduction had been approved, there remained many details to be sorted out. Both sides had strong negotiators—led by Shultz and Shevardnadze—and they had set to work ironing out any remaining wrinkles.

Moreover, the Soviet turnaround was met with some skepticism by many Americans—and most reporters. A clear example of what Reagan was dealing with, and how he was going to handle it, came in an April 28 White House news conference. The first question thrown at him was: "Mr. President . . . do you think Secretary Shultz's opinion that we ought to take the Russians at face value when they say they're talking seriously about arms control, because they want a less threatening and less nuclear world . . . ?" Reagan replied:

> Well, I think that since they—and literally for the first time in history—have actually volunteered a willingness to reduce weapons—if you look back in history, this has never been true of them before . . . I know exactly how George feels about this . . . that doesn't mean that you don't insist on verification and the safeguards that we must have in such an agreement or treaty.
>
> I think that he was simply saying that as long as they've said that, yes, we're going to negotiate with them. But it doesn't mean that you're going to roll over and just give in to something without protecting yourself.

In other words, Reagan would trust the Soviets—as long as he could watch them.

At the end of the press conference one reporter asked, "Does Gorbachev have iron teeth or doesn't he?"

Reagan used his answer to tell the reporter why he thought the Soviets had changed their position:

> No, but I think it is very obvious that he is faced with a tremendous economic problem, and a great deal of that problem has been aggravated, made worse, by their military buildup. And I don't think you have to look for change in philosophy of someone so much as—if it suits their practical ends to have some arms reduction and it suits our policies also— then let's get together.[1]

As the months rolled by, Reagan waited for his most important policy to become a reality. Things were moving slowly, and Reagan was involved with dozens of other policies and problems that were common to all presidents. But his heart lay in the nuclear reduction question.

On June 12, 1987, Reagan spoke at the Brandenburg Gate in West Berlin. Two months had passed with no word from Gorbachev about setting a date for the Washington Summit, and Reagan was getting annoyed with the Soviets for stalling. Also, ever since he had stood in front of the Berlin Wall in 1967, touched it, and reflected on all the Germans who had been shot trying to crawl over or under that wall to freedom, Reagan had felt it was an atrocity that should be torn down. By the day Reagan visited the Berlin Wall, some 760 men, women, and children had been killed by the police who watched the wall.

What he said that day was not approved of by many on his staff, who feared it would upset the Soviets. Reagan just listened to them politely and then gave the speech in spite of their objections. That day, in front of the Berlin Wall, he let his pent-up fury go, and when he was through speaking, he had challenged Gorbachev with words that reverberated around the world.

> We come to Berlin, we American Presidents, because it's our duty to speak, in this place, of freedom. . . . Our gathering today is being broadcast throughout Western Europe and North America. I understand it is being seen and heard as well in the East. . . . To those listening in East Berlin, a special word:
>
> Although I cannot be with you, I address my remarks to you just as surely as to those standing here before me. For I join you, as I join your fellow countrymen in the West, in this firm, this unalterable belief: *Es gibt nur ein Berlin* [There is only one Berlin]. . . .
>
> Today I say: As long as the gate is closed, as long as this scar of a wall is permitted to stand, it is not the German question alone that remains open, but the question of freedom for all mankind.

In the 1950s, Khrushchev predicted: "We will bury you." But in the West today, we see a free world that has achieved a level of prosperity and well-being unprecedented in all human history. In the Communist world, we see failure, technological backwardness, declining standards of health, even want of the most basic kind—too little food. Even today, the Soviet Union still cannot feed itself. . . .

And now the Soviets themselves may, in a limited way, be coming to understand the importance of freedom. We hear much from Moscow about a new policy of reform and openness. Some political prisoners have been released. Certain foreign news broadcasts are no longer being jammed. . . . Are these the beginning of profound changes in the Soviet system? Or are they token gestures, intended to raise false hopes in the West, or to strengthen the Soviet system without changing it? . . . [W]e believe that freedom and security go together, that the advance of human liberty can only strengthen the cause of world peace.

There is one sign the Soviets can make that would be un-mistakable, that would advance dramatically the cause of free-dom and peace.

General Secretary Gorbachev, if you seek peace, if you seek prosperity for the Soviet Union and Eastern Europe, if you seek liberalization:

Come here to this gate!

Mr. Gorbachev, open this gate!

Mr. Gorbachev, tear down this wall. . . .

The totalitarian world produced backwardness because it does such violence to the spirit, thwarting the human impulse to create, to enjoy, to worship. . . .

I noticed words crudely spray-painted upon the wall, perhaps by a young Berliner—"This wall will fall. Beliefs become reality."

Yes, across Europe, this wall will fall.

For it cannot withstand faith; it cannot withstand truth. The wall cannot withstand freedom.[2]

That demand to Gorbachev to "tear down this wall" has become famous around the world. But most people did not understand the depth of belief in human rights that lay behind it, nor did they ever read the part of his speech that said "across Europe, this wall will fall. For it cannot withstand faith; it cannot withstand truth. The wall cannot withstand freedom."

On August 12, Reagan addressed the nation on the goals of his administration:

> Let me turn to the . . . future. There are now 17 months left in this administration, and I want them to be prosperous, productive ones for the American people. . . . My hopes for this country are as fervent today as they were in 1981. Up until the morning I leave this house, I intend to do what you sent me here to do. . . . Let me tell you where I'm going to put my heart and my energies for the remainder of my term.
>
> In the months ahead, I also hope to reach an agreement, a comprehensive and verifiable agreement, with the Soviet Union on reducing nuclear arms. We're making real progress on the global elimination of an entire class of nuclear weapons. . . .
>
> I first proposed this idea to the Soviets back in 1981. They weren't too keen on it and, in fact, walked out of the negotiations at one point. But we kept at it. Until recently, the Soviet Union had insisted on the right to retain some of its INF missiles. But in mid-July, General Secretary Gorbachev announced that he was prepared to drop this demand. . . .
>
> We've come this far because in 1980 you gave me a mandate to rebuild our military. I've done that. And today we're seeing the results. The Soviets are now negotiating with us because we're negotiating from strength. This would be an historic agreement. . . . I am optimistic that we'll soon witness a first in world history—the sight of two countries actually destroying nuclear weapons in their arsenals.
>
> And imagine where that might lead. . . .

My fellow Americans, I have a year and a half before I have to clean out this desk. I'm not about to let the dust and cobwebs settle on the furniture in this office, or on me.

I have things I intend to do, and with your help, we can do them.[3]

Three weeks later, on September 8, 1987, things began to move. With Secretary Shultz preparing to go to Moscow to meet with his counterpart, Reagan chaired an NSPG meeting in the White House Situation Room. Present were twenty-two of his key advisers. Partly to inform his new chief of staff and two new national security staff members, and partly to prepare Shultz for his meeting, Reagan reviewed his arms control positions for those assembled. He began:

For several years we've had consistent arms reduction goals: To get verifiable deep reductions and to preserve our ability to move to a safer world through SDI.

It appears we are near agreement in INF. Now we must finish the task in other areas. I don't accept the suggestions of some that it is too late for us to get a START agreement before I leave office. I want a START agreement, but only if it is a good one, one we can verify and which enhances our security.

At the same time, I believe fully in our policy of seeking a stable transition to strategic defenses. We must set the stage for one day deploying effective defenses, and seek to do so in a manner that will strengthen strategic stability.

George's meeting next week is a chance to move toward these two goals. I want your thoughts today on how we can best use that meeting. Are we better served by movement in our position, or are our current positions the best way to gain our objectives? I'm looking forward to your views so we can help prepare George for his discussions. . . .

With respect to INF issues, as I understand it, we are talking about our positions, not a problem with the Soviets. We need to step up to what we need to agree. Maybe we ought to stick in a few give aways at the same time. But we ought to press forward on decisions.

After long, heated discussion, Reagan stepped in as usual to explain his position and what should be done:

You've got to remember that the whole thing was born of the idea that the world needs to get rid of nuclear weapons.

We've got to remember that we can't win a nuclear war and we can't fight one.

The Soviets don't want to win by war but by threat of war. They want to issue ultimatums to which we have to give in. If we could just talk about the basic steps we need to take to break the log jam and avoid the possibility of war.

I mean, think about it.

Where would the survivors of war live? Major areas of the world would be uninhabitable.

We need to keep it in mind that that's what we're about. We are about bringing together steps to bring us closer to the recognition that we need to do away with nuclear weapons. . . .

Why can't we agree now that if we get to a point where we want to deploy [SDI] we will simply make all the information available about each others system so that we can both have defenses? So that if either side is ready to deploy, both agree to make available to the other all the results of their research. . . .

Once we deploy something, won't they know about the system? So won't they try to counter it anyway? So what difference does it make if they get the information and counter it their way—or if we simply provide it to them? . . .

TOP ~~SECRET~~

NATIONAL SECURITY COUNCIL
WASHINGTON, D.C. 20506

SYSTEM II
90973

National Security Planning Group Meeting
September 8, 1987, 1:15 p.m.-2:15 p.m., Situation Room

SUBJECT: Review of United States Arms Control Positions (S)

PARTICIPANTS:

The President

The Vice President

State:
Secretary George Shultz
Counselor Max Kampelman
Rozanne Ridgway

White House:
Chief of Staff Howard Baker
Frank C. Carlucci
Colin Powell

Treasury:
Secretary James Baker

NSC
Robert E. Linhard
Fritz Ermarth

Defense:
Secretary Caspar Weinberger
Mr. Frank Gaffney

OSTP
William Graham

Energy:
Secretary John Herrington

Special Advisors to the President
Ambassador Paul Nitze
Ambassador Edward Rowny

OMB:
Mr. James Miller

ACDA:
Mr. Kenneth Adelman

CIA:
Mr. William Webster
Mr. Robert Gates

JCS:
General Robert Herres
Vice Admiral Jonathan Howe

Minutes

The meeting opened at 1:15 p.m. in the Situation Room. The
agenda was as shown at Tab A. (S)

Mr. Carlucci: This a meeting we have all been waiting for; an
opportunity to review our options prior to Secretary Shultz's
meeting with his counterpart. Mr. President, would you care to
make any initial remarks before we begin? (S)

~~TOP SECRET~~
DECLASSIFY ON: OADR

TOP ~~SECRET~~

DECLASSIFIED IN PART
NLS _M05-016 # 19280_

Minutes of the September 8, 1987, NSPG meeting.

- 2 -

The President: For several years we've had consistent arms
reduction goals: to get verifiable deep reductions and to
preserve our ability to move to a safer world through SDI. It
appears we are near agreement in INF. Now we must finish the
task in other areas. I don't accept the suggestions of some that
it is too late for us to get a START agreement before I leave
office. I want a START agreement, but only if it is a good one,
one we can verify and which enhances our security. At the same
time, I believe fully in our policy of seeking a stable
transition to strategic defenses. We must set the stage for one
day deploying effective defenses, and seek to do so in a manner
that will strengthen strategic stability. George's meeting next
week is a chance to move toward these two goals. I want your
thoughts today on how we can best use that meeting. Are we
better served by movement in our position, or are our current
positions the best way to gain our objectives? I'm looking
forward to your views so we can help prepare George for his
discussions. (S)

                    *   *   *

The President: With respect to INF issues, as I understand it,
we are talking about our positions, not a problem with the
Soviets. We need to step up to what we need to agree. Maybe we
ought to stick in a few give aways at the same time; but we ought
to press forward on decisions. (S)

                    *   *   *

The President: Well, Cap, I think we have to figure that they're
going to have mobiles, whether we ban them or not, and we will
have to have them too. (S)

                    *   *   *

The President: You've got to remember that the whole thing was
borne of the idea that the world needs to get rid of nuclear
weapons. We've got to remember that we can't win a nuclear war
and we can't fight one. The Soviets don't want to win by war but
by threat of war. They want to issue ultimatums to which we have
to give in. If we could just talk about the basic steps we need
to take to break the log jam and avoid the possibility of war. I
mean, think about it. Where would the survivors of the war live?
Major areas of the world would be uninhabitable. We need to keep
it in mind that that's what we're about. We are about bringing
together steps to bring us closer to the recognition that we need
to do away with nuclear weapons. (S)

Reagan's statements during the September 8, 1987, NSPG meeting.

After about twenty more minutes of discussion, as the meeting was coming to an end, Reagan bared his soul and made this final point:

> There has to be an answer to all these questions because some day people are going to ask why we didn't do something now about getting rid of nuclear weapons.
>
> You know, I've been reading my Bible and the description of Armageddon talks about destruction, I believe, of many cities and we absolutely need to avoid that.
>
> We have to do something now.[4]

On September 21, 1987, Reagan traveled to New York City to address the United Nations' General Assembly. Still hopeful that the Soviets would fulfill their promises, he spoke directly to the question of the Soviet Union and the United States and finished with a quotation from Tocqueville:

> We're heartened by new prospects for improvement in East-West and particularly U.S.-Soviet relations.... We discussed the full range of issues, including my longstanding efforts to achieve, for the first time, deep reductions in U.S. and Soviet nuclear arms. It was 6 years ago that I proposed the zero-option for U.S. and Soviet longer range, intermediate-range nuclear missiles. I'm pleased that we have now agreed in principle to a truly historic treaty that will eliminate an entire class of U.S. and Soviet nuclear weapons....
>
> More than a century ago a young Frenchman, Alexis de Tocqueville, visited America. After that visit he predicted that the two great powers of the future would be, on one hand, the United States, which would be built, as he said, "by the plowshare," and, on the other, Russia, which would go forward, as he said again, "by the sword."

> Yet need it be so? Cannot swords be turned to plowshares? Can we and all nations not live in peace?[5]

Yet Gorbachev and the Politburo, for some reason, were still dragging their feet. It was unclear whether they were getting cold feet on the zero-zero reduction of nuclear missiles or whether they thought that by waiting until the last minute they might force Reagan to relent and agree to condemn his SDI to the laboratory.

So, on Saturday, October 24, while Reagan was up at Camp David in Maryland, he decided to use part of his weekly radio program to nudge Gorbachev. He finished his broadcast that day with this thought:

> I'm sure you are also aware that Secretary Shultz and my national security adviser, Frank Carlucci, were in Moscow this week to talk to the Soviet leaders on the full range of our relations. We're closer now to completing a treaty on eliminating an entire class of U.S. and Soviet intermediate-range nuclear missiles, and progress was made in other areas as well.
>
> No date was set for a summit meeting, but we're in no hurry.
>
> And we certainly will not be pushed into sacrificing essential interests just to have a meeting.
>
> I'll keep you informed as events move forward. Thanks for listening, and God bless you.[6]

That night in his diary, Reagan explained what those words had been intended to tell his listeners—both in the United States and in the Soviet Union:

> I think he [Gorbachev] feels Congress has me on ropes & I need a summit. I told my radio audience I would not give anything away to bring about such a meeting.[7]

Over the years, Reagan's radio broadcasts had been a secret weapon for him. Ever since the 1930s, when he'd called professional baseball games, he'd been a master of the medium. Now, in the White House, he used that radio acumen to talk to millions of people. It is a good bet that the KGB listened to and recorded every broadcast.

The next night, Reagan reported what he saw as more Soviet gamesmanship in his diary:

> Sunday was another beautiful day. Howard B [Baker] called to tell me George S. [Shultz] & Frank C. [Carlucci]—both home now, would come to the W.H. at 5 p.m. for a report on Moscow trip. We left Camp D. at 2:30.
>
> George reported on meeting with Gorbachev, who sort of pounded the table at one point over a State Dept. paper he thought was critical of him.
>
> George pounded the table back & and the air cleared.
>
> We still believe he wants a summit but is playing a game thinking I want a summit so bad I'll pay a price regarding SDI. He's wrong.[8]

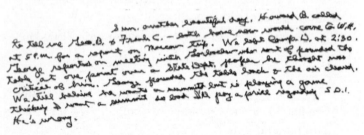

Reagan's personal diary, October 25, 1987.

Two days later, on October 27, 1987, Gorbachev finally gave in.

But Reagan was dealing with more pressing matters that day: Nancy Reagan's mother, Edith Davis, whom he'd always called

"Deede," had died, and Reagan was on his way to her funeral. Reagan wrote in his own hand the eulogy he gave at the service.

In his diary that night he first talked about Deede, and then Gorbachev:

Left at 9 A.M. for Phoenix on our sad journey. Upon arrival we went direct to the mortuary. We saw Deede looking calm & peaceful in her red robe. This was too much for Nancy who broke down sobbing & telling her how much she loved her. I told her Deede knows that now & that she really wasn't in that room with her body, but would be closer to her when we get to her apartment where her long time friends were waiting for us. . . . After a couple of hours I had to get back to the airport. . . . At 2:30 I left & got back to Wash. & the W.H. about 9 P.M.

I should have written that at 8:30 this morning I was in a conference call.

The Soviets blinked.

Shevardnadze speaking for Gorbachev is arriving Thurs. for meetings on INF and plans for the summit.[9]

Reagan's personal diary, October 27, 1987.

On October 30, 1987, it was official: the Soviets had agreed to come to the United States and sign a treaty. Gorbachev was scheduled to set foot on U.S. soil on December 7, 1987, the forty-sixth anniversary of the Japanese attack on Pearl Harbor.

In the White House briefing room, Reagan made the announcement:

> I have just finished meeting with Soviet Foreign Minister Shevardnadze, and Mr. Shevardnadze presented a letter to me from General Secretary Gorbachev, who has accepted my invitation to come to Washington for a summit beginning on December 7th.
>
> At that time, we expect to sign an agreement eliminating the entire class of U.S. and Soviet intermediate-range nuclear forces, or INF. . . . Our proposal will result in the most comprehensive verification regime in history.

The press seemed incredulous that Gorbachev had had a change of heart, as they had reported that the Soviet leader wasn't comfortable coming to Washington at this time. They wanted confirmation that the summit would in fact happen, that every *i* had been dotted and every *t* crossed.

At that point, Secretary Shultz stepped forward and said: "It's not done. But if it doesn't get done, Mr. Shevardnadze and I are going to get kicked in the rear end very hard by our leaders."[10]

As the nuclear summit in Washington drew closer, it was clear that many people were worried by what the agreement could mean. People had gotten used to nuclear weapons and were concerned about how they might defend themselves from non-nuclear attacks. Reagan found such concerns difficult to understand. In his diary on November 3, Reagan recorded a warning call from Shultz:

> George Shultz spoke about our upcoming summit and prospects of getting Senate ratification of INF treaty. Believe it

or not, there are elements who are hinting it would be a bad treaty.[11]

On November 4, Reagan gave a major speech to the people of Western Europe, explaining the details of the nuclear treaty about to be signed. It was broadcast by the U.S. Information Agency on Worldnet television and the Voice of America at 8:00 a.m.

Our plan depended upon unflagging solidarity and steadfastness of purpose, even under immense pressure. And the pressure was put on. Had the nuclear freeze and unilateral disarmament protesters won, Europe would now be condemned to live under the shadow of Soviet nuclear-armed INF missiles. . . . That resolve has now made it possible to achieve an historic agreement—an agreement that will eliminate a whole class of United States and Soviet INF missiles from the face of the planet.

The agreement we are now nearing is based upon the proposal that the United States, in full consultation with allied leaders, put forward in 1981: The zero option. The plan will require the Soviets to remove four times as many nuclear warheads as the United States. Not only will the entire Soviet force of SS-20's and SS-4's be destroyed but also the shorter range SS-12's and SS-23's.

It'll be the first mutual reduction of the world's nuclear arsenals in history. And more than that, the shorter range Soviet missiles that will be eliminated are capable of carrying not just nuclear, but also chemical and conventional warheads. . . .

At this point, Reagan could not resist talking about human rights, and once again challenged General Secretary Gorbachev to tear down the first bricks of the Berlin Wall.

We will closely watch the condition of human rights within the Soviet Union. It is difficult to imagine that a government that continues to repress freedom in its own country, breaking faith with its own people, can be trusted to keep agreements with others . . . [L]et us remember: Denial of the right to emigrate is only a small part of the problem of the repressive Soviet system. . . .

A few months ago, I visited Berlin. I stood there alongside the cruel wall that symbolizes so powerfully the scar that divides the European continent. It's time for that wound to heal and that scar to disappear. Wouldn't it be a wonderful sight for the world to see, if someday General Secretary Gorbachev and I could meet in Berlin and together take down the first bricks of that wall—and we could continue taking down walls until the distrust between our peoples and the scars of the past are forgotten.[12]

About six months later, on December 3, Reagan addressed a number of human rights supporters, including Amnesty International, Helsinki Watch, the National Conference on Soviet Jewry, the Captive Nations Committee, and others.

I appreciate all of you being here. . . . [A]lthough we're making a serious effort to improve relations between the Soviet Union and the United States, we will not do it by compromising our national interests or diminishing our commitment to the universality of human rights. Our dedication to liberty and justice for all is not negotiable. . . .

The goal . . . is not simply arms reduction. Certainly, that's one priority, yet it remains on a par with solving certain bilateral issues: ending regional conflicts and, of course, improving human rights. . . .

Soviet officials not that long ago refused to discuss human rights, claiming it was their internal affair. . . . Well, today our discussions on this issue are wide-ranging, and human rights is accepted as an integral component of our bilateral discussions.

In the last 2 years we've witnessed a loosening of the grip. Over 200 political prisoners have been released from the *gulag*. There's a higher rate of emigration. . . . Earlier this year, for example, there were demonstrations in the Baltic nations on the anniversaries of the Hitler-Stalin pact, and the day marking the Soviet occupation in 1940. The fact that these protests were permitted at all was heartening.

The free people of the West are watching to see if the emigration doors, now cracked, will continue to open. . . . [T]oday we're pleased with . . . any lessening of the iron grip on the freedoms of expressions and religion. . . . The real joy will come . . . not only when prisoners are released, but when the instruments of repression are dismantled, and repressive laws and practices are abolished. . . .

I thank you for all you're doing. God bless you all.[13]

What President Reagan told the human rights supporters that morning was the first time anyone had said that human rights and nuclear arms reductions were of equal importance.

Later that day, some top broadcasters—including Peter Jennings, Dan Rather, and Tom Brokaw—interviewed Reagan in the Oval Office. One of them asked: "Mikhail Gorbachev has a very hard-line view about human rights in his country. He seems not to understand the depth of feeling in America, and even in his own country, about the need for people to have freedom to come and go as they please. Could you not invite some refuseniks to the state dinner next week?"

Reagan answered diplomatically:

Whether that's the place, though, for what you're suggesting, I don't know. . . . [W]e're going to be discussing with him, as we have on all the other occasions—that is human rights— and we have made some headway. . . .

> We've got to make them see that the full human rights, the rights that they agreed to in the Helsinki pact, have got to be observed: the right of people to live where they want to live . . . we're not trying to interfere with their internal workings. . . . But maybe we could make them see that if their people had more of that *glasnost* that he's been talking about they wouldn't want to emigrate.[14]

The intensity of Reagan's concern for human rights came as a surprise to many people, especially when he spoke out so powerfully at the Berlin Wall. But there is no question Reagan felt as strongly, if not more strongly, about human rights as he did about nuclear weapons.

As the number of nuclear weapons declined, people would be safer—that was true. But what good did that safety do if they were still imprisoned in totalitarian countries such as the Soviet Union, living wretched lives? Reagan thought all people on Earth should be free—free to believe in their God, free to talk, and free to move as they wish, even to leave their country.

Also, there was a pragmatic reason for his belief: as soon as a totalitarian country gave its people the freedom to leave, many of them would do so, and the dictatorship would soon crumble. And indeed, as human rights spread through the Soviet Union and the countries it controlled, its empire fell apart. We will never know how much of what happened was a result of Reagan's urgings. All we know is that he pressed the Soviets on the issue time and time again.

At 2:00 p.m. on Monday, December 7, 1987, Mikhail Gorbachev landed on American soil, ready to meet Ronald Reagan the next day. At the time, the scene was utterly surreal: the leader of the most powerful Communist country in the world dropping into the United States to sign a treaty to eliminate thousands of nuclear missiles. True, it had been in the works for some time, but many people, both capitalists and Communists, had never believed it would actually come to pass.

The next day, December 8, was the big day. The treaty had now been under negotiation for over six years, and Reagan and Gorbachev planned to sign that afternoon.

But first there was a meeting in the Oval Office from 11:00 a.m. to 12:30 p.m. The first half of the meeting was a one-on-one discussion between Reagan and Gorbachev. For the second half, they would be joined by George Shultz, Eduard Shevardnadze, Reagan's chief of staff Howard Baker, Politburo member and Gorbachev confidant Aleksander Yakovlev, Colin Powell, and Anatoly Dobrynin—their key advisers.

The one-on-one meeting was classified Secret, and the only others there were the note takers and interpreters—two men from the United States and two from the Soviet Union. Observers likely expected the meeting to be taken up by discussions of what to do about nuclear weapons following the INF treaty, but that was not what took place.[15]

Reagan began by giving Gorbachev a present—"a pair of cuff links, made by an American jeweler, on which was the symbol from Isaiah, the beating of swords into ploughshares." Gorbachev responded saying it was indeed appropriate "on a day in which the two leaders would truly be beating swords into ploughshares by signing the first treaty that did this."

Then Reagan immediately launched into the topic of human rights. He handed Gorbachev "a card listing the names of Soviet citizens to whom he wished the Soviet government to grant exit visas . . . [and] asked that no notes be taken on the American side, because he wanted to make a purely personal suggestion in the area of human rights."

Again, Reagan was quietly, privately making his approach on this subject, as he'd done in Geneva and Reykjavik. And this time the results were better. Gorbachev said he wanted Reagan "to understand that the Soviet government considered human rights a priority issue."

He went on to say that "the question of assuring human rights to a multi-ethnic population was an important question permanently on the Soviet agenda." Then, "turning to emigration," he noted that "some cases were being refused 'for a time,' but the Soviet government would do its utmost to remove this problem from the agenda."

In a surprising turnaround, Gorbachev "added that he always appreciated the tact with which Reagan addressed this delicate and sensitive issue . . . and repeated his assertion that the human rights situation was improving, and that it was a top priority for his government."

Reagan accepted what Gorbachev said, and responded that "he understood that some one-half million Jews sought to leave the USSR for religious-culture freedom. . . . [O]ver the previous weekend 200,000 individuals had gathered to demonstrate on human rights in the USSR."

Gorbachev "acknowledged it and repeated that the USSR considered the matter to be serious and important, which is why it has decided to discuss it with the U.S. government . . . and suggested that this discussion be closed."

He then looked at Reagan and "noted that this had been an important political moment, illustrating how bureaucrats, sometimes very intelligent ones, forget who is really in power—people elect leaders, while officials are merely appointed."

Finally, Gorbachev "proposed that Reagan visit the USSR in June 1988, when the Millennium of Christianity in Russia would be celebrated . . . he could visit churches of numerous Christian denominations in the USSR and see for himself what was happening. . . . [H]e was willing to continue discussing these and other problems, but not today. He and Reagan both agreed to move on." Soon they were joined by their top advisers to discuss nuclear weapons and other matters.

The treaty signing took place at 1:45 p.m. on December 8, 1987, in the East Room at the White House. Before the signing, each man spoke about the importance of this act. First was Reagan:

> Welcome to the White House. This ceremony and the treaty we're signing today are both excellent examples of the rewards of patience. It was over 6 years ago, November 18, 1981, that I first proposed what would come to be called the zero option. It was a simple proposal—one might say, disarmingly simple . . .
>
> For the first time in history, the language of "arms control" was replaced by "arms reduction"—in this case, the complete elimination of the entire class of U.S. and Soviet nuclear missiles. Of course, this required a dramatic shift in thinking, and it took conventional wisdom some time to catch up. Reaction, to say the least, was mixed.
>
> To some the zero option was impossibly visionary and unrealistic; to others merely a propaganda ploy. Well, with patience, determination, and commitment, we've made this impossible vision a reality. . . .
>
> The numbers alone demonstrate the value of this agreement. On the Soviet side, over 1,500 deployed warheads will be removed, and all ground-launched intermediate-range missiles, including the SS-20's, will be destroyed. On our side, our entire complement of Pershing II and ground-launched cruise missiles, with some 400 deployed warheads, will be destroyed. . . .
>
> We can only hope that this history making agreement will not be an end in itself, but the beginning of a working relationship that will enable us to tackle the other urgent issues before us:
>
> - Strategic offensive nuclear weapons
> - The balance of conventional forces in Europe
> - The destructive and tragic regional conflicts that beset so many parts of our globe, and

> • Respect for the human and natural rights God has granted
> to all men.

Then Gorbachev took the floor:

> *I will venture to say that what we are going to do, the signing of
> the first-ever agreement eliminating nuclear weapons, has a universal
> significance for mankind, both from the standpoint of world politics
> and from the standpoint of humanism. For everyone, and above all,
> for our two great powers, the treaty whose text is on this table offers a
> big chance at last to get onto the road leading away from the threat of
> catastrophe. . . .*
>
> *We can be proud of planting this sapling, which may one day
> grow into a mighty tree of peace. . . . As the great American poet and
> philosopher Ralph Waldo Emerson said: "The reward of a thing well
> done is to have done it." So, let us reward ourselves by getting down to
> business. We have covered a 7-year long road, replete with intense work
> and debate. One last step towards this table and the treaty will be
> signed.*
>
> *May December 8, 1987, become a date that will be inscribed in the
> history books, a date that will mark the watershed separating the era of
> a mounting risk of nuclear war from the era of a demilitarization of
> human life.*[16]

The treaty was ratified by the United States Senate on May 27,
1988. It came into force on June 1, 1988. By the treaty's deadline
on June 1, 1991, a total of 2,692 nuclear weapons had been destroyed—846 by the United States and 1,846 by the Soviet Union.
The full title of the treaty signed by President Reagan and Secretary Gorbachev was "The Treaty Between the United States of
America and the Union of Soviet Socialist Republics on the Elimination of Their Intermediate-Range and Short-Range Missiles."[17]
Here is how Reagan described the event in his personal diary
that night:

This is the big day.

Staff meeting was small talk and actually so was NSC because at 10 A.M. a full ceremony on the South Lawn for Gorbachev's arrival. He & Raisa arrived in a limo made in Russia that's bigger than anything we have. After the usual routine he & I went to the Oval Office. All our talk must be through interpreters.

A good rousing meeting—we got into a debate about human rights. He thinks we have fewer of those than they do. After awhile we brought in additional members of our team. It was a good meeting & it's plain he really wants more reduction of nuclear weapons. I think we'll make progress on the START Treaty.

After lunch Nancy & I met he & Raisa and went up to the East Room for the signing of the INF Treaty.

It was TV'd live and really was an historic moment.[18]

That treaty marked the first real reduction in an arms race that, until then, had seemed unstoppable, inevitable. Reagan and Gorbachev proved that idea wrong, setting an example for the rest of the world to follow.

George Shultz summed it up this way:

The results were a tribute to the persistent effort of Ronald Reagan to stick by his basic objectives, to maintain our strength and the cohesion of our alliances, and to be willing to recognize an opportunity for a good deal and a changed situation when he saw one.

President Reagan had the courage of his conviction that Gorbachev represented a powerful drive for a different Soviet Union in its foreign policy and in its conduct of affairs at home. . . . I admired and respected both leaders, and I had told them so.[19]

Chapter 22

~

THE COLD WAR ENDS: 1988

The Cold War is already at an end.
—MARGARET THATCHER, NOVEMBER 28, 1988

As 1988 began, the United States was quiet, prosperous, and at peace. The economy was purring; in January of that year there had been sixty-one consecutive months of economic growth, one of the greatest economic booms in U.S. history. The morale and power of the armed forces had been greatly improved; the U.S. military was now the most powerful fighting force in the world. And, of course, the Soviets and Americans were finally beginning to move past the Cold War.

Yet there were many things Reagan still wanted to do. The economy was doing well, but he knew he could do more. He wanted an "Economic Bill of Rights," a constitutional amendment that would limit government spending, require the federal budget to be balanced, prohibit wage and price controls, require a two-thirds vote of Congress on all major spending, and give the president a line-item veto. And while Reagan beamed when he thought about the INF treaty he had just signed, he had many more thousands of missiles to get rid of—and he still hoped to build "Star Wars" and make it available to all nations.

On January 1, 1988, Reagan broadcast a New Year's message to the people of the Soviet Union, while Gorbachev broadcast his greetings to the United States. Both mentioned the December 1987 signing of the treaty. Reagan noted:

Last month in Washington, we signed the intermediate nuclear forces treaty, in which we agreed to eliminate an entire class of U.S. and Soviet nuclear weapons. . . . It was a history making step toward reducing the nuclear arms of both sides, but it was just a beginning . . . we have a vision of a world safe from the threat of nuclear war, and, indeed, all war. . . . This is also true in the area of human rights . . . human rights, including freedoms of speech, press, worship, and travel . . .

There is no such thing as inevitability in history. We can choose to make the world safer and freer if we have courage. . . . We have been allies in a terrible war. . . . Let us consecrate this year to showing not courage for war—but courage for peace. . . . We owe it to our children and their children and generations to come.

Happy New Year![1]

Gorbachev called the event a good omen and said:

It has brought our two peoples closer together. We are entering the New Year with a hope for continued progress, progress toward a safer world. We are ready to continue, fruitfully, the negotiations on reducing strategic arms. . . . We would like, without delay, to address the problem of cutting back drastically conventional forces and arms in Europe. . . .

One of the features of the past year was the growing mutual interest our two peoples took in each other. Contacts between Soviet and American young people, war veterans, scientists, teachers, astronauts, businessmen, and culture leaders have expanded greatly. . . . There will be profound changes in our country. . . . Human life is equally priceless, whether in the Soviet Union, the United States, or in any other country. So, let us spare no effort to affirm peace on Earth. . . .

In concluding . . . I wish peace, happiness, and joy to every American family. A happy New Year to all of you.[2]

As these men talked, the threat of an all-out nuclear war ebbed away. The heavy burden of fear brought on by the Cold War, the Cuban missile crisis, and mutual assured destruction suddenly became that much less so. The world was still a dangerous place, to be sure, but it had just become incalculably less dangerous.

However, not everyone cheered Reagan's actions. Reagan, like other presidents, received thousands of letters, and he made a habit of reading a sample of them every few weeks, the critical as well as the complimentary. Some, such as John Tringali, who wrote on December 12, 1987, wondered how we could trust Gorbachev: "Will the missiles and warheads . . . be stored and refitted on newer missiles like the SS-25? . . . The Soviet government's (and he is a part of it) single, sole responsibility is the socialization of the entire world. . . . What good are treaties when they are not honored?"

Reagan replied on January 6, 1988:

I'm afraid some of the confused media reporting has led you to some mistaken conclusions. . . . I assure you I hold to the words of Demosthenes 2,000 years ago in the Athenian marketplace when he said, "What sane man would let another man's words rather than his deeds proclaim who is at peace and who is at war with him?"

The treaty we have just signed calls for the destruction of the medium-range nuclear missiles. The verification provisions are the most stringent ever signed in an arms reduction treaty. I assure you we'll carry them out. . . .

I hope this eases some of your concerns.[3]

On Monday night, January 25, 1988, President Reagan addressed a joint session of Congress in his State of the Union speech. It was an odd drama, for his political adversaries now held power in both houses, while Reagan had much good news to report with the booming economy and the thawing of the Cold War. But Reagan did not spend much time crowing on behalf of the Republicans. Instead he quickly turned to the things left to do in the one year he had left.

Here are excerpts from his address that night:

When we first met here 7 years ago it was with the hope of beginning something new for America. . . . If anyone expected just a proud recitation of the accomplishments of my administration, I say let's leave that to history.

We're not finished yet. So, my message to you tonight is put on your work shoes. We're still on the job. . . . In the spirit of Jefferson, let us affirm that in this Chamber tonight there are no Republicans, no Democrats—just Americans.

In international relations, too, there's only one description for what, together, we have achieved: A complete turnabout, a revolution. Seven years ago, America was weak, and freedom everywhere was under siege. Today America is strong, and democracy is everywhere on the move. From Central America to East Asia, ideas like free markets and democratic reforms and human rights are taking hold. . . . We've rebuilt our defenses.

And of all our accomplishments, none can give us more satisfaction than knowing that our young people are again proud to wear our country's uniform.

None of us would have dared imagine 7 years ago, a chance to rid the world of the two great nightmares of the postwar era. I speak of the startling hope of giving our children a future free of both totalitarianism and nuclear terror.

Tonight, then, we're strong, prosperous, at peace—and we are free. This is the State of our Union. . . . [M]y thinking on the next year is quite simple: Let's make this the best of 8. And that means it is all out—right to the finish line.[4]

As the clock ticked down on his presidency, Reagan returned to work on his number one priority—making further progress toward his dream of nuclear disarmament. Yes, the INF treaty had been a historic moment, but a bigger prize was in sight: destroying half of both countries' multi-warhead intercontinental ballistic missiles. Gorbachev had agreed on this idea, but working out the details would be complicated and difficult and would take more time.

On February 9, 1988, Reagan called in twenty-three of his key advisers for an NSPG meeting discussing U.S. options for arms reduction at the upcoming summit in Moscow in May. Reagan, who chaired the meeting as usual, began by laying his thoughts on the table:[5]

> We have important issues to discuss today.
>
> If the Soviets and we have a Moscow summit, it could be the most important meeting of all. We now have a range of arms control options, but depending on how we use our time, our options will narrow. I need your honest assessments of what we can and should achieve in Moscow.
>
> I would like to use the remaining months of this Administration to the best advantage. I meant what I said in the State of the Union—we should all have our work shoes on. At the same time, I know how much must be accomplished before we can conclude another arms agreement with the Soviets.
>
> I will not rush to an agreement for agreements' sake. So we should use this meeting to identify the options that should be protected and the work that is required to protect them. If we are to achieve our objectives, all the departments and agencies will have to work hard and work together.

Then, after listening to General Powell and Secretary Shultz for about fifteen minutes, Reagan added one more thought:

From my past experiences as a labor negotiator, maybe we need to do this:

We need to go for the gold.

You need to put down what the ideal agreement would be. After you've done that, you can decide among ourselves what our bottom lines should be—what we can and what [we] can't give up. . . . Also, where there's no bargaining—those items on which we can't bargain. And we should set up the things that are not essential.

Now, once you have that, then you can see the negotiating pattern of what you absolutely *must* get, what you could try for but you'd still have a good agreement if you didn't get, but the bottom line is you've got to go for the gold.

There are things that we simply can't retreat on. One of them is verification. . . . We must not ignore certain things.

First of all, the situation is not the same as in INF. In this case, the Soviets want a START Treaty too. In INF we were the demandeurs. They had the SS-20's. We had to force them out of them. But in this case, it's very evident that they, too, want a START agreement. They feel they need START. In that context, I can't be too pessimistic. One thing of interest is that they have an innate eye to protect the homeland at all cost, and it may be that they recognized after Chernobyl that facing the nuclear force they face, they can't do this.

So I think we must press.

Powell then summed up what Reagan was saying. "I think we have, therefore, Mr. President," he said, "a decision, and the decision is that we'll go for the gold, and we will drive towards that end. . . . We're going to throw it into overdrive."

On February 26, Reagan chaired another NSPG meeting, this time to prepare for the upcoming NATO summit on March 2–3 in Brussels, Belgium. There was concern that the British and French were very cautious about negotiating with the Soviet Union. Reagan began the meeting:[6]

All 16 Alliance leaders will be attending the NATO Summit in Brussels on March 2–3. This will be the first full NATO summit in six years. The Alliance has much to celebrate, including the INF Treaty, but it also has to confront some important problems.

The task next week will be to keep these problems from disrupting Alliance unity. I am optimistic that this can be done and that the Alliance can reaffirm its proven formula of realism, strength and patience in dealing with the East . . . [E]verybody should understand that I will do all that I can to reach meaningful and useful understandings with the Soviets—not for agreement's sake, but for the security of the Alliance as a whole. . . .

I feel comfortable about the preparations for the Summit. Our objective must be to convince our Allies to keep up their defense expenditures. We must all go through the motion of convincing the Soviets we are serious, and will maintain our guard.

In the final analysis, I do not think General Secretary Gorbachev wants to engage in an arms race with the United States, but our task is to convince him not to try.

On May 4, 1988, just a few weeks before Reagan was scheduled to go to Moscow for his fourth and final summit with the Soviets, he traveled to Chicago, Illinois, to give a long speech on human rights and the Soviet Union. Here are some excerpts:

Today I'd like to take a moment to discuss with you the subject of human rights. We Americans, of course, often speak about human rights, individual liberties, and fundamental freedoms. We know that the promotion of human rights represents a central tenet of our foreign policy. We even believe that a passionate commitment to human rights is one of the special characteristics that help to make America, America. . . . Ultimately, our view of human rights derives from our Judeo-Christian heritage and the view that each individual life is sacred. . . .

Within the Soviet Union, decision making is tightly concentrated at the top. . . . I have in the past stressed these contrasts between the United States and the Soviet Union: The fundamental and profound differences between our philosophies of government and ways of life.

In recent months, the Soviet Union has shown a willingness to respect at least some human rights. . . .

The Soviets should recognize basic human rights because it's the right thing to do. . . . But if they recognize human rights for reasons of their own—because they seek economic growth—well, I want to say here and now—that's fine by me. . . .

We applaud the changes that have been taking place and encourage the Soviets to go further. We recognize that changes occur slowly, but that's better than no change at all. And if I may, I'd like now to share with you a brief summary of the human rights agenda that I'll be discussing in my meeting in Moscow.

It has four aims. First is freedom of religion. . . . Second is freedom of speech. . . . Emigration, third, has long represented a matter of great concern to us. The Universal Declaration states that "Everyone has the right to leave any country, including his own, and to return to his country." Well, it's true that during the past 12 months, the rate of people permitted to leave the Soviet Union has been significantly higher than during the preceding 6 years. . . . We're heartened by this progress. Our hope is that the Soviets grant all their people full and complete freedom of movement. Fourth, making the progress more permanent. . . .

Even more important, this recognition of human rights will advance the cause of peace.[7]

While Reagan's speech was given in Chicago, he was very conscious that he'd be speaking to Gorbachev in a few weeks, and his words were clearly meant to be heard in Moscow. The reporters for the TASS news agency rarely missed what Reagan was saying, especially when it was about the Soviet Union.

On May 27, on the way to Moscow for the summit, Reagan stopped over in Helsinki and spoke to the League of Finnish-American Societies. This speech—about the Helsinki agreement on human rights, to which the Soviet Union was a signatory—rang out even more clearly as a message to the Soviet Union. Here is the essence of Reagan's seven-page speech:

In just 2 days, I will meet in Moscow with General Secretary Gorbachev. It will be our fourth set of face-to-face talks since 1985. . . . We will pursue progress in arms reduction negotiations across the board. . . . And our agenda now includes human rights as an integral component. . . . The General Secretary has spoken often and forthrightly on the problems confronting the Soviet Union . . . things have happened that all of us applaud. The list includes the release from labor camps or exile of people like Andrei Sakharov . . . and many other prisoners of conscience, the publication of books like "Dr. Zhivago," and allowing higher levels of emigration. . . .

There is no true international security without respect for human rights. . . . [T]here are a number of steps, which, if taken, would help ensure the deepening and institutionalization of promising reforms . . . the Soviet leaders could agree to tear down the Berlin Wall, and all barriers between Eastern and Western Europe.[8]

At about 2:00 p.m. on Sunday, May 29, 1988, the Reagans landed in Moscow. Reagan—now seventy-seven years old—had never been to the Communist homeland, and he had obviously looked forward to the journey. It was yet another sign that the Cold War seemed to be quietly, softly, gently sliding away.

As President Reagan walked down the steps to Soviet ground, he was met with what must have been a surprising sight. It was best told by one of the reporters who came with him, Don Oberdorfer of the *Washington Post*:

> President and Mrs. Ronald Reagan, waving . . . stepped out of the plane into the bright sunlight of a magical Moscow. The streets had been cleaned, the trashy residue of the Russian winter had been hauled away, and nearly every place on the official program had been painted or refurbished. The drab, ugly city I had seen in April had become, for a few days at least, a beautiful and gleaming capital.
>
> Reagan's first three summit meetings with Gorbachev had been in winter: the icy blasts of Geneva in November, the frigid gusts of Iceland in October, the short days and chilly nights of Washington in December.[9]

Later, as Reagan arrived at the Kremlin, he commented that his welcome was like summer and, referring to the INF treaty that had just been ratified, said it looked like:

Some of those seeds are beginning to bear fruit.[10]

About an hour later after his plane landed, Reagan was walking into St. Catherine Hall in the Kremlin for a one-on-one meeting with Gorbachev. St. Catherine Hall is famous for its light blue and gold ceilings, about thirty feet high, and huge doors made of gold.

Except for the interpreters and the note takers, the two men were again alone, just as they had been in Reykjavik. And again, their conversation was not what one might have expected. There was little negotiating, despite the fact that the subject of the summit—reducing strategic nuclear weapons—was the heart and soul of the Cold War. All seemed to be settled except for a few details and a signing. Here are excerpts from the interpreters' memoranda of their private meeting:

Gorbachev greeted the president warmly, and said right away that he was:

> *Very determined to continue the growing dialogue which was gaining momentum in Soviet-American relations . . . I think that in recent years, since the statement we signed in Geneva, there are reasons to see change for the better. . . . The most important result of the change is to make the whole international climate better and healthier. Neither side could have done it alone. The Soviet leadership could not have done it alone. The two sides had to do it together . . . the President's personal contribution has counted for a lot.*
>
> *And I am not just saying nice words.*

President Reagan responded:

> Both sides have come a long way since I first wrote to you in 1985. History will record that period positively, and that was true not just for our relations. With the INF Accord, we have made the world a little bit safer with some of the things we have done.

Gorbachev agreed, and Reagan said they still had much to do. Gorbachev then said he would like to return to their first meeting in Geneva:

> *You mentioned it. It was our first meeting, and we would return to it again and again. Looking back to Geneva, from the position achieved today, it is possible to give high marks to the important political statements that we made there.*

There we said in a joint statement that nuclear war cannot be won and must never be fought; that no war was admissible; that neither side sought military superiority. It was a strong statement by the leaders of the two great powers, and it has received much attention in the world.

The discussion continued in the same tone as Reagan moved on to discuss religion and human rights. Gorbachev did not openly agree with many of the ideas that Reagan was urging on him, but he listened respectfully. And in the past year there had indeed been significant changes, with dissidents released from prison and churches rebuilt. Progress was slow, but it was tangible.

As their one-on-one meeting came to a close, Gorbachev said:

I am very pleased with this first discussion. It confirms that the two of us are still on very friendly terms. I hope this means that we are truly beginning to build trust between our two countries. I told Secretary Shultz that we were just beginning to be on good terms with your administration, and along comes an election. But we still want movement; there is still time to accomplish many things.

Reagan answered:

I agree. It is not protocol, but between the two of us we are Mikhail and Ron.

And Gorbachev said:

I had noticed that we were on a first-name basis since the Washington meeting.[11]

After the meeting was over, Reagan returned to Spaso House, where he and Nancy were staying. After a half hour for personal time, he talked to the staff about whether or not he and Nancy should take a walk in Arbat Street. Ron, his son, had told them that artists, musicians, and others congregated on this old Russian street, and that a visit to it would be a way to meet real Russians. The Secret Service objected because of security, but Reagan overrode them, and at 6:05 p.m. he and Nancy were driven to the Arbat. They got out of the car, and once the Russians realized it was Ronald and Nancy Reagan, the Americans were mobbed by delighted, applauding Russians. The Reagans could only stay for a half hour, but were somewhat overwhelmed by the reaction they got, as Reagan explained in his diary that night:

> It was amazing how quickly the street was jammed curb to curb with people—warm, friendly people who couldn't have been more affectionate. In addition to our Secret Service, the KGB was on hand & I've never seen such brutal manhandling as they did on their own people who were in no way getting out of hand.
> Back to Spaso House for the night.[12]

On Tuesday morning, May 31, after a second one-on-one meeting, Reagan had an experience he'd probably only dreamed of: Gorbachev invited him to take a walk in Red Square, and at 11:00 a.m. they headed out for a one-hour stroll in the heart of Communist territory, press in tow. Reagan was fascinated.

At one point a reporter asked Reagan if he still agreed with the statement he made in 1983 that the Soviet Union was an "evil empire." Reagan just turned to him and, obviously pleased with the direction of events, simply said:

> I was talking about another time, another era.

Then another reporter asked Gorbachev and Reagan whether or not they were now old friends. Reagan said:

> Yes.

And Gorbachev said:

> *Da, da.*[13]

In his diary that night, Reagan described the experience:

> Before day was over Gorbachev walked me out into Red Square. It is quite a sight—the expanse is so great it is really something to see. We stopped & talked with several groups of people who were there.[14]

That afternoon, Reagan spoke at Moscow State University, the most prestigious university in the country. Gorbachev had graduated from there in 1955. Behind the podium from which Reagan would speak was a huge bust of Lenin and a banner featuring the Soviet hammer and sickle. It would have been difficult to find a more Communist setting for a speech. Over a thousand Soviet college students and faculty awaited Reagan's words, and they were not disappointed. His message, simultaneously translated, was electric and perhaps subversive.

Jack Matlock, one of Reagan's advisers and an expert on the Soviet Union, was with Reagan that afternoon. Here is how he described the speech:

> Reagan's address to students and faculty at Moscow State University was the centerpiece of his trip. His theme was freedom, and he electrified his audience with a vision of how their future would be brighter as the shackles of totalitarianism were dropped. . . . The prolonged standing ovation he received was probably the most enthusiastic he had witnessed since the demonstration that followed his nomination at the Republican convention.[15]

Below are excerpts of what Reagan said in Moscow that day:

I want to take a little time to talk to you much as I would to any group of university students in the United States. I want to talk not just of the realities of today but of the possibilities of tomorrow.

Standing here before a mural of your revolution, I want to talk about a very different revolution that is taking place right now, quietly sweeping the globe without bloodshed or conflict. Its effects are peaceful, but they will fundamentally alter our world, shatter old assumptions, and reshape our lives. It's easy to underestimate because it's not accompanied by banners or fanfare. It's been called the technological or information revolution, and as its emblem, one might take the tiny silicon chip, no bigger than a fingerprint. One of these chips has more computing power than a roomful of old-style computers.

Like a chrysalis, we're emerging from the economy of the Industrial Revolution—an economy confined to and limited by the Earth's physical resources—into, as one economist titled his book, "The Economy in Mind," in which there are no bounds on human imagination and the freedom to create is the most precious natural resource. Think of that little computer chip. Its value isn't in the sand from which it is made but in the microscopic architecture designed into it by ingenious human minds.

Or take the example of the satellite relaying this broadcast around the world, which replaces thousands of tons of copper mined from the Earth and molded into wire. Even as we explore the most advanced reaches of science, we're returning to the age-old wisdom of our culture, a wisdom contained in the book of Genesis in the Bible: In the beginning was the spirit, and it was from this spirit that the material abundance of creation issued forth.

But progress is not foreordained.

The key is freedom—freedom of thought, freedom of information, freedom of communication. The renowned scientist, scholar, and founding father of this university, Mikhail Lomonosov, knew that.

It is common knowledge," he said, "that the achievements of science are considerable and rapid, particularly once the yoke of slavery is cast off and replaced by the freedom of philosophy."

Some people, even in my own country, look at the riot of experiment that is the free market and see only waste. What of all the entrepreneurs that fail? Well, many do, particularly the successful ones; often several times. And if you ask them the secret of their success, they'll tell you it's all that they learned in their struggles along the way; yes, it's what they learned from failing. Like an athlete in competition or a scholar in pursuit of the truth, experience is the greatest teacher.

And that's why it's so hard for government planners, no matter how sophisticated, to ever substitute for millions of individuals working night and day to make their dreams come true. The fact is, bureaucracies are a problem around the world. . . .

Perhaps most exciting are the winds of change that are blowing over the People's Republic of China, where one-quarter of the world's population is now getting its first taste of economic freedom. At the same time, the growth of democracy has become one of the most powerful political movements of our age.

We Americans make no secret of our belief in freedom. In fact, it's something of a national pastime. Every 4 years the American people choose a new President, and 1988 is one of those years. At one point there were 13 major candidates running in the two major parties, not to mention all the others, including the Socialist and Libertarian candidates—all trying to get my job. About 1,000 local television stations, 8,500 radio stations, and 1,700 daily newspapers—each one an independent, private enterprise, fiercely independent of the Government—report on the candidates, grill them in interviews, and bring them together for debates. In the end, the people vote; they decide who will be the next President. But freedom doesn't begin or end with elections.

Go to any American town, to take just an example, and you'll see dozens of churches, representing many different beliefs—in many places, synagogues and mosques—and you'll see families of every conceivable nationality worshiping together. Go into any schoolroom, and there you will see children being taught the Declaration of Independence, that they are endowed by their Creator with certain unalienable rights— among them life, liberty, and the pursuit of happiness—that no government can justly deny; the guarantees in their Constitution for freedom of speech, freedom of assembly, and freedom of religion.

Go into any courtroom, and there will preside an independent judge, beholden to no government power. There every defendant has the right to a trial by a jury of his peers, usually 12 men and women—common citizens; they are the ones, the only ones, who weigh the evidence and decide on guilt or innocence. In that court, the accused is innocent until proven guilty, and the word of a policeman or any official has no greater legal standing than the word of the accused.

Go to any university campus, and there you'll find an open, sometimes heated discussion of the problems in American society and what can be done to correct them. Turn on the television, and you'll see the legislature conducting the business of government right there before the camera, debating and voting on the legislation that will become the law of the land. March in any demonstration, and there are many of them; the people's right of assembly is guaranteed in the Constitution and protected by the police. Go into any union hall, where the members know their right to strike is protected by law.

As a matter of fact, one of the many jobs I had before this

one was being president of a union, the Screen Actors Guild. I led my union out on strike, and I'm proud to say we won.

But freedom is more even than this. Freedom is the right to question and change the established way of doing things. It is the continuing revolution of the marketplace. It is the understanding that allows us to recognize shortcomings and seek solutions. It is the right to put forth an idea, scoffed at by the experts, and watch it catch fire among the people.

It is the right to dream—to follow your dream or stick to your conscience, even if you're the only one in a sea of doubters. Freedom is the recognition that no single person, no single authority or government, has a monopoly on the truth, but that every individual life is infinitely precious, that every one of us put on this world has been put there for a reason and has something to offer.

America is a nation made up of hundreds of nationalities. Our ties to you are more than ones of good feeling; they're ties of kinship. In America, you'll find Russians, Armenians, Ukrainians, peoples from Eastern Europe and Central Asia. They come from every part of this vast continent, from every continent, to live in harmony, seeking a place where each cultural heritage is respected, each is valued for its diverse strengths and beauties and the richness it brings to our lives. Recently, a few individuals and families have been allowed to visit relatives in the West. We can only hope that it won't be long before all are allowed to do so and Ukrainian-Americans, Baltic-Americans, Armenian-Americans can freely visit their homelands, just as this Irish-American visits his.

Freedom, it has been said, makes people selfish and materialistic, but Americans are one of the most religious peoples on Earth. Because they know that liberty, just as life itself, is not earned but a gift from God, they seek to share that gift with the world.

But I hope you know I go on about these things not simply

to extol the virtues of my own country but to speak to the true greatness of the heart and soul of your land. Who, after all, needs to tell the land of Dostoyevski about the quest for truth, the home of Kandinski and Scriabin about imagination, the rich and noble culture of the Uzbek man of letters Alisher Navoi about beauty and heart? The great culture of your diverse land speaks with a glowing passion to all humanity.

Let me cite one of the most eloquent contemporary passages on human freedom. It comes, not from the literature of America, but from this country, from one of the greatest writers of the 20th century, Boris Pasternak, in the novel "Dr. Zhivago." He writes: "I think that if the beast who sleeps in man could be held down by threats—any kind of threat, whether of jail or of retribution after death—then the highest emblem of humanity would be the lion tamer in the circus with his whip, not the prophet who sacrificed himself. But this is just the point—what has for centuries raised man above the beast is not the cudgel, but an inward music—the irresistible power of unarmed truth."

The irresistible power of unarmed truth.

Today the world looks expectantly to signs of change, steps toward greater freedom in the Soviet Union. We watch and we hope as we see positive changes taking place. There are some, I know, in your society who fear that change will bring only disruption and discontinuity, who fear to embrace the hope of the future—sometimes it takes faith.

We should remember that reform that is not institutionalized will always be insecure. Such freedom will always be looking over its shoulder. A bird on a tether, no matter how long the rope, can always be pulled back. And that is why, in my conversation with General Secretary Gorbachev, I have spoken of how important it is to institutionalize change—to put guarantees on reform. And we've been talking together about one sad reminder of a divided world: the Berlin Wall. It's time to remove the barriers that keep people apart.

Just a few years ago, few would have imagined the progress our two nations have made together. The INF treaty, which General Secretary Gorbachev and I signed last December in Washington and whose instruments of ratification we will exchange tomorrow—[is] the first true nuclear arms reduction treaty in history, calling for the elimination of an entire class of U.S. and Soviet nuclear missiles.

I've been told that there's a popular song in your country—perhaps you know it—whose evocative refrain asks the question, "Do the Russians want a war?"

In answer it says: "Go ask that silence lingering in the air, above the birch and poplar there; beneath those trees the soldiers lie. Go ask my mother, ask my wife; then you will have to ask no more, 'Do the Russians want a war?'"

But what of your one-time allies? What of those who embraced you on the Elbe? What if we were to ask the watery graves of the Pacific or the European battlefields where America's fallen were buried far from home? What if we were to ask their mothers, sisters, and sons, do Americans want war? Ask us, too, and you'll find the same answer, the same longing in every heart. People do not make wars; governments do. And no mother would ever willingly sacrifice her sons for territorial gain, for economic advantage, for ideology. A people free to choose will always choose peace. . . .

Your generation is living in one of the most exciting, hopeful times in Soviet history. It is a time when the first breath of freedom stirs the air and the heart beats to the accelerated rhythm of hope, when the accumulated spiritual energies of a long silence yearn to break free.

We do not know what the conclusion will be of this journey, but we're hopeful that the promise of reform will be fulfilled. In this Moscow spring, this May 1988, we may be allowed that hope: that freedom, like the fresh green sapling planted over Tolstoy's grave, will blossom forth at last in the rich fertile soil of your people and culture. We may be allowed to hope that the marvelous sound of a new openness will keep rising through, ringing through, leading to a new world of reconciliation, friendship, and peace.

Thank you all very much, and *da blagoslovit vas gospod*—God bless you.[16]

Here was Reagan in the heart of Communism, speaking to the best and brightest of that system's new generation, and telling them there was a new world out there if they chose to take it. There was no talk of the Cold War, no talk of military threats. What Reagan told those students is just as right today as it was then.

Many of the Soviet students in the audience were surprised and fascinated. One twenty-five-year-old student, Andrei Fronin, said: "It was not the Reagan we expected. There was nothing old-fashioned or stale about him. He seemed to be so lively, active and thinking. This was a pleasant surprise."

Mikhail Vasyanin, a twenty-year-old student, said: "What I have read a lot about Reagan is that he is a fervent anti-communist. But if an anti-communist could speak so eloquently about principles that are important to us, too, that's impressive."[17]

For the remainder of the Moscow summit, in spite of some heated discussion from time to time, this friendly atmosphere continued, and people on both sides even seemed to be enjoying themselves. For example, on Wednesday, June 1, the last day at the Kremlin, Reagan and Gorbachev had a difference of opinion as they prepared to formally exchange the ratification documents for the INF Treaty. Gorbachev had proposed that Reagan sign the following statement:

Proceeding from their understanding of the realities that have taken shape in the world today, the two leaders believe that no problem in dispute can be resolved, nor should it be resolved, by military means. They regard *peaceful co-existence* as a universal principal of international relations. Equality of all states, non-interference in internal affairs and freedom of socio-political choice must be recognized as the inalienable and mandatory standards of international relations.[18]

When Reagan first glanced at the statement, he had liked it. Indeed, it was a stunning sentiment: it seemed Gorbachev was saying that the Cold War was over, finished, out the door. There was now a new world. Reagan's heart must have beaten a bit faster as he read the words: "the two leaders believe that no problem . . . should be resolved by military means."

But after Reagan reread the statement carefully, he realized that "peaceful coexistence" was a special phrase from the days of détente, one designed to be interpreted as not challenging Soviet dreams of world conquest. So Reagan went over to Gorbachev and said flatly, toe-to-toe:

I don't want to do it.[19]

Then a strange thing happened. What could have been a fight turned into a smile. "Gorbachev was silent momentarily. Then, conceding inability to win the day, he brightened. 'Mr. President, we had a great time,' he said of their fourth summit meeting. He put his arm around Reagan and turned with him to go to the Treaty ceremony, ending their final business meeting."[20]

As Reagan and Gorbachev exchanged signed copies of the INF treaty, the joint statement was modified to eliminate the two words "peaceful co-existence." The key paragraphs read as follows:

Assessing the state of U.S.-Soviet relations, the President and the General Secretary underscored the historic importance of their meetings in Geneva, Reykjavik, Washington, and Moscow in laying the foundation for a realistic approach to the problems of strengthening stability and reducing the risk of conflict.

They reaffirmed their solemn conviction that a nuclear war cannot be won and must never be fought, their determination to prevent any war between the United States and Soviet Union, whether nuclear or conventional, and their disavowal of any intention to achieve military superiority.

The two leaders are convinced that the expanding political dialogue they have established . . . can serve as a constructive basis for addressing not only the problems of the present, but of tomorrow and the next century. It is a process which the President and the General Secretary believe serves the best interests of the peoples of the United States and the Soviet Union, and can contribute to a more stable, more peaceful and safe world.[21]

Sixteen men and women—eight Americans and eight Soviets—contributed to this historic statement. On the American side were George P. Shultz, Frank C. Carlucci, Howard H. Baker, Colin L. Powell, Paul H. Nitze, Edward L. Rowny, Jack F. Matlock, and Rozanne L. Ridgway. The Soviets, many from the Politburo, were Andrei A. Gromyko, Eduard A. Shevardnadze, Aleksander N. Yakovlev, Dimitri T. Yazov, Anatoly F. Dobrynin, Anatoly S. Chernyaev, Aleksander A. Bessmertnykh, and Yuri V. Dubinin.

Many people have argued about exactly when the Cold War ended, and the question can be answered in any number of ways. But that day in Moscow on June 1, 1988, the statement released by the two leaders stated, for all purposes, exactly that: the Cold War was over. The key line: both countries were determined "to prevent any war between the United States and Soviet Union, whether nuclear or conventional," and disavowed "any intention to achieve military superiority."

The Cold War had been with us for so long, had sunk in so deep, that it was difficult to believe it was gone. Other upheavals would follow, but in 1988, the Politburo was alive and well in Moscow, the Soviet Union was still intact . . . and the Cold War had ended peacefully.

Reagan's final night in Moscow was equally memorable. It began with a visit to the Bolshoi Ballet with the Gorbachevs. As Reagan memorably described it:

> From the moment we walked into that famous hall, we were overwhelmed by its beauty. Resplendent in gold and red, richly detailed and elegant, the magnificence of the hall was surpassed only by the grace and elegance of the dancers.
>
> I knew the world was changing when we stood with the Gorbachevs in our box, with the Soviet flag on one side and ours on the other, and "The Star-Spangled Banner" was played. To hear that song, which embodies everything our country stands for, so stirringly played by a Soviet orchestra—was an emotional moment that is indescribable.
>
> Around us were our respective teams of advisers, experts and aides—but for a few moments, at least, official business was far from our minds as we were treated to a performance by one of the world's truly great cultural institutions.[22]

After the performance was over, the Reagans, accompanied by Secretary Shultz and his wife, Obie, were whisked away to dinner at the Gorbachevs' dacha deep in the wooded countryside. A few days later Secretary Shultz sent Reagan a memorandum of the dinner, containing a description Reagan liked enough to publish in his biography:

> While the memory is still fresh, I want to record for you my thoughts on the remarkable evening. . . . [T]he dinner at the Tsarist palace they styled a dacha was an historic occasion between our two countries. . . . The Gorbachevs and Shevardnadzes went out of their way to make it a pleasurable evening. . . .
>
> I was struck by how deeply affected Gorbachev appeared to be by the Chernobyl accident. He commented that it was a

great tragedy which cost the Soviet Union billions of rubles. . . . Gorbachev noted with seemingly genuine horror the devastation that would occur if nuclear power plants became targets in a conventional war much less a full nuclear exchange. . . . Chernobyl has left a strong anti-nuclear streak in Gorbachev's thinking.

Gorbachev showed open pride in your accomplishments together, mentioning that the INF Treaty was an accomplishment for the entire world. . . . In sum, Mr. President, the evening was a fitting climax to your four summits with General Secretary Gorbachev.[23]

But the crowning moment came on the way back from the Gorbachevs' dacha. As their car neared Moscow's Red Square around midnight, Reagan ordered his driver to stop. He and Nancy got out and walked in Red Square for about five minutes. With Reagan as he took his midnight stroll was a military aide with a small black suitcase—Reagan's "football"—at the ready.

The word had spread that Reagan was in Red Square, and some of the press was also there. Reagan described it in his diary:

> On the way back we drove through Red Square so Nancy could see it. Naturally the press was on hand & wanted photos. Believe it or not there were hundreds of people behind a rope there to see & wave at us. I don't know how they find out where we'll be.
>
> It was almost midnight.[24]

There Reagan was, the leader of a country that had long been the Soviet Union's bitter enemy, casually walking arm in arm with his wife in the dark of midnight in the center of Red Square. It was a stunning symbol of the breathtaking changes that had taken place between the United States and the Soviet Union in the seven years since Reagan had become president.

It was a nice ride out in the wooded countryside to a really lovely home & a good time was had by all. On the way back we drove through Red Square so Nancy could see it. Naturally the press was on hand & wanted photos. Believe it or not there were hundreds of people behind a rope there to see & wave at us. I don't know how they find out where we'll be, it was almost midnight.

Reagan's personal diary, June 1, 1988.

Seven years before, Reagan had taken over a weak, sagging economy and an underfunded, dispirited military facing a deadly enemy. The storm clouds hanging over America had seemed dark as he stepped to the helm. Now the clouds had lifted; the economy was booming, American military power and the morale of U.S. troops had leaped forward, and the United States had convinced the Soviets to join it in destroying much of their nuclear stockpile.

In 1989, the Berlin Wall was smashed to pieces, and East Germans walked across the line that had imprisoned them for so many years. Soon the Soviet Union disintegrated, and the tidal wave of change continued to wash away the remnants of Communism. By the early 1990s almost every Communist country, save North Korea and Cuba, was shaking loose old habits and moving toward democracy and free markets.

The Strategic Arms Reduction Treaty (START I), on which Reagan and Gorbachev had worked so hard, was finally signed on July 31, 1991. The agreement provided for huge reductions in stockpiles of ICBMs, sea-launched ballistic missiles (SLBMs), and nuclear weapons on long-range bombers. The reduction of those monster piles of missiles was difficult, but ten years later most of it was accomplished. The Soviets (now Russians) had reduced their ICBM warheads by 4,100, and the Americans had trimmed theirs by 500—leaving 3,500 for the Russians and 2,100 for the Americans. The Americans cut their sea-launched missile warheads by 2,200, leaving them with 3,300—a much larger cut than the Rus-

President and Mrs. Reagan walk alone in Moscow's Red Square
at midnight, June 1, 1988.

sians made, who reduced theirs by 1,600, leaving them with 1,500. Nuclear weapons carried by bombers were cut from 5,300 to 3,000 by the Americans and by the Russians from 1,500 to 900.

The net reduction of the most dangerous nuclear weapons was 38 percent for the United States and 53 percent for the Russians (who had started with far more large ICBMs than the United States).

Jack Matlock, U.S. ambassador to the Soviet Union from 1987 to 1991, elegantly summed up the results of Reagan's work:

> George H. W. Bush boasted during his unsuccessful bid for a second term, "We won the Cold War!" In fact, the Cold War was ended in spirit before he took office as president. All he had to do was set the terms of settlement, and he hesitated for ten months to do that. The tree that bore fruit on the Bush watch had been planted and nurtured by Reagan and Gorbachev.
>
> As for the winners, everyone, including the Soviet Union, won. . . .
>
> Reagan understood this very well. He writes in his memoirs not of a victory of one country over another but of the triumph of one idea over another. . . . It was the Communist system and the ideology that inspired it that lost the competition with liberal democracy and capitalism, not the country it held in its grip for seven decades with catastrophic results.[25]

As for Reagan, his last eight months in the Oval Office after the Moscow visit were primarily devoted to following through on other promises he had made and getting used to a Soviet Union in the throes of revolutionary change.

How did the old duffer accomplish so much? We know he walked into the White House with a clear vision of what he wanted to do. We know that he was a superb writer. We know that he made all the big decisions when he was president. But even now, decades after he left Washington and flew back to his ranch in the mountains of California, he still puzzles people. His spirit seems to stride the country, watching us like a warm and friendly ghost.

On January 11, 1989, Reagan gave his farewell address from the Oval Office, in a moment straight from one of his old movies, where the star mounts his horse and rides off into the sunset, leaving behind a memorable parting line:

> We meant to change a nation, and instead, we changed a world.[26]

Or, as Reagan said when he presented the Ronald Reagan Freedom Award to Mikhail Gorbachev at the Reagan Presidential Library on May 4, 1992:

> It is true that the Cold War is over. Freedom won, as we always knew it would.[27]

GLOSSARY OF ACRONYMS

ABM: Anti-ballistic missile

AFL-CIO: American Federation of Labor and Congress of Industrial Organizations

ASAT: Anti-satellite weapon

ATB: Advanced technology bomber, more commonly the stealth bomber

AWACS: Airborne Warning and Control System

CDE: Conference on Disarmament in Europe

CIA: Central Intelligence Agency

DOD: Department of Defense

FDR: Franklin Delano Roosevelt, the thirty-second president of the United States

FRG: Federal Republic of Germany

GDP: Gross domestic product

GLCM: Ground-launch cruise missile

GNP: Gross national product

GRU: *Glavnoje Razvedyvatel'noje Upravlenije* (Main Intelligence Directorate)

ICBM: Intercontinental ballistic missile

INF: Intermediate-range nuclear force

KGB: *Komityet Gosudarstvennoy Bezopasnosti* (Committee for State Security)

LRINF: Longer-range intermediate nuclear force

MAD: Mutual assured destruction

MBFR: Mutual and balanced force reduction

MX: LGM-118 "Peacekeeper" missile; a land-based intercontinental ballistic missile

NATO: North Atlantic Treaty Organization

NORAD: North American Aerospace Defense Command

NSC: National Security Council

NSDD: National Security Decision Directive

NSPG: National Security Planning Group

OMB: Office of Management and Budget

OPEC: Organization of Petroleum Exporting Countries

PEPAB: President's Economic Policy Advisory Board

PRAVDA: Soviet newspaper known for being an official Communist Party publication

PT: Physical training

RYAN: *Raketno-Yadernoe Napadenie* (nuclear missile attack)

SALT: Strategic Arms Limitation Talks

SALT I/II: Strategic Arms Limitation Treaty

SDI: Strategic Defense Initiative (Star Wars)

SIOP: Single integrated operational plan

SLBM: Submarine-launched ballistic missile

SNDV: Strategic nuclear delivery vehicle

START: Strategic Arms Reduction Talks

TASS: Soviet press agency

TNF: Theater nuclear forces

TOW: Tube-launched, optically tracked, wire-guided

UN: United Nations

USSR: Union of Soviet Socialist Republics

WH: White House, occasionally used by President Reagan as an abbreviation

NOTES

~

The following abbreviations are used in the notes:

RRPL: Ronald Reagan Presidential Library, Simi Valley, California

Public Papers: The Public Papers of the President of the United States: Ronald Reagan

RNPL (YL): Richard Nixon Presidential Library, Yorba Linda, CA

The Reagan Diaries: The Reagan Diaries, ed. Douglas Brinkley (New York: HarperCollins, 2007)

PPP: Pre-Presidential Papers

PHF: Presidential Handwriting File

Reagan, In His Own Hand: eds. Annelise Anderson et al. (New York: Free Press, 2001)

Reagan: A Life in Letters: eds. Annelise Anderson et al. (New York: Free Press, 2003)

Chapter 1: Reagan the Man

1. Nancy Reagan and William Novak, *My Turn: The Memoirs of Nancy Reagan* (New York: Random House, 1989), 106.

2. Richard Wirthlin and Wynton C. Hall, *The Greatest Communicator: What Ronald Reagan Taught Me About Politics, Leadership, and Life* (Hoboken, NJ: John Wiley & Sons, Inc., 2004), 113–14. The quotation is circa March 1983.

3. Edmund Morris, *Dutch: A Memoir of Ronald Reagan* (New York: Random House, 1999), 27–28.

4. Ann Reilly Dowd, "What Managers Can Learn from President Manager Reagan," *Fortune,* September 15, 1986, 41.

5. Meg Greenfield, "How Does Reagan Decide?" *Newsweek,* February 20, 1984, 80.

6. Godfrey Sperling, "Democrat's Strauss Impressed by Reagan Performance But . . . ," *Christian Science Monitor,* May 15, 1981, 10.

7. Dowd, "What Managers Can Learn," 41.

8. Martin Anderson, *Revolution* (San Diego: Harcourt Brace Jovanovich, 1988), 278–95.

9. Dictated letter, Ronald Reagan to John O. Koehler, July 9, 1981, in PR011 321301 Audio. RRPL. Printed in Annelise Anderson et al., *Reagan: A Life in Letters* (New York: Free Press, 2003), 375.

Chapter 2: The Awesome Power of a President

1. National Resources Defense Council. "Global Nuclear Stockpiles 1945–2006," *Bulletin of the Atomic Scientists,* July/August 2006, 66. Also "Table of US Nuclear Warheads" http://www.nrdc.org/nuclear/ nudb/datab9.asp and "Table of USSR/Russian Nuclear Warheads" http://www.nrdc.org/nuclear/nudb/datab10.asp.

2. Ronald Reagan, *An American Life: The Autobiography* (New York: Simon & Schuster, 1990), 257–58.

3. Minutes of the National Security Council, classified Secret/Sensitive, Cabinet Room, The White House, February 6, 1981, 1:30–2:40 p.m., 2. NSC 00001 02/06/1981 [Caribbean Basin, Poland] (1)(2) in Executive Secretariat, NSC: NSC Meeting Files: Records, 1981–88. Box 91282. RRPL.

4. Ibid., 2.

5. Reagan, *An American Life,* 257–58.

6. Richard P. Nathan, "International Change Under Reagan," in John I. Palmer, ed., *Perspectives on the Reagan Years* (Washington, D.C.: Urban Institute, 1986), 141.

7. James M. Perry, "For the Democrats, Pam's Is the Place for the Elite to Meet," *Wall Street Journal,* October 8, 1981, 1.

Chapter 3: Juggling Priorities: 1981

1. Ronald Reagan, "State of the Union," March 17, 1980. Printed in *Reagan, In His Own Hand,* eds. Annelise Anderson et al. (New York: Free Press, 2001), 471–79.

2. Lou Cannon, "Arms Boost Seen as Strain on Soviets," *Washington Post,* June 18, 1980, A3.

3. Ronald Reagan, "A Strategy for Growth: The American Economy in the 1980s," speech before the International Business Council, Chicago, September 9, 1980. RRPL.

4. First Inaugural Address, January 20, 1981, in *Public Papers, 1981,* 1. Handwritten draft in SP100 Inaugural Address, President's [01/20/81 and 1/21/81]. RRPL.

5. Ibid., 3.

6. Executive order 12092 created the Wage and Price Regulatory Program on November 1, 1978; Reagan's Executive Order 12288 revoked it.

7. "Address to the Nation on the Economy, February 5, 1981," in *Public Papers 1981,* 79–83.

8. Ibid.

9. Reagan's personal diary, February 15, 1981, in *The Reagan Diaries,* ed. Douglas Brinkley (New York: HarperCollins, 2007), 4.

10. "Address before a Joint Session of Congress on the Program for Economic Recovery, February 18, 1981," in *Public Papers 1981,* 108–15.

11. Reagan's personal diary, March 2, 1981, as exhibited, RRPL. Photograph in authors' collection.

12. Office of Management and Budget. *Fiscal Year 1982 Budget Revisions,* March 1981.

13. R. W. Apple, "Brezhnev Proposes Talks with Reagan to Mend Relations," *New York Times,* February 24, 1981, A1.

14. "Excerpts from an Interview with Walter Cronkite of CBS News, March 3, 1981," in *Public Papers 1981,* 191–202.

15. Minutes of the National Security Council, classified Secret/Sensitive, Cabinet Room, The White House, February 6, 1981, 1:36–2:40 p.m., 5. NSC 00001 02/06/1981 [Caribbean Basin, Poland] (1)(2) in Executive Secretariat, NSC: NSC Meeting Files: Records, 1981–88. Box 91282. RRPL.

16. Ibid., 4–5.

17. Ibid., 6.

18. Minutes of the National Security Council, classified Top Secret, February 11, 1981, Cabinet Room, The White House, 12 noon–1:30 p.m., 5. NSC 00002 02/11/1981 [Nicaragua Finding and Central America, Cuba Policy, Intelligence, Caribbean, Poland] in Executive Secretariat, NSC: NSC Meeting Files: Records, 1981–88. Box 91282. RRPL.

19. Ibid., 4.

20. Ibid., 5.

21. Minutes of the National Security Council, classified Secret, March 19, 1981, Cabinet Room, The White House, 3:00–4:00 p.m., 2. NSC 00005 03/19/1981 [Pakistan, Sinai Peacekeeping. Foreign Military Sales, Middle East] in Executive Secretariat, NSC: NSC Meeting Files: Records, 1981–88. Box 91282. RRPL.

22. Ibid., 10.

23. Ibid., 11.

24. In 1976 defense experts—primarily Democrats, with some Republicans—had re-created the Committee on the Present Danger to focus attention on the need for stronger defenses. Although Carter, under pressure from the Congress and in response to the Soviet invasion of Afghanistan in December of 1979, had asked for increases in the defense budget, his requests involved spending that took place almost entirely after he left office.

25. U.S. Congressional Budget Office. *Resources for Defense: A Review of Key Issues for Fiscal Years 1982–1986,* GPO, January 1981.

26. National Resources Defense Council. "Global Nuclear Stockpiles 1945–2006," *Bulletin of the Atomic Scientists,* July/August 2006, 66.

27. Reagan's personal diary, June 30, 1981, in *The Reagan Diaries,* 27.

28. Reagan's personal diary, August 3, 1981, in *The Reagan Diaries,* 35.

29. " 'Lyons Carpetbagger' Talks About Conservative Beliefs," *Shreveport Times,* March 1, 1964, 2B–3B.

30. Ronald Reagan. "Peace" Pre-Presidential Papers (PPP), 1921–1980. Box 21. RRPL. Printed in *Reagan: A Life in Letters,* 4–9.

31. "Peace, Speech to the Veterans of Foreign Wars, August 18, 1980," in Reagan-Bush 1980 Campaign: Papers, 1979–80, Box 949. RRPL. Printed in *Reagan, In His Own Hand,* 480–86.

32. Dwight D. Eisenhower's Farewell Address to the Nation, January 17, 1961. The official text differs slightly from Reagan's copy.

33. Ronald Reagan, "Are Liberals Really Liberal?" in speeches and writings pre-1966. Ronald Reagan Subject Collection, Box 1. Hoover Institution Archives. Printed in *Reagan, In His Own Hand,* 442.

Chapter 4: Near Death from an Assassin

1. Letter, Leonid Brezhnev to Ronald Reagan, March 6, 1981, in Executive Secretariat, NSC, Head of State File: Records, 1981–1989, USSR: General Secretary Brezhnev (8190204). Box 38. RRPL.

2. Richard Pipes, through Richard V. Allen, Memorandum for the President, *"Draft of President's Response to Brezhnev Letter,"* March 26, 1981. USSR: General Secretary Brezhnev (8100630)(1)(2) in Executive Secretariat, NSC: Head of State File: Records, 1981–89. Box 37. RRPL.

3. Richard V. Allen, Memorandum to Ed Meese and Jim Baker, *"President's Response to Brezhnev Letter,"* March 30, 1981. USSR: General Secretary Brezhnev (8100630)(1)(2) in Executive Secretariat, NSC: Head of State Files: Records, 1981–89. Box 37. RRPL.

4. Edmund Morris, *Dutch: A Memoir of Ronald Reagan* (New York: Random House, 1999), 431.

5. Reagan's personal diary, written sometime between March 30 and April 11, 1981, in *The Reagan Diaries*, 12.

6. Ibid.

Chapter 5: The Beginning of the End of the Cold War

1. Ronald Reagan, *An American Life* (New York: Simon & Schuster, 1990), 270.

2. Reagan's personal diary, April 18, 1981, in *The Reagan Diaries*, 13.

3. From Richard Pipes's journal, quoted in a letter from Pipes to Annelise Anderson, November 2, 2002. Others attending the meeting were William Stearman, William Nance, Mose Harvey, and Janet Coleson.

4. Reagan's personal diary, April 21, 1981. Quoted in *Reagan: A Life in Letters*, 739.

5. Ibid., April 22, 1981. (Also quoted in *Reagan: A Life in Letters*, 739.)

6. Letter, Ronald Reagan to Leonid Brezhnev, April 24, 1981, in Executive Secretariat, NSC: Head of State Files: Records, 1981–89, USSR: General Secretary Brezhnev (8190204, 8190205). Box 38. RRPL.

7. "Address Before a Joint Session of the Congress on the Program for Economic Recovery, April 28, 1981," in *Public Papers 1981*, 391–94.

8. National Gallup polls of Reagan's popularity, April 13, 1981. Gallup Poll # 172G.

9. Edmund Morris, *Dutch: A Memoir of Ronald Reagan* (New York: Random House, 1991), 439.

10. Reagan's personal diary, April 28, 1981, in *The Reagan Diaries*, 16.

11. Ed Magnuson, "Reagan's Big Win," *Time*, May 18, 1981.

12. Reagan's personal diary, May 28, 1981, in *The Reagan Diaries*, 21.

13. Reagan's personal diary, July 19, 1981, in *The Reagan Diaries*, 34.

Chapter 6: Going for Zero

1. "The President's News Conference, January 29, 1981," Room 450 of the Old Executive Office Building, 4:00 p.m., broadcast live on radio and television, in *Public Papers 1981*, 55–62.

2. Ibid.

3. "Remarks during White House Briefing on the Program for Economic Recovery, February 24, 1981," Room 450 in the Old Executive Office Building, 9:50 a.m., in *Public Papers 1981*, 152–53.

4. Minutes of National Security Council meeting, classified Secret/Sensitive, Cabinet Room, The White House, April 30, 1981, 11:10–12:40 p.m., 4. NSC 00008 04/30/1981 [Theater Nuclear Force—Negotiations Timing, USSR, Arms Control, Nuclear Weapons] (1)–(3). Executive Secretariat NSC: NSC Meeting Files: Records 1981–88. Box 91282. RRPL.

5. "President's News Conference, June 16, 1981," Room 450 in the Old Executive Office Building, 2 p.m., broadcast live on radio and television, in *Public Papers 1981*, 519–26.

6. Minutes of the National Security Council, classified Secret, July 6, 1981, The Cabinet Room, The White House, 11:09–12:22 p.m., 11. NSC 00016 07/07/1981 [East-West Trade Controls, Siberian Pipeline]. Executive Secretariat NSC: NSC Meeting Files: Records, 1981–88. Box 91282. RRPL.

7. Thomas C. Reed, *At the Abyss* (New York: Ballantine Books, 2004), 266–70.

8. Ibid., 267.

9. Gus W. Weiss, "Duping the Soviets: The Farewell Dossier," *CIA Studies in Intelligence*, vol. 39, number 5, 1996.

10. Reed, *At the Abyss*, 267–68.

11. Interview with William P. Clark, June 24, 2005.

12. Reed, *At the Abyss*, 268–69.
13. Minutes of National Security Council meeting, classified Top Secret, Cabinet Room, The White House, October 13, 1981, 2:08–2:51 p.m., 5. NSC 00022 10/13/1981 [Theater Nuclear Forces, Egypt, NATO, Nuclear Weapons, USSR] in Executive Secretariat NSC: NSC Meeting Files: Records, 1981–88. Box 91282. RRPL.
14. Ibid., 6.
15. Ibid., 6.
16. Ibid., 7.
17. Minutes of the National Security Council, classified Secret, Cabinet Room, The White House, November 12, 1981, 4:19–5:17 p.m., 2. NSC 00025 11/12/1981 [Theater Nuclear Forces, NATO, Strategic Forces] in Executive Secretariat NSC: NSC Meeting Files: Records, 1981–88. Box 91282. RRPL.
18. Ibid.
19. Ibid., 4.
20. Ibid.
21. Ibid., 5.
22. Ibid.
23. Ibid.
24. Ibid., 8.
25. Ibid., 9–10.
26. "Remarks to Members of the National Press Club on Arms Reduction and Nuclear Weapons, November 18, 1981," in *Public Papers 1981*, 1026–27.

Chapter 7: The Bond with Pope John Paul II

1. Reagan's personal diary, February 6, 1981, in *The Reagan Diaries*, 3.
2. "A Tale of Two Countries," in PPP Radio Broadcasts, Box 12. RRPL. Printed in *Reagan, In His Own Hand*, 174–77.
3. "Address at Commencement Exercises at the University of Notre Dame, May 17, 1981," in *Public Papers 1981*, 431–35.
4. Reagan's personal diary, May 13, 1981, in *The Reagan Diaries*, 18.
5. Reagan's personal diary, December 12, 1981, in *The Reagan Diaries*, 55.
6. Minutes of President's working lunch with Agostino Cardinal Casaroli, classified Secret, The Map Room, The White House, De-

cember 15, 1981, 12:46–1:46 p.m. in Executive Secretariat, NSC: Subject File: Records, 1981–1985. Memorandums of Conversation–President Reagan (December 1981) (1)(2). Box 49. RRPL.

7. Ibid., 2, 4.

8. Ibid., 4.

9. Ibid.

10. Ibid., 5.

11. Ibid.

12. Ibid., 6.

13. Minutes of the National Security Council, classified Secret, December 21, 1981, The Roosevelt Room, The White House, 10:33–11:48 a.m., 5. NSC 00033 12/21/1981 [Poland, USSR, Export Controls, NATO Speeches], in Executive Secretariat NSC: NSC Meeting Files: Records, 1981–88. Box 91283. RRPL.

14. Ibid., 7.

15. Ibid., 8.

16. Ibid., 12.

17. Ibid.

18. Reagan's personal diary, December 21, 1981, in *The Reagan Diaries,* 57.

19. Reagan's personal diary, December 22, 1981, 58.

20. President Reagan's letter sent to Leonid Brezhnev on December 23, 1981, classified Top Secret Sensitive SPECAT, in Executive Secretariat, NSC: Head of State File: Records, 1981–1989, USSR: General Secretary Brezhnev. Box 38. RRPL.

21. "Address to the Nation about Christmas and the Situation in Poland, December 23, 1981," Oval Office, The White House, 9 p.m., broadcast live on nationwide radio and television, in *Public Papers 1981,* 1185–88.

22. Minutes of the National Security Council, classified Secret, December 23, 1981, The Cabinet Room, The White House, 11:02 a.m.12:22 p.m., 5, 6. NSC 00035 12/23/1981 [Poland], in Executive Secretariat, NSC: NSC Meeting Files: Records 1981–88. Box 91283. RRPL.

23. Reagan's ambassador-at-large, General Vernon Walters, met a couple of times a year with the Pope to keep him informed about U.S. policy and intelligence on matters around the world. CIA director William Casey also stopped at the Vatican on his other travels, and the CIA pro-

vided some funds to the Polish Solidarity movement, often through the AFL-CIO. American Cardinal John Krol, who was close to the Pope, kept in touch with Reagan and others in the administration, especially Casey and William Clark, as did Pio Laghi, the Vatican's envoy to the United States.

24. Letter, Ronald Reagan to Pope John Paul II, January 11, 1982. In Executive Secretariat, NSC: Head of State File: Records, 1981–1989, The Vatican: Pope John Paul II (8100301–8106715). Box 41. RRPL.

Chapter 8: The Nuclear Abolitionist: 1982

1. "Interview in New York City with Members of the Editorial Board of the *New York Post,* March 23, 1982," in *Public Papers 1982 (Book 1),* 362–69.

2. Lou Cannon, *Reagan* (New York: G. P. Putnam's Sons, 1982), 37.

3. The discussion occurred at a meeting Reagan held with his speechwriting staff, probably the meeting held May 18, 1987. Interview with Peter Robinson, June 18, 2007.

4. "Remarks to the Institute for Foreign Policy Analysis at a conference on the Strategic Defense Initiative, March 14, 1988," in *Public Papers 1988 (Book 1),* 330–33.

5. Ronald Reagan with Richard Hubler, *Where's the Rest of Me: The Ronald Reagan Story* (New York: Duell, Sloan & Pearce, 1965), 138–40. Emphasis added. The published version is shorter than the version given here, which is from the 1963 manuscript of this book, 192–95, RRPL.

6. Edmund Morris, *Dutch* (New York: Random House, 1999), 218.

7. Stephen Vaughn, *Ronald Reagan in Hollywood* (New York: Cambridge University Press, 1994), 121–22; Norman Corwin, *United and Other Radio Dramas* (New York: Henry Holt and Company, 1945), 509–15.

8. Ronald Reagan, "My Faith," *Modern Screen,* June 1950, 37, 88–89.

9. "Remarks to National and State Officers of the Future Farmers of America, July 22, 1986," Old Executive Office Building, in *Public Papers 1986 (Book 2),* 980–82.

10. Ronald Reagan's speech at the Eureka College Library dedication, September 28, 1967. http://www.presidentreagan.info/reagan/speeches/eureka_library.cfm.

11. Martin Anderson, *Revolution* (New York: Harcourt Brace Jovanovich, 1988), 71.

12. Reagan's personal diary, February 18, 1982, in *The Reagan Diaries.*

13. Minutes of the National Security Council, classified Top Secret, Cabinet Room, The White House, April 16, 1982, 11:07 a.m.–12:05 p.m., 2. NSC 00045 04/16/1982 [Strategic] in Executive Secretariat, NSC: NSC Meeting Files: Records, 1981–88. Box 91284. RRPL.

14. Ibid., emphasis added.

15. Ibid., 6.

16. Ibid., 8.

17. Minutes of National Security Council meeting, classified Top Secret, Cabinet Room, The White House, April 21, 1982, 10:30–11:40 a.m., 6–8. NSC 00046 04/21/1982 [START] (1)–(5), in Executive Secretariat, NSC: NSC Meeting Files: Records 1981–88. Box 91284. RRPL.

18. Ibid., 8.

19. Letter, Ronald Reagan to Virginia F. Adams, April 21, 1982, in PHF Series II Box 2, Folder 33. RRPL. Printed in *Reagan: A Life in Letters,* 401–02.

20. "Address at Commencement Exercises at Eureka College, Eureka, Illinois, May 9, 1982," 3:23 p.m. in the Reagan Physical Education Center, in *Public Papers 1982 (Book 1),* 580–86.

21. "Remarks and a Question-and-Answer Session with the Student Body of Providence–St. Mel High School in Chicago, Illinois, May 10, 1982," 2:44–3:27 p.m., in *Public Papers 1982 (Book 1),* 600–08.

22. "Address to the United Nations General Assembly Special Session Devoted to Disarmament, New York, New York, June 17, 1982," 11:02 a.m., in *Public Papers 1982 (Book 1),* 784–89.

23. Reagan's personal diary, June 25, 1982, in *The Reagan Diaries,* 91.

24. Ibid.

Chapter 9: "Star Wars"

1. John W. Finney, "Safeguard ABM System to Shut Down: $5 Billion Spent in 6 Years Since Debate," *New York Times,* Washington, D.C., November 25, 1975, 77.

2. Martin Anderson, *Revolution* (Stanford, CA: Hoover Institution Press, 1990), 82–83.

3. Anderson, *Revolution,* 84.

4. Ibid., 94–96.

5. Martin Anderson interview with Ronald Reagan, July 25, 1989. Reagan's office, Los Angeles, California. Reagan requested that certain parts of the interview be held private, and not used until his death.

6. Anderson, *Revolution*, 97.

7. Minutes of the National Security Planning Group, classified Top Secret, January 13, 1983, The Situation Room, 1:05–2:13 p.m., 1. NSPG 0050 01/13/1983 [Arms Control/INF], in Executive Secretariat, NSC: National Security Planning Group (NSPG): Records, 1981–1987. Box 91306. RRPL.

8. Ibid., 4.

9. Ibid., 7.

10. Ibid., 8.

11. Ibid., 9.

12. Ibid., 10–11.

13. Reagan's personal diary, January 13, 1983, in *The Reagan Diaries*, 125. Y. Frank Freeman was the head of Paramount Studios; his nickname was "God." Born in 1865, he lived to be 107 years old. Harry Cohn was with Columbia Pictures.

14. Reagan's luncheon meeting with the Joint Chiefs of Staff, February 11, 1983, The Cabinet Room, The White House, 12:10–1:43 p.m. The President's Daily Diary [02/09/1983–02/17/1983], in Office of the Presidential Diary, The President's Daily Diary, 1981–89. Box 8. RRPL.

15. Reagan's personal diary, February 11, 1983, in *The Reagan Diaries*, 130.

16. Reagan's personal diary, March 7, 1983, in *The Reagan Diaries*, 134–35.

17. Reagan, *An American Life*, 569.

18. "Remarks at the Annual Convention of the National Association of Evangelicals, in Orlando, Florida, March 8, 1983," Sheraton Twin Towers Hotel, 3:04 p.m., in *Public Papers 1983 (Book 1)*, 359–64.

19. Ibid.

20. Ibid.

21. Ronald Reagan, handwritten brief manifesto on negotiating strategy for INF, Camp David, March 19, 1983, printed in *Reagan, In His Own Hand*, 493–95.

22. George P. Shultz, *Turmoil and Triumph* (New York: Charles Scribner's Sons, 1993), 249.

23. "Address to the Nation on Defense and National Security, March 23, 1983." Oval Office, 8:02 p.m., broadcast live on nationwide radio and television, in *Public Papers 1983 (Book 1)*, 437–43.

24. Shultz, *Turmoil and Triumph*, 258.

25. Reagan's personal diary, March 23, 1983, in *The Reagan Diaries*, 139–40.

26. "Question-and-Answer Session with Reporters on Domestic and Foreign Policy Issues, March 29, 1983," Oval Office, 1:44 p.m., in *Public Papers 1983 (Book 1)*, 463–70.

Chapter 10: Close to Nuclear War: 1983

1. Don Oberdorfer, *The Turn* (New York: Poseidon Press, 1991), 66.

2. National Resources Defense Council. "Global Nuclear Stockpiles 1945–2006," *Bulletin of the Atomic Scientists*, July/August 2006, 66. Also "Table of US Nuclear Warheads," http://www.nrdc.org/nuclear/nudb/datab9.asp and "Table of USSR/Russian Nuclear Warheads," http://www.nrdc.org/nuclear/nudb/datab10.asp.

3. Ronald Reagan, *An American Life* (New York: Simon & Schuster, 1990), 273.

4. Oberdorfer, *The Turn*, 29.

5. Christopher Andrew and Vasili Mitrokhin, *The Sword and the Shield* (New York: Basic Books, 1999), 213.

6. Oberdorfer, *The Turn*, 29.

7. Andrew and Mitrokhin, *The Sword and the Shield*, 19, 214.

8. Letter, Ronald Reagan to Yuri Andropov, July 11, 1983, in Executive Secretariat NSC: Head of State File: Records 1981–89. USSR: General Secretary Andropov (8290913, 8391028, 8391032). Box 38. RRPL.

9. Letter, Yuri Andropov to Ronald Reagan, August 4, 1983, in Executive Secretariat NSC: Head of State File: Records 1981–1989. USSR: General Secretary Andropov (8290913, 8391028, 8391032). Box 39. RRPL.

10. Reagan's personal diary, August 8, 1983, in *The Reagan Diaries*, 173. On October 13, 1982, the CIA published a National Intelligence Estimate (NIE 11-13-82) titled "Soviet Ballistic Missile Defense" summarizing the extensive research in which the Soviets were engaged and speculating on the possibility that the Soviets would abandon

the ABM treaty to extend missile defense beyond Moscow. The report was made public in 1996.

11. Letter, Ronald Reagan to Yuri Andropov, August 24, 1983, in Executive Secretariat, NSC: Head of State File: Records, 1981–89, USSR: General Secretary Andropov (8290913, 8391028, 8391032). Box 38. RRPL.

12. Letter, Yuri Andropov to Ronald Reagan, August 27, 1983, in Executive Secretariat, NSC: Head of State File: Records, 1981–89, USSR: General Secretary Andropov (8290913, 8391028, 8391032). Box 38. RRPL.

13. George P. Shultz, *Turmoil and Triumph* (New York: Charles Scribner's Sons, 1993), 361.

14. Scott Shane, "Cold War's Riskiest Moment—Some Think the Fall of 1983 was the Closest the Soviets and the U.S. Came to Nuclear War." *Baltimore Sun,* August 31, 2003, 2A.

15. Andrew and Mitrokhin, *The Sword and the Shield,* 214.

16. Oberdorfer, *The Turn,* 65.

17. Ibid., 66.

18. Reagan's personal diary, November 18, 1983, in *The Reagan Diaries,* 199.

19. Minutes of the National Security Council meeting, classified Secret, The Cabinet Room, The White House, November 30, 1983, 11:02 a.m.–12:12 p.m., 4–6. NSC 00096 11/30/1983 [Strategic Defense] (1)(2) in Executive Secretariat, NSC: NSC Meeting Files: Records, 1981–88. Box 91303. RRPL.

20. "Remarks on a Question-and-Answer Session with Reporters on Strategic Arms Reduction Talks, December 8, 1983," South Portico at the White House, 1:37 p.m., in *Public Papers 1983 (Book 1),* 666–67.

21. This is one of nineteen meetings of the NSC or NSPG that are listed in the White House log of the president's activities but not on the numbered lists of meetings of the NSC and NSPG.

22. Reagan's personal diary, December 9, 1983, in *The Reagan Diaries,* 204.

23. Letter, Ronald Reagan to Mrs. Laurence Clark, December 14, 1983, in PHF Series II, Box 8, Folder 109. RRPL. Printed in *Reagan: A Life in Letters,* 634–35.

24. "Informal Exchange with Representatives of *Le Figaro,* Together with Written Responses to Questions Submitted by the Newspaper, December 22, 1983," in *Public Papers 1984 (Book 1),* 2. (Transcript released January 7, 1984.)

25. Letter, Ronald Reagan to Yuri Andropov, December 23, 1983, in Executive Secretariat NSC: Head of State File: Records, 1981–89, USSR: General Secretary Andropov (8591507, 8490115). Box 38. RRPL.

26. Minutes of National Security Council meeting, classified Secret/Sensitive, The Cabinet Room, The White House, January 13, 1984, 11:04 a.m.–12:07 p.m., 3. NSC 00100 01/13/1984 [MBFR (Mutual and Balanced Force Reductions)] in Executive Secretariat NSC: NSC Meeting Files: Records 1981–88, Box 91303. RRPL.

27. Ibid., 5.

28. Reagan's personal diary, January 13, 1984, in *The Reagan Diaries,* 270.

29. "Address to the Nation and Other Countries on United States–Soviet Relations, January 16, 1984," East Room at the White House, 10:00 a.m., in *Public Papers 1984 (Book 1),* 40–44.

30. Reagan's personal diary, January 16, 1984, in *The Reagan Diaries,* 270–71.

31. "Address before a Joint Session of the Congress on the State of the Union, January 25, 1984," House Chamber of the Capitol, 9:02 p.m., broadcast live on nationwide radio and television, in *Public Papers 1984 (Book 1),* 87–94.

32. Martin Anderson interview with Ronald Reagan, July 25, 1989, Reagan's office, Los Angeles, California.

Chapter 11: Reagan Wins Reelection: 1984

1. Reagan's personal diary, January 27, 1984, in *The Reagan Diaries,* 215.

2. Reagan's personal diary, January 29, 1984, in *The Reagan Diaries,* 216.

3. Letter, Ronald Reagan to Ward Quaal, February 20, 1984, in PHF Series II Box 8 folder 117. RRPL. Printed in *Reagan: A Life in Letters,* 557. (In fact, it was Jesus who said, "Whoever starts to plow and looks back is not fit for the kingdom of God"; Luke 9:62.)

4. "Radio address to the Nation on United States–Soviet Relations, February 11, 1984," Rancho del Cielo, 9:06 a.m., in *Public Papers 1984 (Book 1),* 191–92.

5. Reagan's personal diary, February 22, 1984, in *The Reagan Diaries*, 220–21.

6. Reagan's personal diary for February 25–26, March 1, March 2, and June 14, 1984, in *The Reagan Diaries*, 221–23, 247.

7. Don Oberdorfer, *The Turn* (New York: Poseidon Press, 1991), 79–87.

8. Reagan's personal diary, June 26, 1984, in *The Reagan Diaries*, 250.

9. Letter, Ronald Reagan to Konstantin Chernenko, classified Secret, February 14, 1984, in Executive Secretariat, NSC: Head of State File: Records, 1981–1989, USSR. Box 39. RRPL.

10. Letter, Konstantin Chernenko to Ronald Reagan, February 23, 1984, in Executive Secretariat, NSC: Head of State File: Records, 1981–1989, USSR: General Secretary Chernenko (8490236, 8490283, 8490304) Box 39. RRPL.

11. National Gallup poll, President Reagan vs. Walter Mondale, June 13, 1983 to February 6, 1984.

12. Minutes of the National Security Planning Group, classified Secret/Sensitive, March 27, 1984, The Cabinet Room, The White House, 2:04–3:15 p.m., 4, 5. NSPG Meeting 03/27/1984 [Nuclear Arms Control Discussion] in Executive Secretariat, NSC: System Files: Records, 1981–89, 1984 NSC System II: 91296. RRPL.

13. Ronald Reagan, *Ronald Reagan: An American Life* (New York: Simon & Schuster, 1990), 602.

14. Reagan's personal diary, August 13, 1984, in *The Reagan Diaries*, 259.

15. "Remarks Accepting the Presidential Nomination at the Republican National Convention in Dallas, Texas, August 23, 1984." Dallas Convention Center, 9:11 p.m., in *Public Papers 1984 (Book 2)*, 1174–81.

16. "Interview with Andrew Neil and Jon Connell of the *Sunday Times* of London, September 6, 1984," Oval Office, 4:40 p.m., in *Public Papers 1984 (Book 2)*, 1254–58.

17. "Address to the 39th Session of the United Nations General Assembly in New York, New York, September 24, 1984," 10:31 a.m., in *Public Papers 1984 (Book 2)*, 1355–61.

18. "Key Sections of Speech By Gromyko to the General Assembly," *New York Times*, September 28, 1984, 12A.

19. George P. Shultz, *Turmoil and Triumph: My Years as Secretary of State* (New York: Charles Scribner's Sons, 1993), 482.

20. Four-page document, handwritten by President Reagan, for Andrei Gromyko's visit to the White House, September 28, 1984. Printed in *Reagan, In His Own Hand.* 496–98.

21. Reagan kept the document after the meeting and took it with him when he left the White House in 1989. At Nancy Reagan's request, on October 4, 2000, Martin Anderson examined papers in Reagan's desk, which he was no longer using, and found this document. Accounts of the meeting from both the Soviet and American participants confirm that this is what Reagan said in the meeting.

22. Shultz, *Turmoil and Triumph*, 484.

23. Anatoly Dobrynin, *In Confidence* (New York: Random House, 1995), 556.

24. Shultz, *Turmoil and Triumph*, 484.

25. Dobrynin, *In Confidence*, 555.

26. Oberdorfer, *The Turn*, 92–93. Emphasis added.

27. "Remarks and a Question-and-Answer Session at the Economic Club of Detroit, in Detroit, Michigan, October 1, 1984." Cobo Hall, 12:45 p.m., in *Public Papers 1984 (Book 2)*, 1396–1403.

28. "Debate between President Reagan and Former Vice President Walter F. Mondale in Louisville, Kentucky, October 7, 1984," 9:00 p.m., in *Public Papers 1984 (Book 2)*, 1441–62.

29. Reagan's personal diary, October 6–7, 1984, in *The Reagan Diaries*, 271.

30. Reagan's personal diary, October 18, 1984, in *The Reagan Diaries*, 273.

31. "Debate between President Reagan and Former Vice President Walter F. Mondale, Kansas City, Missouri, October 21, 1984," 7:01 p.m., in *Public Papers 1984 (Book 2)*, 1589–1608.

32. Ibid.

Chapter 12: Reagan's Negotiating Strategy

1. Letter, Presidium of the Supreme Soviet of the USSR to Ronald Reagan, Classified, November 7, 1984, in Executive Secretariat, NSC: Head of State File: Records, 1981–1989, USSR: General Secretary Chernenko (8491139) (1)(2). Box 39. RRPL.

2. Memo, *George Shultz to President Reagan*, Secret/Sensitive, November 5, 1984, in Executive Secretariat, NSC: Head of State File: Records,

1981–1989, USSR: General Secretary Chernenko (8491139) (1)(2). Box 39. RRPL.

3. Oral message, Konstantin Chernenko to Ronald Reagan, Secret, November 8, 1984, in Executive Secretariat, NSC: Head of State File: 1981–1989, USSR: General Secretary Chernenko (8403539). Box 39. RRPL.

4. By January 20, 1989, Shultz and Reagan had met with each other in private meetings 314 times.

5. Reagan's personal diary, November 14, 1984, in *The Reagan Diaries*, 277.

6. Ibid., November 16, 1984, 278.

7. Quoted in George P. Shultz, *Turmoil and Triumph* (New York: Charles Scribner's Sons, 1993), 500.

8. Reagan's personal diary, November 28, 1984, in *The Reagan Diaries*, 282.

9. Minutes of the National Security Planning Group, classified Secret, November 30, 1984, The Situation Room, The White House, 1:45–2:45 p.m., 2. NSPG 0100 11/30/1984 [Arms Control] in Executive Secretariat, NSC: National Security Planning Group (NSPG): Records, 1981–1987, Box 91307. RRPL.

10. Ibid., 2–4.

11. Ibid., 6.

12. Reagan's personal diary, November 30, 1984, in *The Reagan Diaries*, 282–83.

13. Minutes of the National Security Planning Group, classified Secret, December 5, 1984, The Situation Room, The White House, 1:11–2:05 p.m., 3. NSPG 0101 12/05/1984 [Arms Control], in Executive Secretariat, NSC: NSPG: Records, 1981–1987, Box 91307. RRPL.

14. Ibid., 4–5.

15. Letter, President Reagan to General Secretary Chernenko, classified Secret/Supersensitive, December 7, 1984, in Executive Secretariat, NSC: Head of State File: Records 1981–1989, USSR: General Secretary Chernenko (8491237). Box 39. RRPL.

16. Reagan's personal diary, December 7, 1984, in *The Reagan Diaries*, 285.

17. Minutes of the National Security Planning Group, classified Secret/

Sensitive, December 10, 1984, The Situation Room, The White House, 2:10–3:05 p.m., 2–6. NSPG 0102 12/10/1984 [Arms Control] (1)(2), in Executive Secretariat, NSC: National Security Planning Group NSPG: Records, 1981–1987. Box 91307. RRPL.

18. Quoted from Reagan's 1977 radio commentary, "Intelligence," taped March 23, 1977, in PPP Radio Broadcasts, Box 15. RRPL. Printed in *Reagan in His Own Hand,* 117–19.

19. Minutes of the National Security Planning Group, classified Secret/ Sensitive, December 17, 1984, The Situation Room, The White House, 11:21 a.m.–12:12 p.m., 3, 4. NSPG 0104 12/17/1984 [Arms Control] in Executive Secretariat NSC: NSPG: Records 1981–1987. Box 91307. RRPL.

20. Mount Tambora erupted in 1815, changing the weather in 1816.

21. Reagan's personal diary, December 17, 1984, in *The Reagan Diaries.*

22. Reagan's personal diary, December 18, 1984, in *The Reagan Diaries,* 288.

23. Quoted in Shultz, *Turmoil and Triumph,* 507–8.

24. Henry Stanhope, "Gorbachev Links Arm Curb to Star Wars Ban," London *Times,* December 18, 1984, 1.

25. Letter, Konstantin Chernenko to Ronald Reagan, classified Secret/ Sensitive, December 20, 1984, in Executive Secretariat, NSC: Head of State File: Records 1981–1989, USSR: General Secretary Chernenko (8491334). Box 39. RRPL.

26. "Informal Exchange with Reporters on Foreign and Domestic Issues, December 21, 1984," in *Public Papers 1984 (Book 2),* 1901.

27. Minutes of meeting with British prime minister, Margaret Thatcher, classified Secret, Camp David, Maryland, December 22, 1984, 10:40 a.m.–1:25 p.m. Memcon, *Ronald Reagan and Margaret Thatcher at Camp David,* in Executive Secretariat, NSC: VIP Visits: Records, 1981– 1985, United Kingdom: Prime Minister Thatcher Official Visit, 12/22/1984 (1)(2), RAC Box 6–VIP Visits (91440). RRPL.

28. Ibid.

29. Shultz, *Turmoil and Triumph,* 516.

30. "The President's News Conference, January 9, 1985," East Room at the White House, 8:00 p.m., in *Public Papers 1985 (Book 1),* 23–30.

31. "Interview with Ann Devroy and Johanna Neuman of *USA Today,* Jan-

uary 17, 1985," Oval Office, 11:31 a.m., in *Public Papers 1985 (Book 1),* 45–51.

32. "Inaugural Address, January 21, 1985," in *Public Papers 1985 (Book 1),* 55–58. President Reagan spoke at 11:49 a.m. in the Rotunda of the Capitol. Prior to his address, the president repeated the oath of office, again administered by Chief Justice Warren Burger, which he had taken on January 20, 1985. The inaugural ceremony was originally scheduled to take place on the West Portico of the Capitol, but was held inside due to extremely cold weather in Washington.

33. "Address before a Joint Session of the Congress on the State of the Union, House Chamber of the Capitol, February 6, 1985," 9:05 p.m., in *Public Papers 1985 (Book 1),* 130–36.

34. Address by Konstantin Chernenko to the twenty-seventh CPSU Congress, published in *Pravda,* February 23, 1985.

35. Reagan's handwritten note on Chernenko's speech sent to Reagan by George Shultz, February 27, 1985, in PHF Series II, Box 11, Folder 169. RRPL.

36. Reagan's personal diary, March 4, 1985, in *The Reagan Diaries,* 305.

37. "Interview with Morton Kondracke and Richard Smith of *Newsweek,* March 4, 1985," Oval Office, 4:34 p.m. (released on March 11 by Office of the Press Secretary), in *Public Papers 1985 (Book 1),* 258–63.

38. Reagan's personal diary, March 7, 1985, in *The Reagan Diaries,* 306.

39. "Remarks to the United States Negotiating Team for the Nuclear and Space Arms Negotiations with the Soviet Union, March 8, 1985," Roosevelt Room, 10:11 a.m., in *Public Papers 1985 (Book 1),* 254.

40. Edmund Morris, *Dutch* (New York: Random House, 1999), 517.

41. Reagan's personal diary, March 11, 1985, in *The Reagan Diaries,* 307.

Chapter 13: The Ascent of Gorbachev: 1985

1. "Remarks at the Annual Conversation of the National Association of Evangelicals, Orlando, Florida, March 8, 1983," in *Public Papers 1983 (Book 1),* 359–64.

2. "Remarks and Question-and-Answer Session during a White House Briefing for Members of the Magazine Publishers Association, March 14, 1985," Room 450, Old Executive Office Building, in *Public Papers 1985 (Book 1),* 282–85.

3. Letter, Ronald Reagan to General Secretary Gorbachev, Secret/Sensitive, March 11, 1985, in Executive Secretariat, NSC: Head of State File: Records, 1981–1989, USSR: General Secretary Gorbachev (8590272, 8590336). Box 39. RRPL.

4. Letter, General Secretary Gorbachev to President Reagan, classified Secret, March 24, 1985, in Executive Secretariat, NSC: Head of State File: Records 1981–1989, USSR General Secretary Gorbachev. Box 39. RRPL.

5. Memorandum, Secretary Shultz to President Reagan, Secret/Sensitive/Eyes Only for the President and NSC Adviser McFarlane, March 25, 1985, in Executive Secretariat, NSC: Head of State Files: Records 1981–1989, USSR: General Secretary Gorbachev (8590272, 8590336). Box 39. RRPL.

6. Shultz, *Turmoil and Triumph*, 562–71.

7. Letter, President Reagan to General Secretary Gorbachev, Secret/Sensitive, April 30, 1985, in Executive Secretariat, NSC: Head of State File: Records, 1981–1989, USSR: General Secretary Gorbachev. Box 39. RRPL.

8. Letter, General Secretary Mikhail Gorbachev to President Reagan, Secret/Sensitive, June 10, 1985, in Executive Secretariat, NSC: Head of State File: Records, 1981–1989, USSR: General Secretary Gorbachev. Box 40. RRPL.

9. Letter, General Secretary Mikhail Gorbachev to President Reagan, Secret/Sensitive, June 22, 1985, in Executive Secretariat, NSC: Head of State File: Records, 1981–1989, USSR: General Secretary Gorbachev. Box 40. RRPL.

10. "Interview with Representatives of College Radio Stations, September 9, 1985," Roosevelt Room, 4:31 p.m., in *Public Papers 1985 (Book 2)*, 1064–71.

11. Letter, General Secretary Mikhail Gorbachev to President Reagan, Secret/Sensitive, September 12, 1985, in Executive Secretariat, NSC: Head of State File: Records, 1981–1989, USSR: General Secretary Gorbachev (8591009). Box 40. RRPL.

12. Minutes of the National Security Council, classified Secret, September 20, 1985, The Situation Room, The White House, 11:14 a.m.–12:10 p.m., 7, 8. NSC 00121 09/20/1985 [Shevardnadze's Visit] in

Executive Secretariat, NSC: NSC Meeting Files: Records, 1981–88. Box 913 03. RRPL.

13. Reagan lifted the grain embargo April 24, 1981. Reagan is referring here to the long-term grain agreement.

14. Richard Nixon, "How to Live with the Bomb," *National Review,* September 20, 1985, 25.

15. Minutes of the National Security Council, September 20, 1985, 7–8.

16. U.S. Department of State and Defense, "Soviet Strategic Defense Programs," October 1985. American Federation of Scientists. http://www.fas.org/irp/dia/product/ssdp.htm.

17. Reagan's personal diary, October 7, 1985, in *The Reagan Diaries,* 357–58.

Chapter 14: "Star Wars" in Moscow

1. "Radio Address to the Nation on Soviet Strategic Defense Programs, October 12, 1985," Camp David, Maryland, 12:06 p.m., in *Public Papers 1985 (Book 2),* 1240–41.

2. Reagan's personal diary, October 22, 1985, in *The Reagan Diaries,* 361–62.

3. Reagan's personal diary, November 3, 1985, in *The Reagan Diaries,* 365.

4. Reagan's personal diary, November 5, 1985, in *The Reagan Diaries,* 365.

5. "Radio Address to the Nation and the World on the Upcoming Soviet–United States Summit Meeting in Geneva, November 9, 1985," Broadcast from Voice of America Studios, 12:06 p.m., in *Public Papers 1985 (Book 2),* 1362–64.

6. Reagan's personal diary, November 12, 1985, in *The Reagan Diaries,* 368.

7. Reagan's personal diary, November 13, 1985, in *The Reagan Diaries,* 368.

8. Reagan's memo detailing the strategy he will use in negotiations with Gorbachev at the Geneva Summit, circa November, 1985, Jack F. Matlock Jr. personal papers.

9. Reagan is quoting an October 7, 1985, letter he received from Richard Nixon. Post-Presidential Correspondence with Ronald W. Reagan, Box 1, Folder 6. RNPL (YL).

10. Ronald Reagan, *An American Life* (New York: Simon & Schuster, 1990), 637.

11. "Address to the Nation on the Upcoming Soviet–United States Summit Meeting in Geneva, November 14, 1985," Oval Office, 8:00 p.m., broadcast live on nationwide radio and television, in *Public Papers 1985 (Book 2)*, 1388–91.

Chapter 15: The Geneva "Fireside" Summit

1. Ronald Reagan, *An American Life* (New York: Simon & Schuster, 1990), 11.

2. Reagan's personal diary, November 18, 1985, in *The Reagan Diaries*, 369.

3. Jim Kuhn, *Ronald Reagan in Private* (New York: Sentinel, 2004), 168–74.

4. Memcon, Ronald Reagan and Mikhail Gorbachev, tête-à-tête, Château Fleur d'Eau, Geneva, Switzerland, Secret/Sensitive, November 19, 1985, 10:21–11:18 a.m. (D. Zarechnak and N. Uspenskiy, interpreters). In Series III: US–USSR Summits, 1985–1986: Matlock, Jack F., Jr: Files, 1983–1986 Geneva Meeting: Memcons of Plenary Sessions & Tête-à-tête 11/19/1985–11/21/1985 (1)(2). Box 52. RRPL.

5. Memcon, 3:55–4:44 p.m. Reagan and Gorbachev, Geneva, Switzerland, in Series III: US–USSR Summits, 1985–1986: Matlock, Jack F., Jr: Files, 1983–1986 Geneva Meeting: Memcons of Plenary Sessions & Tête-à-Tête 11/19/1985–11/21/1985 (1)(2). Box 52. RRPL.

6. "Interview with Eleanor Clift, Jack Nelson, and Joel Havemann, of *The Los Angeles Times,* June 23, 1986," Oval Office, 11:31 a.m., in *Public Papers 1986 (Book 1)*, 825–32.

7. Martin Anderson, interview with Ronald Reagan, July 25, 1989, Los Angeles, California. Ronald Reagan, *Ronald Reagan: An American Life* (New York: Simon & Schuster, 1990), 637.

8. Edmund Morris, *Dutch: A Memoir of Ronald Reagan* (New York: Random House, 1999), 596, 828.

Chapter 16: The Priority of Human Rights

1. Letter, Ronald Reagan to Leonid Brezhnev, April 24, 1981, in Executive Secretariat, NSC: Head of State File: Records, 1981–1989, USSR: General Secretary Brezhnev (8190204, 8190205). Box 38. RRPL.

2. Ronald Reagan, "America the Beautiful: Commencement Address,"

June 2, 1952, printed in *Echoes from the Woods,* William Woods College, Fulton, Missouri, vol. 39, no. 2, 8–13. Copy in Vertical file, RRPL.

3. Debate between Robert F. Kennedy and Governor Ronald Reagan, CBS Television Network and CBS Radio Network, May 15, 1967, 10:00–11:00 p.m., Charlie Collingwood, host.

4. Richard Reeves, in an interview about Robert Kennedy, Kennedy Presidential Library, February 20, 2006, 19.

5. Ronald Reagan, "Vlasenko," October 2, 1979, in PPP Radio Broadcasts, Box 12, RRPL. Printed in *Reagan: In His Own Hand,* 177–78.

6. Ronald Reagan, "Bukovsky," June 29, 1979, PPP Radio Broadcasts, Box 12, RPPL. Printed in *Reagan, In His Own Hand,* 149–50.

7. Minutes of the National Security Council, classified Top Secret, October 13, 1981, The Cabinet Room, The White House, 2:08–2:51 p.m., NSC 00022 10/13/1981 [Theater Nuclear Forces, Egypt, NATO, Nuclear Weapons, USSR], in Executive Secretariat, NSC: NSC Meeting Files: Records, 1981–88. Box 91282. RRPL.

8. "Address at Commencement Exercise at Eureka College, Eureka, Illinois, May 9, 1982," 3:23 p.m., in *Public Papers 1982 (Book 1),* 580–86.

9. "Address to Members of British Parliament, June 8, 1982," Royal Gallery at the Palace of Westminster in London, England, 12:14 p.m., in *Public Papers 1982 (Book 1),* 742–48.

10. Reagan lifted the grain embargo on April 24, 1981. He met with Dobrynin in February 1983; the Pentecostals were released and allowed to emigrate later that year—and a new long-term grain agreement was concluded.

11. Series III: US–USSR Summits, 1985–1986: Matlock, Jack F., Jr: Files, 1983–1986. Geneva Meeting: Memcons of Plenary Sessions & Tête-à-Tête 11/19/1985–11/21/1985 (1)(2). Box 52. RRPL.

12. George Shultz, *Turmoil and Triumph* (New York: Charles Scribner's Sons, 1993), 602–03.

13. Reagan's personal diary, November 20, 1985, in *The Reagan Diaries,* 370–71.

14. "Address before a Joint Session of the Congress Following the Soviet–United States Summit Meeting in Geneva. November 21, 1985," 9:20 p.m., House Chamber, Capitol broadcast live on nationwide radio and television. In *Public Papers 1985 (Book 2),* 1411–15.

15. "Joint Soviet–United States Statement on the Summit Meeting in Geneva, November 21, 1985," in *Public Papers 1985 (Book 2)*, 1407–11.

Chapter 17: Gorbachev's Gambit

1. Mikhail S. Gorbachev, "Text Excerpts from Gorbachev Arms Statement," Associated Press, January 16, 1986. Emphasis added.
2. Ronald Reagan, *An American Life* (New York: Simon & Schuster, 1990), 650.
3. Reagan's personal diary, January 15, 1986, in *The Reagan Diaries*, 383–84.
4. "Statement on the Soviet Proposal on Nuclear and Space Arms Reductions, January 15, 1986," in *Public Papers 1986 (Book 1)*, 58.
5. Bernard Weinberg, "Reagan 'Grateful' for Soviet Plan on Nuclear Arms," *New York Times*, January 17, 1986, 1.
6. Minutes of the National Security Planning Group, classified Top Secret, Situation Room, The White House, February 3, 1986, 11:16 a.m.–12:21 p.m., 5–6. NSPG 127 02/03/1986 [Arms Control/Gorbachev] in Executive Secretariat, NSC: NSPG: Records 1981–1987, Box 91308. RRPL.
7. Reagan's personal diary, February 3, 1986, in *The Reagan Diaries*, 387–88.
8. Letter, Ronald Reagan to Mikhail Gorbachev, classified Secret/Sensitive, February 16, 1986, in Executive Secretariat, NSC: Head of State File: Records 1981–1989, USSR: General Secretary Gorbachev (8690024, 8690124). Box 40. RRPL.
9. Letter, Ronald Reagan to Mikhail Gorbachev, classified Secret/Sensitive, February 22, 1986, in Executive Secretariat, NSC: Head of State File: Records 1981–1989, USSR: General Secretary Gorbachev (8690024, 8690124), Box 40. RRPL.
10. Letter, Ronald Reagan to Colonel Barney Oldfield, March 17, 1986, in PHF, Series II, Box 15, Folder 233. RRPL.
11. Reagan, *An American Life*, 661.
12. Minutes of National Security Planning Group meeting, classified Secret, The Situation Room, March 25, 1986, 11:04 a.m.–12:05 p.m., introduction by John Poindexter, assistant for National Security Affairs, 1. NSPG 0130 03/25/1986 [Soviet Violations Policy], in Executive Secretariat, NSC: NSPG: Records, 1981–1987. Box 91308. RRPL.

13. Reagan's personal diary, March 25, 1986, in *The Reagan Diaries,* 401.

14. Letter, Mikhail Gorbachev to Ronald Reagan, classified Secret/Sensitive, April 2, 1986, in Executive Secretariat, NSC: Head of State File: Records, 1981–1989, USSR: General Secretary Gorbachev (8690146, 8690267), Box 40. RRPL.

15. Letter, Ronald Reagan to Mikhail Gorbachev, classified Secret/Sensitive, April 11, 1986, in Executive Secretariat, NSC: Head of State File: Records, 1981–1989, USSR: General Secretary Gorbachev (8690146, 8690267), Box 40. RRPL.

16. Meeting of the National Security Planning Group, classified Top Secret, The Situation Room, The White House, April 16, 1986, 10:22–11:24 a.m., 3–4. NSPG 0131 04/16/1986 [Soviet Violations], in Executive Secretariat, NSC: NSPG: Records, 1981–1987. Box 91308. RRPL.

17. Letter, Ronald Reagan to Secretary General Gorbachev, classified Secret/Sensitive, May 23, 1986, in Executive Secretariat, NSC: Head of State File: Records, 1981–1989, USSR: General Secretary Gorbachev (8690389, 8690420), Box 40. RRPL.

18. Letter, General Secretary Gorbachev to President Reagan, classified Secret/Sensitive, June 1, 1986, in Executive Secretariat, NSC: Head of State File: Records, 1981–1989, USSR: General Secretary Gorbachev, Box 40. RRPL.

19. National Resources Defense Council, "Global Nuclear Stockpiles, 1945–2006," *Bulletin of the Atomic Scientists,* vol. 62, no. 4, July/August 2006, 64–66.

20. Meeting of the National Security Planning Group, classified Secret, The Situation Room, The White House, June 6, 1986, 10:58–11:51 a.m., 2. NSPG 0134 06/06/1986 [US–Soviet Relations] (1)(2), in Executive Secretariat, NSC: NSPG: Records, 1981–1987. Box 91308. RRPL.

21. Meeting of the National Security Planning Group, classified Secret, The Situation Room, The White House, June 12, 1986, 2:00–3:05 p.m., 2–3. NSPG 0135 06/12/1986 [US–Soviet Relations], in Executive Secretariat, NSC: NSPG: Records, 1981–1987. Box 91308. RRPL.

22. Meeting of the National Security Council, classified Top Secret, Room 208, Old Executive Office Building, July 1, 1986, 10:55 a.m.–

12:06 p.m., 5. NSC 00132 07/01/1986 [Strategic Defense Initiative] (1)(2), in Executive Secretariat, NSC: NSC Meeting Files: Records, 1981–88. Box 91304. RRPL.

23. Meeting of the National Security Planning Group, classified Secret, The Situation Room, The White House, July 15, 1986, 10:58 a.m.–12:07 p.m., 1, 5. NSPG 136 07/15/1986 [Nuclear Testing], in Executive Secretariat, NSC: NSPG: Records, 1981–1987. Box 91308. RRPL.

24. Reagan, *An American Life*, 665–66.

25. Letter, Ronald Reagan to Mikhail Gorbachev, classified Secret/Sensitive, July 25, 1986, in Executive Secretariat, NSC: Head of State File: Records, 1981–1989, USSR: General Secretary Gorbachev (8690529). Box 40. RRPL.

26. Letter, Mikhail Gorbachev to Ronald Reagan, classified Secret/Sensitive, September 15, 1986 (delivered by Shevardnadze on September 19), in Executive Secretariat, NSC: Head of State File: Records, 1981–1989, USSR: General Secretary Gorbachev. Box 40. RRPL.

27. Reagan's personal diary, September 19, 1986, in *The Reagan Diaries*, 439.

28. Ibid., September 29, 1986, 441.

Chapter 18: Soviet Strategy at Reykjavik: 1986

1. "Statement by Secretary of State George P. Shultz and Remarks by the President on Soviet–United States Relations, September 30, 1986," Briefing Room, The White House, 10:06 a.m., in *Public Papers 1986 (Book 2)*, 1292–99.

2. Kenneth L. Adelman, *The Great Universal Embrace* (New York: Simon & Schuster, 1989), 26.

3. Department of Defense, *Soviet Military Power*, 1985, 55–58.

4. Ibid., 45–46.

5. National Resources Defense Council, "Global Nuclear Stockpiles, 1945–2006," *Bulletin of the Atomic Scientists*, July/August 2006, 64–66. Also "Table of US Nuclear Warheads," http:www.nrdc.org/nuclear/nudb/data9.asp and "Table of USSR/Russian Nuclear Warheads," www.nrdc.org/nuclear/nudb/data10.asp.

6. National Security Archive. "Transcript of Reagan-Gorbachev Summit in Reykjavik: Part 1" FBIS-USR-93-061. http://www.gwu.edu/~nsarchiv/NSAEBB/NSAEBB203/Document10.pdf.

7. Ibid., 3.

8. National Security Archive. "Transcript of Reagan-Gorbachev Summit in Reykjavik: Part 2" FBIS-USR-93-087. http://www.gwu.edu/~nsarchiv/ NSAEBB/NSAEBB203/Document12.pdf.

9. The transcript incorrectly identifies these treaties as START I and START II.

10. National Security Archive. "Transcript of Reagan-Gorbachev Summit in Reykjavik: Part 3" FBIS-USR-93-113. http://www.gwu.edu/~nsarchiv/ NSAEBB/NSAEBB203/Document14.pdf.

11. National Security Archive. "Transcript of Reagan-Gorbachev Summit in Reykjavik: Part 4" FBIS-USR-93-121. http://www.gwu.edu/~nsarchiv/ NSAEBB/NSAEBB203/Document16.pdf.

12. Adelman, *The Great Universal Embrace*, p. 72.

13. National Security Archive, 5.

14. Ibid.

15. Ronald Reagan, *An American Life* (New York: Simon & Schuster, 1990), 675–79.

16. *Time* magazine, front cover, October 20, 1986.

17. "Derailment at Reykjavik." *New York Times*, October 13, 1986, Section A, page 18, editorial.

18. "Cold in Iceland," *Washington Post*, October 13, 1986, page A24, opinion editorial, final edition.

19. Philip Taubman, "The Iceland Summit: 'A Difficult Dialogue'; Gorbachev Angrily Accuses Reagan of Scuttling an Accord at Reykjavik," *New York Times*, October 13, 1986, 8A.

20. Celestine Bohlen and Gary Lee. "Soviet Casts Doubt on U.S. Summit; Gorbachev Gives Bleak Report." *Washington Post*, October 13, 1986, A1.

21. "Address to the Nation on the Meetings with Soviet General Secretary Gorbachev in Iceland, October 13, 1986," Oval Office, 8 p.m., broadcast live on nationwide radio and television, in *Public Papers 1986 (Book 2)*, 1367–71.

22. Anatoly W. Chernyaev, *My Six Years with Gorbachev*, translated and edited by Robert English and Elizabeth Tucker (University Park: Pennsylvania University Press, 2000 [originally published in Russia, 1993]), 86–87.

Chapter 19: The Iran-Contra Controversy

1. David Broder and Paul Taylor, "Senate Contenders Rally Round Reagan or Keep Quiet." *Washington Post,* October 14, 1986, A24.

2. Reagan's personal diary, January 7, 1986, in *The Reagan Diaries,* 381.

3. "Remarks Announcing the Review of the National Security Council's Role in the Iran Arms and Contra Aid Controversy, November 25, 1986," Briefing Room, The White House, 12:03 p.m., in *Public Papers 1986 (Book 2),* 1587–88.

4. "Address to the Nation on the Investigation of the Iran Arms and Contra Aid Controversy, December 2, 1986," Oval Office, noon, broadcast live on nationwide radio and television, in *Public Papers 1986 (Book 2),* 1594–95.

5. Lawrence K. Altman, "Casey's Brain Tumor Is Confirmed as Cancerous," *New York Times,* December 24, 1986, A7.

6. George Shultz, *Turmoil and Triumph* (New York: Charles Scribner's Sons, 1993), 857.

7. Ibid., 854.

8. Ibid., 875.

9. "New Year's Radio Address to the People of the Soviet Union, December 31, 1986," broadcast in the Soviet Union on January 1, 1987 by the Voice of America, in *Public Papers 1986 (Book 2),* 1655–57.

10. Minutes of the National Security Planning Group, classified Top Secret/Sensitive, February 3, 1987, The Situation Room, The White House, 1:47–3:04 p.m., 1. NSPG 143 02/03/1987 [SDI, ABM] (1)–(3), in Executive Secretariat, NSC: NSPG: Records, 1981–1987. Box 91308.

11. Ibid., 11.

12. Ibid., 11–13.

13. Minutes of the National Security Planning Group, classified Top Secret/Sensitive with GRIP attachment, February 10, 1987, The Situation Room, The White House, 11:03 a.m.–12:03 p.m., 1. NSPG 143A 02/10/1987 [Arms Control & SDI] in Executive Secretariat, NSC: NSPG: Records, 1981–1987. Box 91308.

14. Ibid., 3.

15. Ibid.

16. Ibid., 4.

NOTES   427

17. Ibid.

18. Ibid., 5.

19. Ibid., 8.

20. Reagan's personal diary, February 10, 1987, in *The Reagan Diaries*, 474.

21. "Address to the Nation on the Iran Arms and Contra Aid Controversy, March 4, 1987," Oval Office, 9:00 p.m., broadcast live on nationwide radio and television, in *Public Papers 1987 (Book 1)*, 208–11.

22. Ronald Reagan, *An American Life* (New York: Simon & Schuster, 1990), 540–43.

Chapter 20: Gorbachev Caves First: 1987

1. "World Notes Disarmament," *Time* magazine, March 9, 1987.

2. "Remarks to Reporters on Intermediate-Range Nuclear Force Reductions, March 3, 1987," Briefing Room at The White House, 3:30 p.m., in *Public Papers 1987 (Book 1)*, 191–92.

3. "Remarks at a White House Briefing for Members of the National Newspaper Association, March 5, 1987," Room 450, Old Executive Office Building, 11:30 a.m., in *Public Papers 1987 (Book 1)*, 212–15.

4. "Statement on Intermediate-Range Nuclear Force Reductions, March 6, 1987," in *Public Papers 1987 (Book 1)*, 218–19.

5. Reagan's personal diary, Friday, March 6, 1987, in *The Reagan Diaries*, 481.

6. George Shultz, *Turmoil and Triumph* (New York: Simon & Schuster, 1993), 886.

7. Ibid., 889–96.

8. Ronald Reagan, "Are Liberals Really Liberal?" in speeches and writings pre-1966. Ronald Reagan Subject Collection, Box 1. Hoover Institution Archives. Printed in *Reagan, in His Own Hand*, 438–42.

9. Antony C. Sutton, *Western Technology and Soviet Economic Development*, 3 volume series: 1917–1930 (1968), 1930–1945 (1971), and 1945–1965 (1973) with large bibliography (Stanford, CA: Hoover Institution Press).

10. Mikhail Gorbachev, *Memoirs* (New York: Doubleday, 1996), 468.

11. National Security Archive. "Transcript of Reagan–Gorbachev Summit

in Reykjavik: Part 3" FBIS–USR–93–113. http://www.gwu.edu/~nsarchiv/NSAEBB/NSAEBB203/Document14.pdf.

12. Reagan, "Are Liberals Really Liberal?"

Chapter 21: Treaty Signing in Washington

1. "Interview with White House Newspaper Correspondents, April 28, 1987," Oval Office, 2:34 p.m., in *Public Papers 1987 (Book 1)*, 424–29.

2. "Address on East-West Relations at the Brandenburg Gate in West Berlin, June 12, 1987," 2:20 p.m., in *Public Papers 1987 (Book 1)*, 634–37.

3. "Address to the Nation on the Iran Arms and Contra Aid Controversy and Administration Goals, August 12, 1987, Oval Office, 8:00 p.m., broadcast live on nationwide radio and television, in *Public Papers 1987 (Book 2)*, 942–45.

4. Minutes of the National Security Planning Group, classified Top Secret, The Situation Room, The White House, September 8, 1987, 1:13–2:23 p.m., 2, 3, 8–11. NSPG 165 09/08/1987 [Arms Control/Shevardnadze Visit] in Executive Secretariat, NSC: NSPG: Records, 1981–1987, Box 91309. RRPL.

5. "Address to the 42nd Session of the United Nations General Assembly, New York, New York, September 21, 1987," 11:02 a.m., in *Public Papers 1987 (Book 2)*, 1058–63.

6. "Radio Address to the Nation on the Economy and Soviet–United States Relations, October 24, 1987," Camp David, 12:06 p.m., in *Public Papers 1987 (Book 2)*, 1230–31.

7. Reagan's personal diary, October 24, 1987, in *The Reagan Diaries*, 542.

8. Reagan's personal diary, October 25, 1987, in *The Reagan Diaries*, 542.

9. Reagan's personal diary, October 27, 1987, in *The Reagan Diaries*, 542–43.

10. "Remarks and Question-and-Answer Session with Reporters on the Soviet–United States Summit Meeting, October 30, 1987," Briefing Room, The White House, 2:00 p.m., in *Public Papers 1987 (Book 2)*, 1256–58.

11. Reagan's personal diary, November 3, 1987, in *The Reagan Diaries*, 544.

12. "Address to the People of West Europe on Soviet–United States Relations, November 4, 1987," address recorded on November 3, 1987, in

the Roosevelt Room, The White House, broadcast by the U.S. Information Agency on Worldnet television and the Voice of America, 8:00 a.m., November 4, in *Public Papers 1987 (Book 2)*, 1269–74.

13. "Remarks at a White House Briefing for Human Rights Supporters, December 3, 1987," Room 450, Old Executive Office Building, 10:10 a.m., in *Public Papers 1987 (Book 2)*, 1420–21.

14. "Interview with Television Network Broadcasters, December 3, 1987," Oval Office, broadcast nationwide at 8:00 p.m., in *Public Papers 1987 (Book 2)*, 1425–31.

15. One-on-one discussion between Ronald Reagan and Mikhail Gorbachev, December 8, 1987, classified Secret, 11:00 a.m., The Oval Office in the White House.

16. "Remarks on Signing the Intermediate-Range Nuclear Forces Treaty, December 8, 1987," East Room, The White House, 1:45 p.m., in *Public Papers 1987 (Book 2)*, 1455–56.

17. "Intermediate-Range Nuclear Forces Treaty," Wikipedia encyclopedia. http://en.wikipedia.org/wiki/Intermediate_Range_Nuclear_Forces_Treaty.

18. Reagan's personal diary, December 8, 1987, in *The Reagan Diaries*, 555.

19. George Shultz, *Turmoil and Triumph* (New York: Charles Scribner's Sons, 1993), 1015.

Chapter 22: The Cold War Ends: 1988

1. "New Year's Messages of President Reagan and Soviet General Secretary Gorbachev, January 1, 1988." Reagan was recorded on December 23, 1987, at 11:50 a.m. in the Roosevelt Room. Both were televised in the United States and the Soviet Union on January 1, 1988, in *Public Papers 1988 (Book 1)*, 1–3.

2. Ibid.

3. Letter, Ronald Reagan to John Tringali [Mill Valley, California], January 6, 1988. In PHF Series II Box 19 Folder 315. RRPL.

4. "Address before a Joint Session of Congress on the State of the Union, January 25, 1988," House Chamber of the Capitol, 9:07 p.m., address broadcast live nationwide, in *Public Papers 1988 (Book 1)*, 84–90.

5. Minutes of the National Security Planning Group meeting, classified Secret, The Situation Room, The White House, February 9, 1988, 2:03–2:58 p.m., 2, 4, 6–8. NSPG February 9, 1988, 176 in Executive Secretariat, NSC: System Files: 1988: NSC System II 90141. RRPL.

6. Minutes of the National Security Planning Group meeting, classified Secret, The Situation Room, The White House, February 26, 1988, 11:03–11:56 a.m., 1–3. NSPG Minutes February 26, 1988, 177 in Executive Secretariat, NSC: System Files: Records, 1988: NSC System II: 90161 Add On. RRPL.

7. "Remarks and a Question-and-Answer Session with Members of the National Strategy Forum in Chicago, Illinois, May 4, 1988," Palmer House, 2:51 p.m., in *Public Papers 1988 (Book 1)*, 552–58.

8. "Remarks to the Paasikivi Society and the League of Finnish-American Societies in Helsinki, Finland, May 27, 1988," 3:05 p.m., in *Public Papers 1988 (Book 1)*, 656–61.

9. Don Oberdorfer, *The Turn* (New York: Poseidon Press, 1991), 292–93.

10. "Remarks at the Opening Ceremony of the Soviet–United States Summit Meeting in Moscow, May 29, 1988," in St. George's Hall, Grand Kremlin Palace, in *Public Papers 1988 (Book 1)*, 672–74.

11. Memcon, Moscow (Reagan–Gorbachev) Summit 1st Session, May 29, 1988, in Executive Secretariat, NSC: System Files: Records 1981–89, 1988: NSC System 8791367. RRPL.

12. Reagan's personal diary, May 29, 1988, in *The Reagan Diaries*, 613.

13. Oberdorfer, *The Turn*, 299.

14. Reagan's personal diary, May 31, 1988, in *The Reagan Diaries*, 614.

15. Jack F. Matlock, *Reagan and Gorbachev* (New York: Random House, 2004), 301–02.

16. "Remarks and a Question-and-Answer Session with the Students and Faculty at Moscow State University, May 31, 1988," Lecture Hall, 4:10 p.m., in *Public Papers 1988 (Book 1)*, 683–92.

17. Oberdorfer, *The Turn*, 300.

18. Memcon, Moscow (Reagan–Gorbachev) Summit, President Reagan's first one-on-one meeting with General Secretary Gorbachev, St. Catherine Hall, the Kremlin, Moscow, May 29, 1988, 3:26–4:37 p.m., in Executive Secretariat, NSC: System Files: Records, 1981–89, 1988: NSC System 8791367. RRPL.

19. George Shultz, *Turmoil and Triumph* (New York: Charles Scribner's Sons, 1993), 1105.

20. Lou Cannon and Don Oberdorfer, "The Superpowers' Struggle over 'Peaceful Co-existence,' " *Washington Post,* June 3, 1988, A26.

21. "Joint Statement Following the Soviet–United States Summit Meeting in Moscow, June 1, 1988," in *Public Papers 1988 (Book 1),* 698–706.

22. Ronald Reagan, *An American Life* (New York: Simon & Schuster, 1990), 711.

23. Ibid., 710–11.

24. Reagan's personal diary, June 1, 1988, in *The Reagan Diaries,* 614.

25. Jack F. Matlock Jr., *Reagan and Gorbachev: How the Cold War Ended* (New York: Random House, 2004), 315–16.

26. "Farewell Address to the Nation, January 11, 1989," Oval Office 9:02 p.m., broadcast live on nationwide radio and television, in *Public Papers 1988 (Book 2),* 1718–23.

27. Ronald Reagan, "Remarks at Presentation of Ronald Reagan Freedom Award to Mikhail Sergeyevich Gorbachev, Ronald Reagan Presidential Library and Center for Public Affairs, May 4, 1992." RRPL.

ACKNOWLEDGMENTS

~

Many people contributed to the making of this book over the four years we worked on it. But one person stands out, the person who was at Reagan's side for more than fifty years: his wife, Nancy. This book is based on hundreds of documents, many of them classified, and Nancy was central in making it possible to use them in the book.

In talking about her role in preserving Reagan's legacy, Nancy once said, "I just want people to know who Ronnie is." We hope this book has helped to accomplish that goal.

Many people working in the Reagan Presidential Library and the Reagan Foundation were of great help to us as we progressed. Most helpful was Joanne Drake. Joanne had been with Reagan while he was in the White House and was his chief of staff when he returned to California in 1989. Duke Blackwood, executive director of the Reagan Library and of the Reagan Presidential Foundation, and his staff supported our efforts with skill and made several helpful suggestions.

The cornerstone of our book is the classified documents, which are managed by a small group of archivists working in a vault behind four large steel doors. Over several years, Martin Anderson spent hundreds of hours in this vault and witnessed the great care and intelligence with which these archivists dispatch their duties. The two archivists with whom Martin worked directly were Sherrie Fletcher, who handled our requests with skilled professionalism, and Cate Sewell, who also answered innumerable questions. But their whole team, including Mike Duggan, Diane Barrie, and Steve Branch, was enormously helpful in identifying documents critical to our work, including millions of unclassified documents at the Reagan Library and those held by the Reagan Foundation at the library.

These unsung archivists, so few in number, are critical to learning how our most important men and women do what they do in Washington.

Access to the classified documents was assisted by Karl Rove and Ron Soubers, director, Access Management at the National Security Council.

Archivists at the Hoover Institution, especially Carol Leadenham and Linda Bernard, were also helpful. The Hoover Institution holds several collections of papers with Reagan materials, including the Ronald Reagan Subject collection, the Citizens for Reagan collection, and the Deaver & Hannaford collection. Of significant help on our visit to Eureka College were Anthony Glass, college archivist, and Bryan Sajko, the museum curator. Jerry Alfaro of the Lawrence Livermore National Laboratory did a superb job of processing 18,000 pages of the logs of President Reagan's activities in the White House into computer-readable form.

The documents are at the heart of this book, but we also interviewed, formally or informally, many people who were close to President Reagan or active in the Reagan administration. They include Richard V. Allen, Lou Cannon, William P. Clark, Michael Deaver, David Fischer, Peter Hannaford, James Kuhn, Robert Lindsey, Jack Matlock Jr., Robert McFarlane, Edwin Meese III, Herbert Meyer, Betty Murphy, Lyn Nofziger, Michael Novak, Nancy Reagan, Peter Robinson, Edward Rowny, George P. Shultz, Stuart Spencer, Caspar Weinberger, William A. Wilson, and Richard Wirthlin. We also talked about our work with Douglas Brinkley, Jim and Maureen Sanders, Pete Wilson, Neill Ferguson, Michael Boskin, Greg Cumming, and Carl Cannon, as well as others who attended the two conferences George Shultz and Sidney Drell held at the Hoover Institution in 2006 and 2007 on the Reykjavik summit—Max Kampelman, Don Oberdorfer, Henry S. Rowen, David Holloway, Richard Perle, and David Hoffman.

We greatly appreciate the friends and colleagues who took the time to read drafts of the manuscripts for this book and provide us with comments. They include Lou Cannon, John Cogan, Sidney Drell, James Goodby, Jan Hurlbut, George P. Shultz, John Taylor, Darrell Trent, and Lowell Wood.

Our longtime agent John Hawkins, of John Hawkins & Associates, has provided invaluable counsel and judgment.

Our editors at Crown Publishing—Rick Horgan, vice president and executive editor, and Julian Pavia, editor—were of great help to us in rewriting the manuscript and carving a sharper, cleaner story.

The research assistants who labored tirelessly with us did excellent work—everything from reading drafts, suggesting changes and ideas, and finding errors to creating an index to the President's Papers and an index to the final draft. Lillie Robinson, research assistant to Martin Anderson, has worked on this project from its inception in early 2005 and did a superb job in handling the working papers and undertaking myriad tasks such as a compilation of the records of the president's meetings with members of Congress. Heather Campbell, research assistant to Annelise Anderson, read and checked many drafts and compiled a calendar of Reagan's activities during his years with General Electric. Allison Asher, research assistant for Martin, established a system for keeping track of our numerous documents and retrieving them. Lynette Garcia, research assistant for both Martin and Annelise, worked with us for two years on the project, especially on Reagan's meetings with members of the press. Kirstin Julian, research assistant to Martin and Annelise, joined us in the middle of 2007 and did an excellent job in using her training as an archivist to manage documents, check endnotes, and work on the index for the book.

For many years the Hoover Institution at Stanford University has been home to both Annelise and Martin, and its scholarly resources have allowed us to do much work that would otherwise have been impossible. We especially thank John Raisian, the director of the Hoover Institution, for his support.

Finally, we wish to acknowledge with gratitude the funding provided to support the fellows at the Hoover Institution. The most significant grant for this project came from Keith and Jan Hurlbut; others came from Tad Taube of Woodside, California; the late Barton A. Stebbins of Laguna Beach, California; and a neighbor of ours, the Honorable L. W. "Bill" Lane Jr., Portola Valley, California.

INDEX